Qualitative Reading Inventory-3

Lauren Leslie
Marquette University

JoAnne Caldwell
Cardinal Stritch University

Longman

New York • San Francisco • Boston
London • Toronto • Sydney • Tokyo • Singapore • Madrid
Mexico City • Munich • Paris • Cape Town • Hong Kong • Montreal

Publisher: Priscilla McGeehon
Senior Acquisitions Editor: Virginia L. Blanford
Supplements Editor: Jennifer Ackerman
Media Supplements Editor: Mark Toews
Production Manager: Patti Brecht
Project Coordination, Text Design, and Electronic Page Makeup: Pre-Press Company, Inc.
Cover Manager: Wendy Fredericks
Cover Designer: Joseph DePinho
Senior Manufacturing Buyer: Dennis J. Para
Printer and Binder: Webcrafters
Cover Printer: The Lehigh Press, Inc.

Library of Congress Cataloging-in-Publication Data

Leslie, Lauren.
    Qualitative reading inventory, 3 / Lauren Leslie, JoAnne Caldwell.
        p. cm.
    Includes bibliographical references and index.
    Rev. ed. of: Qualitative reading inventory. II. c1995.
    ISBN 0-321-03786-3
    1. Qualitative Reading Invemtory. 2. Reading comprehension–Ability testing. I. Title:
Qualitative reading inventory, three. II. Caldwell, JoAnne. III. Leslie, Lauren.
Qualitative reading inventory, II. IV. Title.

LB1050.75.Q34 L47 2001
372.4–dc21   00-030498

Please visit our website at http://www.awl.com/leslie

ISBN 0-321-03786-3

    4567890—WC—030201

Contents

Preface

Changes in reading-assessment techniques continue to emerge. New research continues to be published. These factors have led to the third edition of the *Qualitative Reading Inventory*. The *QRI–3* continues the emphasis on authentic assessment of children's reading abilities, from the most emergent readers to advanced readers. New to this edition are the inclusion of high school passages, additional passages at the pre-primer through third grade levels, and additional upper middle school passages. Other additions to the *QRI–3* are more direct attention to look-backs and the inclusion of think-alouds as a strategy for analyzing reader cognitions in high school text. We would also like to call your attention to our book-specific website at www.awl.com/leslie.

The *Qualitative Reading Inventory–3* continues the long history of informal reading inventories. Like other informal reading inventories, it provides graded word lists and numerous passages designed to assess the oral reading, silent reading, or listening comprehension of a student. However, the *QRI–3* differs in several ways. The *QRI–3* contains narrative and expository passages at each pre-primer through high school level. All are self-contained selections highly representative of the structure and subject matter of materials found in basal readers and content-area textbooks. Passages at the pre-primer through second grade levels are presented with and without pictures. Maps and illustrations are part of the high school selection. Prior to reading, knowledge of concepts important to an understanding of the passage is assessed, which allows the examiner to label a passage as familiar or unfamiliar to each student. The *QRI–3* measures comprehension in several ways: through an analysis of the student's retelling, through the answers to explicit and implicit comprehension questions, through the use of look-backs that allow readers to search in the text for information to answer questions not previously answered correctly, and through the use of think-alouds to analyze students' thoughts during reading.

This test allows the user to evaluate a reader's comprehension abilities in light of his or her background knowledge about a subject and whether the text was narrative or expository. The reader's answers to explicit and implicit comprehension questions allow the examiner to assess the reader's understanding of the text. The examiner can also assess the reader's understanding of the structure of the text through a qualitative analysis of his or her retelling. Look-backs and think-alouds can be used to assess a reader's awareness and use of various metacognitive strategies for comprehending text.

The *QRI–3* provides a number of diagnostic options that serve a variety of purposes. It can be used to estimate reading levels, suggest directions for instructional intervention, compile a profile of a student's reading ability, or suggest student growth across time. Each examiner is encouraged to decide which of the *QRI–3*'s components meet his or her diagnostic purposes.

We designed the *QRI–3* for students in graduate education courses, reading-assessment specialists, and school district personnel who offer inservice work in reading assessment. If the *QRI–3* is used with preservice education students, an instructor will need to acquaint the student with recent research on factors affecting the reading process. In addition, the *QRI–3* presumes a basic knowledge of informal reading inventories.

Finally, although the *QRI–3* is an informal assessment instrument, we conducted an extensive piloting of the test. In Section 16, we have included a technical manual with reliability and validity data.

Acknowledgments

We would like to extend our appreciation to the following persons who aided in testing, scoring, and interpreting the *Qualitative Reading Inventory–3*:

Nancy Foti, Cardinal Stritch University; Heidi Schaubs, Cardinal Stritch University; Gloria Wiener, Cardinal Stritch University; Dr. Julius Ruff, Associate Professor of History, Marquette University; Dr. Walter Fredericks, Professor of Biology, Marquette University; Katie Barder, Marquette University; Mike Boticki, Marquette University; Paul Hamilton, Marquette University; Vicki Konkey, Marquette University; Marge Laughlin, Marquette University; Nicole Shelley, Marquette University; Ivana Tenuta, Marquette University; Julie Ullman, Marquette University; Kathleen Cepelka, Catholic Memorial High School, Waukesha; Paula Cooper, Salem School District; Cynthia Ellwood, Hartford Avenue School, Milwaukee; Leanne Giese, St. Joseph's School, Grafton; Kathy Lucas, Grafton School District; and Pat Trinitapoli, Elmbrook School District.

The authors are also grateful to the following reviewers:

Mary Alice Barksdale Ladd, University of South Florida; Jack Cassidy, Millersville University of Pennslyvannia; Linda Moxon Cleary, Augusta State University; Timothy Rasinski, Kent State University; and Steven Stahl, University of Georgia.

We would like to thank the Graduate School and School of Education of Marquette University for financial support and research assistant support for Lauren Leslie, and to thank the College of Education of Cardinal Stritch University for support for JoAnne Caldwell during this project.

Lauren Leslie
JoAnne Caldwell

1 Introduction to the Qualitative Reading Inventory–3

The *Qualitative Reading Inventory–3 (QRI–3)* is an individually administered informal reading inventory (IRI) designed to provide diagnostic information about (1) conditions under which students can identify words and comprehend text successfully, and (2) conditions that appear to result in unsuccessful word identification, decoding, and/or comprehension. The *QRI–3* was designed to provide a variety of different opportunities to observe a student's reading behavior. For example, because the *QRI–3* contains narrative and expository passages at each readability level, the examiner can determine the student's relative strengths and weaknesses in both of these types of text. Additional features that promote assessment with the *QRI–3* are presented more fully below.

The *QRI–3* provides a number of assessment options that serve a variety of purposes. The classroom teacher can use the *QRI–3* to estimate student reading level, group students effectively, and choose appropriate textbooks. Student performances on the *QRI–3* can be included in reading portfolios. Reading and assessment specialists can use the *QRI–3* to design and evaluate intervention instruction. Each user will choose different components of the *QRI–3* to administer. Later sections of this manual contain more complete guidelines for assessment alternatives.

The *QRI–3* is not a norm-referenced or standardized instrument. Norm-referenced tests provide comparative data; that is, an individual's score is evaluated in terms of the established norm. Although we conducted extensive piloting on the *QRI–3*, individual subject scores should not be interpreted in comparison to these data. Administration of standardized instruments remains identical across all subjects. However, users of the *QRI–3* should make their own decisions regarding the number and type of passages to administer. The *QRI–3* provides several assessment options, and it is the role of individual examiners to decide which, if any, to use.

The *QRI–3* continues a long history of informal reading inventories. For forty years, informal reading inventories have been used to identify subjects' reading levels—independent, instructional, and frustration—as well as to provide valuable diagnostic information. Like other informal reading inventories, the *QRI–3* provides graded word lists and numerous passages designed to assess the oral and silent reading, and/or listening of students from the pre-primer through the high school level. However, the *QRI–3* differs from other informal reading inventories in several ways.

First, the *QRI–3* provides both narrative and expository text at each level. At the pre-primer through second grade levels, the passages are divided into those with pictures and those without pictures. Passages with pictures are more representative of what beginning readers typically encounter. Comparing performance on passages with and without pictures can suggest the extent to which the student relies on external clues for word identification and comprehension.

Another difference involves assessment of the student's prior knowledge of passage content. Each passage includes at least three questions designed to ascertain whether the student is familiar with the topic of the selection, especially the content tapped by implicit questions. In addition, a prediction task is presented as an option to the examiner. These tasks allow the examiner to label a passage as familiar or unfamiliar to each individual student.

The topics of the pre-primer through second grade passages are generally familiar. At levels three through upper middle school, the topics of the selections vary in their familiarity to the reader. When a reader possesses background knowledge about a topic, he or she will find it easier to comprehend and retain information. Conversely, readers have more difficulty understanding text about an unfamiliar topic. Readers may have different instructional levels for familiar and unfamiliar text. By including passages that vary in familiarity, the *QRI–3* allows the examiner to arrive at a more precise description of a student's reading ability. At the high school level, the topics are representative of typical secondary curricular content and can be assumed to be unfamiliar to most readers. High school students are asked to read for the purpose of learning about such topics. The inclusion of relatively unfamiliar high school passages allows an examiner to assess the student's ability to deal with such material.

The *QRI–3* provides three ways of assessing comprehension: student unaided recall, questions without look-backs, and questions with look-backs. Each passage has an accompanying map for recording and evaluating the retelling. The questions are of two kinds: explicit and implicit. Answers to explicit questions can be found in the text; answers to implicit questions require the reader to make an inference based on a textual clue. The *QRI–3* also employs look-backs as a means of ascertaining whether a student can locate answers to questions. Look-backs allow the examiner to differentiate between comprehension and memory. A reader may comprehend while reading but then forget the information when asked a specific question. If the student can find the correct answer after looking back in the text, the examiner can assume comprehension while reading. The *QRI–3* also offers the opportunity of using think-alouds at the high school level. Asking readers to stop during reading and describe what they are thinking provides information on what readers do as they attempt to comprehend. Do they self-question? Do they make inferences? Do they draw on their prior knowledge? The quality of their comprehension can be evaluated in relation to the number and quality of their comments.

In summary, the *Qualitative Reading Inventory–3* is an informal reading inventory that contains word lists and passages at pre-primer through high school levels. It includes both narrative and expository passages. For each one, we have provided a task to assess the student's prior knowledge for the content of the selection. The *QRI–3* evaluates comprehension by an analysis of retelling, by questions, and through the use of look-backs and think-alouds.

The *QRI–3* provides quantitative scores; however, for many students these scores will depend on the type of text read, their background knowledge, and the manner in which comprehension is assessed. Interpretation of their scores must therefore be qualified by the above factors. For this reason, this inventory has been titled the *Qualitative Reading Inventory–3*.

Section 2 provides the research rationale for the development of the *QRI–3*.

2

Why Another Informal Reading Inventory?

A Research Perspective

Early Reading Assessment: A Developmental Perspective

Factors Related to Comprehension

Text Structure
Prior Knowledge
Oral and Silent Reading
Look-Backs
Think-Alouds

Factors Related to Word Identification

Speed and Automaticity
Oral Reading Miscue Analysis

There are over a dozen informal reading inventories on the market. Why would we want to design another one? The reason is that current research suggests there are factors that affect word identification and comprehension that are not considered together in any other informal reading inventory currently published (Caldwell, 1985). In addition, since the first edition of the *QRI* was published, we have continued to read and conduct research on factors affecting word identification and comprehension. As indicated in Section 1, the *Qualitative Reading Inventory–3 (QRI–3)* reflects several advances based on research.

Early Reading Assessment: A Developmental Perspective

Developmental descriptions of the reading process have been provided by Chall (1983), Hood (1984), Ehri (1991), Gough & Juel (1991), and Spear-Swerling & Sternberg (1996). These descriptions suggest that the knowledge sources that children use to construct meaning from text and the aspects of constructing meaning that give them trouble vary depending on their stage/level of reading acquisition. Children tend to move through several stages as they learn to recognize words and construct meaning. The first stage has been termed the logographic stage (Ehri, 1991) or the stage of visual-cue reading (Spear-Swerling & Sternberg, 1996). Children attempt to identify words on the basis of visual cues as opposed to sound cues. They may use the shape of a word or letter or the presence of a logo as a cue. For example, they can recognize "McDonald's" but only in the presence of the familiar golden arches. They might call any word that ends in "y" "monkey" because the word has a tail at the end, just like a monkey. Children then move into an alphabetic stage (Ehri, 1991) also termed phonetic-cue word recognition (Spear-Swerling & Sternberg, 1996). At this point, they begin to use knowledge of letter-sound relationships in addition to oral language skills, pictures, and knowledge of the purposes of reading (Leslie, 1993). In general, they would understand the text if it were read to them, but they have difficulty making meaning directly from print, without the aid of pictures. They use context to predict text and frequently look at the pictures to initiate or confirm their predictions. They also use pictures to facilitate word identification. The very beginning reader shows a focus on meaning by making meaningful predictions from oral language and pictures, but the words often bear little resemblance to the word in print (Jett-Simpson & Leslie, 1997; Sulzby & Teale, 1991). Gradually, children move to a phase of controlled word recognition (Spear-Swerling & Sternberg, 1996), wherein they make full use of sound-letter relationships but often do so in a laborious manner.

Literacy research has identified the importance of phonological skills to early reading development. Alliteration and rhyme have been theorized by Bradley and Bryant (1985) to be central to learning their orthographic parallels, onsets (f-), and rimes (-un). Instruction in using knowledge of onsets and rimes to identify unknown words has been effective in increasing reading ability (Gaskins, Gaskins, Anderson & Schommer, 1995) as well as phonological skills. The use of known words to identify unknown words is an important development in reading acquisition.

The next stage has been termed sight word reading (Ehri, 1991) or automatic word recognition (Spear-Swerling & Sternberg, 1996). Children recognize many words accurately and automatically with no need of "sounding out." A student who has a large base of sight words may be focused on other aspects of the reading process. This student looks at pictures in a cursory manner prior to or during reading but, in general, uses print for word identification. The student shows a focus on meaning by self-correcting any oral reading miscues that significantly change the meaning of the text. Unlike the very beginning reader, the advanced beginner exhibits a balanced use of cue sources (Clay, 1985; Jett-Simpson & Leslie, 1997). However, as readers become more skilled, they no longer depend on context for word recognition (Stanovich, 1991). Their word recognition is too rapid and automatic for context usage to play a meaningful part. Instead, context becomes a "mechanism in the comprehension process" (Stanovich, 1993–1994, p. 282). For example, readers use context to assign meanings to unknown words.

Still another student may have mastered basic word-recognition skills; can read narrative text with fluency, comprehend it, and retell all major components of the narrative with a single reading; and now focuses on learning how to apply those same strategies to expository text (Chall, 1983). Spear-Swerling and Sternberg (1996) describe this as the strategic reading stage.

This review of the developmental perspective highlights that what we observe depends on the student's development in learning to read. It should be noted that a developmental perspective does not imply rigid stages through which children pass at prescribed rates. Nor should it be inferred that at any point in learning to read, children are focused only on one aspect of reading. On the contrary, the interactive model of reading (Rumelhart, 1977; Stanovich, 1980) describes the interaction of many sources of information that students have available to them as they read. The more information they have in one area, the less they need in another (Stanovich, 1980). In the examples cited previously, children are all attempting to construct meaning from text, but the beginning reader, having less knowledge of the phoneme–grapheme relationships, is using picture cues to aid the process. The most advanced reader described earlier has developed automatic word identification and can free her limited attentional resources to learning different strategies for remembering information from expository text. All students are focused on meaning, but the balance of cue systems used varies with their development. We believe that assessment should observe developmental differences in learning to read. Certain aspects of the *QRI–3* support such observations.

The *QRI–3* includes passages for assessment of earlier stages of beginning reading. The *QRI–3* contains five *pre-primer* passages, four of which are narrative and one expository. Two narratives and the expository text have pictures. All the texts are written to be predictable—that is, they contain repetitive language patterns. Two new pre-primer narratives have rhyming words at the end of sentences. These stories allow examiners to determine if students can use onset and rime patterns to identify unknown words. In addition, two narrative passages each at the primer level and levels one and two include pictures, and each is laid out over several pages. We included pictures to allow examiners to compare students' performance when pictures were available with their performance in the absence of pictures. Our pilot data suggested that at the pre-primer level, texts with pictures were read more accurately. Above the pre-primer level, pictures assisted retelling and comprehension. See Section 16.

Factors Related to Comprehension

Text Structure

Research in the last two decades has described the structures of narrative (Graesser, Golding, & Long, 1991; Johnson & Mandler, 1980; Stein & Glenn, 1979) and expository text (Meyer & Rice, 1984; Weaver & Kintsch, 1991). Narratives, which follow the structure of fables (setting–character–goal/problem–events–resolution) have been found to be easier for children to recall than narratives without the major story components (Stein, 1979; Brennan, Bridge & Winograd, 1986) or with structure disrupted (Mandler & DeForest, 1979). Research with children reveals that throughout the elementary school years, narrative is easier for children to recall and comprehend than expository texts (Berkowitz & Taylor, 1981; Leslie & Caldwell, 1989; Leslie & Cooper, 1993; Leslie, unpublished).

There are many reasons why narrative text holds this privileged status (Graesser & Goodman, 1985; Graesser, Golding & Long, 1991). One reason is structural familiarity: it is highly likely that readers' familiarity with the structure of narratives is greater than their familiarity with the structures of expository text. In the most general sense, narratives are written about people engaging in goal-directed action—that is, the sorts of events that are proposed to be the building blocks of cognition (Mandler, 1984; Nelson, 1986). Children are more likely to have been read narrative than expository texts. Primary-grade instructional materials are predominantly narratives (Durkin, 1981), and the type of narrative most frequently read is the fable. Thus the narrative texts with which children have the most experience have a single, common structure (Mulcahy & Samuels, 1987). In contrast to children's rather stable knowledge of narrative structure, their knowledge of expository structures is variable (Englert & Hiebert, 1984). Children may also be less familiar with any single structure of expository text because of the variety of expository structures, such as compare–contrast, problem–solution, and description, which rarely appear in pure form in student textbooks (Taylor, 1982).

Other reasons why narratives are easier to recall or comprehend may be readers' knowledge of content, or the strategic approaches they employ in reading texts. Although the effects of content knowledge and strategic approaches to reading on comprehension will be discussed separately in detail in this section, it is important to remember that differences between the recall and comprehension of narrative and expository texts may be related to these factors. If students know more about the topics discussed in narrative writings (as compared to those more usually presented in expository texts), then it is likely that they will recall and comprehend more of the narrative text. Only by assessing prior knowledge of concepts will we be able to isolate this effect. Similarly, differences between recall and comprehension of narrative and expository text may be traced to strategic differences. A student reading a narrative for entertainment might read quickly to find out what happened and thus might recall only the action line of the story. However, when reading to remember information for a test, the student might read more slowly, self-test on important main ideas, and so forth.

If structural differences are one of the reasons for the superiority of narrative text, then differences between a student's recall of narrative and expository texts should be evident even when comprehension differences are not significant—if structural knowledge is more important for recall than for comprehension (Kintsch, 1990).

The *QRI–3* contains narrative and expository passages at pre-primer through high school levels. There are four narrative passages and one expository passage at the pre-primer level. There are three narrative and two expository passages at the primer, first grade, and second grade levels, and three narrative and three expository passages at the third through sixth grade levels. There are two literature passages, two social studies passages, and two science passages at the upper middle school level. Finally, at the high school level, there is one extended text in each of three areas: literature, science, and social studies. Our research on the *QRI–3* demonstrated that students' comprehension varies across types of text. See Section 16 for details.

Prior Knowledge

Within the last fifteen years, it has been shown repeatedly that readers with higher prior knowledge, *consistent with the content in the text*, recall and comprehend better than those with less such knowledge (Alvermann, Smith & Readance, 1985; Lipson, 1983). This finding is true for adults (Anderson, Reynolds, Schallert & Goetz, 1977) and children (Pearson, Hansen & Gordon, 1979; Taft & Leslie, 1985). Furthermore, the results can be generalized to poor readers as well as good readers (Taylor, 1979; Stevens, 1980). In fact, research has found that good and poor readers' ability to recall and summarize did not differ significantly if the groups were similar in their levels of knowledge (Recht & Leslie, 1988). The implications of these findings for assessment seem obvious (Johnston, 1984). A student with high knowledge of a particular content that is consistent with the information presented in text will be able to recall more and answer more questions correctly about that content than would be possible on material of the same readability about which the student had less or inconsistent knowledge.

These variations in comprehension as a function of prior knowledge impel us to design new reading-assessment devices. There are many ways in which to measure prior knowledge (Holmes & Roser, 1987): multiple-choice test, interview, oral free association, written free association, open-ended questions, and oral or written prediction. Researchers have found varying correlations among prior-knowledge measures. Recht (1986) found the correlation between multiple-choice tests and free-association measures of prior knowledge to be .92. More recently, however, Valencia, Stallman, Commeyras, Pearson, and Hartman (1991) concluded that interviews, judgments of the likelihood that statements would be included in a passage on a certain topic, and written predictions of content given topical prompts all measure different aspects of prior knowledge. Because they did not measure comprehension, no conclusion can be made about the ability of these measures to predict comprehension, which is termed predictive validity.

Other studies have examined the predictive validity of prior-knowledge measures. Free-association tasks have been shown to be significantly correlated with comprehension of narrative (Langer, 1984; Leslie & Caldwell, 1989; 1990; Leslie & Cooper, 1993) and expository text (Hare, 1982; Langer, 1984; Leslie & Caldwell, 1989; 1990; Taft & Leslie, 1985). Recent research (Leslie & Cooper, 1993) suggests that instructions for the free-association task, which ask for more precise responses rather than general associations, were more predictive of sixth graders' comprehension and retelling of narrative text.

Also, prediction tasks have been shown to correlate somewhat with comprehension, although the findings are less consistent than those using free-association concepts. Valencia and Stallman (1989) found written prediction tasks to be minimally (.23), but statistically significantly, correlated with comprehension of expository text. Leslie and Cooper (1993) gave sixth grade average readers the title of the selection and the concepts to which they had just responded and asked them to make a prediction of what the selection would be about. The prediction score correlated with students' retelling and comprehension of expository text.

The *QRI–3* measures prior knowledge by asking children to answer questions that were written to tap their understanding of key concepts (Langer, 1984). In addition, a prediction task based on the concepts and the title of the selection is provided. Our pilot data suggested that at the first grade level and above, both conceptual knowledge and prediction were significantly correlated with some form of comprehension, be it retelling, answers to questions without look-backs, or answers to questions with look-backs. See Section 16.

Oral and Silent Reading

Although overall differences in oral and silent reading comprehension may be minimal, some children may comprehend better in one mode than in the other. Results of research examining differences between oral and silent reading comprehension are mixed; some studies find no differences (Pinter & Gilliland, 1916; Swalm, 1972) and others find oral superior to silent (Rowell, 1976) or silent superior to oral (Pinter, 1913). The most consistent findings appear to be that poor readers at fourth grade level and below tend to comprehend better when reading orally (Swalm, 1972; Burge, 1983).

In addition to examining comprehension differences between oral and silent reading, rate differences may suggest the reader's level of reading development. Children for whom oral and silent rates are similar may not yet have developed fast and accurate word recognition, called *automaticity*. Generally, authors say that more fluent reading is indicated when a child reads faster silently than orally (Harris & Sipay, 1985). Huey (1968) states that good (fluent) readers read one-and-a-half to two times faster silently than orally. In order to allow comparison of a student's ability in both oral and silent reading, the *QRI–3* includes at least three narratives at pre-primer through second grade levels, two expository passages at primer through second grade levels, and three narrative and three expository passages at levels three through six. At upper middle school level, there are two literature passages, two social studies passages, and two science passages. Each high school passage is divided into three sections, thus allowing for comparison between oral and silent reading if the examiner so chooses.

Look-Backs

The effects of knowledge and application of metacognitive strategies on reading comprehension have been examined extensively during the past decade (for reviews see Baker & Brown, 1984; Paris, Wasik & Turner, 1991). Studies using interviews and observations of students' behavior have found that poor readers rated negative strategies as positive (and vice versa) and failed to ask questions, take notes, or use a dictionary as often as good readers did. Poor readers were also less accurate in applying the monitoring skills useful for resolving comprehension failures. Differences in skilled and less skilled readers' strategy use are particularly obvious when the readers are faced with difficult text (Kletzien, 1991; Zabrucky & Ratner, 1992). Specifically, research on "look-backs" in text containing inconsistencies designed to cause comprehension failure, indicated that students younger than eighth grade rarely used this strategy spontaneously (Garner & Reis, 1981). Various investigators have posited that students may not look back because (1) they do not realize that they have not understood (Markman, 1977; 1979); (2) they realize that the text did not make sense but then make inferences to make sense of the text rather than look back (August, Flavell & Clift, 1984); (3) they have expended so much attention on decoding and meaning construction that they do not have enough resources left to compare new information to prior knowledge and evaluate the consistency between them (Paris, Wasik & Turner, 1991); or (4) they have been unable to form a coherent representation of the text from which to compare and evaluate (Vosniadou, Pearson & Rogers, 1988). However, direct instruction to poor readers over five days improved students' strategic look-backs in text (Garner, Hare, Alexander, Haynes & Winograd, 1984). Thus, through direct instruction with modeling and through explanations of which strategies are important, as well as when and why to use them, young readers can become more strategic.

The *QRI–3* includes the option of asking students to engage in look-backs to resolve comprehension failures. We chose to measure students' ability to perform look-backs rather than including a self-report instrument (Meyers & Paris, 1978; Schmidt, 1990) because we believe that students' abilities to *use* strategies are more important to reading comprehension than their self-report of useful strategies. We recognize that asking students to look back is not the same as spontaneous look-backs, which is the topic of much of the research. We expected students to be able to *use* information from directed look-backs at an earlier age or reading ability level than the research on spontaneous look-backs suggests. We believe that examining whether students can look back when prompted will give valuable information for instruction.

Our pilot research on the *QRI–3* indicated that students with instructional levels at or above third grade were able to increase their explicit and implicit comprehension scores by looking back in the text. See Section 16. Prior to this level, students' focus was on word identification, and look-backs frequently resulted in the student rereading the entire text rather than being able to look back quickly to the section that contained the relevant information.

Think-Alouds

Asking readers to read a selection and think out loud as they do so is a process that can provide valuable information about the strategies that readers use as they attempt to comprehend text. Pressley and Afflerbach (1995) provide a comprehensive summary of studies that have examined this think-aloud process. Readers engaged in a variety of activities as they thought out loud about the text they were reading. They summarized or paraphrased the text; they made inferences; they attempted to isolate important information; they monitored their understanding or lack of it; they reacted personally; they integrated various parts of the text; and they moved beyond literal meaning and attempted to interpret what they were reading. Using think-alouds "has the potential to examine what the reader does to facilitate comprehension" (Myers & Lytle, 1986, p. 140). It offers the opportunity to gather observations about the thinking that occurs during the reading process.

There is evidence that skilled readers and those with higher levels of prior knowledge employ more, and more varied, think-aloud strategies than poorer readers or those struggling with unfamiliar text. In summarizing research on differences in reading skill and think-aloud usage, Goldman (1997) noted that individuals who used a variety of strategies demonstrated better recall. In addition, effective readers engaged in constructive activities; that is, they attempted to build relationships between text ideas. Similarly, Crain-Thoreson, Lippman, and McClendon-Magnuson (1997) reported that successful comprehension was associated with "knowledge-transforming activities" (p. 586). Readers who connected the text to their background knowledge, constructed inferences, and integrated information across the text demonstrated higher comprehension. Myers, Lytle, Palladino, Devenpeck and Green (1990) determined that significant correlations existed between comprehension scores and the type of think-aloud comments made by fourth and fifth graders. Those who constructed more inferences and verbalized more revisions of prior knowledge did better. Zwaan and Brown (1996) found that skilled readers made more explanatory inferences as they attempted to integrate information across the text. Kavale and Schreiner (1979) found that sixth grade above-average readers made more think-aloud comments and more comments directly related to the text, whereas average readers tended to respond with a personal or unrelated comment. Chou-Hare and Smith (1982) found that the number of think-aloud comments correlated positively with reading achievement scores. In light of the above, we decided to emphasize a think-aloud component for high school text as one possible alternative for identifying why a student may demonstrate inadequate comprehension.

Think-aloud procedures are not limited to adult readers. Readers of varying ages have engaged in think-alouds: university students (Garner, 1982); high school students (Olshavsky, 1976–1977; Rogers, 1991); middle school youngsters (Kavale & Schreiner, 1979; Chou-Hare & Smith, 1982; Bereiter & Bird, 1985); and primary school children (Myers, 1988; Myers, Lytle, Palladino, Devenpeck & Green, 1990; Cote & Goldman, 1998; Cote, Goldman & Saul, 1998). Apparently, with appropriate instructions and modeling, learners of most ages can effectively engage in thinking aloud while reading. Afflerbach and Johnston (1984) emphasize the importance of training or modeling when asking readers to engage in think-alouds. Bereiter and Bird

(1985) modeled the think-aloud strategy to seventh and eighth graders and instructed them in identifying and using these strategies. These students made more, and more varied, think-aloud comments than those who were only exposed to modeling. In our pilot, we carefully modeled each of the think-aloud strategies that we intended to score before asking the students to think aloud on their own.

Researchers use a variety of coding systems to classify think-alouds (Olshavsky, 1976–1977; Bereiter & Bird, 1985; Myers, Lytle, Palladino, Devenpeck & Green, 1990; Crain-Thoreson, Lippman & McClendon-Magnuson, 1997; Cote, Goldman & Saul, 1998). Many of these systems are quite similar, varying only in the language used to describe the think-aloud comment. All direct attention to monitoring comments, reasoning comments, restatements or paraphrases, and prediction. For our pilot study, we devised a coding system based on those comments identified most often in the literature. This resulted in an initial list of eleven think-aloud comments. We modified this list to the coding system presented in the *QRI–3* that is based on the results of our pilot study.

Is there a link between the assessment and identification of think-aloud strategies and reading comprehension instruction? Myers (1988) presents a compelling argument for using think-alouds to assess comprehension and to offer suggestions for instruction. However, there is no evidence that identifying an underused or absent think-aloud strategy and instructing students in that strategy will improve reading achievement. Bereiter and Bird (1985) modeled the think-aloud strategy to seventh and eighth graders and instructed them in identifying and using these strategies. After instruction, these students demonstrated higher scores on standardized reading measures than those who had been exposed only to modeling or to exercises that directed students to make specific think-aloud comments but offered no explanation for doing so. Nist and Kirby (1986) suggest that modeling the think-aloud process may be an effective form of comprehension instruction. Wade (1990) suggests that teachers can use think-aloud data to identify directions for instruction. She describes several types of comprehenders on the basis of their think-aloud comments and offers instructional suggestions for each. Non–risk takers who tend to repeat segments of text and do not develop hypotheses for new meaning need to be shown how to draw on prior knowledge and textual clues to generate inferences. Non-integrators develop new hypotheses for every text segment and fail to integrate old and new information. Such readers might benefit from constructing semantic maps and visualizing relationships between text segments. Schema imposers retain an initial hypothesis despite contradicting information. They should be encouraged to entertain multiple perspectives or alternative interpretations. Storytellers who depend more on prior knowledge than on text content need to ask questions to determine whether their own experiences actually do match information presented in the text. Pressley and Afflerbach (1995) comment that strategy instruction present in many classrooms actively teaches readers to engage in many of the strategies identified in the think-aloud literature, such as predicting, self-questioning, summarizing, and checking understanding. They admit that it is not certain that such instruction leads to growth in reading expertise. However, they are confident that long-term use of such strategies "must increase their use somewhat" (p. 314).

Olson, Duffy, and Mack (1984) and Myers and Lytle (1986) describe traditional achievement measures as having predictive validity. That is, good performance on these measures tends to predict average or above-average classroom performance. However, such measures are limited in that they do not assess process. They lack prescriptive validity: they offer no suggestions for increasing learning. Think-aloud data may be a process measure that can suggest instructional directions. For this reason, we have included think-alouds in the *QRI–3*. Our pilot data suggested that, on the high school level passages, think-aloud statements that indicated understanding of the text were positively correlated with retelling, inferences generated during retelling, or comprehension with look-backs. See Section 16.

Factors Related to Word Identification

Speed and Automaticity

The ability to recognize words is characterized by accuracy, automaticity, and speed (Ehri & Wilce, 1979). As readers practice the accurate identification of words, they begin to read these words with less conscious attention to letter–sound matching and, therefore, more rapidly. Although automaticity and speed in word identification are different constructs (Stanovich, Cunningham & West, 1981), reading rate can suggest the presence of automaticity.

Perfetti's (1985, 1988) verbal efficiency theory hypothesizes that children who do not develop the ability to read words accurately and quickly will encounter difficulty in comprehension. Because most of their attention is directed toward identifying individual words, they are unable to access word meanings efficiently and integrate sentence meanings across an entire passage. LaBerge and Samuels (1985) also stress the importance of fast and accurate automatic word identification. Both word identification and comprehension require attention on the part of the reader. Attentional resources are limited. The more attention that is directed to word identification, the less is available for comprehension.

The *QRI–3* measures word-identification speed (and automaticity) in two ways. The timed portion of the word lists provides one measure. Our pilot data showed that the number of words read within one second predicts reading rate in context better than the total number of words read correctly.

Some may argue that the use of word lists for assessment is not an authentic task. We agree. Readers do not curl up with a good list of words. However, the ability to identify words accurately and quickly *out of context* is a characteristic of the skilled reader (Perfetti, 1983, 1988; Stanovich, 1980, 1991). Therefore, using word lists may provide an important piece of assessment information. Readers who take more than one second to identify a word accurately may not have achieved automaticity for that word.

The *QRI–3* provides another measure of word-identification speed: rate of reading as measured in words per minute on the passages. Definitive research in this area has been elegantly reviewed by Carver (1990). Carver describes five different reading processes: memorizing, learning, rauding, skimming, and scanning. Memorizing involves the slowest reading rate, and scanning is the fastest. Rauding is the process normally used by readers for relatively easy material. Rauding occurs at a generally constant rate for individuals, and speed of word identification is the factor that most affects that rate.

Reading rate is affected by a variety of factors (Carver, 1990). Rate varies with the purpose of the reader and the process chosen. For example, a reader engaged in the rauding process may well shift to the learning process if the material becomes relatively difficult. This shift would result in a slower reading rate. In this example, we can note that text difficulty, as determined by the structure of the text, the familiarity of the content, and the difficulty level of the author's vocabulary, can be important determiners of reading rate. Reading rate can vary according to the mode of reading (oral versus silent), the age of the reader, and reading skill. Finally, reading rate is also determined by individual cognitive processing speeds. The complexity of variables affecting rate suggest that hard-and-fast norms may be impossible to formulate. In Section 10, we offer some general suggestions for evaluating reading rate that are based on our pilot data.

Since the late 1960s, Goodman (1969) has drawn attention to the rich information that an assessment specialist can gain from examining how a student's oral reading deviates from the written text. Prior to Goodman, assessment specialists only analyzed how deviations from print (then called errors) reflected what the reader did not know about sound–symbol correspondences. Goodman's research encouraged others to go beyond what appeared to be wrong with the reader and attend to the cue systems that the reader was using when his or her reading deviated from the print. Goodman calls these deviations *miscues* because he believes that they indicate how the reading process was miscued by characteristics of the text and by prior knowledge of the reader. Goodman's work has led assessment specialists to examine what miscues tell us about how readers are using the cue systems. Two of the cue systems discussed by Goodman that are pertinent to the *QRI–3* are the graphophonic cue system and the semantic cue system.

Graphophonic cues refer to the relationships between graphemes (letters) and phonemes (the smallest units of sound). If a reader says the word "was" for "saw," one can infer that the reader is utilizing graphic cues because the letters are the same in both words. However, the phonemic similarity is low; these words don't sound alike at all. On the other hand, a reader who identifies "horse" as "house" is using both graphic and sound cues.

Semantic cues are meaning cues. They are obtained from the semantic content of what is being read. For example, if a reader reads the sentence "I received six presents for my birthday" as "I received six gifts for my birthday," we can infer that the reader is using semantic information in saying "gifts" for "presents." The reader is not using graphophonic cues, because these words do not share similar letters or sounds.

Leslie and Osol (1978) and Leslie (1980) examined how the quantity of miscues related to the quality of miscues. They asked whether the acceptability of miscues decreases as the reader makes more and more miscues. The results showed that as the percentage of miscues increased, the proportion that changed the author's meaning and was left uncorrected also increased. As the reader makes more and more deviations from text, she or he begins to lose meaning, which is reflected in miscues of less quality.

These findings support the 90% oral reading accuracy recommended by Betts (1946) and endorsed by Harris and Sipay (1985) as the cutoff for frustration-level reading. The oral reading research suggests that reading with less than 90% accuracy may result in an inability to obtain meaning. The research points to an implication, which hasn't been tested, that students reading materials with which they frequently make more than 10% errors will not learn to correct errors that change meaning. Furthermore, they may learn to expect reading not to make sense (Bristow, 1985).

Another factor that has been shown to affect the quality of miscues is prior knowledge. Taft and Leslie (1985) found that students with prior knowledge about content made fewer miscues that changed the author's meaning than students who had little knowledge about the content area. Those with little knowledge made a higher proportion of miscues that were graphically similar to the word in print. The results suggested a trade-off between the use of semantic and graphic cues. When more semantic cues are available, readers may not need to pay so much attention to graphic cues. Conversely, a reader who does not have enough semantic information will rely on graphic cues (Stanovich, 1980).

Users of the *QRI–3* can examine oral reading behavior quantitatively and qualitatively. The quantitative criteria used to determine independent, instructional, and frustration levels follows the recommendations of Harris and Sipay (1985). Our pilot data suggests that the best predictor of instructional-level comprehension is 95% for Acceptable Accuracy. Acceptable Accuracy is the measure of accuracy attained when only uncorrected, meaning-change miscues are counted.

We encourage qualitative analysis of the reader's use of semantic and graphic cues to ascertain how much attention the reader is paying to meaning and how much attention is paid to the graphic elements of the text. In addition, because prior knowledge has been found to influence miscue patterns (Taft & Leslie, 1985), the assessment specialist can examine whether the use of the semantic and graphic cues changes as a function of degree of familiarity with the text.

3 A General Description of the Qualitative Reading Inventory–3

The Word Lists

The Passages

Pre-primer, Primer, First Grade, and Second Grade Passages
Third Grade Through Upper Middle School Passages
High School Passages
Measures of Comprehension

The Word Lists

Each of the *QRI–3*'s ten word lists contains twenty words that we have selected from passages at the same level of readability. For example, the primer word list contains words from the primer passages.

The word lists are designed:

1. To assess accuracy of word identification
2. To assess speed and automaticity of word identification
3. To determine the starting point for reading the initial passage

The Passages

The passages to be read orally or silently assess the subject's ability to read and comprehend different types of text. Table 3.1 presents the *QRI–3* passages grouped according to readability level and text type.

Pre-primer, Primer, First Grade, and Second Grade Passages

At the pre-primer readability level, there are five passages. Four are narratives and one is expository. Two of the narratives and the expository passage are presented with pictures. The primer, first grade, and second grade

TABLE 3.1

Passages on the *Qualitative Reading Inventory–3*

Readability Level	Narrative	Expository

Pre-primer	"Lost and Found"
	"Spring and Fall"
	"Who Do I See?"
	  (pictures)
	"Just Like Mom"
	  (pictures)
		"People at Work"
		  (pictures)

Primer	"A Trip"
	"Fox and Mouse"
	  (pictures)
	"The Pig Who Learned
	  to Read" (pictures)
		"Who Lives Near
		  Lakes?"
		"Living and Not
		  Living"

First	"Mouse in a House"
	"Marva Finds a Friend"
	  (pictures)
	"The Bear and Rabbit"
	  (pictures)
		"Air"
		"What You Eat"

Second	"What Can I Get for
	  My Toy?"
	"The Lucky Cricket"
	  (pictures)
	"Father's New Game"
	  (pictures)
		"Seasons"
		"Whales and Fish"

Third	"The Trip to the Zoo"
	"A Special Birthday
	  for Rosa"
	"The Friend"
		"Cats: Lions and Tigers
		  in Your House"
		"Where Do People
		  Live?"
		"Wool: From Sheep
		  to You"

Fourth	"Johnny Appleseed" "Amelia Earhart" "Sequoyah"	"The Busy Beaver" "Saudi Arabia" "The City of Cahokia"
Fifth	"Martin Luther King, Jr." "Christopher Columbus" "Margaret Mead"	"The Octopus" "Getting Rid of Trash" "Laser Light"
Sixth	"Pele" "Abraham Lincoln" "Andrew Carnegie"	"Computers" "Predicting Earthquakes" "Ultrasound"

	Literature	Social Studies	Science

Upper Middle
School
	"Biddy Mason"
	"Malcolm X"
		"Lewis and Clark"
		"Ferdinand
		  Magellan"
			"Fireworks"
			"Life Cycles of
			  Stars"

High School	"Where the
	  Ashes Are"
		"World War I"	"Characteristics
			  of Viruses"

readability levels have five passages—three narrative and two expository. At each level, two of the narrative passages are presented with pictures. Research suggests that emergent readers depend on picture context for both word identification and passage comprehension. In addition, text with pictures more closely approximates the type of selections presented to beginning readers. However, good readers are not dependent on pictures for word identification (Stanovich, 1991), and it may be important to ascertain whether word identification differs when pictures are present as opposed to when they are absent. The diagnostician can assess the effect of pictures on a subject's word identification and/or comprehension by contrasting performance on passages with and without pictures.

In addition to the narrative selections, there are one or two expository passages at each level. Because the amount of expository material is increasing in basal readers, and because children have had difficulty making the transition from narration to exposition, we felt that it was important to include expository material at all levels. The inclusion of expository material also makes the *QRI–3* more usable by teachers working with adult beginning readers who might be put off by children's narratives. Examiners who give passages from pre-primer through second grade will be able to ascertain the subject's relative strengths in recalling and comprehending narrative versus expository material. In addition, we have included enough passages to assess differences between oral and silent reading, which, if they are likely to occur, should be more predominant at these early reading levels.

All passages contain concept questions that are designed to measure prior knowledge of the major concepts within each passage. Each passage assesses knowledge of three to four concepts. Scores on the concept task should help the examiner to determine whether the subject possesses knowledge of basic concepts necessary to comprehend the selection.

Third Grade Through Sixth Grade Passages

The passages for use from third grade through sixth grade include three narrative and three expository passages at each level. The narratives for fourth through sixth grades are biographies of famous people who had a goal or dream. Two of the people are relatively well known (such as Martin Luther King) and/or contain concepts that should be familiar to the readers because similar concepts were included in several content area texts at that level (such as Abraham Lincoln). We chose biographies in order to provide a more controlled assessment of prior knowledge. For example, it is easier to assess prior knowledge of Abraham Lincoln than to evaluate a student's knowledge of the content of a fictional narrative. In addition, the purpose of biographies is to inform (Brewer, 1980). Thus the purpose for reading these narratives is the same as for our expository passages. This control allows us to examine the effect of text structure without the confounding of purpose. The other passage in each level is about a person likely to be unknown to the readers (such as Andrew Carnegie). Because both familiar and unfamiliar topics are included, *QRI–3* results can be useful in suggesting why subjects are having trouble in comprehension.

The expository passages are descriptive science and social studies materials written about various topics. As in the narratives, two of the passages are about relatively familiar topics (such as an octopus) and one is on a less familiar topic (such as ultrasound). We included passages that, according to our pilot data, offered a range in familiarity. Again, we did so because of research findings suggesting that the level of prior knowledge is an important determinant of reading comprehension.

Upper Middle School Passages

At the upper middle school level, there are six passages. Two passages are representative of middle school literature selections and are biographical or autobiographical in nature. Two passages represent science content, and two represent social studies content.

All the passages on levels four through upper middle school were taken from published literature, science texts, and social studies texts, so they are representative of the material that readers at these grade levels are exposed to in class. Prior-knowledge tasks were designed for each passage to assess reader familiarity with or prior knowledge of the important concepts included in the selection. This should help the examiner determine whether high or low comprehension scores on a passage were due, in part, to the level of prior knowledge a subject had about the topic. Because of the variety and number of the passages we have provided, test administrators can examine differences in comprehension of familiar versus unfamiliar material, narrative versus expository material, and oral versus silent reading.

The pre-primer through upper middle school passages are designed:

1. To determine a student's independent, instructional, and/or frustration levels for word identification in context
2. To determine a student's independent, instructional, and/or frustration levels for comprehension
3. To assess a student's ability to read different types of text: narrative and expository text; text with and without pictures (pre-primer through grade two); and text of varying familiarity
4. To assess a student's ability to comprehend in different modes: oral and silent
5. To assess a student's ability to use look-backs to locate missing or incorrect information

High School Passages

At the high school level, we have included three passages taken from representative literature, social studies, and science texts. Readability formulas for determining text level are not useful at the high school level. Different formulas provided us with a wide range of readability levels for a single selection. For example, the social studies passage was leveled anywhere from grade eight to grade twelve, depending on the formula used. Readability levels for the science passage ranged from grade eight through fifteen. The literature passage was leveled somewhat lower but with the same wide range of scores. We reasoned that readability levels mattered less than the content typically chosen for high school textbooks. We therefore chose selections that were very representative of high school content across several publishers.

All high school passages represent relatively unfamiliar topics: the Vietnam War, World War I, and viruses. Each passage is divided into three sections preceded by a prior-knowledge and prediction task and followed by a retelling grid and ten questions. The second section of each selection contains suggestions for modeling the think-aloud process to and with the student. The text is divided at certain points, and suggested modeling comments are included. The third section is similarly divided, and space is provided for the examiner to write the student's think-aloud comments.

The passages are designed:

1. To determine a student's independent, instructional, and/or frustration levels for comprehension
2. To assess a student's ability to read different types of text: narrative and expository text and relatively unfamiliar text
3. To assess a student's ability to use look-backs to locate missing or incorrect information
4. To assess the variety and quality of a student's think-alouds

Measures of Comprehension

The *QRI–3* assesses comprehension of all passages in two ways: retelling and questions. In addition, in passages at the third grade through high school levels, the examiner may utilize look-backs to evaluate quality of comprehension further. In the high school passages, the examiner may employ think-alouds as a further assessment of comprehension quality.

Retelling. After reading the selection, the student is asked to retell the passage as though she or he were telling it to someone who never heard it before. The student's retelling is scored from a map of important idea units, or propositions, contained in the passage. For example, "John Chapman was born in Massachusetts," contains two propositions: John Chapman was born, and he was born in Massachusetts.

What the student is able to retell can provide information about the reader's ability to recall important ideas that are structured in some logical way. For example, in recalling goal-based stories, a student who knows the structure of stories may retell the passage in the order of a well-structured narrative: setting–character–goal/problem–events–resolution. In exposition, examiners should note whether a student recalls main ideas first, followed by supporting details.

Questions. Next the examiner asks the student two types of questions. Questions with answers stated explicitly in the text are called *text-explicit questions.* Questions with answers that the subject must infer from information in the text are called *text-implicit questions.* Answers to the text-implicit questions are based on the interaction of text information and prior knowledge. However, correct answers to text-implicit questions must be tied to information in the story and not simply derived from prior knowledge. Independent, instructional, and frustration levels for comprehension are derived from scores on the question measure.

The comprehension measures are designed:

1. To assess the quality of the reader's unaided recall
2. To arrive at independent, instructional, and frustration levels for text comprehension

Look-Backs. At levels three through high school, the examiner may use look-backs to assess comprehension further. After scoring the questions, the examiner can ask the student to look back in the text to locate missing information or to correct erroneous answers. Look-backs allow the examiner to differentiate between comprehension during reading and memory after reading. Students may understand a concept while reading but then promptly forget it. As a result, they are unable to answer an explicit or implicit question.

Look-backs are particularly informative when the student has read unfamiliar and/or difficult, concept-dense text. Skilled readers can generally employ skimming or rereading to locate information. Less skilled readers are unable to do this successfully.

Think-Alouds. At the high school level, the examiner can ask the student to think aloud while reading. The examiner asks the student to stop at designated segments of text and describe what he or she is thinking at that point. A think-aloud scoring grid is provided to help examiners keep track of the type of comments made by the reader.

In summary, the *QRI–3* consists of graded word lists and narrative and expository passages. The word lists and passages, which range from pre-primer to high school level, vary in familiarity, and prior knowledge is assessed before the student reads each passage. Comprehension is assessed through retelling, questions, look-backs, and think-alouds.

Section 4 describes the assessment information provided by the *QRI–3*.

4 Information Provided by the Qualitative Reading Inventory–3

Finding Reading Levels

The Independent Level
The Instructional Level
The Frustration Level
Level Variety

Determining Reader Strengths and Needs

Finding Reading Levels

The *Qualitative Reading Inventory–3* can provide two kinds of information: the student's reading levels and his or her reading strengths and/or needs. When used to determine a student's reading levels, the *QRI–3* can help find the level at which a student can read independently, can read with instructional guidance, and can read with frustration.

The Independent Level

This is the level at which a student can read successfully without assistance. Oral reading should be fluent and free from behaviors such as finger pointing and overt signs of tension. The student's accuracy in word recognition while reading orally should be 98% or higher. Silent reading should also be free from finger pointing. For both oral and silent reading, comprehension should be excellent. The reader should be able to answer 90% or more of the questions correctly.

An examiner should choose materials written at this level for the student's free-reading pleasure or for tasks that the reader is expected to perform independently. It is also wise to choose materials at an independent level for reading-strategy instruction or fluency practice. This allows the reader to learn and practice a strategy on relatively easy text before transferring to more challenging material.

The Instructional Level

This is the level at which a student can read with assistance from a teacher. Both oral and silent reading should be free from behaviors that often indicate serious difficulty, such as finger pointing or tension. Although oral reading may be less fluent at this level than at the independent level, it should retain some sense of rhythm and expression. The examiner should use a criterion of 95% accuracy when counting only those miscues that changed the meaning of the passage. Our pilot data revealed that 95% acceptable accuracy best predicts comprehension at the instructional level. The examiner who is counting all miscues should use a criterion of 90% accuracy, and the subject should correctly answer 70% of the questions asked.

Materials written at this level should be chosen for reading and content-area instruction. This placement assumes that the teacher will introduce words and concepts that are likely to be unfamiliar to the readers. She or he presents the identification and meaning of these concepts and provides appropriate background knowledge necessary for understanding the material. Obviously, when students are placed at the instructional level, the teacher should not say, "Read Chapter 5 and we'll have a test tomorrow."

The Frustration Level

At this level, the student is completely unable to read the material with adequate word identification or comprehension. Signs of difficulty and tension are evident. Oral reading lacks fluency and expression; a word-for-word, halting style is common. Accuracy of word recognition is less than 90%, and less than 70% of the questions are answered correctly. Teachers should avoid materials at this level.

Level Variety

Whereas it was once common, it is now simplistic to talk about a single independent, instructional, or frustration level for an individual. The act of reading is highly complex and contextual. When students possess extensive prior knowledge about a topic, they can read and comprehend at a higher level than in unfamiliar material. This is well illustrated by the difficulty that mature readers often have with an income tax form or the language of an insurance policy. Text structure also affects a student's reading ability. The diverse structure and concept density of expository material makes it more difficult to comprehend than narrative text. Whether a student reads orally or silently can affect comprehension, depending on the age of the subject. Younger, less fluent readers generally do better in oral reading, whereas older readers are often constrained by the performance aspect of oral reading, and their comprehension suffers accordingly. The variety of passages in the *Qualitative Reading Inventory–3* allows the examiner to evaluate the effects of background knowledge, text structure, and reading mode on the independent, instructional, and frustration levels of the reader. It is not inconceivable that a single reader may have different levels for familiar and unfamiliar text, for narrative and expository material, and for oral and silent reading modes. The presence or absence of pictures may affect performance. Levels may also vary depending on whether the examiner is assessing comprehension with or without look-backs. A student may be at a frustration level for answering questions without referring to the text but may achieve an instructional level when allowed to utilize the look-back strategy.

Which reading level is most important? Given the constraints of time, few examiners would be able to determine all possible reading levels that a student might have. Based on individual purposes and needs, each examiner will have to choose which reading level to isolate for a given student. Which level best estimates the overall reading ability of the student? Determination of the familiar narrative reading level seems most essential. Because reading familiar narrative text is generally easier than dealing with expository and unfamiliar material, the familiar narrative level probably represents a reader's best effort. However, in unfamiliar, concept-dense, and lengthy texts, the level attained after look-backs may represent the reader's best effort.

Determining Reader Strengths and Needs

The major purpose of the *QRI–3* is to indicate the conditions under which a student would perform successfully or unsuccessfully in reading. Assessment specialists once believed that a student had a reading disability if there was a substantial difference between his or her expectancy level or reading potential and his or her instructional level in familiar material. Expectancy level or reading potential was generally based on IQ. However, this has been seriously questioned (Aaron, 1997). For this reason, it may be easier to speak of reading disability in terms of a discrepancy between the child's reading level and her or his chronological grade level.

For most readers with serious disabilities, strengths and needs in reading are evident. The *QRI–3* was designed to identify these strengths and needs by providing more information about why a student is not reading well. Following are questions that the *QRI–3* was designed to answer.

Can the Student Identify:
words accurately?
words automatically?

When Reading Orally, Does the Student:
correct word-identification errors that do not make sense?
make word-identification errors that are contextually appropriate?
make word-identification errors that suggest use of graphic or letter cues?

Can the Student Comprehend Successfully in:
narrative material?
expository material?
familiar material?
unfamiliar material?
material with pictures (pre-primer through second grade)?
material without pictures?

Can the Student
answer explicit questions?
answer implicit questions?
use look-backs to locate information in text?
think aloud during reading?

What Is the Quality of the Student's Recall?
Does the student organize recall in stories according to elements of story structure?
Does the student organize recall in exposition according to main idea and details?

The sections that follow will illustrate how the *QRI–3* can answer the above questions. Table 4.1 provides a summary of the options offered by the *QRI–3*.

TABLE 4.1

Assessment Options of the *Qualitative Reading Inventory–3*

Determination of a Student's Reading Levels

Independent
Instructional
Frustration
In:
　Narrative text
　Expository text
　Text read orally
　Text read silently
　Familiar text
　Unfamiliar text
　With look-backs
　Without look-backs
　Text with pictures (pre-primer through second grade)
　Text without pictures

Description of a Student's Strengths and Needs in Reading

Word-Identification Ability
In isolation
　Accuracy
　Automaticity
In context
　Oral reading of passages
　Accuracy
　Automaticity/rate
　Miscue analysis
　　Use of graphic/letter cues
　　Use of semantic cues
　　Use of self-corrections

Comprehension Ability
Ability to comprehend narrative text
Ability to comprehend expository text
Ability to comprehend familiar text
Ability to comprehend unfamiliar text
Ability to comprehend after oral reading
Ability to comprehend after silent reading
Ability to comprehend with look-backs
Ability to comprehend without look-backs
Ability to answer explicit questions
Ability to answer implicit questions
Ability to comprehend with pictures
Ability to comprehend without pictures
Ability to recall
　Completeness of recall
　Organization of recall
　Accuracy of recall

Prior Knowledge
Conceptual-question task
Prediction task

Think-Alouds
Variety of think-alouds
Quality of think-alouds

5 Uses of the Qualitative Reading Inventory–3

The Examiner as a Reflective Decision Maker

The Classroom Teacher

Using the *QRI–3* to Estimate Reading Level
Using the *QRI–3* to Match Students to Appropriate Text
Using the *QRI–3* for Reading Portfolios
Using the *QRI–3* to Verify a Suspected Problem

The Reading-Assessment Specialist

Using the *QRI–3* to Determine Reading Level
Using the *QRI–3* to Indicate Growth
Using the *QRI–3* to Describe Specific Reading Behavior as a Guide for
Intervention Instruction

In order to use the *QRI–3* to its best advantage without undue testing and interpretation time, the user must be a decision maker. The examiner must decide what information he or she wants to obtain about the student and how to use the *QRI–3* to obtain it. He or she need not determine a complete range of levels (independent, instructional, and frustration) for each student. He or she need not administer both word lists and passages to each student. He or she need not determine familiar/unfamiliar, narrative/expository, and oral/silent levels for each student. And he or she does not have to use all options (recall, questions, look-backs, think-alouds, and miscue analysis). This would be extremely time-consuming and, in many cases, totally unnecessary. The examiner must decide beforehand what information will be most helpful and choose the passages and options accordingly. In some cases, he or she may administer only one or two passages to estimate a reading level or to confirm the existence of a problem in a specific area, such as expository text. In other cases, the examiner may choose to engage in a more complete assessment of a reader's strengths and needs.

The *QRI–3* can be utilized effectively by the classroom teacher or the reading-assessment specialist. Both can choose those components of the inventory that will best suit their needs.

<table>
<tr><td>

The Classroom Teacher

</td><td>

Using the QRI–3 to Estimate Reading Level

The *QRI–3* can be effectively used by the classroom teacher to estimate the reading level of individual children. This is important for a variety of reasons. First, reading instruction is characterized by different organizational formats. Some classrooms group children according to reading ability; others employ a less structured approach, with groups of children and/or individuals reading selections that they have chosen. Some classrooms depend on basal reading series for instructional materials; others follow a literature-based approach and use a variety of trade books. Whichever format is used, its success depends on placing children in materials appropriate to their reading level.

The movement away from basal reading series to a literature-based approach has presented the classroom teacher with the problem of estimating an individual's reading level. Some school districts require that a child's reading level be placed on a report card or in a cumulative folder. Parents often ask for an estimation of reading level. Is their child performing at the level of his or her peers? Formerly, a classroom teacher could use a child's performance in a specific basal reader as an indication of individual level. If a child experienced success in a basal at grade level, the classroom teacher could assume that the child was on level. Similarly, performance in a higher or lower basal could suggest a reading level above or below grade placement. However, current basals are more focused on the content, quality, and kind of the literature selections included in the basal. They are less focused on a uniform reading level or a reading level that closely matches the grade level for which the basal is intended. Trade books do not always come marked with reading levels. Although some suggest appropriate grade levels for use, this is sometimes based on the topic and not on the difficulty level of the text.

In estimating individual reading levels, the classroom teacher does not have the luxury of ample time for assessment activities. Administration of the *QRI–3* should involve only a few passages. The teacher should choose a narrative at the appropriate grade level—for example, a third grade passage for use with third graders. The teacher should have the child read orally or silently, depending on which mode is primarily utilized in the classroom. We recommend using oral administration for second grade and below and using silent administration for third grade and above. If the teacher is listening to the child read orally, he or she should count all reading miscues and use a 90% cut-off score. It takes less time to count all miscues than to evaluate which ones represent meaning-change miscues and which do not. Again, because it is easier, the teacher should ask the comprehension questions as opposed to scoring recall.

If the student achieves at an instructional level, the teacher can estimate that the child is at least at grade level. The teacher has the option to move up to the next-higher passage in order to determine whether the child can read higher-level passages. If the student is at a frustration level, the teacher should administer the next-lower passage in order to determine the instructional level. Usually the teacher needs administer only two passages in order to determine reading level. It is not necessary to exercise the options of miscue analysis or unaided recall, nor is it necessary to contrast various types of text. It is important to remember that this offers only an estimate of

</td></tr>
</table>

reading level, because many other variables affect whether or not a child can comprehend a specific selection. Section 14 contains examples of the use of *QRI–3* passages to estimate reading level.

Using the QRI–3 to Match Students to Appropriate Text

Once the teacher has an estimate of reading level, he or she can match this level to a specific guided reading-group placement or basal text. Of course, if the school's basal reader has its own informal reading inventory (IRI), we suggest using this instead of the *QRI–3* for several reasons. First, the passages in the basal IRI are often taken directly from the book that will be used for instruction; thus one can tell how well the child will do on that material. Second, basal IRIs often utilize questions similar to those in the teacher's manual. For these reasons, a child's performance on the basal IRI should be most like his or her classroom performance.

The teacher can also use the *QRI–3* to place students in appropriate content textbooks. Some classrooms provide a range of such textbooks to use with the students. Matching an individual's reading level to a content text involves the same process as above. However, instead of using narrative passages from the *QRI–3* to estimate reading level, the teacher should use expository ones.

Matching an individual's reading level to trade book selection represents a less exact process. Because few trade books are designated as written at specific reading levels, the teacher cannot expect to match a child who is at a third grade instructional level on the *QRI–3* with a trade book leveled at grade three. Even if this were possible, it would not necessarily ensure success. Children can read more difficult books on very familiar topics or on topics of great interest to them.

Of course, the best way to estimate whether a child can handle a specific book is to listen to him or her read several pages from the book in question, note word-recognition skill, and ask for a brief recall. However, this can represent a very time-consuming process for a classroom teacher. An individual child may need to try out several trade books before finding an appropriate one. In addition, a teacher rarely deals with only one child but instead has an entire class to match to appropriate books. Administration of the *QRI–3* can offer a viable alternative. If the teacher has an instructional level from the *QRI–3*, he or she can use this as a rough estimate of ability level. If a tradebook is marked as suitable for a specific grade and if the child's instructional level matches this grade, there is a strong probability that the child can handle the selection with relative success.

Many classrooms are compiling classroom libraries. It is important that these libraries represent a range of difficulty levels so that appropriate text is available to all students. If the *QRI–3* has been used as an estimate of individual levels, this can be used to ensure that the teacher includes the necessary span of materials in the library.

Using the QRI–3 for Reading Portfolios

The concern for authentic assessment has led many classroom teachers to employ reading portfolios as an integral part of their assessment. The *QRI–3* can become one component of a reading portfolio. Asking a student to read a passage and then recall it is an authentic task that parallels the actual reading process. Although using actual trade books or textbooks can serve the same purpose, the *QRI–3* offers the convenience of scoring protocols and leveled passages with reliability and validity data on the questions and the difficulty of the passages.

There are several ways in which the *QRI–3* can be used in a reading portfolio. First, the classroom teacher can administer the *QRI–3* to obtain an estimate of reading level and can place the scored protocol in the child's portfolio. If this is done at the beginning of the year, the same passage or another of the same genre or level of difficulty can be administered at the end of the year or at the end of a grading period to evaluate growth. The two scored protocols can be clipped together with a brief teacher comment on the student's progress. The protocol can also be shared with the student and used as a vehicle for student self-assessment of progress.

The reading portfolio can contrast the student's performance on narrative and expository text. Both can be administered and then re-administered at a later date. Again, both the teacher and the student can offer comments on performance growth.

QRI–3 passages can be used for student self-analysis, an important component of a portfolio. The teacher can choose a passage at an appropriate grade level and have the student engage in activities designed to foster self-awareness of strategic reading. Of course, this can be done with any trade book or textbook. However, using *QRI–3* passages allows the teacher to assess a child's performance in leveled material. The teacher can conveniently choose different passages to correspond to the different ability levels in the classroom. The passages can be easily duplicated, without violating copyright, for students to write on. Several activities for student self-analysis follow. These activities can be done in the presence of the teacher as a form of conferencing, in cooperative groups, or individually.

- Have the student read a passage orally or silently and underline all new or unknown words. Have the student suggest possible strategies for determining the pronunciation and/or meaning of the words. The student should then attempt to utilize the suggested strategies and comment on her or his success.
- Have the student read a passage orally or silently and write down his or her recall without looking back at the passage. The recall could also be read into a tape recorder. The student should then return to the passage and evaluate the completeness of the recall.
- Have the student read a passage into a tape recorder and listen to the tape. Using a teacher-provided checklist, the student can evaluate her or his accuracy, fluency, and expression.
- Have the student read a passage and answer the accompanying questions. The student can then correct the answers, using the passage as a guide. The student should correct explicit questions by underlining the answer in the passage. The student should correct implicit questions by underlining the clue provided in the passage. After correction, the student can evaluate his or her success.

Using the **QRI–3** to Verify a Suspected Problem

In some cases, the classroom teacher may suspect that poor performance in science, social studies, or other content classes may be due to a specific reading difficulty. The teacher can use appropriate passages from the *QRI–3* to verify the existence of such a problem.

To Verify a Possible Problem with Expository Text. The teacher should choose an expository passage that is probably familiar to the student and that corresponds to the reading level of the content textbook used in the class. Because most content reading is done silently, he or she should have the student read the passage in this mode and then ask the accompanying questions. The teacher can employ look-backs if he or she chooses.

To Verify a Possible Problem with Unfamiliar Topics. The teacher should choose a narrative or expository passage that is probably unfamiliar to the student. He or she should choose this passage to correspond to the reading level of the textbook used. The student should read it orally or silently and answer the questions that follow. We strongly suggest that the student be encouraged to look back in the text to correct erroneous answers or find forgotten information. It is common for students to demonstrate poor comprehension after the first reading of an unfamiliar text. However, comprehension often improves when the student looks back in the text. If time permits, it may be helpful to contrast this passage with a familiar one at the same level in order to note whether comprehension differences are indeed present in familiar and unfamiliar text with or without look-backs.

To Verify a Possible Problem with Silent Reading Comprehension. The teacher should choose a narrative passage that is likely to be familiar to the child. Many children who are effective oral readers and comprehenders often experience difficulty in making a transition to independent silent reading. He or she can ask the child to read the passage silently and then can ask the accompanying questions. If time permits, he or she can contrast this with a similar passage read orally, timing both. If the child's rate of silent reading is similar to his or her oral reading rate, this may indicate that the child is not engaging in effective silent reading strategies.

To Verify a Possible Problem with Ineffective Note Taking. The teacher should choose a familiar expository passage at a level that corresponds to the level of the content textbook. He or she should ask the student to read silently and take notes on the important parts of the passage. An alternative would be to have the student underline the important parts as he or she reads. The teacher can then examine these notes and/or underlining to ascertain whether the reader has internalized effective note-taking strategies for finding important elements in the text.

To Verify a Possible Problem with Recall Following Reading. The teacher should choose a familiar passage at a level that corresponds to the textbook being used by the subject. He or she should ask the student to read silently and then should ask for unaided recall. The teacher can compare this recall to the retelling scoring sheet in order to evaluate the quality of the reader's memory for what was read. Then he or she can ask the accompanying questions and contrast the subject's ability to give correct answers with his or her ability to offer unaided recall of a selection.

The classroom teacher can utilize the *QRI–3* effectively to determine reading group and textbook placement and to verify the existence of a suspected problem. Because of time constraints, the teacher will rarely employ all the diagnostic options provided by the *QRI–3* but will instead choose one or two passages to serve a very specific purpose.

The Reading-Assessment Specialist

The reading-assessment specialist can be a school-based reading specialist or a reading clinician employed by a university reading clinic or a private educational institution. The role of the reading specialist often involves determining whether a student qualifies for exceptional educational placement or for other forms of reading intervention. The reading specialist may assess individually those students suspected of having a reading problem and may act as part of a multidisciplinary team that evaluates a student in areas other than reading. Once a reading problem is verified, the reading specialist plays a key role in planning intervention instruction.

The function of the reading clinician is to provide a complete assessment of the reading behavior of disabled readers. Often these students have been referred for clinical diagnosis as a verification of district placement. Some are students in schools that do not provide extensive assessment or intervention services. Many are "gray area" children, who have not met district criteria for special services but are experiencing difficulties in the classroom.

In many school districts, criteria for reading intervention involve scores obtained on individualized, standardized, norm-referenced tests. These tests seldom present reading in a natural context. That is, they tend to include word lists, multiple-choice vocabulary tests, and comprehension assessments based on brief, isolated passages. In addition, although some may provide a valid estimate of a student's instructional reading level (Blanchard, Borthwick & Hall, 1983; Smith & Beck, 1980), others may be of limited use in ascertaining the level of text that a student can read successfully.

The *QRI–3* provides both the reading specialist and the reading clinician with a tool for observing the reading behavior of a subject in a context that more closely approximates a classroom setting. It can be used to indicate the level at which a reader can succeed in different types of text. Neither the reading specialist nor the reading clinician has unlimited time for assessment. Both must choose those parts of the *QRI–3* that will offer the most valuable diagnostic information for a given student. Three general diagnostic areas are important: determination of the student's reading level, indication of reading growth following intervention, and description of specific reading behaviors as a guide for intervention instruction.

Using the QRI–3 to Determine Reading Level

The reading-assessment specialist generally has several kinds of data to use in estimating which passages to administer in determining a student's instructional level. Because of time constraints, it is important to avoid administration of unnecessary selections. Classroom information may be a viable starting point. For example, if the student is not functioning successfully in the second grade classroom, this suggests that first grade may represent an appropriate instructional level, and the validation of level may begin with a selection at that level. The score on a standardized reading test may also provide a starting point. We suggest administering a passage that is one or two grade levels below the grade equivalent attained on a test. By careful use of existing data, the reading-assessment specialist can use a minimum number of *QRI–3* passages to ascertain level placement for the student. Of course, if time permits, the word lists can also be used as a guide for passage administration.

Although the familiar narrative level is most important, in that it probably represents the student's best effort, the reading-assessment specialist may choose to exercise one of the following options.

- If the familiar instructional level was obtained through oral reading, the examiner may choose to verify this level in silent reading. A discrepancy between the student's oral and silent reading comprehension may suggest which mode to stress during instruction.
- If the reading level was obtained by reading a text with pictures, the specialist may choose to compare this with performance on a text without

pictures. If a student performs less well on the text without pictures, this may suggest excessive reliance on pictures for word identification.

- The examiner may choose to determine the student's instructional level for familiar expository text as a guide to the type of instructional materials to select. For example, a lower level for expository text may suggest that this type of material should receive primary emphasis.
- Finally, the examiner may choose to ascertain a level for unfamiliar text. Most readers do score at a lower level for unfamiliar material, but designation of a specific level for unfamiliar material can help the assessment specialist plan specific background enhancement activities for the student.

Using the QRI–3 to Indicate Growth

Many schools and school districts are implementing structured intervention programs or designing intense instructional units for development of reading skill. The teacher or intervention specialist can use the *QRI–3* for a pre and post analysis of reading growth following such programs. Several studies have suggested that passages on the QRI are sensitive to immediate and long-term change (Leslie & Allen, 1999; Caldwell, Fromm & O'Connor, 1998; Regner, 1992; Glass, 1989).

Pre and post assessment can take two forms. The specialist can administer a passage before the intervention and then administer the same passage after the intervention, noting such elements as a decrease in oral reading miscues, an increase in rate, and an increase in the number of questions answered correctly and the number of ideas recalled. Prior to intervention, the specialist will want to determine the highest instructional level and then re-administer that same passage at the close of the intervention. Of course, the pre and post passages must be administered in the same way. Both should employ either oral or silent reading, and both should focus on the same comprehension components (retelling, questions, and/or look-backs).

A second option is to administer a different passage prior to and after the intervention. This may be a more viable option if the duration of the intervention is relatively short and the specialist is concerned that memory for the initial passage may confound performance on the same passage. If the specialist chooses this option, the two passages should be as similar as possible. They should be at the same readability level, of the same structure (narrative or expository), and of the same level of familiarity. Table 16.4 presents pilot comprehension scores for all passages that illustrate the difficulty of passages *within* each level.

Using the QRI–3 to Describe Specific Reading Behaviors as a Guide for Intervention Instruction

The reading-assessment specialist may already know the student's reading level or may choose not to use the *QRI–3* to determine placement levels. However, selected passages and assessment options on the *QRI–3* can be used effectively to isolate areas for intervention emphasis. Again, it must be stressed that the assessment specialist is a decision maker. He or she should ask, "What do I want to know about this student?" and then should choose *QRI–3* components accordingly. Some possible assessment questions are presented below, and the *QRI–3* components that can be used to answer each one are listed. Guidelines for using these components are given in greater depth in the following sections of the manual.

How Accurate Is the Student in Identifying Words? The total score on the word lists and the number of miscues made during oral reading of the passages can provide this information.

How Automatic Is the Student in Identifying Words? The timed administration of the word lists can suggest a level of automaticity. Automaticity can also be inferred from the student's oral and silent reading rate on the passages. Accuracy and automaticity can be contrasted.

What Word Identification Strategies Are Used by the Student? The reading-assessment specialist can evaluate the nature of the miscues made on the word lists or when reading the passages by engaging in miscue analysis. Does the student use graphic or letter cues? Does the child recognize rhyming words? Is the child able to use a known word to identify an unknown word? Does the student self-correct miscues that do not make sense, which suggests that some self-monitoring or comprehension is present? Does the student use semantic cues and produce miscues that do not distort text meaning? An examination of miscues can often suggest which phonics principles are known, which are unknown, and/or which are consistently misapplied.

Is There a Difference Between a Student's Ability to Identify Words in Isolation and Words in Context? If the student has a higher level of word-identification skill when reading passages than when reading word lists or when reading text with pictures than when reading text without pictures, this may suggest effective use of context by a beginning reader or excessive use of context by the older and poorer reader. Context-free word identification is characteristic of a skilled reader, whose word-identification levels in isolation and context should be similar (Perfetti, 1985, 1988; Stanovich, 1980, 1991). The assessment specialist can also contrast the student's ability to identify specific words on the word lists with her or his ability to identify those same words in the passages. All list words are underlined in the passages wherever they occur at that level. For example, the word "in" on the pre-primer list is underlined wherever it occurs in the pre-primer passages.

Which Types of Text Can the Student Handle Most Successfully? The examiner can compare narrative and expository text. This is probably more important for upper-level students. The examiner can also compare content areas for upper middle school students and high school students. Does the student perform more effectively in social studies, science, or literature passages? For younger children and those reading at pre-primer through second grade levels, the examiner can contrast reading when pictures are present and reading when they are absent.

Which Modes of Reading Represent a Strength for the Student? The examiner can compare oral and silent reading comprehension to determine which mode to emphasize during instruction. Then he or she can compare comprehension following listening with that following reading. Listening comprehension is often regarded as representative of a child's comprehension potential in the absence of decoding problems (Gough & Juel, 1991; Stanovich, 1991).

How Does the Student Perform in Familiar and Unfamiliar Text? The examiner can note any differences between performance on familiar and unfamiliar text. Students may not comprehend as well in unfamiliar text, but the examiner can note whether this difference represents a change in instructional level. Lower levels in word identification in unfamiliar text may suggest that the student is overly dependent on familiar context for word identification.

Does the Student Effectively Use Look-Backs? The examiner can compare the student's ability to answer explicit and implicit questions with and without look-backs. The ability to look back in the text and locate information is a characteristic of effective readers. At the upper levels and in unfamiliar, concept-dense text, performance in answering questions without look-backs is less important than answering questions accurately when allowed to look back. Memory constraints placed upon students who are struggling with such text argues that effective use of look-backs may represent a more realistic picture of a student's reading performance.

What Comprehension Strategies Does a Student Employ While Reading? The use of think-alouds can offer the examiner evidence of the comprehension strategies used by the student during the act of reading. Does the student self-question? Does the student construct inferences? Does the student recognize his or her understanding or lack of it? Does the student summarize and/or paraphrase parts of the text before moving on to the next segment? The presence of such strategies can suggest an interactive and involved reader. Conversely, their absence can suggest the need for a metacognitive instructive focus.

The reading-assessment specialist will have to decide which of the above questions will be most helpful in describing the reading behavior of an individual and in planning suitable intervention instruction. No two students are the same, and it is likely that the assessment specialist will use different components for different students. Because the *QRI–3* is not a standardized instrument, the assessment specialist can decide which options to choose, given the constraints of time and the needs of each individual student. Table 5.1 summarizes the various uses of the *QRI–3*.

TABLE 5.1

Uses of the *Qualitative Reading Inventory–3*

Use the *QRI–3* to Determine Reading Level

- Find the instructional level for familiar text.
    Choose a passage on the basis of word lists and/or classroom performance.
    Find the instructional level for narrative text.
    Use oral or silent reading, depending on the passage level: oral reading for pre-primer through grade five, silent reading for grades six through high school.
    Count miscues according to Total Accuracy or Total Acceptability.
    Ask comprehension questions.
- Find the instructional level for expository text.
- Find the instructional level for unfamiliar text.

Use the *QRI–3* to Indicate Growth:
Diagnostic Options

- Choose the *QRI–3* components that will best assess the effectiveness of the intervention.
    Oral or silent reading
    Retelling or questions
    Rate
    Narrative or expository text
    Look-backs or no look-backs

TABLE 5.1 *(Continued)*

Uses of the *Qualitative Reading Inventory–3*

Use the *QRI–3* to Indicate Growth:
Diagnostic Options *(Continued)*

- Find the highest instructional level for familiar text.
- Use the same passage as the pre-test and as the post-test.
  Or
- Use similar passages as the pre-test and the post-test.
- Administer the pre and post measures in the same way.

Use the *QRI–3* to Plan Supportive or Remedial Instruction:
Diagnostic Options

- Find the word identification accuracy level.
    Administer the word lists.
    Find the instructional level for Total Number Correct.
    Administer the passages.
    Find the word identification accuracy level in familiar text.
- Find the word identification automaticity level.
    Administer the word lists.
    Find the instructional level for Total Correct Automatic.
- Contrast accuracy and automaticity.
    Contrast the word-list levels for Total Correct Automatic with the Total
        Number Correct.
    Evaluate word identification accuracy on oral passage reading in
        relation to rate of reading.
- Describe word identification strategies.
    Do miscue analysis on passage miscues.
    Use of self-correction
    Use of graphic or letter cues, particularly rhyme at the pre-primer level
    Use of meaning cues
- Compare word identification in isolation and in context.
    Contrast instructional level of Total Number Correct on the word lists
        with instructional level in passage reading.
- Contrast narrative and expository text.
- Contrast text with pictures and text without pictures (pre-primer through
        grade two).
- Contrast oral and silent reading comprehension.
- Contrast reading comprehension and listening comprehension.
- Contrast familiar and unfamiliar text.
- Utilize alternative administration procedures for assessing strategic
        reading.
    Contrast comprehension with and without look-backs.
    Contrast the quality and variety of think-alouds with the quality of
        comprehension.

6 Administration and Scoring of the Qualitative Reading Inventory–3

Preparation for Testing

To ensure the best possible testing environment, the examiner should administer the *QRI–3* in a quiet place that is free from distractions. Before meeting the student, the examiner should gather all materials and place them in the testing room: the word lists, passages to be read, accompanying sheets for examiner recording, tape recorder, stopwatch or timer, clipboard, paper, and pencils.

It is often difficult to determine how many scoring sheets to prepare, especially if the examiner has never met the student. It is better to prepare too many than not enough; otherwise, the examiner may have to leave the room to obtain more. We recommend that the examiner prepare a kit of scoring sheets for all the passages and organize them according to grade level. The examiner can then be assured of having the correct passages on hand. The examiner may wish to laminate the student's copy of each passage or to encase it in a plastic cover for protection.

Before beginning the testing, the examiner should strive to put the student at ease. Engaging in conversation about the student's interests, feelings toward school and other subjects, or favored activities can act as an effective icebreaker as well as provide valuable information. Some students are concerned with the use of a stopwatch or with the examiner writing. Sitting across from the student can make the act of writing somewhat less noticeable. Using a clipboard that rests on the examiner's lap and a stopwatch that rests on a chair placed to one side can also make these items less obtrusive.

We highly recommend that the entire testing session be taped, especially in the early stages of learning how to administer the *QRI–3*. Even experienced examiners often find a tape helpful in scoring. Some students are upset by the use of a tape recorder. Explaining the need for this and allowing the student to experiment with it may help to alleviate anxiety.

If the examiner is using the word-identification lists to estimate a starting point for passage administration, he or she gives those to the student first and scores them immediately in order to estimate which passages to administer. Next, the examiner administers the prior-knowledge task for a passage before the student reads the passage. This task allows the examiner to determine whether the content of the passage is familiar to the reader. It need not be scored before proceeding; however, the examiner should estimate familiarity with the text topic. Third, the examiner gives the student the passages. If the passages are being used to determine an instructional level, the examiner must score oral reading accuracy and responses to comprehension questions in order to know what additional passages to administer. We recommend that during the actual administration, the examiner determine oral reading accuracy by counting all errors or miscues. This allows for a quick estimation of the word-identification level so that the examiner can ascertain which passage to administer next. After the administration, if desired, the examiner can determine passage level by counting only those miscues that change meaning.

Finally, the amount of time spent in administering the *QRI–3* will vary depending on the assessment questions posed by the examiner. It is important that the examiner be sensitive to the student's energy level and attention span. Frequent short breaks are often helpful. If somewhat lengthy testing is required, there is no reason why testing should not be scheduled across several days, if this can be arranged.

7

Administration and Scoring of the Qualitative Reading Inventory–3

The Word Lists

Purposes for Administering the Word Lists

Estimating the Starting Point for Passage Administration
Estimating Automatic Word Identification
Estimating Knowledge of Letter–Sound Matches
Analyzing the Differences Between Word Identification in Isolation
  and in Context

Procedures for Administering the Word Lists

General Procedures
Instructions to the Student
The Beginning Point
Recording Subject Responses: Accuracy and Automaticity

Procedures for Scoring the Word Lists

Criteria for Determining Reading Levels from Word Recognition Scores
  in Isolation
Estimating the Starting Point for Passage Administration
Estimating Automatic Word Identification
Additional Diagnostic Uses of the Word Lists

Purposes for Administering the Word Lists

Estimating the Starting Point for Passage Administration

The word lists can help the examiner decide which level of passage to administer to the student first. The word lists provide a quick estimate of the student's word-identification ability. If the examiner has little information about a student's performance, the lists may help the examiner estimate the level on which to begin testing. If the student has problems with word identification, his or her performance on the word lists will indicate a realistic beginning point for passage administration. If, however, the student can identify words well but has problems in comprehension, the word lists may suggest a starting point that will be too difficult for the reader to comprehend. Our pilot data suggested a relationship between performance on the word lists and word recognition in context. See Section 16.

Estimating Automatic Word Identification

The examiner can estimate automaticity of word identification by counting the number of seconds that it takes the student to read each word on the word lists. If a student reads a word within one second, we can assume that the student has identified the word automatically without needing to sound it out by applying decoding rules. The more words that a reader identifies automatically, the more likely that she or he will be a fluent reader in the corresponding level of passages.

Words that are automatically identified have often been termed sight vocabulary. It was thought that a direct link occurred between the visual aspects of a word and word meaning. However, automatic word identification may involve a strong sound component (Ehri, 1992). Therefore, "sight vocabulary" may be a misnomer, and we prefer to use the term "automatic word identification."

Estimating Knowledge of Letter–Sound Matches

All other words that the student reads correctly beyond a one-second limit are probably read via decoding ability; that is, the student is matching letters and sounds in order to identify the word. The examiner can examine correct and incorrect pronunciations in order to assess the letter–sound matches that the student knows and those that might need emphasis in an intervention program.

Analyzing the Differences Between Word Identification in Isolation and in Context

Many words on the word lists were taken from the passages. Thus the examiner can determine how well the reader is able to use context to identify words by examining whether the student can identify words in a passage that she or he could not identify in isolation. If the reader cannot identify more words in context than in isolation and the words are within a frequency range appropriate for his or her instructional reading level, then instruction on context utilization may be in order. The words underlined in the passages are those that appear on the word list of the same readability level.

Procedures for Administering the Word Lists

General Procedures

The student is given the list of words and is asked to pronounce them. As this is done, the examiner records the answers on the accompanying scoring

---

sheet, carefully differentiating between words identified automatically and those identified after some delay. Those identified automatically are marked in the Identified Automatically column; those identified after some delay are recorded in the Identified column. There are several ways to administer the lists. Each may seem awkward at first, but with practice, the examiner will soon choose the one with which she or he is most comfortable.

The examiner can sit next to or across from the student and cover each word with an index card, which is then moved down to reveal the word. Immediately after the word is completely exposed, the examiner says mentally "one thousand and one." This acts as the equivalent of one-second timing. If the student has not pronounced the word within that time frame, any attempt, correct or otherwise, is marked in the Identified column. Older students may choose to move the card themselves, and the examiner must watch when the word is uncovered and say mentally "one thousand and one" in order to estimate their ability to pronounce words automatically.

The examiner may also choose to place individual words on index cards. Each word should be printed on both sides of the card. The student reads one side, and the other side provides a way for the examiner to keep track of which word is being read. The examiner presents the words one at a time. The words known automatically are placed in one pile, those identified after some delay in another, and those not known in a third pile. The first pile is recorded in the Identified Automatically column and the last two in the Identified column.

The examiner may find it more comfortable to dispense with cards and simply hand the list to the student to read at his or her own pace. The important thing is to keep track of automatic pronunciation by saying mentally "one thousand and one."

Another alternative is to utilize a window card, which is illustrated in Figure 7.1. Using a piece of cardboard, the examiner cuts a rectangular slit that corresponds in length to the longest word in a list. (We have provided a pattern for this card in Figure 7.1.) When the examiner places the card over each word, the student sees only one word at a time, which prevents her or his becoming distracted by previous words or those that must be identified next.

FIGURE 7.1

Pattern for a Word List Window Card

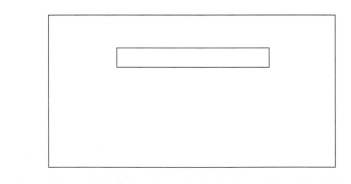

As the examiner juggles the word lists and the timing, recording the student's answers may seem difficult at first. Until she or he becomes more accustomed to timing, listening, and recording all at once, the examiner should tape the entire session.

Instructions to the Student

The examiner should introduce the word lists to the student by saying, "I have some lists of words that I want you to read one at a time. Some of the words will be easy for you, and some I expect to be very hard. Don't worry. You are not expected to know all of them. If you don't know a word right away, try your best to figure it out. I cannot help you in any way, and I cannot tell you whether you are right or wrong. Just do your very best. Are you ready?"

The Beginning Point

Whether the examiner is using the word lists to estimate automatic word identification or to suggest a level for passage administration, she or he must determine a realistic beginning point. In order to avoid initial frustration, the examiner should begin with a word list two or more years below the student's chronological grade placement. This is especially important if the examiner suspects a serious reading problem. For example, the pre-primer or primer list is a good starting point for children in first through third grades. She or he should begin with the second or third grade list for students in grades four through six. The fourth and fifth grade lists can be beginning points for those in sixth grade and above. It is better to begin too low than to place the subject in a frustrating situation immediately. Little time will be lost if the list is too easy, and the initial experience of success may put the student more at ease.

Recording Subject Responses: Accuracy and Automaticity

There are two things for the examiner to keep track of while administering these lists: accuracy of identification and automaticity of response. *Accuracy* refers simply to whether or not the student reads the word correctly. If the student makes an error, the examiner should write down the phonetic equivalent of the mispronunciation. For example, if the student reads "live" with a long "i" sound, the examiner should use the – mark above the "i." If the student changes the word quite a bit, the examiner should write the best phonetic equivalent. This information provides an indication of how the student approaches word identification. If a student self-corrects an error, the examiner should write "C" and count it as correct. If the student skips a word, the examiner should write "d.k." (don't know).

Automaticity of response refers to whether or not the student gives a response (correct or not) within one second. To provide a realistic estimate of one second, the examiner can say mentally, "one thousand and one." Any response begun within one second is recorded in the Identified Automatically column. If the response is correct, the examiner should simply put a "C" in the column. If it is incorrect, she or he should write the phonetic equivalent.

If the student takes more than one second to begin a response, the examiner should record the response in the Identified column. If it is a correct response, the examiner should put a "C" in the Identified column. If it is incorrect, she or he should write the phonetic equivalent. It is possible for a student to give an incorrect response within one second but then correct it. In this case the word is a correct decoded word. Figure 7.2 contains an example of recorded and scored word lists.

FIGURE 7.2

Examiner Word Lists

Third				Fourth		
	Identified Automatically	*Identified*			*Identified Automatically*	*Identified*
1. lunch	c			1. escape	escarp	sc
2. celebrate	c			2. desert		c
3. believe	belief			3. crop	c	
4. claws		c		4. islands		c
5. lion		c		5. chief		chif
6. rough	rug	sc		6. mounds		munds
7. wear	c			7. busy	c	
8. tongue		c		8. pond		c
9. crowded	c			9. signs		c
10. wool	c			10. ocean	c	
11. removed	removed	sc		11. pilot		plot
12. curious		kircus		12. fame		fim
13. sheep		c		13. precious		DK
14. electric		c		14. settlers		settle
15. worried	c			15. guarded		guard
16. enemies	enemy			16. passenger		passed
17. glowed		c		17. boundaries		DK
18. clothing		c		18. communicate		DK
19. swim		c		19. adventurer		aventrer
20. entrance	entray	sc		20. invented		c

Third			Fourth		
Total Correct Automatic	6 /20 =	30 %	**Total Correct Automatic**	3 /20 =	15 %
Total Correct Identified	11 /20 =	55 %	**Total Correct Identified**	6 /20 =	30 %
Total Number Correct	17 /20 =	85 %	**Total Number Correct**	9 /20 =	45 %

LEVELS		
Independent	**Instructional**	**Frustration**
18–20	14–17	below 14
90–100%	70–85%	below 70%

Procedures for Scoring the Word Lists

Scoring procedures vary depending on the purpose for administering the word list. Finding a beginning point for passage administration simply involves counting the number of correct responses in both the Identified Automatically and the Identified columns. Independent, instructional, and frustration levels are determined from this total. If the purpose of administering the word list is to estimate automatic word identification, then the examiner must count the Identified Automatically column separately from the total correct in both columns. The following sections explain these two scoring procedures in more depth.

Criteria for Determining Reading Levels from Word-Recognition Scores in Isolation

The following criteria (McCracken, 1966) help determine levels for word identification on the word lists.

Independent	Total correct:	90% and above	18–20 words
Instructional	Total correct:	70%–89%	14–17 words
Frustration	Total correct:	Less than 70%	13 words or less

The above guidelines are included on each word list to facilitate scoring.

Estimating the Starting Point for Passage Administration

The examiner should administer the first list and score it immediately to determine which level it represents. If the student scores at an instructional or frustration level, the examiner should move down until the student attains an independent level. Then the examiner should continue upward until the student reaches a frustration level. The examiner may also stop before the frustration level if the student reaches a word list that corresponds to his or her chronological grade placement. These levels suggest what passages may represent a realistic starting point. Word identification in isolation is a rough predictor of the level of passage that a student can decode reasonably well. If a student scores at an independent or instructional level on a word list, she or he will probably decode a passage of similar readability level with some measure of success.

Students often score at an independent or instructional level across several lists. For example, a student may score at an independent level for the primer and first grade lists and at an instructional level for lists two through four. If the examiner wants to be safe and present an initial passage that will ensure success, she or he should choose one that corresponds to the highest independent level attained on the lists. If the examiner is operating under narrow time constraints, she or he can estimate the level for the beginning passage from the lowest instructional level attained on the word lists.

Word-list scores for Chris, a third grader, provide an example of how to estimate a starting point for passage administration. Initially, Chris was asked to read the first grade list. He scored at an independent level. The second grade list was administered, and again, he attained an independent level. Chris scored at an instructional level for the third and fourth grade lists and reached frustration at the fifth grade level. The examiner chose to administer a second grade passage first in order to ensure that Chris met with success with his initial attempt at oral reading. (However, a third grade passage would also have been a viable starting point.) Chris scored at an independent level in second grade text and attained an instructional level in third grade text.

When Joe, a fifth grader, read a third grade list, he scored at frustration level. The examiner moved to lower levels, and Joe scored at an instructional level for second grade and at an independent level for first grade. The first passage chosen for Joe to read was at a second grade level, which was his anticipated instructional level.

There are two types of readers whose levels the word-list scores will not predict accurately. One is a reader who makes exceptionally good use of context and, thus, whose capabilities in context far exceed her or his word identification in isolation. The word-list scores will underestimate this reader's capabilities. The other type of reader has comprehension problems but also has excellent word-identification capabilities. This subject's abilities will be overestimated by the word-list scores.

Estimating Automatic Word Identification

A student's ability to identify words automatically is estimated as the number of words correctly read within one second. On each list this number is written in the column marked Identified Automatically. The examiner should count the number correct on each list to arrive at an independent, instructional, or frustration level for automatic word identification. Then she or he should count the total number correct on both the Identified Automatically list and the Identified list and use this to arrive at a level for total word identification. She or he should compare the two in order to decide whether automatic word identification represents a weakness for the student.

One example is Chris, a third grader. His scores on the word lists were as follows:

First:	*Total Score:*	Independent level
	Identified Automatically score:	Independent level
Second:	*Total Score:*	Independent level
	Identified Automatically score:	Instructional level
Third:	*Total Score:*	Instructional level
	Identified Automatically score:	Frustration level
Fourth:	*Total Score:*	Frustration level
	Identified Automatically score:	Frustration level

Obviously, for the second through the third grade, Chris's levels for automatic word identification fall below his level for total word identification. This may suggest a possible weakness. It needs to be supported by assessment of Chris's word-identification ability in context, specifically by assessment of his ability to read selected passages at the same grade levels.

Caution: The graded word lists do not represent a natural reading situation and do not assess a student's comprehension ability. Also, some students identify words more effectively in context than in a list format. Therefore, a student's scores on an isolated list should never be used to estimate his or her overall reading ability.

Additional Diagnostic Uses of the Word Lists

Because many of the words on the lists are contained in the passage of corresponding readability, the examiner can choose to note whether a word missed on the list was identified correctly in context. Although this may involve only a small number of words, it can reveal a reader who is not utilizing context effectively.

The examiner can also note the accuracy of the student's decoding attempts within the untimed format. For example, are there any consonant or vowel sounds that are missed consistently? Does the student attempt to apply phonetic strategies to irregular words? Which phonetic principles are applied erroneously? Word-list administration can provide the examiner with a tool for probing into the student's strategies for pronouncing words. For example, the examiner can direct the student to various parts of unknown words and model word-analysis strategies to see whether she or he can take advantage of them. The examiner can cover up parts of words and uncover them sequentially for the subject to pronounce. The examiner can contrast an unknown word with one of similar spelling and/or pronunciation to see whether the student can transfer knowledge of that word to the unknown one. Any success achieved through examiner aid should be noted on the scoring sheet, but a student should not receive credit for it when the diagnostician is determining independent, instructional, and frustration levels for word identification in isolation.

Caution: A student's ability to decode words in isolation may be very different from her or his ability to identify words in context (Nicholson, Lillas & Rzoska, 1988). Therefore, any diagnostic decisions made on the basis of word-list information should be corroborated by the student's performance while identifying words in the context of *QRI–3* passages.

## 8

Administration and Scoring of the Qualitative Reading Inventory-3

Assessment of Prior Knowledge

Assessing Prior Knowledge

Conceptual-Questions Task
Prediction Task

Assessing Prior Knowledge

Because students' knowledge has such a powerful effect on comprehension, it is important to determine whether the selection read by the student contains familiar or unfamiliar concepts. Understanding what students know and what they do not know about important concepts or ideas in the selection allows the examiner to evaluate comprehension difficulties in relation to students' knowledge base. The *QRI–3* provides two methods for assessing prior knowledge: conceptual questions and predictions. Before reading a passage, a student should be asked to participate in one or both activities so that the examiner can assess his or her familiarity with the topic of the selection. A student's lack of knowledge of the concepts, or a knowledge of the concepts that differs from that reflected in the text may explain difficulty in comprehension. Engaging in the conceptual questions and/or prediction tasks prior to reading can also serve to activate any background knowledge that the student has for the information contained in the selection. If this knowledge is consistent with text information, facilitation of comprehension will occur. Our pilot data suggested a strong relationship between prior knowledge and comprehension at first grade level and above. In fact, prior knowledge predicted passage comprehension more frequently than did a general measure of reading achievement. This latter finding illustrates the value of measuring prior knowledge in reading assessment. See Section 16.

Conceptual-Questions Task

General Procedures. For each passage there are three to five questions judged to be important to comprehension of the passage. Some questions were chosen because they represented the topic of the selection (such as a class trip, uses of computers, soccer, or viruses) or because they represented the person the selection was about (such as Martin Luther King, Jr., or Amelia Earhart). Other questions were included because we believed that if students understood them, they would be more likely to answer the implicit comprehension questions correctly (for example, questions involving animal defenses in the fifth grade passage "The Octopus" and changing seasons in the second grade passage "Seasons").

The questions are on the examiner's copy of the passage, directly under the title of the passage. The examiner should ask all these questions before the student reads the passage. The examiner should ask all questions for each passage that the student reads.

Instructions for the conceptual-questions task are as follows: "Before you read, I want to know what you already know about some ideas in the text. I will ask you a few questions to find out."

Scoring the Conceptual-Questions Task. Each question is scored according to a 3-2-1-0 system, where 3 is the best score. The examiner can use the following guidelines for assigning scores.

3 Points: **A precise definition, or a definitional response to a phrase, or an answer to a question specifically related to passage content**
   Examples:
   What does "learning to read" mean to you? pronouncing and understanding words
   Why do people work? to get money for their families
   When do you see turtles outside? in summer when it's hot, because turtles like the sun
   What do flowers need to grow? sunlight, water, and food
   What are the problems with living in the desert? it's very hot and there's little water
   Who was Christopher Columbus? a man who sailed the ocean and landed in America
   What is Washington, D.C.? where our nation's capital is and national laws are made there
   How do companies make a profit? they make more money than they spend
   What happens to products after recycling? they get made into other things
   What is a biography? it is about a person's life and it's written by another person
   What does it mean to emulate someone? you admire and look up to someone and try to be like them
   What is circumnavigation? sailing around the world
   What do nuclear reactions produce? energy, heat, and radiation
   What is a civilian? a person not in the military
   What are some causes of wars? people want independence, they fight over land, and they think they are treated unfairly
   What does it mean to classify something? to put things into groups according to how they are alike and different

   A Synonym
   Examples:
   What does "trade" mean to you? to bargain
   What are claws? nails

What is fall? autumn
What is a biography? a life story
What does it mean to emulate someone? to imitate
What does escalation mean? to go up
What is an invasion? an attack
What is a membrane? a layer or a covering in the body
What does it mean to classify something? categorize

2 *Points:* An Example of the Concept
Examples:
What does "doing something new" mean to you? getting a new toy and
    playing with it
Where do people work? at hospitals
What is working at home? cleaning house, washing dishes
What does "being afraid of animals" mean to you? grizzly bear
What is "racism"? people who don't like black people because they are black
"What are changes in computers?" they can do things faster
What are animal defenses? bite; spit; hunch their backs
What are evils of slavery? people telling others what to do and whipping
    them
What does the word "articulate" mean? like when you say something
    really clear so people understand it
What is slavery? you buy a person and make them work
How do stars change over time? from a baby star to a normal one to a
    dead one
What does the word "marveled" mean? you are in awe because you see
    something really spectacular
What does "allied" mean? Germany and Russia were allies
What are ethnic minorities? Islamic or Jewish people in our country
What is mass? an object like a chair or a computer

A *Specific* Attribute or Defining Characteristics
Examples:
What is a Mom? a human being, someone who takes care of you
What is a bear? furry with a black nose
What is an octopus? thing with eight legs with suction cups
How is steel made? from iron
What is an earthquake? when the earth shakes
What is circumnavigation? to circle around something
What is a settlement? it's land but it has homes on it.
What do you know about Vietnam? the United States was in a war there
What does "interception" mean? get something meant for someone else
    like in football
What does "idealism" mean? dreaming of a perfect society
What is a compromise? striking a deal
What does "infectious" mean? something that could go into your body
    and spread

A Function
Examples:
What is a class trip? learn something new
What is taking notes? so you remember something
Why do people use maps? to find their way
What is Washington, D.C.? city where Martin Luther King, Jr., did his "I
    Have a Dream" speech
What is the purpose of recycling? to use something again
What is an autobiography? you can learn about people by reading them

What is gravity? it pulls us down and keeps us down
What is a disinfectant? you use it to clean out wounds
What was the League of Nations? They were supposed to keep peace
What is DNA? it makes you what you are, like your size and hair color and stuff like that
What is a virus? it can make you sick

1 Point: A General Association
Examples:
What does "going to work" mean to you? leaving the house
What does "trade" mean to you? you trade something
Who was Sacajawea? an Indian name
What is laser light? beams of light flying all over
What does "size of earthquakes" mean to you? big
Who were Lewis and Clark? men
What is slavery? a bad thing
What does it mean to be courageous? do something that will touch someone else's life
What is a convoy? things staying together
What is an armistice? it has something to do with war
What does "interception" mean? how you get something
What is a virus? you get them in a computer

Isolation of Prefix, Suffix, or Root Word
Examples:
What is circumnavigation? circumference
What is archeology? archeologist
What is an octopus? eight
What is ultrasound? a noise
What are protestations? protests
What are tracers? you trace with them
What does "unrestricted" mean? not restricted
What does re-education mean? educate again

Firsthand, Personal Associations
Examples:
What does "people reading stories" mean to you? baby sister picks them
What does "learning to read" mean to you? I learned to read in first grade
What is a school trip? my mother came on our field trip
What does "an old house for sale" mean to you? we just sold our house
What are new toys? I get new toys for Christmas
What are fireworks? I get bottle rockets
What do you know about Vietnam? My father was there
What is DNA? I remember it from *Jurassic Park*

0 Points: Sound-Alikes
Examples:
What is a bear? wear
What is fall? wall

Unconnected Responses
Examples:
What does "looking for something" mean to you? Batman
Who was Martin Luther King, Jr.? wears a crown

No Response or I Don't Know

Interpreting the Conceptual-Questions Scores. Generally, we have found that students who score at least 55% of the points possible on the concept task score above 70% on comprehension questions on the related passage. See Section 16 for details.

Prediction Task

General Procedures. After administration of the conceptual-questions task, the examiner may choose to administer the prediction task. If so, the examiner should say, "Given that the title of the passage is _____, and it includes the ideas _____, _____, and _____ (naming all the concepts within the questions), what do you think the passage will be about? I want you to take a guess or make a prediction about what you think the passage will be about." For example, on the third grade selection "The Trip to the Zoo," the instructions would be phrased, "Given that the title of the passage is 'The Trip to the Zoo' and that it has the ideas 'class trip,' 'taking notes,' 'being by yourself,' and 'why people use maps,' what do you think the story will be about?" If the student simply restates the title of the passage, the examiner should provide a *general* probe for more information. For example, if the student says, "Amelia Earhart," say, "What about Amelia Earhart?"

Scoring the Prediction Task. Leslie and Cooper (1993) examined three ways of scoring the prediction task and found that one of them significantly correlated with retelling and comprehension among sixth graders. Further piloting of the task at other reading levels and ages found that the same method of scoring was related to retelling and/or comprehension at second and third grade reading levels. Thus we have chosen to score the prediction task by counting the number of idea statements the student predicts *that are contained in the passage either explicitly or implicitly.* By idea statements, we mean any proposition (verb and accompanying nouns) contained in the selection or implied by the selection. The following list provides students' predictions and our scoring from passages at diverse levels. The idea statements are in italics.

> *Pre-primer Story:* **"Just Like Mom"**
> **2 Ideas:**
> —*Mom is going to work* and having a good day. Dad is doing something at the end. *The girl does everything the Mom does.*
> —*Mom is working at home* and *going to work.*
> **1 Idea:**
> —*Mom is working.*
> —What a Mom is and *Mom going to work*
> —*Working with Mom*
> **0 Ideas:**
> —Mom
>
> *Primer Story:* **"The Pig Who Learned to Read"**
> **2 Ideas:**
> —*The pig that just learned to read* and *he liked it*
> —*A pig that heard people read* and *learned to read*
> **1 Idea:**
> —*A pig learning how to read*
> —*A pig that learns to read*
> **0 Ideas:**
> —The pig who told the boy how to read

Primer Story: **"Who Lives Near Lakes?"**

1 Idea:

—*People who live near lakes*

0 Ideas:

—*Fish*

First-Level Story: **"The Bear and the Rabbit"**

3 Ideas:

—*Having no one to play with; the bunny would be afraid of the bear; and will make friends*

2 Ideas:

—*It's about a bear and a rabbit; the rabbit is scared of the bear*

1 Idea:

—*It's about friendship*

—*About a rabbit that's scared of animals*

First-Level Passage: **"What You Eat"**

1 Idea:

—*Different kinds of foods*

—*Trying to keep healthy*

Second-Level Passage: **"What Can I Get for My Toy?"**

1 Idea:

—*Person getting toys*

—*A kid who wants to trade for toys*

Second-Level Passage: **"Whales and Fish"**

2 Ideas:

—*How fish get born; how animals live in the sea*

1 Idea:

—*Animals in the sea*

Third-Level Passage: **"The Trip to the Zoo"**

5 Ideas:

—*Somebody who is going to a zoo on a field trip gets lost; looks at a map; and finds his way back*

3 Ideas:

—*Taking a trip; and taking notes; and having a map for directions*

1 Idea:

—*About going to the zoo*

0 Ideas:

—Things you can see, touch, or use

Third-Level Passage: **"Cats: Lions and Tigers in Your House"**

1 Idea:

—*Cats protecting themselves; lions, tigers, and cat families*

0 Ideas:

—Cats

Fifth-Level Passage: **"Martin Luther King, Jr."**

3 Ideas:

—*Washington, D.C., where the marches are; segregation; and what Martin Luther King, Jr. did for black people*

2 Ideas:

—*Why blacks and whites didn't like each other back then and what Martin Luther King, Jr. did about it*

1 Idea:
—*His life and what he wanted to do*

Fifth-Level Passage: **"Getting Rid of Trash"**
3 Ideas:
—*About taking trash; recycling it;* and *making it into other things*
1 Idea:
—*Trash and recycling it*

Sixth-Level Passage: **"Andrew Carnegie"**
2 Ideas:
—*A man who made steel;* and *made a lot of money*
1 Idea:
—*How steel is made* and they raise money; *about a steel-making factory*

Sixth-Level Passage: **"Predicting Earthquakes"**
1 Idea:
—*About earthquakes and how animals can tell if they're coming*
—*How animals sense earthquakes*

Upper Middle School Passage: **"Lewis and Clark"**
2 Ideas:
—*Two people exploring* or *going a great distance; Lewis and Clark going north;* and an *expedition* mapping the United States

Upper Middle School Passage: **"Biddy Mason"**
2 Ideas
—*About a slave* who *does something brave*

Upper Middle School Passage: **"Life Cycles of Stars"**
3 Ideas
—*What stars are made of* and *the life of a star* and *what happens when fusion occurs*

Interpretation of the Prediction Scores. As you can see from the predictions made by students, most students gave only one or two idea statements in their predictions. There seem to be three levels of quality in predictions. First, there are young readers, who only restate the title and do not integrate the concepts at all. Second, there are students who integrate some of the concepts and make a prediction using them. For example, on "The Trip to the Zoo," a student predicts, "taking a trip and taking notes and having a map for directions." Finally, there is the occasional student who is so knowledgeable about the concepts as to make a prediction that sums up many main ideas contained in the selection. For example, a sixth grade student who read the upper middle school passage "Fireworks" and predicted, "It's about how fireworks are made from different chemicals and how they get all the colors and why they are dangerous. It will probably talk about the kinds of injuries that happen and maybe the laws that ban fireworks. I think it will explain who can use them and who can't."

In summary, predictions should be evaluated in light of the above examples, which are from our pilot data on average readers. Qualitative judgments can be made by examining whether or not students have integrated any of the concepts with the title in order to make predictions. Recognize that this skill, like all other skills, is learned and is subject to instruction. If we want children to make good predictions, we have to teach them how by modeling.

9

Administration and Scoring of the Qualitative Reading Inventory–3

The Passages

Purposes for Administering the Passages

There are three main purposes for administering the passages.

1. Determination of a Student's Independent, Instructional, and/or Frustration Levels. This involves two steps: determining levels for word identification in context and determining levels for comprehension.

Word Identification in Context. The examiner determines these levels for word identification in context by asking the student to read graded passages orally. The examiner records the errors/miscues made by the student and then counts them to arrive at a designation of level. The miscues can be counted in two ways, depending on the preference or philosophy of the examiner. He or she can count all miscues regardless of quality and use this total to determine the level. We call this *Total Accuracy*. Alternatively, the examiner can choose to count only those miscues that change or distort passage meaning. This is referred to as *Total Acceptability*. Section 10 explains how to identify, count, and score miscues.

Comprehension. The examiner determines a student's independent, instructional, and frustration levels for comprehension by asking the student to read graded passages orally or silently and answer questions based on passage content. The examiner counts the number of correct answers to determine the designation of level. Section 11 explains the scoring of comprehension questions.

2. Assessment of a Student's Ability to Read Different Types of Text. The examiner can ask the student to read narrative and expository text, familiar and unfamiliar text, text with and without pictures (pre-primer through grade two). He or she can determine independent, instructional, and frustration levels for each type of text depending upon her or his diagnostic purposes. Not all levels should be determined for all passage types. To do so would require an inordinate and unrealistic amount of time. Determination of a familiar level is most important. For most students, determination of this level in narrative text is the primary concern. Narrative text is generally easier than expository text, so assessment of familiar levels in this genre tends to represent a student's best effort.

3. Assessment of a Student's Ability to Comprehend in Different Modes. The examiner can ask the student to read orally or silently. Then he or she determines independent, instructional, and frustration levels in oral reading from two scores: the number of miscues made while reading orally and the number of questions answered correctly. Guidelines for determining a total passage level for oral reading are explained later in this section. The examiner determines silent reading levels on the basis of the number of comprehension questions answered correctly. Section 11 contains guidelines for determining silent reading comprehension.

Assessment Options

Administration of the passages can also involve several diagnostic options.

1. Assessment of Prior Knowledge. There are two options for determining a student's prior knowledge for the topic of a passage: the conceptual-questions task and the prediction task. See Section 8 for an explanation of the use of both.

2. Oral Reading Miscue Analysis. There are three types of miscues made while reading orally: whole-word substitutions, such as "tried" for "trade"; nonword substitutions, such as "trad" for "trade"; and omissions and insertions of words.

The examiner asks two questions about each miscue: Was the miscue semantically acceptable in that passage meaning was not changed or distorted, and/or was it self-corrected by the student? Was the miscue graphically similar to the original word? See Section 10 for an explanation of analyzing and interpreting oral reading miscues.

3. Assessment of Comprehension Through Unaided Recall. The examiner can ask students to retell the passage as though they were telling it to someone who had never read it. He or she can then record the number of ideas recalled by the student and map them on a retelling scoring sheet. This recall can be evaluated for completeness, accuracy, sequence, and use of narrative and expository structure. (See Section 11 for guidelines on recording and interpreting unaided recall.) The quality of unaided recall can be contrasted with the student's ability to answer explicit and implicit questions about passage content.

4. Assessment of Comprehension Through Look-Backs. After asking the student to answer questions, the examiner can then ask the student to look back in the text to locate answers to missed questions and/or to find answers to incorrect responses.

5. Assessment of Comprehension Through Think-Alouds. In the high school passages, the examiner can model the think-aloud process and then ask the student to think aloud while reading.

Examiners must choose purposes that are germane to their diagnostic needs. Seldom will an individual diagnostician utilize all the diagnostic options of the *QRI–3*. Examiners must ask themselves, "What are my purposes in administering the passages?" and choose the level and types of passages accordingly.

General Procedures for Administering the Passages

General Administration Guidelines

First, the examiner must choose a passage for the student to read, using the conceptual-questions and/or prediction tasks to determine the student's familiarity with the topic of the selection. He or she should then ask the student to read the passage orally or silently.

If the student reads the passage orally, the examiner should record the student's miscues (substitutions, omissions, and insertions) on the examiner copy of the passage. The examiner should also time the student's rate of oral reading. Once the student completes the passage, the examiner removes it and assesses comprehension by asking the reader to retell what he or she remembers, to answer explicit and implicit questions, or to do both. If the student reads the passage silently, the examiner obviously cannot mark oral miscues. Instead, he or she can time the student's rate of reading and assess comprehension in the above manner.

The examiner should then determine whether the total performance on the passage represents an independent, instructional, or frustration level for the student. These levels are obtained from two scores. The total number of oral reading miscues determines the level for word identification in context. The percentage of questions answered correctly determines the level for comprehension. The examiner then compares these two scores to determine a general passage level.

Instructions to the Student

"I have some passages for you to read. Some you will read orally and some silently. I will be making some notes as you read, and because I cannot remember everything you say, I will also be taping you. I cannot help you in any way. If you come to a word you do not know, just do the best you can and continue on. Afterwards I will ask you to tell me what you can remember about the passage just as if you were telling it to someone who had never heard it before. I will also ask you some questions about what you have read. Ready? The first passage is called —.''

Passage Selection

As a decision maker, the examiner must choose, in accordance with his or her purposes, the number and type of passages to administer. However, examiners often ask several questions regarding passage administration.

Which Level of Passage Should I Begin With? An examiner can use the word lists to estimate a beginning point. He or she does not want to start too low, nor does he or she want the passage to be too difficult. Meeting frustration at the beginning of a diagnostic session can prejudice the student against the entire process. He or she should choose a level where the student has attained the independent level on the accompanying word list. (See Section 7 for an explanation of using the word lists to select a beginning point.) If the examiner has data to suggest a viable starting point, such as test scores or reading-group placement, he or she does not have to use the word lists for this purpose.

Must I Find Independent, Instructional, and Frustration Levels for All Types of Text? No. To do so would demand an unrealistic amount of time, and student fatigue would be a very real concern. Determination of an instructional level is of primary importance in most cases. Determination of an instructional level in familiar text is more important than level determination in unfamiliar text. Once the examiner obtains the instructional level, he or she can often estimate the independent and frustration levels.

Do I Have to Administer All Passages Within a Readability Level? No. The passages chosen will depend on the examiner's purpose in giving the *QRI–3*. Assessment specialists may well use more passages than a classroom teacher attempting to determine an instructional level for text placement.

How Can I Select Passages for Pre- and Post-testing? If you wish to use *QRI–3* for pre- and post-testing, you have several options. You can administer the same passage as your pre and post measure. Or you can administer two passages at the same readability level. If you choose this option, you must select passages that are somewhat similar. They should both be either narrative or expository. They should be of roughly the same length and familiarity. However, even within a single readability level, passages can vary in difficulty. Section 16 indicates which passages tend to be more difficult at each readability level. You may wish to choose the easier passage as the pre-test and the more difficult one as the post-test. In this way, gains made on the post-test will tend to be a more accurate indicator of actual growth.

What Types of Passages Should I Start With? Determining the student's instructional level for familiar text is the first step. Within this parameter, an examiner can select either narrative or expository text. For younger readers, we suggest that text with pictures often provides an effective starting point. For students suspected of reading at levels six through high school, choice of narrative or expository text depends on the instructional needs and known capabilities of the student. Very often, students are performing acceptably in reading or literature classes but are experiencing difficulties in content-area classes. For these students, beginning in expository text would be more crucial than in narrative. If the examiner has no clear direction as to the desired text type, familiar narrative assessment represents a good beginning point. Because it is generally easier than expository text, it tends to lead to initial experiences of success on the part of the student and to represent his or her best effort.

Which Mode Should I Use, Oral or Silent? We suggest that examiners use an oral reading format with younger children and with older students suspected of reading below the third grade level. The examiner can estimate this by the word-list scores. At this point, students are still learning how to read, and listening to oral reading performance can offer much valuable information. However, if time permits, asking younger children to read a familiar narrative silently can sometimes provide information about how well they are making the transition to silent reading.

For students reading at levels three through five, the examiner should use a combination of oral and silent reading. At these levels, oral reading miscues can provide important information. Once an instructional level is established for narrative material, the examiner may wish to change to a silent reading mode. It is better to evaluate ability in expository text through silent reading, because most students are expected to read expository material silently in school. For students reading at levels six through high school, silent reading is the best format because individuals do little oral reading at these levels.

How to Find an Instructional Level

Finding the Instructional Level in Familiar Text

The examiner can use the word lists or his or her knowledge of the student to choose a beginning passage that will probably offer an initial experience of success to the reader. The passage should be a familiar narrative. If he or she is using the word lists, he or she can choose a passage of the same readability level as the highest word list on which the student scored at an independent level (see Section 7). The examiner should ask the student to read the passage orally and answer the questions. Then the examiner can count the oral reading miscues to determine a level for word identification in context. (See Section 10 for guidelines for counting miscues and using this count to arrive at independent, instructional, and frustration levels.) The examiner then counts the questions answered correctly to determine the comprehension level. (See Section 11 for guidelines for scoring comprehension.) Once the examiner has the word-identification (WR) and comprehension (Comp) levels, he or she is ready to determine total passage level using the following guidelines:

WR: Independent	+	Comp: Independent	=	Independent Level
	+	Comp: Instructional	=	Instructional Level
	+	Comp: Frustration	=	Frustration Level
WR: Instructional	+	Comp: Independent	=	Instructional Level
	+	Comp: Instructional	=	Instructional Level
	+	Comp: Frustration	=	Frustration Level
WR: Frustration	+	Comp: Independent	=	Instructional Level
	+	Comp: Instructional	=	Frustration Level

If the student reads silently, the examiner can determine the total passage level by the comprehension score.

If the student scores within the independent or instructional range on the first passage, the examiner should choose another familiar narrative passage at the next-higher level. He or she should continue moving upward until the student reaches a frustration level. If the student reaches a frustration level on the first passage, the examiner should move downward until the student reaches an instructional level. There may be times when the examiner will not choose to find the highest instructional level. The student may reach an instructional level at her or his chronological grade level. If that happens, determining that the student can read above chronological grade placement or ascertaining the exact frustration level may have little value.

Once the examiner has found the student's instructional level, he or she may choose to have the student read the other familiar narrative passage at that level. If the student reads the first passage orally, he or she should read the second one silently. This allows the examiner to assess the student's ability in both oral and silent reading. If performance is different, the student may be experiencing discrepancies between the two modes. If the student read the first passage silently, the examiner may choose to verify the attained level by asking the student to read the second one silently also. Verification of levels and comparison of oral and silent reading provide for a more in-depth assessment; however, they are options that the examiner may choose to bypass in the interest of time.

Finding the Instructional Level in Other Types of Material

Once the examiner has determined the familiar narrative instructional level, he or she may wish to contrast this level with the level attained in other types of text: text with and without pictures (pre-primer through grade two), unfamiliar selections, and expository text. For expository text, the examiner should begin at the instructional level attained in familiar narratives and move up or down as indicated by the student's performance. For unfamiliar text, the examiner should begin one level lower than the level attained in familiar material. Table 9.1 provides instructions for finding an instructional level. Table 9.2 presents the criteria for establishing these levels.

TABLE 9.1

How to Find an Instructional Level

1. Use the *word lists* to choose a beginning level.
   Select a passage at the same readability level as the highest independent level attained by the student on the word lists.

   OR

   Use *other* data to choose a beginning level.

   Select a passage at a readability level that your data suggest will provide the student with a successful experience.

2. Select a familiar narrative passage at the appropriate beginning level as determined above.

3. Have the student *read the passage orally* (if using passages for primer through fifth grades) or *silently* (if using passages for grade six through high school) and *answer the questions.*

4. Determine the *total passage level:* a combination of the level for word recognition and the level for comprehension.

5. *Move to the next highest level* if the student scores at an independent or instructional level

---

TABLE 9.1 *(Continued)*

How to Find an Instructional Level

Move to the next lowest level if the student scores at a frustration level.

6. *Stop* when the student reaches his or her highest instructional level.

OR

Stop when the student reaches an instructional level at his or her chronological grade level.

7. Options
   a. Once you have the highest instructional level, you may *verify this level* by having the student read another familiar passage at that level orally or silently. If you began with text accompanied by pictures, you may verify the level in text without pictures.
   b. To determine a level for *familiar expository text* or text with and without pictures, begin with a passage at the familiar instructional level as determined in the above procedure.
   c. To determine a level for *unfamiliar text,* begin with a passage one level below the familiar instructional level.
   d. To determine a *listening* level, begin with a passage one level below the student's chronological grade placement.

TABLE 9.2

Criteria: Independent, Instructional, and Frustration Levels

Independent Level:

The level at which a student can read and comprehend without assistance.
Word Identification in Isolation: 90% or higher
Obtained from word lists
Word Identification in Context: 98% or higher
Obtained from oral reading of passages
Comprehension: 90% or higher

Instructional Level:

The level at which a student can be instructed profitably.
Word Identification in Isolation: 70% to 89%
Obtained from word lists
Word Identification in Context:
Obtained from oral reading of passages
90% to 97%: Total Accuracy
95% to 97%: Total Acceptability
Comprehension: 70% to 89%

Frustration Level:

The level at which a student is completely unable to read with adequate word identification or comprehension.
Word Identification in Isolation: Less than 70%
Obtained from word lists
Word Identification in Context:
Obtained from oral reading of passages
Less than 90%: Total Accuracy
Less than 95%: Total Acceptability
Comprehension: Less than 70%

(continued)

TABLE 9.2 *(Continued)*

Criteria: Independent, Instructional, and Frustration Levels

Formula for Determining Percentages:

Word Identification in Isolation (word lists):
  Number of words correctly identified ÷ total number of words on the
    list (20).
Word Identification in Context (oral reading of passages):
  (Number of words in passage − number of miscues) ÷ number of
words in passage
Comprehension (questions):
Number of questions correctly answered ÷ total number of questions

Rate:

To obtain the reading rate in words per minute, use the following formula:
WPM = (Number of words in the passage × 60) ÷ number of seconds it
  took to read the passage

10 Administration and Scoring of the Qualitative Reading Inventory–3

Word Identification in Context: Oral Reading

Recording Oral Reading Miscues

Counting Oral Reading Miscues

Counting Total Accuracy
Counting Total Acceptability

Analyzing Oral Reading Miscues: Miscue Analysis

Recording Miscues
Counting Miscues
Analyzing the Miscues

Evaluating Automaticity

Recording Oral Reading Miscues

When the student is reading orally, the examiner marks any miscues the student makes. It is helpful to tape the oral reading segment; then the examiner will be sure to catch the miscues. As one becomes more proficient in recording student miscues, the tape becomes less important. We suggest the following system for recording miscues:

> *Substitution:* Write what the student said over the word as it appears in print.

Omission: Circle the omitted word.

Insertion: Write in the insertion and mark it with a $\wedge$.

Self-correction: If a student corrects a miscue, write the miscue and mark it with "C."

Reversal: If the student transposes two words or phrases, such as "Said John" for "John said," mark the reversal with a $\cap$ symbol.

Punctuation ignored: Mark an "X" on any punctuation that the reader ignores.

Examples:

TEXT: Once there was a very (big) bear. X

loved C   *dark*
He lived in the $\wedge$ woods.

One day his father saw the big bear crying.

Why are you crying, his father said.

In this example, the student omitted "big" in the first sentence and ignored the period by continuing to read. In the second sentence, she or he said "loved" for "lived" and self-corrected. The student also inserted "dark." In the last sentence, she or he read, "said his father" instead of, "his father said."

Most IRIs allow the examiner to offer assistance to the student when she or he encounters an unfamiliar word. We do not recommend this. It is impossible to assess the effect of word identification on comprehension if the student is given the correct pronunciation for key words in the passage. If a student is unable to identify a word, gently ask him or her to move on. Figure 10.1 offers additional examples of recorded miscues.

Counting Oral Reading Miscues

Examiners can count miscues in two ways. The examiner can determine independent, instructional, and frustration levels by counting all miscues. We call this *Total Accuracy.* Or the examiner may choose to count only those miscues that change or distort passage meaning. We call this *Total Acceptability.* It is not necessary to do both. *Total Accuracy* is perhaps the easier and less time-consuming to score. The examiner does not have to spend time deciding whether or not miscues distort meaning. However, the diagnostic philosophy of the examiner will determine which scoring system to use. If the examiner decides to use *Total Acceptability*, during the actual administration, the examiner may find it easier to count all miscues in order to determine whether to move up or down a level. She or he can then determine *Total Acceptability* after completing the test administration.

FIGURE 10.1   Example of Reading and Scoring Miscues

wet ¹ _mc_   _went_ ² _mc_
It was a warm spring day. The children were going on a trip. The trip was

aminals ³ _mc_
to a farm. The children wanted to see many animals. They wanted to write

_4 mc_   _gone_ ⁵ _mc_   _the_ ⁶
down(all)they saw. They were going to make a book for their class. On the

pumpkin ⁷ _mc_   ⁸
way to the ⋀farm the bus broke (down.) The children thought their trip was over.

stepped ⁹ _mc_   10   _won't_ ᶜ 11
Then a man stopped his car. He helped(to)fix the bus. The bus ⋀started again.

was ᶜ 11
The children said, "yea!" The children got to the farm. They saw a pig. They

13 _hens_   _looked_ 14 _mc_   _looked_ 15 _mc_
saw a hen and cows. They liked petting the kittens. They learned about milking

and 16
cows. They liked the trip to the farm. They wanted to go again. (119 words)

The following miscues were substitutions:
   #1, 2, 3, 5, 6, 9, 12, 13, 14, 15, 16
The following miscues were insertions:
   #7, 11
The following miscues were omissions:
   #4, 8, 10
The following miscues were meaning-change miscues. They changed the meaning of the text or they were not self-corrected.
   #1, 2, 3, 4, 5, 7, 9, 14, 15

Counting Total Accuracy

Any deviation from the printed text is counted as a miscue. This includes

   insertions
   omissions
   substitutions
   reversals
   self-corrections

We do not count repetitions, hesitations, and omission of punctuation because they tend to be scored unreliably (Hood, 1975–1976). Also, repetitions and hesitations may indicate uncertainty on the part of the subject or a desire to clarify meaning that was missed. It can also be argued that they do not alter the text materially and therefore do not truly represent an error (McKenna, 1983).

Miscues made on proper names represent a special problem because of the extreme variability in pronunciation of some names. We recommend the following: If the student pronounces a proper name as a nonsense name—a name the examiner has never heard—and repeatedly calls the character by that name, the examiner should count it as one miscue. For example, if the student consistently refers to "Maria" as "Marin," these deviations count as one miscue. If, however, the student refers to "Maria" as "Marin," "Morin," and "Meres," each deviation is a separate miscue.

If a student makes the same miscue on the same word several times in the passage and it does not change the meaning of the passage, the examiner should count it as one miscue. For example, if a student consistently refers to "puppy" as "pup" or to "planes" as "airplanes," the deviations count as one miscue. If, however, the consistent miscue changes meaning, such as "poppy" for "puppy" or "please" for "planes," each pronunciation counts as a separate miscue. When a single word is repeated numerous times throughout a passage, students often pronounce it identically several times and then change to another pronunciation. How should this be scored? We recommend that each mispronunciation of the word be scored as a separate miscue. Examiners should assign *one* point to several miscues only if the mispronunciation does not change meaning and is consistent across the entire passage.

If a student omits an entire line, it is counted as one miscue because the omission represents a loss of place, not a conscious omission because of inability to identify words. Obviously, in this case, the student is not monitoring comprehension. However, counting each omitted word as a separate miscue could distort the final level designation.

Variations in pronunciations due to articulation difficulties or regional dialects should not be counted as oral reading miscues unless the student has been observed to pronounce the word or word part correctly. For example, if a student who speaks one of the black dialects omits the "s" or "ed" marker sometimes but reads it in other cases, it should be counted as an oral reading miscue. The examiner should not assume that a student of a specific race speaks or does not speak a particular dialect, but she or he should determine speaking patterns through casual conversation with the student before, during, and after testing.

The examiner should count the total number of miscues and use this result to determine whether the student's performance reflects an independent, instructional, and/or frustration level. For ease and accuracy in scoring, we recommend that she or he number the miscues. The following criteria determine level designations for word identification in context:

Total Accuracy

Independent Level:	98% accuracy
Instructional Level:	90% to 97% accuracy
Frustration Level:	less than 90% accuracy

The examiner can determine percentages by subtracting the number of miscues from the number of words in the passage (listed at the bottom of his or her copy of the passage). This yields the number of words read correctly. She or he then divides this by the number of words in the passage, rounding upward to find the percent of Total Accuracy. She or he may also wish to use the guidelines given at the bottom of each passage, which indicate how many miscues result in independent, instructional, and frustration level reading. Examiners who use these will not need to determine percentages.

Example: "A Trip" has 119 words. A student made 8 total miscues.

$$119$$
$$\underline{-8}$$
$$111 \div 119 = 93\% \text{ Total Accuracy}$$

For Total Accuracy, the student scored within the criteria for the instructional level for word identification in context.

Counting Total Acceptability

Acceptable miscues are those that do not change or distort passage meaning. What is counted as a miscue that changes meaning? A meaning-change miscue is any deviation from the printed text that results in an ungrammatical sentence or in a grammatical sentence that differs from the author's intended meaning. This includes

insertions
omissions
substitutions

If the student self-corrects a miscue, it is not counted as changing meaning.

If a student mispronounces a proper name, it does not count as a meaning-change miscue unless the gender of the character is changed. For example, if a student mispronounces "Lopez" as "Lopz," it is not counted as a meaning-change miscue. If a student mispronounces "Maria" as "Mary," do not count it as a meaning-change miscue. However, the substitution of "Mark" for "Mary" is counted as a miscue that changes meaning. A nonword substitution for a common proper name such as "Marin" for "Mary" is not counted as a meaning-change miscue if the student *consistently* offers this pronunciation. If, however, the student pronounces the name differently or correctly in other parts of the text, it is counted as a meaning-change miscue.

Nonword substitutions such as "piloneer" for "pioneer" are always counted as changing meaning. If the same nonword miscue is repeated several times, we advise counting it each time because it distorts meaning and adversely affects comprehension.

If a student consistently makes the same miscue on the same word and it changes meaning, the examiner should count each miscue separately, because each mispronunciation, however consistent, distorts the meaning of the text in some way.

In order to judge whether a miscue results in a meaning change, the examiner should read the miscue in the context of the sentence. If it is ungrammatical and is not corrected by the subject, it is scored automatically as a meaning change. If it is grammatical, the examiner will have to decide whether it is semantically synonymous with what the author meant.

Examples:

TEXT:
Marin   her   monkeys'   when
Maria went with the group to the monkey house where she

watch   others
spent a long time watching the chimps groom each other.

The substitutions of "Marin," "her," and "monkeys" do not change the meaning of the text. "Marin" was a consistent miscue for this subject throughout the passage. The substitutions of "when," "watch," and "others" are not acceptable. They do not make grammatical sense. Tables 14.2 and 14.3 contain additional examples of meaning-change miscues.

The examiner should count the number of miscues that change or distort text meaning. For ease in scoring, we recommend marking each meaning-change miscue as "M. C." One may also keep track by highlighting or underlining meaning-change miscues. The examiner can then use this number to determine the level designations for Total Acceptability. The following criteria determine level designations for word identification in context (see Section 16 for a further explanation of these criteria).

Total Acceptability

Independent Level:	98% Total accuracy
Instructional Level:	95% to 97% Total accuracy
Frustration Level:	less than 94% Total accuracy

The examiner counts the meaning-change miscues and subtracts the result from the number of words in the passage. Then she or he divides this by the number of words in the passage, rounding upward to find the percentage of Total Acceptability. She or he may also use the guidelines given at the end of the passage, which indicate how many meaning-change miscues result in an independent, instructional, or frustration reading level.

Example: "A Trip" has 119 words. A student made a total of 8 miscues. Four of these were meaning-change miscues.

$$119$$
$$\underline{-4}$$
$$115 \div 119 = 96.6 = 97\% \text{ Total Acceptability}$$

For Total Acceptability, the student scored within an instructional level for word identification in context.

Analyzing Oral Reading Miscues: Miscue Analysis

Recording Miscues

Examiners can qualitatively analyze any miscues that the student makes while reading passages orally. This analysis provides a rich body of information about the student's reading strategies. The Miscue Analysis Worksheet in Table 10.1 provides a format for analyzing the student's miscues qualitatively. Generally, the examiner will analyze all miscues made during oral reading. If the student reads enough passages, the examiner can analyze any miscues made at independent and instructional levels (as determined by the total passage level) separately from those made at the frustration level. Generally, students employ different strategies as they move into frustration-level text, where meaningful context is not generally available to the reader.

1. The examiner writes the miscue in the first column and the text word in the second column. She or he should write substitutions and insertions as said by the student. Omissions are indicated by a dash.
2. Columns three and four evaluate the graphic similarity of the miscue to the text word. If the miscue resembles the text word in the initial letter/s, the examiner places a check in column three. Initial similarity occurs, for example, when the miscue and the text word begin with the same letter ("call" for "claw") or the miscue and the text word share a

TABLE 10.1

Miscue Analysis Worksheet

Subject _____ Level of Miscues: Independent/Instructional   Frustration

MISCUE	TEXT	GRAPHICALLY SIMILAR Initial	Final	Semantically Acceptable	Self-Corrected
Column Total		_____	_____	_____	_____
Total Miscues		_____	_____	_____	_____
Column Total / Total Miscues = %		_____	_____	_____	_____

common letter pattern ("broke" for "bright"). If the miscue resembles the text word in the final letter/s, the examiner places a check in column four. Examples include a miscue and a text word that end with the same letter or letter pattern ("fits" for "fins" or "decks" for "ducks") and a shared common ending ("looked" for "watched" or "going" for "sailing"). Why not record miscue and text similarities in the middle position? It has been our experience that the majority of miscues do involve a medial error, probably because vowel sounds are more variable than consonants and thus are more readily confused by readers, particularly those experiencing difficulty. Recording initial and final similarity is sufficient to suggest that the student is attempting to pay attention to letter-sound matching.

3. Column five evaluates semantic or contextual acceptability. Did the miscue retain the author's meaning? If the miscue was acceptable, the examiner places a check in this column. Semantically acceptable miscues suggest that the student is paying attention to meaning during the reading process. An example is the substitution of "takes" for "drink" in the sentence "The baby drinks milk from its mother for about a year."

4. Column six evaluates the number of self-corrections made by the student. Self-corrections suggest that the reader is comprehending during the reading process and thus is able to note a miscue that distorts the author's meaning. Self-corrections can also indicate attention to graphic cues. An example would be the reader who self-corrects a semantically acceptable miscue such as "put" for "divided" in the sentence "When they got to the zoo, their teachers divided the children into four groups."

Once the examiner has recorded all miscues, she or he must total each column as indicated on the worksheet. Now she or he can analyze the word-identification strategies of the subject.

Counting Miscues

The examiner should first count the total number of miscues made by the student (column one). Then the number of checks in each of columns three through six should be counted. The examiner can determine the percentage of miscues in each category by dividing the column total by the number of total miscues as recorded in column one. For example, if the subject made a total of 23 miscues and 15 of these were similar in the initial position, $15/23 = 65\%$.

Analyzing the Miscues

The Miscue Analysis Worksheet can indicate the strategies used by the student when reading orally. The percentages should not be interpreted rigidly; no percentage limits are given. Rather, they should be used as a means of noting general patterns of reader behavior. The following guidelines may be helpful.

1. If the worksheet shows a high percentage of semantically acceptable miscues and/or self-corrections, the reader is probably comprehending during the reading process. Of course, an observation like this needs to be made in relation to the student's comprehension score on the passages.

2. If the worksheet shows a high percentage of initial and final graphic similarity coupled with a low percentage of acceptable or self-corrected miscues, the reader may be paying more attention to decoding words than to the meaning of the text.
3. If the worksheet shows a high percentage of initial graphic similarity and a low percentage of final similarity, the reader may be paying attention only to the beginnings of words. Some children use only the initial letter/s as a basis for guessing the rest of the word.
4. If the worksheet shows a low percentage of initial and final graphic similarity coupled with a low percentage of acceptability and/or self-corrections, the reader may be a "wild guesser," one who is unable to use either phonics or context effectively.

As we mentioned previously, the examiner may analyze all miscues or only those made at independent and instructional levels versus those made at a frustration level. Comparing the types of miscues made at the independent/instructional levels with those made at the frustration level typically shows that the reader makes relatively more miscues acceptable to the author's meaning when reading independent/instructional text. As the reader moves into frustration text, the number of acceptable miscues and self-corrections tends to drop.

Evaluating Automaticity

Rate of oral and silent reading can suggest automaticity of word identification. If a reader reads relatively quickly, one can assume that the words are no longer being decoded. Instead, the reader is processing the words as whole units. Words recognized in this way are often termed *sight vocabulary*.

The *QRI–3* provides the examiner with the means of determining oral and silent reading rates as measured in words per minute. The number of words in the passage multiplied by 60 and divided by the number of seconds it took to read the passage will yield a word-per-minute score.

Both oral and silent reading rates are quite variable. They vary across passages. More difficult and/or unfamiliar passages tend to be read more slowly. Reading rate also varies according to reader purpose. If the reader is reading in order to learn or remember text content, this is typically done at a slower rate than pleasure reading. Reading rate also varies across individuals. Some readers are naturally faster than others, a phenomenon that may be attributed to speed of cognitive processing (Carver, 1990). For these reasons, any guidelines for evaluating reading rate must be interpreted as general in nature.

Our pilot data reflect normal readers reading at their instructional level. We found that there was wide variation in the rates, despite a steady growth in rate as reading level increased. We offer these rates, based on means and standard deviations, as *suggestive* of the rates of typical readers when processing text at their instructional level. Some drop in silent reading rate occurred at the upper middle school and high school levels. We believe this was due to the increased length and difficulty of some passages, as well as the fact that the high school passages were being read by eighth graders. Silent rates are not offered for pre-primer through first grade levels. Readers who are instructional at these levels have seldom made a transition to silent reading.

TABLE 10.2

Ranges of Oral Reading Rates of Students Reading at Instructional Level

Level	Oral Words per Minute
Pre-primer	13–35
Primer	28–68
First	31–87
Second	52–102
Third	85–139
Fourth	78–124
Sixth	113–165

TABLE 10.3

Ranges of Silent Reading Rates of Students Reading at Instructional Level

Level	Silent Words per Minute
Second	58–122
Third	96–168
Fourth	107–175
Sixth	135–241
Upper Middle School	73–370
High School	65–334

11 Administration and Scoring of the Qualitative Reading Inventory–3

Comprehension

Retelling

General Procedures
Scoring
Analysis of Retelling

Questions

General Procedures
Scoring the Questions

Criteria for Determining Reading Levels

An examiner can assess a student's comprehension of orally and silently read passages in two ways. He or she can ask the student to retell the selection and/or ask questions about the selection. The percentage correct on questions is used for assigning independent, instructional, and frustration levels. The examiner can evaluate the retelling qualitatively against a map composed of the important ideas contained in the passage. Examiners will use the questions more often than retelling; however, if an examiner should elect to do both, he or she should ask for the retelling before asking the questions. For that reason, we will look at retelling first.

General Procedures

After the student has finished reading the selection, the examiner should remove the passage and ask the student to retell it as if it were being told to someone who had never read or heard it before. After the student has retold as much as he or she can, the examiner should ask whether there is anything else he or she would like to say. If the student says that he or she can remember nothing, the examiner can draw the student's attention to the title of the passage and ask whether he or she can remember what the author wrote about it. The examiner should not offer more extensive hints or direct suggestions, such as "Can you remember what Johnny Appleseed's journey was like?" The examiner will find it helpful at first to tape the retelling and use the tape for scoring at a later time. As he or she becomes familiar with the individual passages, he or she can often score the retelling directly onto the Retelling Scoring Sheet as the student is talking.

Scoring

Scoring is determined by comparing the idea units recalled by the student with those on the Retelling Scoring Sheet. The scoring sheet was designed on the basis of an examination of the idea units most frequently recalled by students in our piloting sample, as well as a theoretical analysis of the important units. The scoring sheets for the high school passages were also designed from these two components, but we also used teacher judgments about what were the most important ideas in the passage as well as what they thought a student would normally recall after an initial reading. The examiner should place a check next to each explicit idea listed on the scoring sheet that was recalled by the student. As an option, the examiner may wish to indicate the sequence of the recalled ideas by using a number instead of a check mark; however, this is not necessary. He or she can write in any additional recalled ideas, such as explicit ideas not listed on the scoring sheet or inferences made by the student.

The following paragraph is Peter's retelling of "Johnny Appleseed"; it is accompanied by a scoring example in Figure 11.1.

> *Johnny, all the men nicknamed him Johnny Appleseed because he had planted a lot of apple trees, because he had lived in Massachusetts and he went down west to put in a lot of apple trees. While he was planting a lot of apple trees, miles and miles, he had crossed rivers and all that through the forest where Indians and that were there. His clothes were wet and torn in the knees and used his shirt for a pillow or something. He still didn't give up. And he didn't have any shoes or nothin'. He lived like raggy and then the apple trees that are here weren't really here before.*

Obviously, a student will not recall in the exact words of the text, and synonyms and paraphrases are acceptable. The examiner will have to decide whether the subject's recall matches the meaning of the text.

Our pilot data indicated that recall for the high school passages did not vary significantly among the three content areas of literature, social studies, and science. Students reading these lengthy and difficult passages recalled few explicit details. Their recall tended to take the form of summary or gist statements. For example, one student recalled the first part of "Where the Ashes Are" by saying," It's about a boy caught in the middle of a war." Similarly, another student retold the second section of "World War I" by saying,

FIGURE 11.1

Retelling Scoring Sheet for Johnny Appleseed

Setting / Background

____ John Chapman was born

____ in 1774.

____ He became a farmer

____ grew crops.

____ John liked

____ to grow

____ and eat apples.

____ People were moving west.

____ Apples were a good food

____ for settlers to have.

Goal

____ John decided

_5_ to go west.

____ He wanted

_3_ to plant apple trees.

Events

____ John got many seeds

____ from farmers

____ who squeezed apples

____ to make a drink

____ called cider.

____ He left

____ for the frontier.

____ He planted seeds

____ as he went along.

____ He gave them away.

____ John walked miles.

_6_ He crossed rivers

_7_ and went through forests.

____ He was hungry

____ and wet.

____ He had to hide

_8_ from Indians

____ unfriendly Indians.

_9_ His clothes were torn.

____ He used a sack

____ for a shirt

____ and he cut out holes

____ for the arms.

_11_ He wore no shoes.

Resolution

____ John's fame spread.

_1_ He was nicknamed

_2_ Johnny Appleseed.

____ Settlers accepted seeds

____ gratefully.

____ Thanks to Johnny Appleseed

_12_ trees grow

_13_ in many parts

____ of America.

Other ideas recalled including inferences

4 lived in Massachusetts

10 didn't give up

"It's about how the war ended and what the guys who won wanted to get for themselves and the part that Wilson played with his ideas for peace." Such summary statements represent few ideas that are explicitly stated in the text, but they do demonstrate the student's overall understanding of the passage and should be written down. At the end of each Retelling Scoring Sheet, there is space to write in any summary statements that were part of the retelling.

Analysis of Retelling

Although the retelling is not used to determine independent, instructional, and frustration levels, it can provide valuable information with implications for instruction. For example, if the student does not retell the central parts of a narrative, the student may not have an understanding of story structure. Similarly, if the student does not organize an expository retelling around the main idea and supporting details, the student may not understand the structure of paragraphs in exposition.

The examiner should use the retellings to answer the following questions:

1. Do the retellings of narrative material retain the basic structure of the narratives? Is the most important information included?
2. Do the retellings of expository material retain the main idea and supporting detail structure of the selection? Is the most important information included?
3. Are the retellings sequential?
4. Is the recall accurate?

Peter's recall of "Johnny Appleseed" can be evaluated in the following way. Although his recall was not offered in a sequential manner, Peter included information related to all four categories of story structure: the setting/background, the goal, the events, and the resolution. This suggests that Peter has somewhat internalized the structure of the story and is using it to help his recall.

Evaluating the retelling of the longer selections at the upper middle school and high school levels poses a somewhat different problem. Because of the length of these selections and their concept density, it is unrealistic to expect a complete and lengthy retelling. We suggest that you use the following guidelines to evaluate the retellings of the longer selections.

1. Did the retelling contain appropriate summary/gist statements or main idea statements?
2. Did the retelling support the summary/gist statements or main idea statements with any details?
3. Was the retelling generally specific? Did it contain vague and general statements?
4. Was the retelling generally accurate?

The contrast between Carol's and Terrie's retellings of the first section of "World War I" is instructive.

Carol's retelling:

How World War I got started in 1914 because Serbia killed some guy and what countries were involved like Britain, France, and Germany and how the U.S. got into it because Germany attacked supply ships and then asked Mexico to fight us.

Terrie's retelling:

It was about the reasons that started World War I and the countries that were involved and how they were fighting and who was fighting and what started it. The Serbian leader got killed for being too close to Serbia. It talked about Russia pushing Germany back. And it talked about what the empires were and where they were.

Carol's retelling contained three summary or gist statements: how World War I started, what countries were involved, and how the United States got into it. She expanded these with supporting details. Her retelling was generally specific and accurate.

Terrie mentioned two summary or gist statements: the reasons that started World War I and the countries that were involved. However, she repeated these in different words and offered few specific details. Her comments about the Serbian leader were inaccurate, as was her statement that Russia pushed Germany back. Her statement about "empires" indicates that she paid attention to the map but only in a very general fashion. Terrie's retelling suggests a less complete memory for the text than Carol's.

A comparison of Carl's and Mark's retellings of the first section of "Characteristics of Viruses" also illustrates differences in quality of recall on the high school passages.

Carl's retelling:

Viruses are not cells. They're infectious and harm other cells. They have two parts. Some contain DNA and others have RNA which are the hereditary genes. Viruses are simple and they don't eat. They only have five genes while humans have a lot. There was a diagram of the flu virus. It has an envelope which protects the virus.

Mark's retelling:

It told what viruses are made of and that there are different kinds. There are different layers of the virus and a middle part. They can infect people but not all are infectious but most of them are. They have DNA and some have RNA. There were a lot of scientific terms like "capsule."

Carl began his retelling by defining a virus. He mentioned two main ideas, that viruses have two parts and their simplicity. For each, he recalled a few specific details. He also paid attention to the diagram and seemed to integrate this with the text. His retelling was sequential and specific.

Mark offered two summary/gist statements: what viruses are made of and that there are different kinds. He offered a few rather general comments in support of these, and he inaccurately stated that not all viruses are infectious. He confused the term "capsule" with "capsid" and seemed more aware of the terminology in the selection than of what it meant in relation to the topic. His retelling was less coherent than Carl's and suggests an incomplete understanding of the selection.

Questions

General Procedures

After the student has retold to the best of his or her ability, the examiner should ask the comprehension questions and score them according to the suggestions provided. There are two types of questions. Explicit questions have answers that are stated directly in the passage. These questions assess whether the student can understand and remember information stated directly by an author. For implicit questions, the reader must use clues in the passage to make inferences in order to answer correctly. These questions assess the reader's inferencing abilities.

Scoring the Questions

We suggest that answers be scored as either right or wrong with no half points given. This is because the awarding of half credit tends to be unreliable. In addition, our piloting was done on the basis of either right or wrong answers. Of course, the examiner should give credit for any answer that includes the same information in different words.

If the question is an explicit question, the answer *must* come from the passage. You cannot count as correct an answer that comes from prior knowledge (even if it is accurate). For example, on the third grade passage "Cats: Lions and Tigers in Your House," explicit questions ask the reader to name ways in which lions, tigers, and cats are alike. If a student says that they all have sharp teeth or all have fur, this would be an incorrect answer. Such information is accurate, but it is not stated explicitly in the passage.

Similarly, an implicit question cannot be considered correct if the answer is not related to a clue in the passage. Again, if the answer comes from prior knowledge only, it is not counted as correct. For example, for the "Amelia Earhart" passage, one implicit question is "Why do you think her plane was never found?" A student may answer, "because it burned up," which is a reasonable answer drawn from his or her background. However, the clues in the passage suggest that it crashed into an ocean and probably sank. When the student's answer to an implicit question obviously comes from background knowledge, the examiner can acknowledge its reasonableness and then ask, "But what do the clues in the passage tell you?"

The pre-primer passages do not have implicit comprehension questions. However, the student may answer an explicit question by using information from the pictures. We have chosen to score such a response as a correct answer to an implicit question. For example, on "Just Like Mom," one question is "Name one thing that the girl can do just like Mom." One of the most common responses was "water the flowers." That response comes from the fourth picture. However, the text says, "I can work at home." Thus the child's response is an incorrect answer to the explicit question, but is counted as a *correct* implicit response. A question asked about "People at Work" is "What is one thing that people do at work?" A common response was "fix things." This is counted as a correct implicit response, because although the text says, "Other people make things at work," children interpret the picture as someone fixing the bicycle.

You must score the questions as you go along. The scores tell you when to move to higher passages and when to stop.

Criteria for Determining Reading Levels

Passages have five, six, eight, or ten questions. The following guide indicates the number of correct questions needed to attain an independent level (90% or above), an instructional level (67% to 89%), and a frustration level (below 67%). The following criteria for use on each passage are also provided on the examiner's question page.

Five questions: Independent level: 5 correct
                     Instructional level: 4 correct
                     Frustration level: 0–3 correct
Six questions: Independent level: 6 correct
                     Instructional level: 4 correct
                     Frustration level: 0–3 correct
Eight questions: Independent level: 8 correct
                     Instructional level: 6–7 correct
                     Frustration level: 0–5 correct
Ten questions: Independent level: 9–10 correct
                     Instructional level: 7–8 correct
                     Frustration level: 0–6 correct

Analysis of a student's ability to answer explicit and implicit questions can provide valuable information. An examiner should analyze a student's performance at independent and instructional levels separately from that at frustration level. For each grouping, he or she should count the total number of explicit questions asked of the student and the total number answered correctly. To arrive at a percentage, he or she must divide the total correct by the total asked, repeating the procedure for implicit questions. A substantial difference between these two scores, such as 50% on several passages, may suggest that the student needs instruction either in remembering what the author stated explicitly in the text or in using clues in the text to make inferences, depending on which score is higher.

12 Administration and Scoring of the Qualitative Reading Inventory–3

Assessing Strategic Reading

Look-Backs

Think-Alouds

Think-Aloud Statements That Indicate Understanding of the Text
Think-Aloud Statements That Indicate Lack of Understanding

Assessing Note-Taking Ability

Assessing Listening Comprehension

The following procedures can offer valuable insights into a student's strengths and weaknesses in strategic reading. The examiner can choose to administer one or more of them in addition to or in lieu of the assessment measures explained in the preceding sections. The examiner must decide which procedures will offer the most meaningful information.

Look-Backs

During the normal administration procedures, the examiner asks the student to answer questions without the benefit of the accompanying text. Student success in doing this is heavily dependent on memory for what was read. It is impossible to know whether an incorrect or missing answer resulted from poor comprehension during reading or poor memory after reading. As students read longer and more concept-dense text, such as the high school passages included in the *QRI–3*, memory constraints may interfere with the ability to answer explicit or implicit questions. This is especially true when the student is struggling with unfamiliar text.

Think about the last time you read a selection on a very unfamiliar topic. You probably comprehended what you were reading, but afterwards you may have been able to recall only a small portion of it. If someone asked you a direct question, you may not have been able to provide the answer. Did this mean that you were a poor reader? On the contrary, a quick skimming of the text would have improved your recall immeasurably. Similarly, looking back in the text would have allowed you to locate the answer to the question you were asked.

Skilled readers employ the look-back strategy naturally and efficiently as a way of increasing and maintaining comprehension. Our pilot data suggested that students with instructional levels at or above third grade could do this readily. See Section 16. For this reason, we recommend adding look-backs to the process of assessing comprehension. After scoring the questions and determining the comprehension level, the examiner can give the student the text and ask whether she or he can look back to locate answers that were unknown and/or to correct erroneous answers. Score the look-backs as correct or incorrect, and use this result to determine a level for comprehension with look-backs. The *QRI–3* provides space on the scoring sheet to record Comprehension Without Look-Backs and Comprehension with Look-Backs.

If a student can locate answers and/or correct errors, she or he probably understood the text, at least after rereading it. The initial problem may have been one of memory or purpose. If, however, the student cannot locate or correct an answer, perhaps the problem lies with basic understanding of what she or he read.

Students vary in their ability to use look-backs. For some, it is an effortless procedure. They seem to know exactly where to look to find the information. Others do not seem to know how to begin. They begin to reread the entire selection laboriously or to stare helplessly at the page and look to the examiner for guidance. In such cases, the examiner may point to the area where the relevant material can be found. However, in order to receive credit for a look-back, the student should exhibit relatively independent performance. If the examiner has to point out where the information can be found or has to offer supportive hints, no credit should be given. For example, after reading a section of the high school passage on viruses, Sally was unable to look back to find the correct answer to an implicit question. The examiner pointed out where the information could be found (the illustration) and offered a few suggestions about what Sally knew and what information she should look for. Sally eventually arrived at the correct answer, but she did not receive credit for a successful look-back because it was not an independent performance on her part.

Answering implicit questions demands some background knowledge from the reader as well as identification of clues provided by the author. If a student look-back is unsuccessful, the examiner can probe to see whether the student's inability to answer an implicit question is due to lack of background or to lack of attention to the clues in the text. For example, the examiner can tell the student the correct answer and ask him or her to find the clue in the text. The examiner can also point out the clue and see whether the student can use it to arrive at the correct answer. Such procedures provide valuable diagnostic information, but the student should not be given credit for such examiner-supported answers.

Scoring comprehension without look-backs may underestimate a student's comprehension. For example, Jonah read the "Life Cycles of Stars" passage and, when answering questions without look-backs, attained a frustration score of 40%. When he was allowed to look back, he raised his comprehension score to 90%, an independent level.

Without Look-Backs		With Look-Backs	
Number Correct Explicit: _3_		Number Correct Explicit: _5_	
Number Correct Implicit: _1_		Number Correct Implicit: _4_	
Total: _4_		Total: _9_	
____ Independent:	8 correct	_X_ Independent:	8 correct
____ Instructional:	6–7 correct	____ Instructional:	6–7 correct
_X_ Frustration:	0–5 correct	____ Frustration:	0–5 correct

Many students in our pilot study who read the high school passages attained frustration levels in their initial attempts to answer questions. However, the majority were able to raise their scores to an instructional or independent level following look-backs. For this reason, we believe that any determination of reading level on the high school passages *should be based on the use of look-backs*. In other words, comprehension with look-backs is most representative of reading performance on the high school passages. For all passages from third grade through upper middle school, we believe that a level based on a combination of questions answered without *and* with look-backs is more representative of what skilled readers do when faced with concept-dense and unfamiliar text. See Section 16.

There are other ways to utilize the look-back procedure to obtain information about a student's reading needs. The examiner can choose a passage that proved difficult to the student and ask the student to look back and indicate specific parts that she or he found especially troublesome. The examiner either can direct the student to indicate a specific word that she or he does not know or can ask the subject to identify "something you found hard or something you didn't understand." Once the examiner isolates a segment of text, she or he can ask a few questions to confirm that the chosen element actually was difficult and was not selected at random. If the student says that everything was hard, the examiner should reverse the procedure and ask her or him to find one or two things that were a bit easier than the rest.

The examiner can ask the student to look back and define or explain certain key vocabulary words contained in a passage. This may be especially helpful if the student has evinced poor comprehension. The examiner can ascertain whether the student knows the meaning of words that were pronounced correctly, as well as words that were pronounced incorrectly, during passage reading. After silent reading, the examiner can ask the student to define and pronounce certain key words contained in the passage. Inability to do either may be an indication of why the student's comprehension was low.

Think-Alouds

Think-alouds are a reader's verbalizations in reaction to reading a selection. They can be made before, during, or after reading. Think-alouds provide a way of "gathering information about individual readers' ongoing thinking processes and metacognitive behavior" (Brown & Lytle, 1988, p. 96). When using think-alouds during reading, the examiner asks the student to read the passage and stop at set points to "think out loud" and share efforts to understand, judge, reason, and monitor. Although this can be done in any text, the high school passages are specifically designed to facilitate use of the think-aloud process.

We recommend that the first section be read by the student without any attempt to think aloud. This allows for a comparison of comprehension in text with and without think-alouds. The second section is constructed to offer suggestions to the examiner for modeling the think-aloud process. We have included modeling comments that the examiner can make to demonstrate how to think aloud during the reading process. We recommend that this be an interactive dialogue between the examiner and the student. The examiner shares his or her think-aloud comments and then asks the student to offer one in kind.

The third section is designed so the examiner can write in the student's think-aloud comments. In this section, the student is basically on his or her own, reading the text silently and thinking out loud whenever the word STOP is encountered.

On the basis of the research literature on think-alouds (see Section 2) and our pilot study, we constructed a system for coding different types of think-alouds. The majority of think-aloud comments exhibited by students in our pilot were paraphrasing or summarizing the text segment, questioning, and making new meaning, such as drawing an inference or a conclusion. Questioning think-alouds tended to fall into two categories: questions that indicated understanding of the text and questions that indicated lack of understanding. Other, less frequent think-aloud comments involved indicating understanding or lack of it, reporting a match, absence of or conflict with prior knowledge, and identifying personally. We divided the think-aloud comments into two categories: those that indicated understanding of the text and those that indicated lack of understanding. Our pilot data supported the validity of this classification in that a negative correlation existed between statements representing understanding and statements representing lack of understanding for all content areas. In other words, students who made more think-aloud statements that indicated understanding made significantly fewer that indicated lack of understanding. See Section 16.

Think-Aloud Statements That Indicate Understanding of the Text

Paraphrasing or summarizing. The student repeats the content of the text segment and basically preserves the language of the author.

"Where the Ashes Are"

Dad and the men were taken inside the guesthouse. Women and children were led to another building, a rectangular one with thick walls and a little door. The gunfire and bombs didn't bother them anymore; they were used to it. There were ten families.

"World War I"

The Allies want Germany to pay money for damages right away, a lot of money with interest. They only let Germany have a few warships and no airplanes or submarines. Wilson is hoping the League of Nations will help in the future.

"Characteristics of Viruses"

The text is saying that viruses are really diverse so they classify them by what they look like or how they invade a host.

Making New Meaning. The student makes an inference, draws a conclusion, or engages in reasoning.

"Where the Ashes Are"

I bet Mom is lying to the kids so they won't feel bad 'cause she probably knows something really bad is going to happen to them or their dad.

I can just picture a lot of people lying there helpless.

"World War I"

This was dangerous because they could start another war because of all the resentment that they had to move around and change borders.

Creating more countries and putting them under France and Britain will just create offspring, Little Frances and Britains. It doesn't seem logical.

"Characteristics of Viruses"

It's unusual that viroids have nothing, no capsid, to protect them. It doesn't seem like they would be able to survive.

Viruses are really smart. They can do a lot of things.

Questioning That Indicates Understanding. The student asks a question that is based on understanding of the text, such as questioning the motivation of a character, applying text content to a similar situation, or projecting text content into a future point in time.

"Where the Ashes Are"

Did the people treat the father bad and is that why he is not acting too happy to see his wife and child?

What is the mother thinking as she is sitting there? Is she worried about her husband?

"World War I"

Did Germany pay the two billion and did they go bankrupt?

What was the timeline for the mandates to get independence? How long in the future?

"Characteristics of Viruses"

Why does the polio virus only replicate in humans but the rabies virus replicates both in animals and humans?

How is the structure of a viroid simpler than a virus?

Noting Understanding. The student recognizes that she or he understands what was read.

"Where the Ashes Are"

I wasn't sure what was going on about the bathtub but now I get it. They probably didn't have any running water.

At first I didn't know what re-education was and now I do. It is where you get beaten to do work.

"World War I"

I guess it makes sense. The winners really want to rub the losers' nose in it. That's why they billed Germany for all that money

At first I wasn't sure what they were doing but now I get it. If they cut up the big countries into little ones, they won't be that much of a threat.

"Characteristics of Viruses"

Hey, this is yucky. You can get a tumor from a virus.

It makes sense that some viruses only go into animals and not humans. After all, we are built differently from animals.

Reporting Prior Knowledge. The student reports a match with what was previously known or indicates that prior knowledge was absent or in conflict with the text.

"Where the Ashes Are"

I knew some cultures call years by animal names but I don't know why.

That word [pointed to "dispassionately"]. I remember it was part of a vocabulary lesson but I guess I didn't learn it very well.

"World War I"

I didn't realize how many new countries started after World War I.

I read about the League of Nations and I don't think it worked.

"Characteristics of Viruses"

I didn't know viruses had different shapes, I thought they were all the same.

I know about HIV; I've heard about it.

Identifying Personally. The student relates the text to personal experiences, makes a judgment of some sort on the basis of personal experiences, states interest or lack of it, or indicates like or dislike for a topic.

"Where the Ashes Are"

I think it was really sad that he had to see his father tied up and taken away. He was just a little boy.

The father has no expression on his face. If it were me, I would be thrilled to see my child.

"World War I"

I'm glad someone else thinks that what they are doing is unjust. Thirty-two billion is a bit much!

I'm really not into wars, especially one that happened a long time ago.

"Characteristics of Viruses"

I thought animals could get polio. My cat got flu. It makes me feel better that they can't get polio.

I feel sorry for the animals that die from these diseases.

Think-Aloud Statements That Indicate Lack of Understanding

Questioning That Indicates Lack of Understanding. The student asks questions about character motivation or the applications of a concept that indicate lack of understanding. The student also asks about the meaning of words or concepts.

"Where the Ashes Are"

Why is the mother just sitting there in the basement gossiping with everyone and not doing something? [The mother was actually sitting quietly and saying nothing.]

Why did the mother take the dirty water to her husband? Why didn't she just get clean water? [Indicates a lack of understanding of their prisoner status.]

"World War I"

What is a war-guilt clause?

Why did the empires allow themselves to be broken up? [Indicates lack of understand that they were divided because they lost the war.]

"Characteristics of Viruses"

What kind of capsules do viroids have? How big are they? [Confuses "capsule" with "capsid".]

Does a prion make DNA from RNA? [Indicates lack of understanding that prions have neither DNA nor RNA.]

Noting Lack of Understanding. The student clearly states that she or he is confused about something.

"Where the Ashes Are"

I am really confused about what is happening, especially about this bathtub thing.

I don't get this whole part about the sister and why she kept wanting to wash her hands.

"World War I"

This doesn't make sense to me. They created all these countries and said it was the right of self-determination. The people didn't form their own nations. The Allies did it.

I have no idea what a buffer zone is supposed to do. Is it a good thing?

"Characteristics of Viruses"

I'm having some trouble here. It sounds like if you get a virus you can get a tumor or HIV. That doesn't seem right.

I hope this chart will help me understand what they are talking about. I am really mixed up with all this DNA and RNA stuff.

Think-aloud scoring sheets are provided after each passage. Alys read the third section of "Where the Ashes Are." Her think-aloud comments were as follows:

Why would a little boy lead everyone into the basement? (Questioning that indicates understanding.)

The mother must be really very worried with her husband taken away and her one daughter mentally ill. (Making new meaning.)

I picture a lot of people all jammed into this room. What are the soldiers going to do to them? (Making new meaning and Questioning that indicates understanding.)

Did the boy wonder if his mother would come back? I would have been terrified. (Questioning that indicates understanding and Identifying personally.)

They don't sound too organized about helping the wounded. (Making new meaning.)

The mother is avoiding answering the boy's questions. (Making new meaning.)

The dirty water will be dangerous for her husband to drink. It's probably infected and I know that infection can spread fast. (Making new meaning and Reporting prior knowledge.)

The prisoners who were curled up might have been tortured. (Making new meaning.)

What did they do to him during those sixteen years? I don't know how the boy could stand it. If it was my father—well—I don't even want to think about it. (Questioning that indicates understanding and Identifying personally.)

Think-Aloud Statements That Indicate Understanding

Paraphrasing or summarizing	0
Making new meaning	6
Questioning understanding	4
Noting understanding	0
Reporting prior knowledge	1
Identifying personally	2

Think-Aloud Statements That Indicate Lack of Understanding

Questioning no understanding	0
Noting lack of understanding	0

There were nine STOP points in the selection "Where the Ashes Are" but Alys made a total of thirteen think-aloud comments. This is because she verbalized two different comments at several STOP points. For example, she commented, "I picture a lot of people all jammed in this room (Making new meaning). What are the soldiers going to do to them (Questioning that indicates understanding)?" All of her comments indicate that she was understanding what she was reading.

Does any one kind of think-aloud comment or any specific combination of comments indicate better comprehension as measured by retelling and answers to questions with and without look-backs? Think-aloud statements that indicated understanding, especially summarizing or paraphrasing and making new meaning through inferencing were significantly correlated with retelling, inferences made during retelling, or comprehension with look-backs. See Section 16 for details. It would seem that what a reader thinks about during reading has some effect on comprehension, just as reader prior knowledge does. We believe that use of think-alouds, like assessment of prior knowledge, can offer an interesting and perceptive window into the reading process.

Students exhibited a variety of think-aloud patterns. Some used one exclusively, such as Lannie, who only summarized or paraphrased. Others, like Alys, exhibited a variety of patterns. There were a number of students in our pilot who could offer no comments whatsoever. The examiner must evaluate the variety and quality of a student's think-aloud comments in relation to several factors: the student's retelling and/or comprehension, the content area that was read, and the relative unfamiliarity of the text. If a student uses only one form of think-aloud and that student exhibits marginal comprehension, the examiner may be justified in suggesting that the student develop other think-aloud strategies. It is probably easier to identify personally in a literature selection than in a science or social studies text, so lack of this think-aloud comment should not be regarded negatively when students are reading science or social studies. In an unfamiliar text, summarizing or paraphrasing may be all a reader can do, at least during an initial reading. We suspect that think-alouds are very idiosyncratic to readers and are affected by such things as difficulty level, familiarity, and interest. The examiner may have to evaluate each student individually in light of such factors.

Guiding students through the think-aloud process is time-consuming. As with many of the options on the *QRI–3*, the examiner must be a decision maker and choose those components that will offer the information she or he feels is most meaningful.

Assessing Note-Taking Ability

Once the examiner determines an instructional level, she or he can use a parallel passage to assess the student's ability to take notes. We recommend using expository text. This can be done in two ways. The examiner can give the student a copy of the passage and ask her or him to read with pencil in hand, underlining those parts of the selection that seem most important. Or the examiner can ask the student to read a selection and take notes on it as if studying for a test. Either procedure can identify a student who is unable to isolate the main ideas of a selection and/or engage in efficient note-taking procedures. The examiner may wish to map the student's note-taking efforts on the Retelling Scoring Sheet to indicate whether the more important points are included.

Assessing Listening Comprehension

Often, beginning readers and readers who have severe decoding problems cannot successfully read and comprehend material at the primer level. In such cases, it is wise to assess the level of material that the student can understand if the material is read to him or her. This will suggest whether the student can profit from orally presented material at his or her grade level. An examiner can also find a listening level for students whose comprehension is severely below grade placement. In this case, a listening level can indicate whether or not the student can comprehend apart from reading.

Listening comprehension is evaluated in the same way as oral and silent reading. The only difference is that after assessing the student's prior knowledge, the examiner reads the passage to the student. The student retells what she or he heard and/or answers specific questions. It is most important to determine listening levels in familiar narrative text, although the examiner can choose to determine listening levels in expository and unfamiliar text as well.

13

Summarizing the Results of the Qualitative Reading Inventory–3

Organizing the Data

The Student Profile Sheet
The Comparisons Sheet: Describing Specific Reading Behaviors
Word Identification
Comprehension

The major strength of the *QRI–3* is that it provides a profile of the strengths and needs of an individual reader across different types of text according to the student's prior knowledge. In order to facilitate such comparisons, we have provided two summary sheets: The Student Profile Sheet and the Comparisons Sheet (see Tables 13.1 and 13.2).

Organizing the Data

The Student Profile Sheet

The examiner should fill out the Student Profile Sheet using the following abbreviations:

Familiar: F	Unfamiliar: UF	
Narrative: N	Expository: E	
Pictures: P	No Pictures: NP	
Independent: Ind	Instructional: Ins	Frustration: Fr

Obviously, the completeness of the Student Profile Sheet will depend on the extent and complexity of the assessment. For some students, an examiner will enter data for only a few passages. Other students will be represented by a much more detailed profile sheet. In addition, examiners can

TABLE 13.1

Qualitative Reading Inventory–3

Student Profile Sheet

Name _____ Birthdate _____ Grade _____

Sex _____ Date of Test _____ Examiner _____

Word Identification

Grade

Level/% Automatic

Level/% Total

Oral Reading

Passage Name

Readability Level

Passage Type

Level/% Total Accuracy

Level/% Total Acceptability

Familiar/Unfamiliar: %

Retelling: %

Explicit Correct

Implicit Correct

Level/% Comprehension

Explicit Correct: Look-backs

Implicit Correct: Look-backs

Level/% Comprehension: Look-backs

Rate

Total Passage Level

Silent Reading

Passage Name

Passage Section (High School)

Readability Level

Passage Type

Familiar/Unfamiliar: %

Retelling: %

Correct Explicit

Correct Implicit

Level/% Comprehension

Correct Explicit: Look-backs

Correct Implicit: Look-backs

Level/% Comprehension: Look-backs

Rate

choose not to fill in certain portions. For example, an examiner may choose to record levels, but not percentages, for Total Accuracy and/or Total Acceptability. An examiner may elect to determine levels from Total Acceptability only. In this case, the spaces for Total Accuracy would remain blank. Similarly, an examiner may elect to record the comprehension level without recording the number of explicit and implicit questions answered correctly. When recording the data, the examiner should:

1. Begin with the lowest level of list or passage administered and move to the right with successively higher levels.
2. Organize the passages into groupings: narrative, expository, familiar, unfamiliar, pictures, and no pictures.
3. When recording scores, record the information for familiar narratives first.
4. When recording scores, record the information from text with pictures before that from text without pictures.
5. After listing results for familiar narratives, record scores for unfamiliar narratives.
6. Record familiar expository scores, and then record unfamiliar expository scores.
7. If passages were administered to assess listening comprehension, group these to the far right on the Profile Sheet and draw a line separating them from passages administered orally or silently.

Section 14 contains an example of a completed Student Profile Sheet.

The Comparisons Sheet: Describing Specific Reading Behaviors

We have provided Table 13.2 to facilitate comparison of a student's reading ability across different contexts. The Comparisons Sheet is organized according to different questions that an assessment specialist might ask about a student. Answering these questions can provide important information for planning intervention instruction. The assessment specialist should complete the sheet by reporting the highest instructional levels attained by a student. If an instructional level is not available, the examiner can choose to report independent or frustration levels.

Word Identification

The Comparisons Sheet allows the examiner to describe the student's word-identification accuracy, word-identification automaticity, strategies used for word identification, and word identification in isolation and in context.

How Accurate Is the Student in Identifying Words? Total scores on the word lists and word-identification levels on oral passage reading will allow the examiner to ascertain the student's accuracy in identifying words. Accurate word identification is a critical component of skilled reading (Gough & Juel, 1991), and the majority of poor readers are deficient in this respect. The student's accuracy level should parallel his or her chronological grade placement. The greater the gap between word-identification accuracy and chronological grade placement, the more serious the reading problem.

How Automatic Is the Student in Identifying Words? Reading fluency is dependent on an extensive sight vocabulary, or automaticity in identifying

TABLE 13.2

Comparisons: Describing Specific Reading Behaviors

Student _____

WORD IDENTIFICATION

How Accurate Is the Student in Identifying Words?
  Word-Lists Total Score: Level   _____
  Passage Reading
    Word Identification: Level   _____

How Automatic Is the Student in Identifying Words?
  Word-Lists Timed Score: Level   _____
  Oral Passage Reading: WPM   _____
  Silent Passage Reading: WPM   _____

What Strategies for Word Identification in Context Are Used by the Student?
  Percent: Graphically Similar Miscues:
    Initial Position   _____
    Final Position   _____
  Percent: Acceptable Miscues   _____
  Percent: Self-corrected Miscues   _____

**Is There a Difference Between a Student's Ability to Identify Words
in Isolation and Words in Context?**
  Word-Lists Total Score: Level   _____
  Passage Reading
    Word Identification: Level   _____

COMPREHENSION

Which Types of Text Can the Student Handle Most Successfully?
Narrative Text: Level   _____
Expository Text: Level   _____
Text with Pictures: Level   _____
Text Without Pictures: Level   _____

Which Modes of Reading Represent a Strength for the Student?
Oral Reading: Level   _____
Silent Reading: Level   _____

How Does the Student Perform in Familiar and Unfamiliar Text?
Familiar Text: Level   _____
Unfamiliar Text: Level   _____

How Does the Student Perform with Look-Backs and Without Look-Backs?
Without Look-Backs: Level   _____
With Look-Backs: Level   _____

What Comprehension Strategies Does the Student Employ While Reading?

What Is the Extent of the Student's Reading Problem?
Highest Instructional Level   _____
Chronological Grade Placement   _____

words. If a reader must pause and decode the majority of words, her or his fluency will suffer and comprehension will probably be hindered. The timed score on the word lists gives the examiner one measure of word-identification automaticity. If the level for words pronounced automatically on the word lists is lower than the total level for word identification, the subject may profit from procedures to increase automatic word identification. Reading rate attained on the passages is another measure that suggests automaticity of word identification. If a student reads very slowly, the examiner should recommend instructional interventions to increase fluency.

What Strategies for Word Identification Are Used by the Student? A marked difference between word-identification scores in text with pictures and in text without pictures may suggest excessive use of context, especially in older readers. The results of miscue analysis can also suggest strategies used by the student in identifying words. A high percentage of graphically similar words suggests that the student is paying attention to letter cues. Errors in word identification indicate that the student does not have an accurate representation of the target word in memory (Perfetti, 1991). The examiner can note which letter–sound matches are known and which need instructional emphasis. Self-corrected miscues or miscues that do not seriously change the meaning of the text indicate that the student is comprehending as she or he is reading. If a subject's comprehension is poor after reading, this may indicate that attention to word identification is disrupting the recall process.

Is There a Difference Between a Student's Ability to Identify Words in Context and Words in Isolation? The examiner should compare the student's highest instructional level for words recognized in isolation with those recognized when reading within the context of a passage. For many readers, the instructional levels attained on the word lists will closely parallel the instructional levels achieved for word accuracy in familiar text. However, some readers recognize far more words in context. If the oral reading of these students is fluent and expressive, a lower score on the list probably does not represent a serious area of concern. However, if oral reading is slow and halting, lower scores on the word lists could indicate lack of automaticity in word identification. Occasionally a student will have better word-identification scores in isolation than in context. This may be a function of classroom instruction that has focused on word lists. Also, less skilled readers may be less threatened by a word list than by a passage.

Comprehension

The examiner can use the Comparisons Sheet to compare a student's comprehension in a variety of contexts. These comparisons are based on total passage levels. For oral reading, the word-identification and comprehension levels together determine the total passage level (see Section 9). For silent reading, total passage levels are drawn from the comprehension score.

What Types of Text Can the Student Handle Most Successfully? The examiner should compare the student's levels in narrative and expository text. Many readers, especially those below fourth grade, will score a year or two below their familiar narrative level when asked to read expository text. Because content-area material is primarily exposition, the student will have difficulty comprehending this material. She or he will need instruction in expository text structure, including typical paragraph structure. For levels pre-primer through grade two, the examiner can also compare a student's performance in text with and without pictures. Emerging readers naturally depend on a picture context for both word identification and comprehension. However, skilled readers are less dependent on such contextual aids (Stanovich, 1980). A student whose success in word identification is dependent on pictures needs to learn strategies for context-free and automatic decoding. A student whose success in comprehension is dependent on pictures should be exposed to instruction in prereading activities such as prediction and to self-monitoring strategies during reading.

What Modes of Reading Represent a Strength for the Student? The examiner should compare the student's oral and silent reading comprehension. It is natural for young readers to do better in oral reading because of the emphasis on this mode during the early elementary grades. As the student moves through the grades, she or he must become increasingly efficient at silent reading. A middle school student whose instructional level for oral reading is higher than for silent reading will be at a disadvantage in coping with the demands of textbook reading. Such a reader needs practice in silent reading.

How Does the Student Perform on Familiar and Unfamiliar Text? The examiner can compare levels in familiar and unfamiliar text. For levels three through upper middle school, the *QRI–3* provides passages that offer both familiar and unfamiliar content. Most readers will score at a higher level in familiar text for both narrative and expository material. It is likely that a student may score a year below the familiar instructional level when reading unfamiliar material. A fifth grade student reading at the fifth grade level in familiar text but only at the third grade level in unfamiliar material may have extreme difficulty with content-area subjects where she or he is less likely to be familiar with the material.

How Does the Student Perform with Look-Backs and Without Look-Backs? To what extent can the student raise his or her comprehension score by engaging in look-backs? Are look-backs more effective for explicit questions or can the students use look-backs to find clues that suggest correct answers to implicit questions? Does the student use look-backs more effectively with one type of text (narrative versus expository; familiar versus unfamiliar) or with one mode of reading (oral versus silent)?

What Comprehension Strategies Does the Student Employ While Reading? Did engaging in think-alouds have any effect on comprehension? In other words, if all three sections of the high school passage were administered, was there a difference in the student's comprehension between the first passage without think-alouds and the second and third passages with think-alouds? Do the types of think-alouds suggest effective or ineffective strategies? For example, reacting personally may be more appropriate in literature selections than in social studies or science text. Was the student even able to offer think-alouds? Some of the students in our pilot study were unable to construct a think-aloud statement independently. Did the student offer a variety of think-alouds or tend to stay with one type? Variety may indicate a more involved and interactive reader than one who reacts in the same way to different segments of text.

What Is the Extent of the Student's Reading Problem? To identify a serious reading disability, the examiner can compare the student's highest instructional level with her or his chronological grade placement. Reading disability was once defined as the discrepancy between reading level and a student's potential as indicated by IQ, but this definition has been seriously questioned (Aaron, 1997). It is more valid to define reading disability as a serious discrepancy between the chronological grade level of the student and the level at which a student can read familiar narrative material. A serious discrepancy is defined by Spache (1981) as follows:

One year for first through third graders
Two years for fourth through sixth graders
Three years for seventh graders and above

The seriousness of the disability is obviously dependent on the size of the discrepancy. For example, a third grader reading at a primer level would be more disabled than one reading at a first grade level. Another consideration is the grade level at which the student is reading. A student who cannot read primer material has not learned to read. A student who is having trouble at the second or third grade level may be able to read but lacks fluency and automaticity at that level. Children reading beyond the third grade level may have learned to read, but they may not have learned how to read *to learn*. An older student who has not learned how to read despite years of instruction is obviously more disabled than one who knows how to read but cannot handle the demands of reading to learn.

14 Examples of Using the Qualitative Reading Inventory–3

Using the QRI–3 in the Classroom to Estimate Reading Level

Caryl
Ryan
Hannah
Jonah

Using the QRI–3 for Reading Portfolios

Ricardo
Deatura

Using the QRI–3 to Design Intervention Instruction

Amanda
Perry
Troy
Alicia
Jamie

Using the QRI–3 for Indicating Growth

"Elm Street School"

Using the QRI–3 in the Classroom to Estimate Reading Level

Caryl

Caryl is in second grade. Her teacher spends several weeks at the beginning of each school year observing the reading strengths and needs of the class. Then, in early October, she forms three groups for guided reading. The teacher wants to be sure that each child is appropriately placed, and whenever she is unsure of placement, she uses the *QRI–3* for further assessment. Caryl's work suggested that she was somewhat uncomfortable with some of the reading activities the class had engaged in during the preceding month.

The teacher chose two passages with pictures from the *QRI–3*: the first-grade "Marva Finds a Friend" and the second grade "The Lucky Cricket." The conceptual-questions task indicated that Caryl was familiar with the concepts present in "Marva," and she scored at an independent level for Total Accuracy and for comprehension. The teacher then asked Caryl to read "The Lucky Cricket." Caryl scored at an instructional level for word identification and comprehension. To verify this, the teacher asked Caryl to read a text without pictures, "What Can I Get for My Toy?" While her word identification and comprehension scores remained at an instructional level, they were much lower than her scores on "The Lucky Cricket." The teacher placed Caryl in the middle group but noted that Caryl may be too dependent on pictures for both word identification and comprehension.

Ryan

Ryan, a third grader, transferred from another school, and records from his previous school were not available. His teacher wanted an estimate of Ryan's reading level in order to place him in appropriate instructional materials and to assist him in selecting books.

The teacher chose a second grade narrative with pictures from the *QRI–3*, "The Lucky Cricket." For the third grade selection, she chose "The Trip to the Zoo," a text with no pictures. Ryan was nervous at the prospect of reading alone to a new teacher, so she asked him to read the second grade passage first, hoping he would experience success and become more comfortable with the assessment process. Ryan had no difficulty with the concepts of "luck," "cricket," and "surprised," and he scored at an instructional level for word identification as measured by Total Accuracy. He also scored at an instructional level for comprehension. The teacher next asked a more relaxed Ryan to read the third grade selection. This topic was also familiar to him, as suggested by the conceptual-questions task, and Ryan again attained an instructional level for both word identification and comprehension. The teacher was satisfied that Ryan would not experience problems in keeping up with his peers, but she wanted to be sure that he would be appropriately challenged in his selection of books for pleasure reading. She asked Ryan if he would read one more passage. Flushed with success, he eagerly agreed. The teacher chose the fourth grade selection "Johnny Appleseed," a person who was familiar to Ryan. She asked Ryan to read silently, and he scored at a low instructional level for comprehension. However, when given the opportunity to look back in the text, he scored at an independent level. The teacher noted that if the material was familiar and if the text was available for rereading, Ryan could successfully function above the third grade level.

Hannah

Hannah, a sixth grader, qualified for placement in a Learning Disabilities program as a result of Multidisciplinary Team (M-Team) Staffing. Her school places such students in the regular classroom, supported by a learning disabilities specialist. In social studies and science, the classroom teacher presents concepts orally and through demonstration. Then students read assigned texts at their level. Hannah's reading level, as indicated by standardized tests administered during the M-Team Staffing, was 4.5. In order to determine which text would be most appropriate for Hannah, the learning disabilities specialist asked Hannah to read the second grade passage "Whales and Fish." The conceptual-questions task indicated that this was somewhat unfamiliar to Hannah; however, she scored at an instructional level for both word identification and comprehension. The specialist then asked Hannah to read a third-grade passage, "Wool: From Sheep to You." The topic of this selection was also unfamiliar to Hannah, and although she scored at an instructional level for word identification, she placed at a frustration level for comprehension. Accordingly, the specialist noted that the standardized measure overestimated Hannah's reading skill and that Hannah would be most comfortable reading third grade textbooks.

Jonah

Jonah, an eighth grader, wanted to attend the same high school as several of his friends. This school was noted for high expectations and a strong academic focus. Jonah's parents were concerned that it might be too difficult for him, and they asked the reading assessment specialist to evaluate his potential. The specialist asked Jonah to name his most difficult subject. It was science. She then asked him to read the upper middle school passage "Life Cycles of Stars." Jonah's recall was sparse, but his answers to questions placed him at an instructional level. On the first section of the high school passage "Characteristics of Viruses," Jonah's recall consisted of several general ideas. "It's about viruses and how they act and what they are like." He scored at the frustration level for answering questions. However, when allowed to look back in the text, Jonah scored at the instructional level. The assessment specialist asked Jonah to read the first section of another high school passage, "World War I," and the pattern was repeated. She reported to Jonah's parents that Jonah might have to work very hard in his chosen high school but that his skill in utilizing look-backs would provide a valuable strategy for success.

Using the QRI–3 for Reading Portfolios

Ricardo

Ricardo is a fourth grade student whose classroom teacher uses reading portfolios as a key component of his student assessment. At the beginning of the first semester, the teacher asked all students in the class to read silently the fourth grade expository passage "Saudi Arabia." Without looking back at the passage, they wrote down what they recalled and answered the questions. The teacher then asked the students to look back in the text and verify whether their answers were correct. If they were in error, the students corrected their answers. If, as in the case of implicit questions, they were unsure, the teacher asked the students to write why they were unsure. The teacher then scored the written recalls and the questions with and without look-backs according to the protocol sheets provided in the *QRI–3*. Ricardo' s recall was both sparse and inaccurate. He scored at the frustration level for questions both without and with look-backs. For several implicit questions, Ricardo was unsure whether his answer was correct or incorrect. The teacher then asked Ricardo and other children like him who demonstrated poor comprehension to read the passage again. Each child orally read "Saudi Arabia" individually to the teacher, who scored word identification according to Total Accuracy. Ricardo scored at an instructional level for word identification, so the teacher judged that Ricardo's poor performance in comprehension was not due to difficulties with word identification.

The teacher then shared the protocols with Ricardo, and they discussed his strengths and needs. Ricardo and his teacher decided that one goal for the coming semester would be to learn to use look-backs to improve his comprehension. A second goal would be to locate text cues to inference questions. The protocols, together with the teacher's and Ricardo's notes from the conference, were dated and placed in his portfolio.

The teacher held conferences with Ricardo's classmates in a similar fashion. He asked those whose word identification was below fourth grade to read easier passages until he located their word-identification instructional level. He then assessed their comprehension of this text. The teacher used his findings to set instructional objectives not only for individuals but also for the entire class.

After a semester of effort, Ricardo again read "Saudi Arabia" silently, wrote down his recall, answered the questions, and looked back to correct them. His recall was much more nearly complete and his ability to answer questions without look-backs placed him at an instructional level. His ability to answer questions with look-backs placed him at an independent level. Ricardo's teacher asked him to read silently another fourth grade expository passage, "The City of Cahokia" and he performed similarly. Both Ricardo and his teacher were pleased with his progress. All protocols were dated, clipped to the original set, and placed in Ricardo's portfolio, along with Ricardo's own analysis of his efforts and progress.

Deatura

Deatura is a first grader whose teacher used the *QRI–3* to maintain an ongoing record of Deatura's developing word-identification skills. At the beginning of the year, Deatura read the pre-primer word list. Her protocol was scored, dated, and placed in her portfolio. At that time, Deatura knew only six words and scored at the frustration level.

Deatura's teacher administered the pre-primer list on two other occasions during the first three months of first grade. When Deatura approached an instructional level, her teacher asked her to read the pre-primer text with pictures "Who Do I See?" Although Deatura clearly enjoyed the predictable rhyme pattern of this selection, she scored at a low instructional level (90%) for word identification. When asked to read "Lost and Found," a predictable text without pictures and rhyme, she met frustration.

Deatura's teacher administered these two passages several additional times over the next months. Deatura first achieved a solid instructional level on "Who Do I See?" and was obviously aided by the rhyming pattern. However, by February, Deatura had achieved a strong instructional level for word identification on "Lost and Found." Her teacher then moved into primer-level text and repeated the process with "Fox and Mouse," a narrative with pictures, and "A Trip," a narrative without pictures. Deatura's teacher placed all protocols, suitably dated, in Deatura's portfolio, along with other oral reading samples and observational comments. She used these to choose classroom reading activities for Deatura, to fill out her progress report, and to discuss her growth as a reader with her parents during conference times.

Using the QRI–3 to Design Intervention Instruction

Amanda

Amanda, a third grader, was referred to the school reading specialist. Her teacher described Amanda as a capable decoder and a fluent, expressive oral reader. School records indicated that Amanda had done well in first and second grades. However, during the first semester of third grade, she began to experience difficulties. Her performance in reading class was inconsistent, and her achievement in science and social studies activities was poor.

Word Identification

How Accurate Is the Student in Identifying Words? Because Amanda was described as a capable decoder and a fluent oral reader, the *QRI–3* word lists were not administered either to evaluate word-identification ability or to suggest a starting point for passage administration. In order to ensure that Amanda met with initial success, the examiner first asked her to read a second grade familiar narrative with pictures, "The Lucky Cricket." She scored at an independent level for word identification and at an instructional level for comprehension. The examiner then asked Amanda to read the third grade narrative "The Trip to the Zoo." The concept task indicated that this was a very familiar topic to Amanda, and she scored at an instructional level for word identification and comprehension.

How Automatic Is the Student in Identifying Words? On both the second and third grade passages, Amanda's oral reading rate was acceptable. She read both fluently and expressively, which suggested that at her level, automaticity of word identification was not a problem.

What Strategies for Word Identification Are Used by the Student? Amanda scored at a third grade instructional level for word identification. Because word-identification accuracy did not seem to be a problem, the examiner chose not to analyze Amanda's miscues.

Is There a Difference Between a Student's Ability to Identify Words in Isolation and Words in Context? Again, because word identification was not a problem for Amanda, the examiner chose to ignore this question.

Comprehension

Which Types of Text Can the Student Handle Most Successfully? The examiner then asked Amanda to read a third grade expository passage orally. The passage "Wool: From Sheep to You" dealt with concepts unfamiliar to Amanda. Although her word-identification score placed her in the instructional range, she scored at a frustration level for comprehension. This suggested to the examiner that Amanda's problems might rest in the area of expository text or with unfamiliar text. Accordingly, the examiner asked Amanda to read another third grade passage, "Cats: Lions and Tigers in Your House." This selection contained concepts that were very familiar to Amanda, who had two cats of her own. Again, she scored at a frustration level for comprehension. The examiner noted that Amanda's problem was probably in the area of expository text structure.

Which Modes of Reading Represent a Strength for the Student? The examiner chose to verify Amanda's third grade instructional level in silent reading, thinking that her problem might be due to poor silent reading strategies. However, Amanda silently read a familiar passage, "A Special Birthday for Rosa," with an acceptable rate and scored at an instructional level for comprehension.

How Does the Student Perform in Familiar and Unfamiliar Text? Amanda's performance on the unfamiliar third grade "Wool" passage was very similar to her performance on the familiar "Cats" selection. For both, she scored at a frustration level for comprehension. At her level, prior knowledge did not seem to be an issue.

Summary The results of the *QRI–3* suggest that Amanda is indeed a capable decoder and does not require any supportive instruction in this area. In addition, Amanda is able to comprehend familiar narrative text, and there are no major differences in her ability to understand following oral or silent reading, However, Amanda experiences some difficulty in dealing with expository material. As a result, Amanda may perform at a higher level in narrative reading than in content-area texts, and her inconsistent performance in class activities may be due to the structure of the specific selections. The results of the assessment suggest that Amanda could profit from supportive instruction in reading and understanding expository text.

Perry

Perry is in the second half of third grade. He was referred for M-Team Staffing assessment by his teacher, who described him as "having a lot of problems with reading and keeping up with the class." Perry had experienced reading difficulties since first grade, and his parents had provided private tutoring to supplement the regular classroom instruction. As part of the M-Team, the reading-assessment specialist evaluated Perry's reading ability. Perry was clearly unhappy about having to read by himself and confided to the specialist that he hated reading.

Word Identification

How Accurate Is the Student in Identifying Words? The examiner asked Perry to read the pre-primer word list, and he scored at an instructional level. He achieved the same level on the primer list. Perry met frustration with the first grade words, recognizing barely half of them.

When the examiner asked Perry to read a passage, he instantly refused, saying it would be too hard. When the examiner noted how well he had done on the first two word lists, Perry replied that "words are ok but sentences aren't." The examiner chose the easiest passage on the *QRI–3*, a pre-primer passage with both pictures and a predictable structure. She gently coaxed Perry into trying "Who Do I See?" He scored at an instructional level for word identification, offered a complete and accurate recall, and achieved at an instructional level for comprehension. Perry was obviously relieved at his success. The examiner then asked Perry to read orally the primer passage with pictures, "Fox and Mouse." Perry scored at an instructional level for word identification and comprehension. His recall, again complete, contained elements obviously drawn from the accompanying pictures. When asked to read "A Trip," a primer text without pictures, Perry's recall was sparse. He scored at a frustration level for word identification but at an instructional level for comprehension. The words he was able to identify carried enough of the text content for Perry to offer adequate answers to the questions. The examiner asked Perry to read the first grade text with pictures, "The Bear and the Rabbit." Perry had so much difficulty and became so upset that the examiner stopped halfway through the passage. The examiner noted that Perry was most comfortable identifying words at a pre-primer level but could handle primer text if given additional support such as pictures.

How Automatic Is the Student in Identifying Words? On the word lists, there was little difference between the total number of words identified correctly and the number of words pronounced automatically. When Perry knew a word, he seemed to know it automatically. However, when he was reading the passages, Perry's rate was very slow, fluctuating between 15 and 30 words per minute. He lost his place several times, and it was clear that Perry was reading the passages much like a word list, approaching each word as an individual unit unconnected to the words that preceded or followed it.

What Strategies for Word Identification Are Used by the Student?
The examiner formally analyzed Perry's miscues. The majority were graphically similar in the initial and final positions, indicating that Perry was paying attention to letter–sound matching and word endings such as "ing" and "ed." However, there were few self-corrections or semantically acceptable miscues. Perry either knew the word or he didn't. If he didn't, he attempted to decode but usually ended with a nonword substitution or the substitution of a real word with similar beginning and ending letters, such as "liked" for "looked." Perry clearly needs some workable strategies for identifying unfamiliar words and checking that the resulting pronunciation makes sense within the context of the passage.

Is There a Difference in the Student's Ability to Identify Words in Isolation and Words in Context? No difference was noted. Perry scored at the same level for both the word lists and the passages.

Comprehension

Which Types of Text Can the Student Handle Most Successfully?
Perry was asked to read only narrative passages; however, they were presented with and without pictures. Perry was more successful with text with pictures at the primer level. However, at the first grade level, he met too many unfamiliar words, and pictures were of no help. This suggests that Perry can use picture clues in those situations in which he can successfully identify most of the words.

Which Mode of Reading Represents a Strength for the Student? Because of Perry's low instructional level, he was not asked to read silently.

How Does the Student Perform on Familiar and Unfamiliar Text?
Perry was not asked to read unfamiliar text, again because of his low reading level.

Summary Perry is an almost fourth grader who is most comfortable at a pre-primer level but can handle primer text if given pictorial support. His primary problem is accuracy in word identification. When Perry knows a word, he pronounces it quickly. However, when meeting an unknown word, he lacks effective strategies for identifying the word or checking its semantic acceptability. Instruction in word identification strategies is recommended.

Troy

Troy is in his first semester of high school. His grades after the first grading period consisted primarily of D's. The guidance counselor asked the reading-assessment specialist to evaluate Troy's reading ability.

Word Identification

How Accurate Is the Student in Identifying Words? The specialist asked Troy to read the upper middle school word lists. He scored at an independent level. She then asked Troy to read the high school lists. Again Troy attained an independent level. He read the words fluently and with confidence.

How Automatic Is the Student in Identifying Words? Troy read the upper middle school passages "Biddy Mason" and "Life Cycles of Stars." He also read the first section of the high school passage "Characteristics of Viruses." In all three cases, his reading rate suggested the same word-recognition fluency as demonstrated by his word-list performance.

Comprehension

Which Types of Text Can the Student Handle Most Successfully? Troy silently read a literature selection at the upper middle school level, "Biddy Mason." He read fluently, but his recall was sparse. He scored at a frustration level for comprehension without look-backs but raised this to an instructional level when allowed to look back. He then read "Life Cycles of Stars." Again, his reading rate indicated fluency, but Troy recalled little and scored at a frustration level for comprehension without look-backs. He managed to raise this to an instructional level when allowed to look back, but it was not a completely independent performance on his part. The specialist noted that better performance on the literature selection than on the science one paralleled his grades. Troy had received a C for his English grade but a D- for science. The specialist asked Troy to read the high school passage "Characteristics of Viruses."

After completing the first section, Troy demonstrated the same comprehension pattern as on "Life Cycles of Stars." The specialist then modeled think-alouds during the second section but, because of time constraints, did not ask Troy to retell or to answer questions. Troy seemed to enjoy the process, but his think-aloud comments were identical to the examiner's and often took the form of "I thought that too." On the third section, Troy evinced extreme difficulty in phrasing independent think-alouds. At several stop points, he was unable to offer anything. On others, Troy paraphrased the text, and because he kept his eyes on the page, the examiner suspected that he was actually rereading the segment.

How Does the Student Perform on Familiar and Unfamiliar Text? The conceptual-questions task indicated that Troy was more familiar with the concepts in "Biddy Mason" than in "Life Cycles of Stars" or "Characteristics of Viruses." However, his performance on "Biddy Mason" was only marginally better. As a high school student, Troy will be expected to read much unfamiliar text, and he needs strategies for doing so successfully.

How Does the Student Perform with Look-Backs and Without Look-Backs? Troy was able to raise his comprehension level on all passages when given the opportunity to look back in the text. The examiner asked Troy whether he employed look-backs on a regular level. He replied that he generally read assignments only once and seldom looked back, because it "takes too much time." The specialist pointed out how looking back had improved his performance and suggested that he do it regularly.

What Comprehension Strategies Does the Student Employ While Reading? Troy seems to possess few active comprehension strategies. He admitted that he seldom looked back while reading, and he found it extremely difficult to think aloud while reading.

Summary Although Troy has no problems in identifying words, he is not an interactive reader. He does not use look-backs effectively, and his inability to offer any independent think-aloud comments suggests that he is merely reading the words and hoping that comprehension will magically occur. Troy needs to become more metacognitive as he reads. He needs to pause during reading and ask himself what he understood and what confused him. He needs to become more adept at using look-backs to refine his comprehension.

Alicia

Alicia is a high school junior who plans to attend college. She has had much difficulty in high school, and her grades reflect this. She puts a lot of effort into her school work but seldom attains a grade higher than C. The guidance counselor, concerned that Alicia might not find success in college, suggested that the reading specialist evaluate her potential.

Word Recognition

How Accurate Is the Student in Identifying Words? The reading specialist administered the eighth grade and high school word lists to determine whether Alicia's difficulties might be in the area of word recognition. For both lists, Alicia achieved at an independent level for words correctly identified. She was not, however, fluent in word recognition but paused often before pronouncing each word.

How Automatic Is the Student in Identifying Words. As noted above, Alicia demonstrated lack of fluency in reading the word lists. Her performance in reading the high school selections silently confirmed that one of Alicia's problems could be a slow reading rate. If she is paying too much attention to word pronunciation, this may be detrimental to her comprehension.

What Strategies for Word Identification Are Used by the Student? Alicia made too few word-identification errors to indicate any specific strategy. Her accuracy in word identification suggests that she has developed an efficient way of pronouncing unfamiliar words. However, it is not a fluent strategy, as evidenced by the pauses she made before pronouncing word-list words and by her slow reading rate.

Comprehension

How Does the Student Perform with and Without Look-Backs? The reading specialist asked Alicia which subject area was her favorite: literature, social studies, or science. Alicia indicated a preference for social studies and stated that she hated science and hoped not to take it in college. The specialist asked Alicia what course of studies she intended to pursue in college. Alicia was unsure but thought she might want to be a teacher or go into some form of radio or television work. The specialist chose the high school passage "World War I" for Alicia to read.

The conceptual-questions task suggested that this material was relatively unfamiliar to Alicia. She read the first section of "World War I" slowly and deliberately. Her recall consisted of a few summary statements and a few explicit details. For example, she recalled that the selection was "how the war started and who fought who and why the United States got into it. There was something about a telegram asking Mexico to fight us." She scored at a frustration level for answering questions without look-backs but was able to raise this to an instructional level with look-backs. Alicia was able to locate both explicit and implicit answers in the text, but it was a somewhat slow and deliberate process. The specialist asked Alicia whether she would return on another day to continue the assessment process. Alicia agreed, and they set a date during one of Alicia's free periods.

What Comprehension Strategies Does the Student Employ While Reading? Two days later, Alicia returned to the specialist. She seemed nervous and stated that she really should be studying for a quiz that was coming up that day. The specialist suggested that another time might be more convenient, and Alicia eagerly agreed. A week later, Alicia returned and read the second part of "World War I" while the specialist modeled think-alouds. Alicia eagerly participated in the process, and many of her think-alouds involved noting lack of understanding. The specialist asked Alicia what strategies she employs when she doesn't understand what she is reading. Alicia shrugged and said, "I read it over, I guess." The specialist asked if this helped, and Alicia stated, "Sometimes but not a lot." Her recall of the second section of "World War I" again consisted of summary statements, and her use of lookbacks raised her from a frustration to an instructional level. There was no time to continue with the third segment, partly because of Alicia's extremely slow reading rate. However, Alicia agreed to return on another day.

At the third meeting, Alicia read the last part of "World War I" and engaged in thinking aloud on her own. Her first think-aloud comment noted lack of understanding. The specialist asked Alicia to indicate clearly what she didn't understand. Alicia said, "The whole thing." The specialist then went through the text segment with Alicia, asking a variety of questions. "Do you know the meaning of this word?" "Does this sentence make sense?" "What part of this sentence is difficult for you?" In this way, the specialist was able to demonstrate to Alicia that she actually understood most of the segment and that her problem centered on lack of knowledge of Wilson's Fourteen Points and why Germany would want these included in a peace treaty. Similarly, after the second STOP, Alicia and the specialist, working together, determined that "buffer zone" was the issue. For the third STOP, Alicia's lack of understanding focused on the functions of the League of Nations, and she was encouraged to hypothesize what these might be. The specialist and Alicia continued with this process, and Alicia began to understand that it was her responsibility to determine exactly what she didn't understand, as opposed to saying "everything." Time ran out, but Alicia was clearly eager to engage in more practice with the specialist.

The specialist asked Alicia whether she read for pleasure. Alicia replied that she did not have the time. The specialist suggested that Alicia make the time to read easy and enjoyable material so that she could increase her reading rate. The specialist offered to identify some possible books for this, and she and Alicia set a date for continued practice.

Jamie

Jamie was referred to a private Reading Clinic for evaluation of his reading ability. He had always experienced problems in school, and he had been retained in second grade. Presently a fifth grader, Jamie had been tested several times for Exceptional Educational Placement but had never qualified. His parents intended to place him in another school, and they wanted a complete evaluation of his reading to be part of his records. Figure 14.1 presents a summary of the results.

Word Identification

How Accurate Is the Student in Identifying Words? The reading-assessment specialist knew from information provided by Jamie's present

FIGURE 14.1

Qualitative Reading Inventory–3

Student Profile Sheet

Name _Jamie_   Birthdate _11/12_   Grade _5 (retained)_

Sex _M_   Date of Test _11/8_   Examiner _YC_

Word Recognition

Grade	3	4	5						
Level/% Automatic	70 ins	55 fr	25 fr						
Level/% Total	85 ins	65 fr	40 fr						

Oral Reading

Passage Name	Zoo	Amelia	Columbus		Beavers				
Readability Level	3	4	5		4				
Passage Type	N	N	N		E				
Level/% Total Accuracy	95 ins	95 ins	88 fr		95 ins				
Level/% Total Acceptability	96 ins	98 ins	91 fr		97 ins				
Familiar/Unfamiliar: %	F	F	F		F				
Retelling: %	4	4	3		2				
# Explicit Correct	3	3	2		0				
# Implicit Correct	88 ins	75 ins	63 fr		25 fr				
Level/% Comprehension									
# Explicit Correct: Look-backs					3				
# Implicit Correct: Look-backs					1				
Level/% Comprehension: Look-backs					50% fr				
Rate									
Total Passage Level	ins	ins	fr		fr				

Silent Reading

Passage Name	John								
Passage Section (High School)									
Readability Level	4								
Passage Type	N								
Familiar/Unfamiliar: %	F83								
Retelling: %	1%								
# Correct Explicit	3								
# Correct Implicit	2								
Level/% Comprehension	50% fr								
# Correct Explicit: Look-backs	3								
# Correct Implicit: Look-backs	2								
Level/% Comprehension: Look-backs	50% fr								
Rate									

school that he was reading at a third grade level. The examiner asked Jamie to read the third grade word list, and he scored at an instructional level. He met frustration on the fourth grade list but, with a score of 65%, was close to the cut-off. On the fifth grade list, Jamie met frustration.

The examiner chose a third grade familiar passage, "The Trip to the Zoo," for Jamie to read orally. He scored at an instructional level for word identification. On the fourth grade passage "Amelia Earhart," he also scored at an instructional level but met frustration for word identification on the fifth grade "Christopher Columbus." Both the word lists and the passages suggest that Jamie's ability to identify words accurately is at a fourth grade instructional level.

How Automatic Is the Student in Identifying Words? On the word lists, no differences were evident between the total number of words pronounced correctly and those pronounced automatically. Both seemed to present a weakness for Jamie. Jamie's rate on the passages ranged from 50 to 60 words per minute. He tended to read in a deliberate and monotone fashion, which suggested that his primary attention was directed toward word identification.

What Strategies for Word Identification Are Used by the Student? The examiner analyzed Jamie's miscues both at an instructional level (Figure 14.2) and at a frustration level (Figure 14.3). She chose to analyze miscues made on "The Trip to the Zoo" and "Amelia Earhart" as representative of a clear instructional level. Miscues made on "Christopher Columbus" reflected a clear frustration level. At an instructional level, 37% of Jamie's miscues were graphically similar in the initial position and 22% in the final position; 41% were semantically acceptable, and he self-corrected 19%. In frustration text, 68% of Jamie's miscues were similar in the initial position and 56% in the final position; 13% were semantically acceptable, and he self-corrected only 8%. When Jamie meets unfamiliar text, his primary strategy is to decode phonetically. Unfortunately, he does not check that the resulting pronunciation makes sense either as an actual word or in the context of the passage.

Is There a Difference Between a Student's Ability to Identify Words in Isolation and Words in Context? No differences were noted.

Comprehension

Which Types of Text Can the Student Handle Most Successfully? The examiner asked Jamie to read three narratives: "The Trip to the Zoo," "Amelia Earhart," and "Christopher Columbus." Jamie scored at an instructional level for both word identification and comprehension for the third and fourth grade texts. However, his retelling was extremely sparse and reflected only a few isolated ideas offered in a nonsequential manner. The examiner also asked Jamie to read the fourth grade expository passage "The Busy Beaver." Although Jamie achieved an instructional level for word identification, he met frustration for comprehension. When Jamie was asked to look back in the text, he was unable to improve his score beyond a frustration level. This suggests that expository text may present more of a problem for Jamie than narrative.

Which Modes of Reading Represent a Strength for the Student? Jamie was asked to read the fourth grade passage "Johnny Appleseed" silently. He scored at the frustration level for comprehension, which suggests that silent reading may also pose a problem for Jamie. Again lookbacks did not help.

FIGURE 14.2

Miscue Analysis Worksheet

Subject _Jamie_　　　　　Level of Miscues:　　　Independent/Instructional　　　Frustration

MISCUE	TEXT	GRAPHICALLY SIMILAR Initial	Final	Semantically Acceptable	Self-Corrected
class	classes	✓	✓		
then	when		✓		✓
grade	graders	✓		✓	
lots	lot	✓		✓	
teacher	teachers	✓		✓	
was	–				✓
Lopzek	Lopez	✓		✓	
into					
Mary	Maria	✓			✓
they	she				
–	that			✓	
–	of				
the	–			✓	
place	pace	✓	✓		✓
the	his			✓	
piloneer	pioneer	✓	✓		
–	too			✓	
ocean	–			✓	
do	be				
–	also			✓	
fly	flying	✓			
she	–				
also	as				
Column Total Total Miscues Column Total / Total Miscues = %		—— —— ——	—— —— ——	—— —— ——	—— —— ——

Miscue Analysis Worksheet

FIGURE 14.2   *(Continued)*

Miscue Analysis Worksheet

Subject _Jamie (cont.)_   Level of Miscues: Independent/Instructional   Frustration

MISCUE	TEXT	GRAPHICALLY SIMILAR Initial	Final	Semantically Acceptable	Self-Corrected
frightened	frightening	✓			
to	it				
fault	failure				✓
—	ocean			✓	
Column Total		10	6	11	5
Total Miscues		27	27	27	27
Column Total / Total Miscues = %		37%	22%	41%	19%

FIGURE 14.3 ·

Miscue Analysis Worksheet

Subject _Jamie_   Level of Miscues: Independent/Instructional   (Frustration)

MISCUE	TEXT	GRAPHICALLY SIMILAR Initial	Final	Semantically Acceptable	Self-Corrected
a	—				
determinded	determined	✓	✓		
—	an				
rou tee	route	✓	✓		
Indians	Indies	✓	✓		
was	world	✓			
for time	fortune	✓			
thor ree	theory	✓	✓		
—	the			✓	
mĕ rit	merit	✓	✓		
careful	costly	✓			
fïñ ence	finance	✓	✓		
ex pen sion	expedition	✓	✓		
soap lies	supplies	✓	✓		
it	in	✓			✓
explored	unexplored	✓	✓		
solers	sailers	✓	✓		
the	—			✓	
—	too				
—	so				
mutter	mutiny	✓			
were	had				✓
finis shed	finished	✓	✓		
Column Total Total Miscues Column Total / Total Miscues = %		—— —— ——	—— —— ——	—— —— ——	—— —— ——

(continued)

FIGURE 14.3 *(Continued)*

Miscue Analysis Worksheet

Subject _Jamie (cont.)_   Level of Miscues: Independent/Instructional   ⟨Frustration⟩

MISCUE	TEXT	GRAPHICALLY SIMILAR Initial	Final	Semantically Acceptable	Self-Corrected
vorge	voyage	✓	✓		
—	he			✓	
treatened	threatened	✓	✓		
the journey	—			✓	
front	farther	✓			✓
wel cōme	welcome	✓	✓		
clumed	claimed	✓	✓		
it	—			✓	
inhabitats	inhabitants	✓	✓		
the	he		✓		
men	mistakenly	✓			
rōte	route	✓	✓		
of	—				
died	did	✓	✓		
Indians	Indies	✓	✓		
Column Total		26	20	5	5
Total Miscues		38	38	38	38
Column Total / Total Miscues = %		68%	53%	13%	8%

How Does the Student Perform on Familiar and Unfamiliar Text?   The examiner administered the conceptual-questions task for "Sequoyah" and "The City of Cahokia." She had hoped that "Sequoyah" would prove unfamiliar to Jamie so she could assess his ability to handle unfamiliar material in a narrative structure. Because Jamie seemed more comfortable with a narrative format, this would allow her to assess the effect of topic unfamiliarity on his word identification and comprehension. Unfortunately, Jamie had just completed a unit on Native Americans in social studies, and he knew quite a bit about Sequoyah and the Cherokee nation. The concept task indicated that Cahokia was unfamiliar. However, because Jamie had experienced difficulty with expository structure in familiar text, the examiner did not feel that poor performance could be ascribed to lack of topic knowledge. Jamie was growing tired, so the examiner ended the session.

Summary   Jamie needs instruction in several areas. Word-identification accuracy was at a fourth grade level, two years below Jamie's chronological grade placement if his retention in second grade is taken into account. His primary strategy for identifying unfamiliar words is to attempt to decode phonetically. Because he pays little attention to the resulting meaning, this practice does not work well for him. Jamie's slow reading rate suggests that he has not developed automaticity of word identification but, instead, is still decoding words he has met many times before.

Jamie's ability to comprehend familiar narrative text is also two years below his grade placement, with some problems suggested in silent reading. Expository text seems to present another problem for Jamie.

The examiner suggested a program that revolved around silent reading of expository text focusing on the use of look-backs. In addition, she suggested instruction in word-identification strategies The examiner also recommended that Jamie engage in much silent reading of easy text in order to develop automaticity in word identification. Repeated reading of text was also suggested as a way of building reading fluency.

Using the QRI–3 for Indicating Growth

"Elm Street School"

Two learning support teachers in a small urban elementary school were unhappily aware that some children in the school were not reading as well as they could. These children were receiving extra support in their classrooms during literacy instruction, but it was clear that they needed more help. Accordingly, the two teachers designed structured lesson plans to be used in a pull-out program. The children, second through fifth graders, remained in their regular classroom for literacy instruction but were tutored four days a week. Each tutoring session lasted for thirty minutes, and children were paired for these lessons according to their reading level. Each lesson involved repeated reading of familiar text, direct instruction in sound-letter matching, and the introduction of a new selection through supported oral reading and discussion of story structure.

The two teachers did not have unlimited time for testing. They felt that the *QRI* was a more authentic assessment instrument than a standardized norm-referenced measure, and they carefully chose the *QRI* components that would provide them with the most useful information. They knew their children exhibited difficulties in word identification, so they chose oral reading as the mode of assessment. For scoring word identification, they used Total Accuracy as opposed to Total Acceptability, because it takes less time to mark each error than to decide whether or not a miscue changed meaning. The teachers determined the highest instructional level in familiar narrative text for each child for both word identification and comprehension. They used these as their pre-test measure.

The tutoring continued from October to the middle of May. At that time, the two teachers administered the same passages as a post-test, again using oral reading as the mode of assessment. For each child, they determined the highest instructional level for both word identification and comprehension.

They compared the pre and post *QRI* measures in several ways (Caldwell, Fromm & O'Connor, 1998). They assigned a number to each level. An instructional pre-primer level was assigned level 1, an independent pre-primer level was assigned 1.5, and so on. Using this scheme, they found that the average gain in levels was 2.8 for word identification and 2.0 for comprehension. Six children gained one level for word identification. Four children gained two levels, four gained three levels, three gained four levels, and one child gained five levels. For comprehension, one child made no gain, eight children gained one level, six gained two levels, one gained three levels, one gained four levels, and one gained five levels. The two teachers also compared the pre and post percentages for word recognition and comprehension. They found statistically significant gains for word recognition but nothing significant for comprehension. Although the students raised their comprehension from one grade level to a higher one, they still tended to be at an instructional level so their percentages remained approximately the same. The teachers were well pleased with their intervention and felt that the *QRI* was a sensitive and valid measure of reading growth following intervention.

15 Test Materials

Subject Word Lists

Examiner Word Lists

Pre-Primer Level Passages

"Lost and Found"
"Spring and Fall"
"Who Do I See?"
"Just Like Mom"
"People at Work"
Examiner Copies

Primer Level Passages

"A Trip"
"Fox and Mouse"
"The Pig Who Learned to Read"
"Who Lives Near Lakes?"
"Living and Not Living"
Examiner Copies

Level One Passages

"Mouse in a House"
"Marva Finds a Friend"
"The Bear and the Rabbit"
"Air"
"What You Eat"
Examiner Copies

Level Two Passages

"What Can I Get for My Toy?"
"The Lucky Cricket"
"Father's New Game"
"Whales and Fish"
"Seasons"
Examiner Copies

Level Three Passages

"The Trip to the Zoo"
"A Special Birthday for Rosa"
"The Friend"
"Cats: Lions and Tigers in Your House"
"Where Do People Live?"
"Wool: From Sheep to You"
Examiner Copies

Level Four Passages

"Johnny Appleseed"
"Amelia Earheart"
"Sequoyah"
"The Busy Beaver"
"Saudi Arabia"
"The City of Cahokia"
Examiner Copies

Level Five Passages

"Martin Luther King, Jr."
"Christopher Columbus"
"Margaret Mead"
"The Octopus"
"Getting Rid of Trash"
"Laser Light"
Examiner Copies

Level Six Passages

"Pele"
"Abraham Lincoln"
"Andrew Carnegie"
"Computers"
"Predicting Earthquakes"
"Ultrasound"
Examiner Copies

Upper Middle School Passages

Literature :	"Biddy Mason"	
	"Malcolm X"	
Social Studies:	"Lewis and Clark"	
	"Ferdinand Magellan"	
Science:	"Fireworks"	
	"Life Cycles of Stars"	
	Examiner Copies	

High School Passages

Literature :	"Where the Ashes Are"
Social Studies:	"World War I"
Science:	"Characteristics of Viruses"

can	keep
who	need
I	not
work	what
write	children
at	thing
with	was
my	animal
he	they
too	were
the	saw
in	want
she	every
other	went
make	like
place	from
go	said
to	live
see	comes
do	help

bear	morning
father	tired
find	shiny
sound	old
friend	trade
song	promise
thought	pieces
there	picked
run	push
then	though
move	begins
knew	food
eat	light
air	ends
bread	clue
afraid	breathe
wind	insects
heard	weather
put	noticed
looked	money

Subject Word Lists

lunch	escape	attend
celebrate	desert	protest
believe	crop	movement
claws	islands	sailor
lion	chief	month
rough	mounds	threatened
wear	busy	continue
tongue	pond	tales
crowded	signs	creature
wool	ocean	wavelengths
removed	pilot	laser
curious	fame	focuses
sheep	precious	arrested
electric	settlers	poison
worried	guarded	route
enemies	passenger	convince
glowed	boundaries	giant
clothing	communicate	pollution
swim	adventurer	aluminum
entrance	invented	finance

Subject Word Lists

sewed	commissioned	armaments
controlled	arduous	alliance
championships	nebula	enzyme
messenger	remembered	parasite
fortune	settlement	escalation
memories	emulate	convoy
abolish	articulate	opulence
earthquake	encyclopedia	armistice
volunteers	ammonium	idealism
machines	crucial	immunodeficiency
businesses	gravity	mediated
shrinking	nuclear	mandates
research	navigated	infectious
abdomen	tumultuous	nucleic
slavery	straits	chromosome
howled	initiated	protestations
homogenized	rebellion	disinfectant
connection	opportunity	liberated
fashioned	skirmish	chauffeur
behavior	meticulous	retrovirus

Examiner Word Lists

Pre-primer

	Identified Automatically	Identified
1. can	_____	_____
2. who	_____	_____
3. I	_____	_____
4. work	_____	_____
5. write	_____	_____
6. at	_____	_____
7. with	_____	_____
8. my	_____	_____
9. he	_____	_____
10. too	_____	_____
11. the	_____	_____
12. in	_____	_____
13. she	_____	_____
14. other	_____	_____
15. make	_____	_____
16. place	_____	_____
17. go	_____	_____
18. to	_____	_____
19. see	_____	_____
20. do	_____	_____

Total Correct Automatic	_____ /20 =	_____%
Total Correct Identified	_____ /20 =	_____%
Total Number Correct	_____ /20 =	_____%

Primer

	Identified Automatically	Identified
1. keep	_____	_____
2. need	_____	_____
3. not	_____	_____
4. what	_____	_____
5. children	_____	_____
6. thing	_____	_____
7. was	_____	_____
8. animal	_____	_____
9. they	_____	_____
10. were	_____	_____
11. saw	_____	_____
12. want	_____	_____
13. every	_____	_____
14. went	_____	_____
15. like	_____	_____
16. from	_____	_____
17. said	_____	_____
18. live	_____	_____
19. comes	_____	_____
20. help	_____	_____

Total Correct Automatic	_____ /20 =	_____%
Total Correct Identified	_____ /20 =	_____%
Total Number Correct	_____ /20 =	_____%

LEVELS		
Independent	**Instructional**	**Frustration**
18–20	14–17	below 14
90–100%	70–85%	below 70%

Examiner Word Lists

First

	Identified Automatically	Identified
1. bear	_____	_____
2. father	_____	_____
3. find	_____	_____
4. sound	_____	_____
5. friend	_____	_____
6. song	_____	_____
7. thought	_____	_____
8. there	_____	_____
9. run	_____	_____
10. then	_____	_____
11. move	_____	_____
12. knew	_____	_____
13. eat	_____	_____
14. air	_____	_____
15. bread	_____	_____
16. afraid	_____	_____
17. wind	_____	_____
18. heard	_____	_____
19. put	_____	_____
20. looked	_____	_____

Total Correct Automatic _____ /20 = _____%

Total Correct Identified _____ /20 = _____%

Total Number Correct _____ /20 = _____%

Second

	Identified Automatically	Identified
1. morning	_____	_____
2. tired	_____	_____
3. shiny	_____	_____
4. old	_____	_____
5. trade	_____	_____
6. promise	_____	_____
7. pieces	_____	_____
8. picked	_____	_____
9. push	_____	_____
10. though	_____	_____
11. begins	_____	_____
12. food	_____	_____
13. light	_____	_____
14. ends	_____	_____
15. clue	_____	_____
16. breathe	_____	_____
17. insects	_____	_____
18. weather	_____	_____
19. noticed	_____	_____
20. money	_____	_____

Total Correct Automatic _____ /20 = _____%

Total Correct Identified _____ /20 = _____%

Total Number Correct _____ /20 = _____%

Level 1

Level 2

LEVELS		
Independent	Instructional	Frustration
18–20	14–17	below 14
90–100%	70–85%	below 70%

Examiner Word Lists

Third

	Identified Automatically	Identified
1. lunch	_____	_____
2. celebrate	_____	_____
3. believe	_____	_____
4. claws	_____	_____
5. lion	_____	_____
6. rough	_____	_____
7. wear	_____	_____
8. tongue	_____	_____
9. crowded	_____	_____
10. wool	_____	_____
11. removed	_____	_____
12. curious	_____	_____
13. sheep	_____	_____
14. electric	_____	_____
15. worried	_____	_____
16. enemies	_____	_____
17. glowed	_____	_____
18. clothing	_____	_____
19. swim	_____	_____
20. entrance	_____	_____

Total Correct Automatic _____ /20 = _____%

Total Correct Identified _____ /20 = _____%

Total Number Correct _____ /20 = _____%

Fourth

	Identified Automatically	Identified
1. escape	_____	_____
2. desert	_____	_____
3. crop	_____	_____
4. islands	_____	_____
5. chief	_____	_____
6. mounds	_____	_____
7. busy	_____	_____
8. pond	_____	_____
9. signs	_____	_____
10. ocean	_____	_____
11. pilot	_____	_____
12. fame	_____	_____
13. precious	_____	_____
14. settlers	_____	_____
15. guarded	_____	_____
16. passenger	_____	_____
17. boundaries	_____	_____
18. communicate	_____	_____
19. adventurer	_____	_____
20. invented	_____	_____

Total Correct Automatic _____ /20 = _____%

Total Correct Identified _____ /20 = _____%

Total Number Correct _____ /20 = _____%

LEVELS		
Independent	Instructional	Frustration
18–20	14–17	below 14
90–100%	70–85%	below 70%

Level 3

Level 4

Examiner Word Lists

Fifth

	Identified Automatically	Identified
1. attend	_____	_____
2. protest	_____	_____
3. movement	_____	_____
4. sailor	_____	_____
5. month	_____	_____
6. threatened	_____	_____
7. continue	_____	_____
8. tales	_____	_____
9. creature	_____	_____
10. wavelengths	_____	_____
11. laser	_____	_____
12. focuses	_____	_____
13. arrested	_____	_____
14. poison	_____	_____
15. route	_____	_____
16. convince	_____	_____
17. giant	_____	_____
18. pollution	_____	_____
19. aluminum	_____	_____
20. finance	_____	_____

Total Correct Automatic	_____ /20 =	_____%
Total Correct Identified	_____ /20 =	_____%
Total Number Correct	_____ /20 =	_____%

Sixth

	Identified Automatically	Identified
1. sewed	_____	_____
2. controlled	_____	_____
3. championships	_____	_____
4. messenger	_____	_____
5. fortune	_____	_____
6. memories	_____	_____
7. abolish	_____	_____
8. earthquake	_____	_____
9. volunteers	_____	_____
10. machines	_____	_____
11. businesses	_____	_____
12. shrinking	_____	_____
13. research	_____	_____
14. abdomen	_____	_____
15. slavery	_____	_____
16. howled	_____	_____
17. homogenized	_____	_____
18. connection	_____	_____
19. fashioned	_____	_____
20. behavior	_____	_____

Total Correct Automatic	_____ /20 =	_____%
Total Correct Identified	_____ /20 =	_____%
Total Number Correct	_____ /20 =	_____%

LEVELS		
Independent	**Instructional**	**Frustration**
18–20	14–17	below 14
90–100%	70–85%	below 70%

Level 5

Level 6

Examiner Word Lists

Upper Middle School

	Identified Automatically	Identified
1. commissioned	_____	_____
2. arduous	_____	_____
3. nebula	_____	_____
4. remembered	_____	_____
5. settlement	_____	_____
6. emulate	_____	_____
7. articulate	_____	_____
8. encyclopedia	_____	_____
9. ammonium	_____	_____
10. crucial	_____	_____
11. gravity	_____	_____
12. nuclear	_____	_____
13. navigated	_____	_____
14. tumultuous	_____	_____
15. straits	_____	_____
16. initiated	_____	_____
17. rebellion	_____	_____
18. opportunity	_____	_____
19. skirmish	_____	_____
20. meticulous	_____	_____

Total Correct Automatic	_____	/20 = _____	%
Total Correct Identified	_____	/20 = _____	%
Total Number Correct	_____	/20 = _____	%

High School

	Identified Automatically	Identified
1. armaments	_____	_____
2. alliance	_____	_____
3. enzyme	_____	_____
4. parasite	_____	_____
5. escalation	_____	_____
6. convoy	_____	_____
7. opulence	_____	_____
8. armistice	_____	_____
9. idealism	_____	_____
10. immunodeficiency	_____	_____
11. mediated	_____	_____
12. mandates	_____	_____
13. infectious	_____	_____
14. nucleic	_____	_____
15. chromosome	_____	_____
16. protestations	_____	_____
17. disinfectant	_____	_____
18. liberated	_____	_____
19. chauffeur	_____	_____
20. retrovirus	_____	_____

Total Correct Automatic	_____	/20 = _____	%
Total Correct Identified	_____	/20 = _____	%
Total Number Correct	_____	/20 = _____	%

LEVELS		
Independent	**Instructional**	**Frustration**
18–20	14–17	below 14
90–100%	70–85%	below 70%

Lost and Found

I lost my cat.

Where was she?

I looked inside the house.

I looked under the bed.

I looked outside too.

I lost my dog.

Where was he?

I looked inside the house.

I looked under the bed.

I looked outside too.

I found my cat.

I found my dog.

Where were they?

They were in the same place.

They were under the table.

Spring and Fall

I like the spring.

When I can do many things.

I can play with my dog.

I can play with a frog.

I can play in the rain.

I can go see a train.

I like the fall.

I can do it all.

I can read a book.

I can help Mom cook.

I can ride my bike.

I can go on a hike.

In the spring and fall, there is much to do.

But what I like best is going to the zoo.

Who Do I See?

Who do I see on the log?

Oh! I bet it is a frog.

Who do I see on the plant?

Oh! I bet it is an ant.

Who do I see on the rug?

Oh! I bet it is a bug.

Who do I see in the truck?

Oh! I bet it is a duck.

And who is dancing a happy jig?

It must be that silly pig.

Just Like Mom

I can write.

Just like Mom.

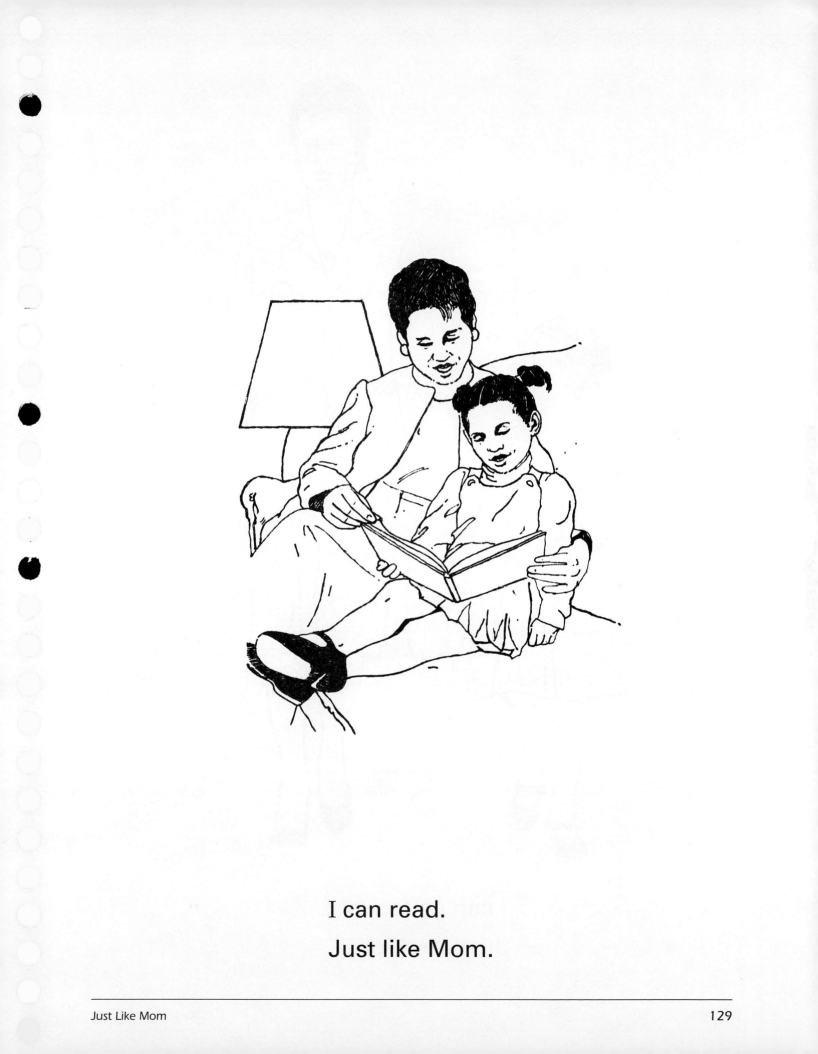

I can read.

Just like Mom.

I can go to work.

Just like Mom.

I can work at home.

Just like Mom.

I can work with numbers.

Just like Mom.

I can do lots of things.

Just like Mom.

People at Work

Some people work at home.

Other people go to work.

Why do people work?

People work to make money.

People work at many things.

Some people write at work.

Other people read at work.

Some people make things at work.

Other people sell things at work.

People work together.

Level: Pre-primer

Narrative

Concept Questions:

What does it mean when something is lost?

_____

_____

_____ (3-2-1-0)

What does it mean when something is found?

_____

_____

_____ (3-2-1-0)

What does "looking for something" mean to you?

_____

_____

_____ (3-2-1-0)

Score: _____ /9 = _____ %

_____ FAM _____ UNFAM

Prediction:

_____

_____

Lost and Found

I lost my cat.

Where was she?

I looked inside the house.

I looked under the bed.

I looked outside too.

I lost my dog.

Where was he?

I looked inside the house.

I looked under the bed.

I looked outside too.

I found my cat.

I found my dog.

Where were they?

They were in the same place.

They were under the table. (64 words)

Number of Miscues
(Total Accuracy): _____

Number of Meaning-Change Miscues
(Total Acceptability): _____

Total Accuracy		Total Acceptability
0–1 miscue	____ Independent	____ 0–1 miscue
2–6 miscues	____ Instructional	____ 2–3 miscues
7+ miscues	____ Frustration	____ 4+ miscues

Rate: $64 \times 60 = 3{,}840/$____ seconds = ____ WPM

Retelling Scoring Sheet for Lost and Found

Events

____ I lost my cat.
____ Where was she?
____ I looked
____ inside the house.
____ I looked
____ under the bed.

____ I looked
____ outside too.
____ I lost my dog.
____ Where was he?
____ I looked
____ inside the house.
____ I looked
____ under the bed.
____ I looked
____ outside too.
____ I found my cat.
____ I found my dog.
____ Where were they?
____ They were in the same place.
____ They were under the table.

Other ideas recalled, including inferences:

Questions for Lost and Found

1. What did the person in the story lose?
   Explicit: cat or dog

2. What else did the person in the story lose?
   Explicit: cat or dog, depending upon the answer above.

3. Where did the person in the story look?
   Explicit: inside the house, under the bed, or outside

4. Where else did the person in the story look?
   Explicit: inside the house, under the bed, or outside, depending on the answer above.

5. Where did the person find the dog and cat?
   Explicit: in the same place or under the table

> Number Correct Explicit: ____
>
> **Total:** ____
>
> ____ Independent: 5 correct
>
> ____ Instructional: 4 correct
>
> ____ Frustration: 0–3 correct

Level: Pre-primer

Narrative

Concept Questions:

What does the word "spring" mean to you?

_____

_____

_____ (3-2-1-0)

What does the word "fall" mean to you?

_____

_____

_____ (3-2-1-0)

What does "doing something you like best" mean to you?

_____

_____

_____ (3-2-1-0)

Score: _____ /9 = _____ %

_____ FAM _____ UNFAM

Prediction:

_____

_____

Spring and Fall

I like the spring.

When I can do many things.

I can play with my dog.

I can play with a frog.

I can play in the rain.

I can go see a train.

I like the fall.

I can do it all.

I can read a book.

I can help Mom cook.

I can ride my bike.

I can go on a hike.

In spring and fall, there is much to do.

But what I like best is going to the zoo.

(84 words)

Number of Miscues
(Total Accuracy): _____

Number of Meaning-Change Miscues
(Total Acceptability): _____

Total Accuracy			Total Acceptability
0–2 miscues	____	Independent ____	0–2 miscues
3–8 miscues	____	Instructional ____	3–4 miscues
9+ miscues	____	Frustration ____	5+ miscues

Rate: $49 \times 60 = 2,940/$____ seconds = ____ WPM

Retelling Scoring Sheet for Spring and Fall

Details

____ I like the spring.
____ When I can do
____ many things.
____ I can play
____ with my dog.
____ I can play
____ with a frog.
____ I can play
____ in the rain.
____ I can go.
____ see a train.
____ I like the fall.

____ I can do it all.
____ I can read
____ a book.
____ I can help Mom
____ cook.
____ I can ride
____ my bike.
____ I can go
____ on a hike.
____ In spring
____ and fall
____ there is much to do.
____ But what I like
____ best
____ is going
____ to the zoo.

Other ideas recalled, including inferences:

Questions for Spring and Fall

1. What can the person in the story play with in the spring?
   Explicit: a dog <u>or</u> a frog

2. Name another thing the person can do in the spring.
   Explicit: play with a dog or frog (depending on above), or play in the rain, or go see a train.

3. What can the person in the story ride on during the fall?
   Explicit: a bike

4. What can the person in the story help Mom do?
   Explicit: cook

5. What does the person like to do best?
   Explicit: go to the zoo

Number Correct Explicit: ____

Total: ____

____ Independent: 5 correct

____ Instructional: 4 correct

____ Frustration: 0–3 correct

Level: Pre-primer

Narrative

Concept Questions:

What is a frog?

_____

_____

_____ (3-2-1-0)

What is a bug?

_____

_____

_____ (3-2-1-0)

What is a pig?

_____

_____

_____ (3-2-1-0)

Score: _____ /9 = _____ %

_____ FAM _____ UNFAM

Prediction:

_____

_____

Who Do I See?

Who do I see on the log?

Oh! I bet it is a frog.

Who do I see on the plant?

Oh! I bet it is an ant.

Who do I see on the rug?

Oh! I bet it is a bug.

Who do I see in the truck?

Oh! I bet it is a duck.

And who is dancing that happy jig?

It must be that silly pig. (69 words)

Number of Total Miscues
(Total Accuracy): _____

Number of Meaning-Change Miscues
(Total Acceptability): _____

Total Accuracy		**Total Acceptability**
0–1 miscue	____ Independent	____ 0–1 miscue
2–7 miscues	____ Instructional	____ 2–3 miscues
8+ miscues	____ Frustration	____ 4+ miscues

Rate: 69 × 60 = 4,140/____ seconds = ____ WPM

Retelling Scoring Sheet for Who Do I See?

Events

____ Who do I see
____ on the log?
____ Oh! I bet
____ it is a frog.
____ Who do I see
____ on the plant?
____ Oh! I bet
____ it is an ant.
____ Who do I see
____ on the rug?
____ Oh! I bet
____ it is a bug.
____ Who do I see
____ in the truck?
____ Oh! I bet

Level: Pre-primer

____ it is a duck.
____ And who is dancing
____ a jig
____ a happy jig?
____ It must be that pig
____ that silly pig.

Other ideas recalled, including inferences:

Questions for Who Do I See?

Note: If a question is answered with direct reference to pictures as opposed to text, score the answer as implicitly correct.

1. What was on the log?
   Explicit OR Implicit from picture: a frog

2. What was on the plant?
   Explicit OR Implicit from picture: an ant

3. Where was the bug?
   Explicit: on the rug

4. Where was the duck?
   Explicit OR Implicit from picture: in the truck

5. What was the pig doing?
   Explicit: dancing a happy jig. *Note:* If the student says "dancing," count that as a correct *implicit* answer. Count it as an explicit answer (judged to be from print) only if the word "jig" is included.

Number Correct Explicit: ____

Number Correct Implicit
        (from pictures): ____

                Total: ____

____ Independent: 5 correct

____ Instructional: 4 correct

____ Frustration: 0–3 correct

Level: Pre-primer

Narrative

Concept Questions:

What is a Mom?

_____

_____

_____ (3-2-1-0)

What does "working at home" mean to you?

_____

_____

_____ (3-2-1-0)

What does "going to work" mean to you?

_____

_____

_____ (3-2-1-0)

Score: _____ /9 = _____ %

_____ FAM _____ UNFAM

Prediction:

_____

_____

Just Like Mom

I can write.

Just like Mom.

I can read.

Just like Mom.

I can go to work.

Just like Mom.

I can work at home.

Just like Mom.

I can work with numbers.

Just like Mom.

I can do lots of things.

Just like Mom. (44 words)

Number of Total Miscues
(Total Accuracy): _____

Number of Meaning-Change Miscues
(Total Acceptability): _____

Total Accuracy		**Total Acceptability**
0–1 miscue	____ Independent	____ 0–1 miscue
2–4 miscues	____ Instructional	____ 2 miscues
5+ miscues	____ Frustration	____ 3+ miscues

Rate: $44 \times 60 = 2{,}640/$ ____ seconds = ____ WPM

Retelling Scoring Sheet for Just Like Mom

____ I can write.
____ Just like Mom.
____ I can read.
____ Just like Mom.
____ I can go to work.
____ Just like Mom.
____ I can work
____ at home.
____ Just like Mom.
____ I can work
____ with numbers.
____ Just like Mom.
____ I can do lots
____ of things.
____ Just like Mom.

Other ideas recalled, including inferences:

Level: Pre-primer

Questions for Just Like Mom

Note: If a question is answered with direct reference to pictures as opposed to text, score the answer as implicitly correct.

1. Name one thing the girl can do just like Mom.
   Explicit: write, read, go to work, work at home, or work with numbers
   Implicit: water the flowers, walk to work, or write numbers

2. Name another thing the girl can do just like Mom.
   Explicit: read, write, go to work, work at home, or work with numbers, depending on the answer above
   Implicit: same as #1

3. What can the girl work with just like Mom?
   Explicit: numbers
   Implicit: pencils, paper

4. Where can the girl work just like Mom?
   Explicit: at home or she can go to work
   Implicit: in the garden

5. Where is another place the girl can work just like Mom?
   Explicit: at home or at her workplace, depending on the answer above
   Implicit: same as #4

Number Correct Explicit: ____

Number Correct Implicit
      (from pictures): ____

   Total: ____

   ____ Independent: 5 correct

   ____ Instructional: 4 correct

   ____ Frustration: 0–3 correct

Level: Pre-primer

Expository

Concept Questions:

Where do people work?

_____

_____

_____ (3-2-1-0)

Why do people work?

_____

_____

_____ (3-2-1-0)

What are different kinds of jobs?

_____

_____

_____ (3-2-1-0)

Score: _____ /9 = _____ %

_____ FAM _____ UNFAM

Prediction:

_____

_____

People at Work

Some people work at home.

Other people go to work.

Why do people work?

People work to make money.

People work at many things.

Some people write at work.

Other people read at work.

Some people make things at work.

Other people sell things at work.

People work together. (49 words)

Number of Total Miscues
(Total Accuracy): _____

Number of Meaning-Change Miscues
(Total Acceptability): _____

Total Accuracy		**Total Acceptability**
0–1 miscue	____ Independent	____ 0–1 miscue
2–5 miscues	____ Instructional	____ 2 miscues
6+ miscues	____ Frustration	____ 3+ miscues

Rate: 49 × 60 = 2,940/____ seconds = ____ WPM

Retelling Scoring Sheet for People at Work

Details

____ Some people work
____ at home.
____ Other people go to work.
____ Why do people work?
____ People work to make money.
____ People work
____ at many things.
____ Some people write
____ at work.
____ Other people read
____ at work.
____ Some people make things
____ at work.
____ Other people sell things
____ at work.
____ People work
____ together.

Level: Pre-primer

Other ideas recalled, including inferences:

Questions for People at Work

Note: If a question is answered with direct reference to pictures as opposed to text, score the answer as implicitly correct.

1. Where do people work?
   Explicit: at home or they go to work

2. What is one thing that people do at work?
   Explicit: write, read, make things, or sell things
   Implicit: fix things

3. What is another thing that people do at work?
   Explicit: write, read, make things, or sell things, depending on answer above
   Implicit: fix things

4. What is another thing that people do at work?
   Explicit: write, read, make things, or sell things, depending on answers to previous questions
   Implicit: fix things

5. What is another thing that people do at work?
   Explicit: write, read, make things, or sell things, depending on answers to previous questions
   Implicit: fix things

Number Correct Explicit: ____

Number Correct Implicit
   (from pictures): ____

   Total: ____

   ____ Independent: 5 correct

   ____ Instructional: 4 correct

   ____ Frustration: 0–3 correct

A Trip

It was a warm spring day.

The children were going on a trip.

The trip was to a farm.

The children wanted to see many animals.

They wanted to write down all they saw.

They were going to make a book for their class.

On the way to the farm the bus broke down.

The children thought their trip was over.

Then a man stopped his car.

He helped to fix the bus.

The bus started again.

The children said, "Yea!"

The children got to the farm.

They saw a pig.

They saw a hen and cows.

They liked petting the kittens.

They learned about milking cows.

They liked the trip to the farm.

They wanted to go again.

Fox and Mouse

Fox wanted to plant a garden.

Mouse helped him.

They put the seeds in the ground.

They watered the seeds.

Then they waited.

One night Mouse went to the garden.

He dug up one of the seeds.

He wanted to see if it was growing.

The seed looked good to eat.

"It is only one seed," thought Mouse.

"Fox will not know who ate the seed."

The next night Mouse went to the garden again.

He dug up one seed and ate it.

He did this every night.

After a few weeks, all the seeds were gone.

"I wonder why the seeds didn't grow," said Fox.

Mouse didn't say a word.

So Fox planted more seeds.

And Mouse helped him.

The Pig Who Learned to Read

Once there was a pig.

His name was Pete.

He lived on a farm.

He was not like other pigs.

He was special.

He wanted to learn to read.

His father said, "But pigs can't read!"

"I don't care," said Pete.

"I want to read."

One day Pete went to a boy who lived on a farm.

"Teach me to read," he said.

The boy said, "But you're a pig. I don't know if I can.

But I'll do what my mother and father did with me."

Every night before bed, the boy read to the pig.

The pig loved the stories.

He liked one called "Pat the Bunny" best.

A week later Pete asked to take the book to the barn.

He looked at the words.

He thought about what the boy had said.

He did that every day.

One day he read a story to the boy.

He was so happy!

After that he read to the other animals every night.

The boy was happy too, because he'd taught his first
pig to read.

Who Lives Near Lakes?

Many animals live near lakes.

Turtles sit on rocks.

They like to be in the sun.

You can see ducks near a lake.

There may be baby ducks.

The babies walk behind the mother duck.

There are fish in lakes.

You can see them when they jump out of the water.

People live near lakes too.

They like to see the animals.

Living and Not Living

Some things around us live.

Others are not living.

Things that live need air.

Things that live need food.

Things that live need water.

Things that live move and grow.

Animals are living things.

Plants are living things.

Is paper living?

No, but it comes from something living.

Paper comes from trees.

Is a wagon living?

No, it moves but it is not living.

Narrative

Concept Questions:

What is a farm?

_____

_____

_____ (3-2-1-0)

What happens when a car or bus breaks down?

_____

_____

_____ (3-2-1-0)

What is a school trip?

_____

_____

_____ (3-2-1-0)

Score: _____ /9 = _____ %

_____ FAM _____ UNFAM

Prediction:

_____

_____

A Trip

It was a warm spring day. The children were going on a trip. The trip was to a farm. The children wanted to see many animals. They wanted to write down all they saw. They were going to make a book for their class. On the way to the farm the bus broke down. The children thought their trip was over. Then a man stopped his car. He helped to fix the bus. The bus started again. The children said, "Yea!" The children got to the farm. They saw a pig. They saw a hen and cows. They liked petting the kittens. They learned about milking cows. They liked the trip to the farm. They wanted to go again. (119 words)

Number of Total Miscues
(Total Accuracy): _____

Number of Meaning-Change Miscues
(Total Acceptability): _____

Total Accuracy		**Total Acceptability**
0–2 miscues ____	Independent ____	0–2 miscues
3–12 miscues ____	Instructional ____	3–6 miscues
13+ miscues ____	Frustration ____	7+ miscues

Rate: 119 × 60 = 7,140/____ seconds = ____ WPM

Retelling Scoring Sheet for A Trip

Setting/Background

____ The children were going on a trip
____ to a farm.

Goal

____ The children wanted to see animals
____ and write down all they saw.
____ They were going to make a book
____ for their class.

Events

___ On the way
___ to the farm
___ the bus broke down.
___ A man stopped his car.
___ The man helped
___ to fix the bus.
___ The children got to the farm.
___ They saw a pig
___ a hen
___ and cows.
___ They liked
___ petting kittens.
___ They learned
___ about milking cows.

Resolution

___ They liked their trip
___ and wanted to go again.

Other ideas recalled, including inferences:

Questions for A Trip

1. Where were the children going?
   Explicit: on a trip to a farm

2. What did they want to see?
   Explicit: many animals, or names of at least two types of animals

3. Who do you think went with the children on the trip?
   Implicit: their teacher. If the child says, "Bus driver," ask, "Who else went with them besides the bus driver?"

4. What happened on the way to the farm?
   Explicit: the bus broke down

5. What would have happened *to their trip* if the man hadn't stopped his car?
   Implicit: they wouldn't have gotten to the farm, they got to the farm late

6. What did the children learn at the farm?
   Explicit: about getting milk from cows. If the child says "About cows," say, "What about cows?"

Number Correct Explicit: ____

Number Correct Implicit: ____

Total: ____

___ Independent: 6 correct

___ Instructional: 4–5 correct

___ Frustration: 0–3 correct

Primer

Narrative

Concept Questions:

What are seeds?

_____

_____

_____ (3-2-1-0)

What do gardens need to grow?

_____

_____

_____ (3-2-1-0)

What do mice eat?

_____

_____

_____ (3-2-1-0)

Score: _____ /9 = _____ %

_____ FAM _____ UNFAM

Prediction:

_____

_____

Fox and Mouse

Fox wanted to plant a garden.

Mouse helped him.

They put the seeds in the ground.

They watered the seeds.

Then they waited.

One night Mouse went to the garden.

He dug up one of the seeds.

He wanted to see if it was growing.

The seed looked good to eat.

"It is only one seed," thought Mouse.

"Fox will not know who ate the seed."

The next night Mouse went to the garden again.

He dug up one seed and ate it.

He did this every night.

After a few weeks all the seeds were gone.

"I wonder why the seeds didn't grow," said Fox.

Mouse didn't say a word.

So Fox planted more seeds.

And Mouse helped him. [122 words]

Number of Total Miscues
(Total Accuracy): _____

Number of Meaning-Change Miscues
(Total Acceptability): _____

Total Accuracy		**Total Acceptability**
0–3 miscues	____ Independent ____	0–3 miscues
4–12 miscues	____ Instructional ____	4–6 miscues
13+ miscues	____ Frustration ____	7+ miscues

Rate: 122 × 60 = 7,440/____ seconds = ____ WPM

Retelling Scoring Sheet for Fox and Mouse

Setting/Background

____ Fox wanted to plant a garden.
____ Mouse helped him.
____ They put seeds
____ in the ground.
____ They watered the seeds.
____ Then they waited.

Goal

___ One night
___ Mouse went to the garden.
___ He dug up one of the seeds.
___ He wanted to see
___ if it was growing.

Events

___ The seed looked good to eat.
___ "It is only one seed,"
___ thought Mouse.
___ Fox will not know
___ who ate the seed.
___ The next night
___ Mouse went to the garden again.
___ He dug up one seed
___ and ate it.
___ He did this
___ every night.
___ After a few weeks
___ all the seeds were gone.

Resolution

___ "I wonder
___ why the seeds didn't grow?"
___ said Fox.
___ Mouse didn't say a word.
___ So Fox planted more seeds.
___ And Mouse helped him.

Other ideas recalled, including inferences:

Questions for Fox and Mouse

1. What did Fox want to do?
   Explicit: to plant a garden

2. What did Fox and Mouse do?
   Explicit: put seeds in the ground *and* watered them. *Note:* If child says only one part ask, "What else did they do?"

3. Why did Mouse dig up the first seed?
   Explicit: to see if it was growing

4. What did Mouse do with the first seed that he dug up?
   Explicit: ate it

5. Why didn't the garden grow?
   Implicit: because Mouse ate all the seeds in the garden

6. Why did Mouse help Fox plant the garden again?
   Implicit: because he had eaten all the seeds, felt bad, and was Fox's friend. *Note:* the student needs to indicate either that Mouse felt responsible or that he wanted to help his friend, or both.

Number Correct Explicit: ____

Number Correct Implicit: ____

Total: ____

___ Independent: 6 correct

___ Instructional: 4–5 correct

___ Frustration: 0–3 correct

Level: Primer

Narrative

Concept Questions:

What is doing something new?

_____

_____

_____ (3-2-1-0)

What is learning to read?

_____

_____

_____ (3-2-1-0)

What does it mean when people read stories to you?

_____

_____

_____ (3-2-1-0)

Score: _____ /9 = _____ %

_____ FAM _____ UNFAM

Prediction:

_____

_____

The Pig Who Learned to Read

Once there was a pig. His name was Pete. He lived on a farm. He was not like other pigs. He was special. He wanted to learn to read. His father said, "But pigs can't read!" "I don't care," said Pete. "I want to read."

One day Pete went to a boy who lived on the farm. "Teach me to read," he said. The boy said, "But you're a pig. I don't know if I can. But I'll do what my mother and father did with me." Every night before bed the boy read to the pig. The pig loved the stories. He liked one called "Pat the Bunny" best. A week later Pete asked to take the book to the barn. He looked at the words. He thought about what the boy had said. He did that every day. One day he read a story to the boy. He was so happy! After that he read to the other animals every night. The boy was happy too, because he'd taught his first pig to read. (176 words)

Number of Total Miscues
(Total Accuracy): _____

Number of Meaning-Change Miscues
(Total Acceptability): _____

Total Accuracy		**Total Acceptability**
0–4 miscues	____ Independent	____ 0–4 miscues
5–18 miscues	____ Instructional	____ 5–9 miscues
19+ miscues	____ Frustration	____ 10+ miscues

Rate: 176 × 60 = 10,560/____ seconds = ____ WPM

Retelling Scoring Sheet for The Pig Who Learned to Read

Setting/Background

____ There was a pig
____ named Pete.

Level: Primer

Goal

____ He wanted to learn
____ to read.
____ His father said,
____ "Pigs can't read."
____ Pete said,
____ "I don't care."

Events

____ He went to a boy
____ who lived on a farm.
____ He said,
____ "Teach me
____ to read."
____ The boy said,
____ I'll do
____ what my mother
____ and father did.
____ Every night
____ before bed,
____ the boy read
____ to the pig.
____ The pig loved the stories.
____ Pete took the book
____ to the barn.
____ He looked at the words
____ every day.
____ One day
____ the pig read a story
____ to the boy.
____ He was so happy.

Resolution

____ He read
____ to the animals
____ every night.
____ The boy was happy.
____ He taught the pig
____ to read.

Other ideas recalled, including inferences:

Questions for The Pig Who Learned to Read

1. Who was this story about?
   Explicit: Pete the pig

2. What did Pete want?
   Explicit: to learn to read

3. What did Pete do to get what he wanted?
   Explicit: he asked the boy who lived on the farm to teach him

4. Why was the boy not sure he could teach the pig to read?
   Implicit: because pigs didn't learn to read or because the boy had never taught anyone to read before

5. What did the boy do to teach Pete to read?
   Explicit: he read to him every night

6. What did the pig do in order to learn how to read?
   Implicit: he matched the words with what the boy had said. He did that every day.

Number Correct Explicit: ____

Number Correct Implicit: ____

Total: ____

____ Independent: 6 correct

____ Instructional: 4–5 correct

____ Frustration: 0–3 correct

Level: Primer

Expository

<table>
<tr><td>

Concept Questions:

What are animals who live near lakes?

_____

_____

_____ (3-2-1-0)

When do you see turtles outside?

_____

_____

_____ (3-2-1-0)

Why do people live near lakes?

_____

_____

_____ (3-2-1-0)

Score: _____ /9 = _____ %

_____ FAM _____ UNFAM

Prediction:

_____

_____

</td></tr>
</table>

Who <u>Lives</u> Near Lakes?

Many <u>animals</u> <u>live</u> near lakes.

Turtles sit on rocks.

<u>They</u> <u>like</u> to be in the sun.

You can see ducks near a lake.

There may be baby ducks.

The babies walk behind the <u>mother</u> duck.

There are fish in lakes.

You can see them when <u>they</u> jump out of the water.

People <u>live</u> near lakes too.

<u>They</u> <u>like</u> to see the <u>animals</u>. (62 words)

<table>
<tr><td>

Number of Total Miscues
(Total Accuracy): _____

Number of Meaning-Change Miscues
(Total Acceptability): _____

Total Accuracy		**Total Acceptability**
0–1 miscue	____ Independent	____ 0–1 miscue
2–6 miscues	____ Instructional	____ 2–4 miscues
7+ miscues	____ Frustration	____ 5+ miscues

Rate: 62 × 60 = 3,720/ ____ seconds = ____ WPM

</td></tr>
</table>

Retelling Scoring Sheet for Who Lives Near Lakes?

Main Idea

____ Many animals live
____ near lakes.

Details

____ Turtles sit
____ on rocks.
____ They like to be in the sun.
____ You can see ducks
____ near a lake.
____ There may be baby ducks.
____ The babies walk
____ behind the mother duck.
____ There are fish
____ in lakes.
____ You can see them
____ when they jump
____ out of the water.

____ People live near lakes too.
____ They like
____ to see the animals.

Other ideas recalled, including inferences:

Questions for Who Lives Near Lakes?

1. What did the passage say turtles sit on?
   Explicit: rocks

2. When would turtles sit on rocks?
   Implicit: when it is sunny

3. Where do baby ducks walk?
   Explicit: behind the mother duck

4. What other animal besides a turtle and ducks does the passage talk about?
   Explicit: fish

5. When can you see fish?
   Explicit: when they jump out of the water

6. Why do people live near lakes?
   Implicit: they like to see animals

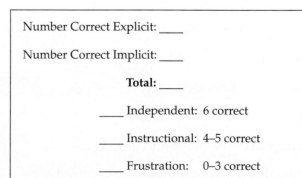

Number Correct Explicit: ____

Number Correct Implicit: ____

Total: ____

____ Independent: 6 correct

____ Instructional: 4–5 correct

____ Frustration: 0–3 correct

Level: Primer

Expository

Concept Questions:

What do plants need to grow?

_____

_____

_____ (3-2-1-0)

What do living things do?

_____

_____

_____ (3-2-1-0)

What are things that have never been alive?

_____

_____

_____ (3-2-1-0)

Score: _____ /9 = _____ %

_____ FAM _____ UNFAM

Prediction:

_____

_____

Living and Not Living

Some things around us live.

Others are not living.

Things that live need air.

Things that live need food.

Things that live need water.

Things that live move and grow.

Animals are living things.

Plants are living things.

Is paper living?

No, but it comes from something living.

Paper comes from trees.

Is a wagon living?

No, it moves but it is not living. (64 words)

Number of Total Miscues
(Total Accuracy): _____

Number of Meaning-Change Miscues
(Total Acceptability): _____

Total Accuracy		**Total Acceptability**
0–1 miscue	____ Independent	____ 0–1 miscue
2–6 miscues	____ Instructional	____ 2–3 miscues
7+ miscues	____ Frustration	____ 4+ miscues

Rate: 64 × 60 = 3,840/____ seconds = ____ WPM

Retelling Scoring Sheet for Living and Not Living

Main Idea

____ Some things live.

____ Others are not living.

Details

____ Things that live

____ need air,

____ food,

____ and water.

____ They move

____ and grow.

____ Animals are living.

____ Plants are living.

____ Paper is not living.

____ It comes from something living.

___ It comes from trees.
___ A wagon is not living.

Other ideas recalled, including inferences:

Questions for Living and Not Living

1. Name two things that living things need.
   Explicit: air, food, water

2. What do living things do?
   Explicit: move and grow

3. What two things did your reading say were living things?
   Explicit: animals and plants

4. What causes a plant to die?
   Implicit: it doesn't have food or water or air

5. What living thing does paper come from?
   Explicit: trees

6. Why isn't a wagon that moves a living thing?
   Implicit: it does not grow

Number Correct Explicit: ____

Number Correct Implicit: ____

Total: ____

____ Independent: 6 correct

____ Instructional: 4–5 correct

____ Frustration: 0–3 correct

Mouse in a House

Once there was a mouse.

He lived in a wall of an old house.

Each night the mouse went to the kitchen.

He wanted to find something to eat.

The man who lived in the house heard the mouse.

He knew the mouse lived in the wall.

But he didn't mind.

Then one day the man decided to sell the house.

He loved the old house.

But it was too big.

He put an ad in the paper.

It said, "100-year-old house for sale.

Call 224-3414."

Many people called and wanted to visit the house.

Two people came on Sunday.

They walked up the old stairs.

When they got to the top, the mouse ran down the wall.

He ran up and down the inside of the wall.

Up and down.

The people heard the mouse.

They said, "We don't want the house."

The mouse was very happy.

He was afraid that new people would try to get rid of him.

Every time someone visited the house, the mouse would do the same thing.

He would run up and down the wall between the first and second floors.

Every time, the people left without buying the house.

Then a family came to see the house.

The house was just the right size for them.

When they walked up the stairs, the mouse ran up and down the wall.

They heard him and said, "Oh, you have a mouse.

We love the house so much we'll buy it mouse and all."

Marva Finds a Friend

One rainy day Marva heard a funny sound.

She looked out the window and saw a little gray cat with white feet.

It was wet and it looked hungry.

Marva went out and picked up the cat.

Then she brought it inside.

She and her mother took a soft towel and dried it.

Mother gave the cat some food.

And the cat ate it all up!

Marva said, "I will name this cat Boots. I will take care of it."

"I hope you don't belong to anyone," Marva said.

"Now, Marva, this cat may belong to somebody," her mother said. Marva felt sad.

She said to Boots. "But I want you to be *my* cat."

That night Marva's mother looked in the newspaper.

She saw an ad that read, "Lost. Gray cat with white feet. Call 376-2007."

Marva started to cry.

"But I want to keep Boots," she said.

"It's not right, Marva, we have to call," said her mother.

Marva knew her mother was right.

The next day a woman and a girl Marva's age came to the house.

When the girl saw Boots she cried, "That's my cat, Boots!"

"But I called her Boots too," Marva said.

The girl took Boots in her arms.

She thanked Marva and her mother for taking care of Boots.

Then she said, "I live on the next street.

Why don't you come over tomorrow and play with me and Boots?"

Marva was sad to give up Boots, but she was happy that she'd made a new friend.

Marva's mother now knew what to get Marva for her birthday!

The Bear and the Rabbit

Once there was a very big bear.

He lived in the woods.

He was sad because he didn't have anyone to play with.

He said to his father, "How can I find a friend?"

His father said, "By being you."

"But all the animals are afraid of me," said the bear.

"I can't even get near them."

But one day the bear was sitting by a river.

He was singing softly to himself.

A rabbit lived near the river.

He looked out of his hole when he heard the bear's song.

He thought, "Anyone who sings like that must be nice.

Maybe I don't need to be afraid of him.

It would be nice to have a friend."

The rabbit went and got his horn.

Very softly he began to play.

His music went well with the bear's song.

The bear looked around.

He couldn't see the rabbit.

Slowly, the rabbit walked up to the bear.

He kept playing and the bear kept singing.

They were both happy that they had found a friend.

And a bird joined in the song.

Air

Air is all around us.

But we can't see it.

How do we know it is there?

There are many ways.

We can see what air does.

Moving air is called wind.

Wind moves plants.

Wind moves dirt.

Strong winds can move heavy things.

Strong winds can even move a house.

We can weigh air.

We can weigh two balloons.

The one with a lot of air weighs more.

We can see what air does.

We can weigh air.

Then we know it is there.

What You Eat

People eat many kinds of foods.

The different kinds of foods are called food groups.

There are four food groups.

One food group is the cereal and bread group.

Cereals and breads are foods made of grain.

It is good to eat them three times a day.

Another food group is the dairy group.

Milk and cheese are part of the dairy group.

You should have milk three times a day, too.

Another food group is fruit and vegetables.

Did you know that tomatoes are a fruit?

The fourth group is the meat group.

Meat, eggs, and fish are part of this group.

You should eat some of these foods every day.

Eating the right foods makes you grow and keeps you
   healthy.

Narrative

Concept Questions:

How do people feel about mice?

_____

_____

_____ (3-2-1-0)

What does "an old house for sale" mean to you?

_____

_____

_____ (3-2-1-0)

What does "a mouse inside a house" mean to you?

_____

_____

_____ (3-2-1-0)

Score: _____ /9 = _____ %

_____ FAM _____ UNFAM

Prediction:

_____

_____

Mouse in a House

Once there was a mouse. He lived in a wall of an old house. Each night the mouse went to the kitchen. He wanted to find something to eat. The man who lived in the house heard the mouse. He knew the mouse lived in the wall. But he didn't mind.

Then one day the man decided to sell the house. He loved the old house. But it was too big. He put an ad in the paper. It said, "100-year-old house for sale. Call 224-3414." Many people called and wanted to visit the house. Two people came on Sunday. They walked up the old stairs. When they got to the top, the mouse ran down the wall. He ran up and down the inside of the wall. Up and down. The people heard the mouse. They said, "We don't want the house." The mouse was very happy. He was afraid that new people would try to get rid of him.

Every time someone visited the house, the mouse would do the same thing. He would run up and down the wall between the first and second floors. Every time, the people left without buying the house. Then a family came to see the house. The house was just the right size for them. When they walked up the stairs, the mouse ran up and down the wall. They heard him and said, "Oh, you have a mouse. We love the house so much we'll buy it, mouse and all." (254 words)

Level 1

Level: One

Number of Total Miscues
(Total Accuracy): _____

Number of Meaning-Change Miscues
(Total Acceptability): _____

Total Accuracy		Total Acceptability
0–6 miscues ____ Independent	____	0–6 miscues
7–26 miscues ____ Instructional	____	7–13 miscues
27+ miscues ____ Frustration	____	14+ miscues

Rate: 254 × 60 = 15,240/ ____ seconds = ____ WPM

Retelling Scoring Sheet for Mouse in a House

Setting/Background

____ There was a mouse.
____ He lived
____ in a wall
____ of a house.
____ Each night
____ the mouse went
____ to the kitchen
____ to find something to eat.
____ The man who lived in the house
____ heard the mouse.
____ He knew
____ that the mouse lived
____ in the wall.
____ He didn't mind.

Goal

____ The man decided
____ to sell the house.
____ The mouse was afraid
____ that the people would try
____ to get rid of him.

Events

____ The man put an ad
____ in the paper.
____ It said,
____ Call 224-3414.
____ Two
____ people came
____ on Sunday.
____ They walked up the stairs.
____ The mouse ran up
____ and down.
____ The people heard the mouse.
____ They said,
____ "We don't want the house."
____ When someone visited the house,
____ the mouse ran up
____ and down.

Resolution

____ A family came
____ to see the house.
____ The house was right
____ for them.
____ They said
____ "You have a mouse.
____ We love the house.
____ We'll buy the house
____ mouse and all."

Other ideas recalled, including inferences:

Questions for Mouse in a House

1. Where did the mouse live in the house?
   Explicit: in a wall

2. What did the old man decide to do?
   Explicit: sell the house

3. What did the mouse do when people came to visit the house?
   Explicit: run up and down the inside of the walls

4. How many floors did the house have?
   Implicit: two

5. Why didn't some people want to buy the house?
   Implicit: they didn't want a mouse in their house

6. Why did the last family buy the house even though it had a mouse?
   Explicit: it was the right size for them

Number Correct Explicit: _____

Number Correct Implicit: _____

Total: _____

_____ Independent: 6 correct

_____ Instructional: 4–5 correct

_____ Frustration: 0–3 correct

Narrative

Level 1

Concept Questions:

What is a newspaper advertisement?

_____

_____

_____ (3-2-1-0)

What do you do to take care of a pet?

_____

_____

_____ (3-2-1-0)

What should a child do if he or she finds something that belongs to someone else?

_____

_____

_____ (3-2-1-0)

Score: _____ /9 = _____ %

_____ FAM _____ UNFAM

Prediction:

_____

_____

Marva Finds a Friend

One rainy day Marva heard a funny sound. She looked out the window and saw a little gray cat with white feet. It was wet and it looked hungry. Marva went out and picked up the cat. Then she brought it inside. She and her mother took a soft towel and dried it. Mother gave the cat some food. And the cat ate it all up! Marva said, "I will name this cat Boots. I will take care of it." "I hope you don't belong to anyone," Marva said. "Now, Marva, this cat may belong to somebody," her mother said. Marva felt sad. She said to Boots. "But I want you to be *my* cat."

That night Marva's mother looked in the newspaper. She saw an ad that read, "Lost. Gray cat with white feet. Call 376-2007." Marva started to cry. "But I want to keep Boots," she said. "It's not right, Marva, we have to call," said her mother. Marva knew her mother was right.

The next day a woman and a girl Marva's age came to the house. When the girl saw Boots she cried, "That's my cat, Boots!" "But I called her Boots too," Marva said. The girl took Boots in her arms. She thanked Marva and her mother for taking care of Boots. Then she said, "I live on the next street. Why don't you come over tomorrow and play with me and Boots?" Marva was sad to give up Boots, but she was happy that she'd made a new friend. Marva's mother now knew what to get Marva for her birthday! (264 words)

Level: One

Level 1

Number of Total Miscues
(Total Accuracy): _____

Number of Meaning-Change Miscues
(Total Acceptability): _____

Total Accuracy		**Total Acceptability**
0–5 miscues ___ Independent	___	0–5 miscues
6–26 miscues ___ Instructional	___	6–13 miscues
27+ miscues ___ Frustration	___	14+ miscues

Rate: 264 × 60 = 15,840/ ___ seconds = ___ WPM

Retelling Scoring Sheet for Marva Finds a Friend

Setting/Background

___ One rainy day
___ Marva heard a sound
___ a funny sound.
___ She looked out
___ and saw a cat
___ a little cat
___ a gray cat
___ with white feet.
___ It was wet
___ and it looked hungry.
___ Marva picked up the cat.
___ She brought it inside.
___ Mother gave the cat some food.
___ And the cat ate it all up!

Goal

___ Marva said,
___ "I will name this cat Boots.
___ I will take care of it."
___ "This cat may belong to somebody,"
___ her mother said.
___ Marva felt sad.
___ "But I want you to be *my* cat."

Events

___ That night
___ Mother looked in the newspaper.
___ She saw an ad that read,
___ "Lost.
___ Gray cat
___ with white feet."
___ Marva started to cry.
___ "But I want to keep Boots."
___ "We have to call,"
___ said her mother.
___ The next day
___ a woman
___ and a girl came to the house.
___ The girl cried,
___ "That's my cat, Boots!"
___ The girl took Boots.
___ She thanked Marva
___ and her mother.

Resolution

___ The girl said,
___ "Why don't you come over
___ and play with Boots
___ and me?"
___ Marva was sad
___ to give up Boots,
___ but she was happy
___ that she'd made a new friend.
___ Marva's mother knew
___ what to get Marva
___ for her birthday.

Other ideas recalled, including inferences:

180

QRI–3   Test Materials

Questions for Marva Finds a Friend

1. What did Marva find outside her window?
   Explicit: a cat

2. What did Marva's mother do with the cat?
   Explicit: dried it with a towel *or* gave it some food

3. What did Marva want to do with the cat?
   Explicit: keep it

4. What did Marva's mother do after she looked in the newspaper?
   Implicit: called the phone number listed in the paper

5. What happened the next day?
   Explicit: people that owned the cat came over and got the cat.

6. How are Marva and the girl who owned the cat alike?
   Implicit: they both liked cats

Number Correct Explicit: ____

Number Correct Implicit: ____

Total: ____

____ Independent: 6 correct

____ Instructional: 4–5 correct

____ Frustration: 0–3 correct

Level 1

Level: One

Narrative

The Bear and the Rabbit

Once there was a very big bear. He lived in the woods. He was sad because he didn't have anyone to play with. He said to his father, "How can I find a friend?" His father said, "By being you." "But all the animals are afraid of me," said the bear. "I can't even get near them."

But one day the bear was sitting by a river. He was singing softly to himself. A rabbit lived near the river. He looked out of his hole when he heard the bear's song. He thought, "Anyone who sings like that must be nice. Maybe I don't need to be afraid of him. It would be nice to have a friend." The rabbit went and got his horn. Very softly he began to play. His music went well with the bear's song. The bear looked around. He couldn't see the rabbit. Slowly, the rabbit walked up to the bear. He kept playing and the bear kept singing. They were both happy that they had found a friend. And a bird joined in the song. (181 words)

Retelling Scoring Sheet for The Bear and the Rabbit

Setting/Background

____ There was a bear
____ who was big.
____ He was sad
____ because he didn't have anyone
____ to play with.

Goal

____ He asked his father
____ "How can I find a friend?"

Events

____ His father said,
____ "By being you."
____ "But all the animals are afraid of me,"
____ he said.
____ The bear was sitting
____ by the river.
____ He was singing
____ softly.
____ A rabbit lived there.
____ He looked out
____ of his hole
____ when he heard the song.
____ He thought
____ the bear was nice.
____ The rabbit went
____ and got his horn.
____ He began to play.
____ His music went well
____ with the bear's song.
____ The rabbit walked to the bear.
____ The bear kept singing.

Resolution

____ They were both happy
____ that they had found a friend.
____ A bird joined in.

Other ideas recalled, including inferences:

Questions for The Bear and the Rabbit

1. Why was the bear sad at the beginning of the story?
   Explicit: because he didn't have anyone to play with

2. Why did the father think that the bear could find a friend just by being himself?
   Implicit: the bear was nice and being nice makes friends

3. What was the bear doing as he sat by a river?
   Explicit: singing

4. What did the rabbit think when he heard the bear singing?
   Explicit: that the bear must be nice; he doesn't have to be afraid of him; it would be nice to have a friend

5. What did the rabbit do?
   Explicit: went and got his horn; played his horn

6. Why did the bear and the rabbit become friends?
   Implicit: because of their love of music

Number Correct Explicit: ____

Number Correct Implicit: ____

Total: ____

____ Independent: 6 correct

____ Instructional: 4–5 correct

____ Frustration: 0–3 correct

Level: One

Expository

Concept Questions:

What is air?

_____

_____

_____ (3-2-1-0)

What can wind do?

_____

_____

_____ (3-2-1-0)

How do we know there is air?

_____

_____

_____ (3-2-1-0)

Score: _____ /9 = _____ %

_____ FAM _____ UNFAM

Prediction:

_____

_____

Air

Air is all around us.

But we can't see it.

How do we know it is there?

There are many ways.

We can see what air does.

Moving air is called wind.

Wind moves plants.

Wind moves dirt.

Strong winds can move heavy things.

Strong winds can even move a house.

We can weigh air.

We can weigh two balloons.

The one with a lot of air weighs more.

We can see what air does.

We can weigh air.

Then we know it is there. (92 words)

Number of Total Miscues
(Total Accuracy): _____

Number of Meaning-Change Miscues
(Total Acceptability): _____

Total Accuracy		**Total Acceptability**	
0–1 miscue	____ Independent	____	0–1 miscue
2–8 miscues	____ Instructional	____	2–5 miscues
9+ miscues	____ Frustration	____	6+ miscues

Rate: $92 \times 60 = 5{,}520/$____ seconds = ____ WPM

Retelling Scoring Sheet for Air

Main Idea

____ Air is all around us.

____ But we can't see it.

____ How do we know it is there?

____ We can see

____ what air does.

Details

___ Moving air
___ is called wind.
___ Wind moves plants.
___ Wind moves dirt.
___ Strong winds can move
___ heavy things.
___ Strong winds can move a house.

Main Idea

___ We can weigh air.

Details

___ We can weigh
___ two balloons.
___ The one with lots of air
___ weighs more.

Main Idea Restatement

___ We can see what air does.
___ We can weigh air.
___ Then we know it is there.

Other ideas recalled, including inferences:

Questions for Air

1. How do we know air is there?
   Explicit: we can see what air does; or air moves things (reader can answer things, dirt, plants, or houses); or we can weigh air

2. How else do we know air is there?
   Explicit: any other of the above answers

3. What does air move?
   Explicit: plants or dirt or houses

4. What else does air move?
   Explicit: any other of the above answers

5. How do we know that wind could move a car?
   Implicit: it can move heavy things; or it can move a house

6. Why does a flat tire weigh less than a tire that is not flat?
   Implicit: the flat tire does not have as much air

Number Correct Explicit: ____

Number Correct Implicit: ____

Total: ____

___ Independent: 6 correct

___ Instructional: 4–5 correct

___ Frustration: 0–3 correct

Expository

Concept Questions:

What are foods made from milk?

_____

_____

_____ (3-2-1-0)

What are foods made from grain?

_____

_____

_____ (3-2-1-0)

What are different kinds of meat?

_____

_____

_____ (3-2-1-0)

Score: _____ /9 = _____ %

_____ FAM _____ UNFAM

Prediction:

_____

_____

What You Eat

People eat many kinds of food.

The different kinds of foods are called food
    groups.

There are four food groups.

One food group is the cereal and bread group.

Cereals and breads are foods made of grain.

It is good to eat them three times a day.

Another food group is the dairy group.

Milk and cheese are part of the dairy group.

You should have milk three times a day, too.

Another food group is fruit and vegetables.

Did you know that tomatoes are a fruit?

The fourth group is the meat group.

Meat, eggs, and fish are part of this group.

You should eat some of these foods every day.

Eating the right foods makes you grow and
    keeps you healthy. (123 words)

Number of Total Miscues
(Total Accuracy): _____

Number of Meaning-Change Miscues
(Total Acceptability): _____

Total Accuracy		Total Acceptability
0–3 miscues	____ Independent	____ 0–3 miscues
4–12 miscues	____ Instructional	____ 4–6 miscues
13+ miscues	____ Frustration	____ 7+ miscues

Rate: $123 \times 60 = 7380/$____ seconds = ____ WPM

Retelling Scoring Sheet for What You Eat

Main Idea

____ Different kinds of food are called food
        groups.
____ There are four food groups.

Level: One

Details

___ One group is the cereal
___ and bread group.
___ Cereals
___ and breads are foods
___ made of grain.
___ It is good
___ to eat them
___ three times
___ a day.
___ Another group is the dairy group.
___ Milk
___ and cheese are part of this group.
___ You should have milk
___ three times
___ a day.
___ Another group is fruits
___ and vegetables.
___ Tomatoes are a fruit.
___ The fourth group is the meat group.
___ Meat,
___ eggs,
___ and fish are part of this group.
___ You should eat these
___ every day.
___ Eating foods
___ the right foods
___ makes you grow
___ and keeps you healthy.

Other ideas recalled, including inferences:

Questions for What You Eat

1. What food group does butter belong to?
   Implicit: dairy

2. What are cereals and breads made of?
   Explicit: grain

3. What two food groups should you have
   three times a day?
   Explicit: cereals and dairy

4. What kind of food is a tomato?
   Explicit: fruit

5. Name one member of the meat group
   other than meat.
   Explicit: eggs, fish

6. To what food group does a chicken belong?
   Implicit: meat

Number Correct Explicit: ____

Number Correct Implicit: ____

Total: ____

____ Independent: 6 correct

____ Instructional: 4–5 correct

____ Frustration: 0–3 correct

What Can I Get for My Toy?

It was a Saturday morning. John looked at the toys in his room. They were all old and he wanted something new. John went to his mother. "All my toys are old," he said. "I want something new to play with." His mother looked at him, "John, we don't have the money to buy you anything new. You'll have to find a way to make something new." John went back to his room and looked around at the toys. There were many toys that were fun. But he had played with them so much that they weren't fun anymore. Then he had an idea. His friend Chris wanted a truck just like his red truck. And John wanted a car like the one Chris got for his birthday. Maybe they could trade. John ran down the street to Chris's house. "Hey, Chris, would you trade your car for my truck?" "Sure," said Chris, "I'll trade. Later we can trade something else. That way we'll always have something new to play with."

The Lucky Cricket

Once upon a time there was a young girl by the name of Ling-Ling. She was playing in a garden one day and found a cricket. "Crickets are lucky," she said. "I will keep this cricket and it will bring me luck." Ling-Ling put the cricket in her pocket. The cricket heard Ling-Ling and said to himself, "I'm not lucky! How can I be lucky? I'm just a cricket."

Ling-Ling looked up at the sky. As she did, a lovely crane landed beside her. The crane looked at Ling-Ling for a long time before it nodded its head at her and flew away. "How lucky I am to have seen this beautiful crane," said Ling-Ling. "It must be because of my lucky cricket!" Again, the cricket heard Ling-Ling. "The crane did not come because of me. I am not lucky. Ling-Ling is wrong."

Then Ling-Ling walked onto a bridge. As she looked into the stream below, she saw a beautiful goldfish. She sat on the bridge to look at the fish more closely. The fish stopped swimming and looked into Ling-Ling's eyes. "What a beautiful fish," said Ling-Ling. "How lucky I am to have seen it. It must be because of my lucky cricket!" Again, the cricket heard her and thought, "The fish did not come to Ling-Ling because of me. I am not lucky. I want to get out of here."

Ling-Ling got up and saw a shiny stone in the water. "I will take that stone to my grandmother," thought Ling-Ling, and she reached to pick it up. Just then the cricket jumped out of her pocket and landed on her neck. Ling-Ling was surprised and pulled her hand back. As she looked down she saw a water snake coiled around the stone. "If I had picked up that stone, the snake would have bitten me," she said. "My lucky cricket saved me."

"I did save her!" said the cricket "If I hadn't jumped on her, she would have picked up that stone with the snake. Maybe I am lucky after all."

Father's New Game

It was a cold winter day. Too cold for Mary and Susan to go outside. They wanted something interesting to do. They went to their father and asked if he would take them to a movie. He said, "I'm sorry, girls. Someone is coming to see why the washer isn't working. If you'll play by yourselves for a while, I'll think of a new game for you. But you must promise to stay in your room until I call you." "Okay," said Mary and Susan.

Father wrote notes on pieces of paper and left them around the house. Each note gave a clue as to where to find the next note. Just as the person came to look at the washer, father called to them. "Mary, Susan, you can come out now!" Then he went into the basement.

Mary and Susan came out of their room. They didn't see anything to play with. They thought that their father had forgotten to think of a new game for them to play. Then Susan noticed a piece of paper on the floor. She picked it up and read it aloud. "I'm cold but I give off heat. I'm light when I'm open but dark when I'm closed. What am I? Open me and you'll find the next clue." The girls walked around their house thinking. They came into the kitchen and looked around. "That's it!" yelled Mary. "The refrigerator!" She opened the door and found the next clue taped to the inside of the door. The girls were off again in search of the next clue. After an hour they had found five clues. The person who had fixed the washer was just leaving as Susan found the last clue. It read, "Nice job, girls. Let's go to a movie!"

Whales and Fish

Whales and fish both live in the water, but they are different in many ways. Whales are large animals that live in the water. Even though whales live in the water, they must come to the top of the water to get air. When they come to the top of the water, whales breathe in air through a hole in the top of their heads. At the same time they blow out old air. Whales don't get air like fish. Fish take in air from the water.

Mother whales give birth to live whales. The baby whale must come to the top of the water right away for air. The baby drinks milk from its mother for about a year. Then it finds its own food. Fish have babies in a different way. Most mother fish lay eggs. The babies are born when the eggs hatch. Right after they are born, the baby fish must find their own food.

Whales and fish are alike in some ways too. Whales and fish have flippers on their sides. They also have fins on their tails. Flippers and fins help whales and fish swim. Fins move and push the water away.

Seasons

There are four seasons in a year. They are spring, summer, fall, and winter. Each season lasts about three months. Spring is the season when new life begins. The weather becomes warmer. Warm weather, rain, and light make plants grow. Some plants that looked dead during the winter grow again. Tulips are plants that come up every spring.

Summer begins on June 20th for people who live in the United States. June 20th is the longest day of the year for us. We have more sunlight that day than on any other day. Insects come out in summer. One bug that comes out in summer likes to bite. The bite hurts and it itches. Do you know what that bug is? It's the deerfly.

Summer ends and fall begins during September. In fall we continue to get less light from the sun. In the North, leaves begin to die. When they die they turn brown. Then they fall off. Nuts fall from trees. They are saved by squirrels to eat in the winter.

Winter begins just a few days before Christmas. December 21st is the shortest day of the year for us. We have less light that day than on any other day. In winter many animals have to live on food that they stored during the fall. There are no green plants for the animals to eat. Winter ends when spring begins on March 20th. The seasons keep changing. Plant life begins and ends each year.

Level: Two

Narrative

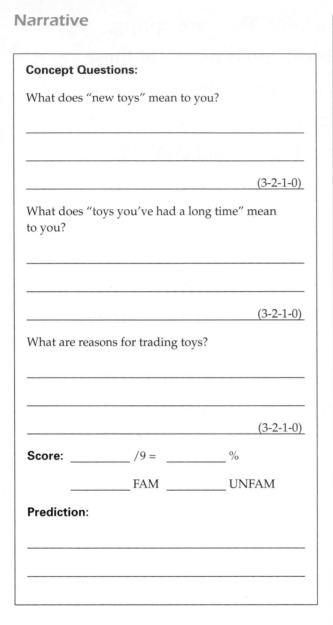

Concept Questions:

What does "new toys" mean to you?

_____

_____

_____ (3-2-1-0)

What does "toys you've had a long time" mean to you?

_____

_____

_____ (3-2-1-0)

What are reasons for trading toys?

_____

_____

_____ (3-2-1-0)

Score: _____ /9 = _____ %

_____ FAM _____ UNFAM

Prediction:

_____

_____

What Can I Get for My Toy?

It was a Saturday morning. John looked at the toys in his room. They were all old and he wanted something new. John went to his mother. "All my toys are old," he said. "I want something new to play with." His mother looked at him. "John, we don't have the money

to buy you anything new. You'll have to find a way to make something new." John went back to his room and looked around at the toys. There were many toys that were fun. But he had played with them so much that they weren't fun anymore. Then he had an idea. His friend Chris wanted a truck just like his red truck. And John wanted a car like the one Chris got for his birthday. Maybe they could trade. John ran down the street to Chris's house. "Hey, Chris, would you trade your car for my truck?" "Sure," said Chris. "I'll trade. Later we can trade something else. That way we'll always have something new to play with." (175 words)

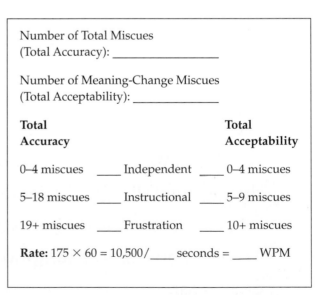

Number of Total Miscues
(Total Accuracy): _____

Number of Meaning-Change Miscues
(Total Acceptability): _____

Total Accuracy		**Total Acceptability**
0–4 miscues	____ Independent	____ 0–4 miscues
5–18 miscues	____ Instructional	____ 5–9 miscues
19+ miscues	____ Frustration	____ 10+ miscues

Rate: 175 × 60 = 10,500/____ seconds = ____ WPM

Level: Two

Retelling Scoring Sheet for
What Can I Get for My Toy?

Setting/Background

___ John looked at his toys.
___ They were old.

Goal

___ John wanted something
___ that was new.

Events

___ John went to his mother.
___ "My toys are old,"
___ he said.
___ "I want something
___ new
___ to play with."
___ His mother looked
___ at John.
___ "We don't have money
___ to buy something
___ new."
___ John had played with his toys
___ so much
___ that they weren't fun
___ anymore.
___ His friend
___ Chris wanted a truck
___ just like his truck
___ his red truck
___ and John wanted a car
___ like Chris's car.
___ Maybe they could trade.
___ John ran
___ down the street
___ to Chris's house.
___ "Would you trade your car
___ for my truck?"
___ "Sure,"
___ said Chris.

Resolution

___ "We can trade something else
___ later.
___ We'll always have something
___ new
___ to play with."

Other ideas recalled, including inferences:

Questions for
What Can I Get for My Toy?

1. At the beginning of the story, what did John tell his mother he wanted?
   Explicit: something new to play with

2. Why did John want a new toy to play with?
   Implicit: because he had played with his old toys so much they weren't interesting to him anymore; he got bored with them.
   Note: broken is not acceptable—the story discusses his boredom and indicates that his toys were desired by another child.

3. What did John's mother say when he asked her to buy something new for him?
   Explicit: they didn't have the money to buy anything new; he'd have to make something new

4. What did John do to get what he wanted?
   Explicit: he went to his friend's house and asked him to trade toys with him

5. Why was trading a good idea?
   Implicit: the boys would always have something new to play with; boys had new toys without spending money

6. At the end of the story, what did his friend suggest that they do?
   Explicit: trade again later

7. In the future what must both boys have for trading to make them both happy?
   Implicit: toys that the other boy wanted

8. Why do you think that the boys will trade again?
   Implicit: they will get bored with the toys they traded; they will want a new toy again

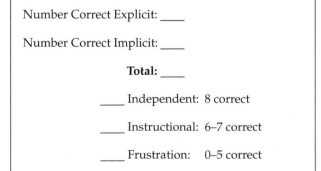

Number Correct Explicit: ____

Number Correct Implicit: ____

Total: ____

____ Independent: 8 correct

____ Instructional: 6–7 correct

____ Frustration: 0–5 correct

Level 2

Narrative

Concept Questions:

What does it mean if something is lucky?

_____

_____

_____ (3-2-1-0)

What is a cricket?

_____

_____

_____ (3-2-1-0)

What does "coiled" mean?

_____

_____

_____ (3-2-1-0)

How could a bird communicate with a person?

_____

_____

_____ (3-2-1-0)

Score: _____ /12 = _____ %

_____ FAM _____ UNFAM

Prediction:

_____

_____

The Lucky Cricket

Once upon a time there was a young girl by the name of Ling-Ling. She was playing in a garden one day and found a cricket. "Crickets are lucky," she said. "I will keep this cricket and it will bring me luck." Ling-Ling put the cricket in her pocket. The cricket heard Ling-Ling and said to himself, "I'm not lucky! How can I be lucky? I'm just a cricket."

Ling-Ling looked up at the sky. As she did, a lovely crane landed beside her. The crane looked at Ling-Ling for a long time before it nodded its head at her and flew away. "How lucky I am to have seen this beautiful crane," said Ling-Ling. "It must be because of my lucky cricket!" Again, the cricket heard Ling-Ling. "The crane did not come because of me. I am not lucky. Ling-Ling is wrong."

Then Ling-Ling walked onto a bridge. As she looked into the stream below, she saw a beautiful goldfish. She sat on the bridge to look at the fish more closely. The fish stopped swimming and looked into Ling-Ling's eyes. "What a beautiful fish," said Ling-Ling. "How lucky I am to have seen it. It must be because of my lucky cricket!" Again, the cricket heard her and thought, "The fish did not come to Ling-Ling because of me. I am not lucky. I want to get out of here."

Ling-Ling got up and saw a shiny stone in the water. "I will take that stone to my grandmother," thought Ling-Ling, and she reached to pick it up. Just then the cricket jumped out

Level 2

of her pocket and landed on her neck. Ling-Ling was surprised and pulled her hand back. As she looked down, she saw a water snake coiled around the stone. "If I had <u>picked</u> up that stone, the snake would have bitten me," she said. "My lucky cricket saved me." "I did save her!" said the cricket. "If I hadn't jumped on her, she would have <u>picked</u> up that stone with the snake. Maybe I am lucky after all."

[346 words]

Number of Total Miscues
(Total Accuracy): _____

Number of Meaning-Change Miscues
(Total Acceptability): _____

Total Accuracy			**Total Acceptability**
0–8 miscues	____ Independent	____	0–8 miscues
9–36 miscues	____ Instructional	____	9–17 miscues
37+ miscues	____ Frustration	____	18+ miscues

Rate: 346 × 60 = 20,760/____ seconds = ____ WPM

Retelling Scoring Sheet for The Lucky Cricket

Setting/ Background

____ Once upon a time
____ there was a girl
____ by the name of Ling-Ling.
____ She was playing
____ and found a cricket.

Goal

____ "Crickets are lucky,"
____ she said.

____ "I will keep this cricket."
____ Ling-Ling put the cricket
____ in her pocket.
____ The cricket said to himself,
____ "I am not lucky."

Events

____ Ling-Ling looked at the sky.
____ A crane landed beside her.
____ The crane looked at Ling-Ling
____ for a long time
____ before it flew away.
____ "How lucky I am
____ to have seen this beautiful crane,"
____ said Ling-Ling.
____ "It must be because of my lucky cricket."
____ The cricket heard Ling-Ling.
____ "I am not lucky."
____ Ling-Ling walked onto a bridge.
____ She saw a goldfish.
____ The fish stopped swimming
____ and looked into Ling-Ling's eyes.
____ "What a beautiful fish,"
____ said Ling-Ling.
____ "How lucky I am to have seen it.
____ It must be because of my lucky cricket."
____ The cricket thought
____ "I am not lucky.
____ I want to get out of here."
____ Ling-Ling saw a shiny stone
____ in the water.
____ She reached to pick it up.
____ The cricket jumped
____ out of her pocket
____ and landed on her neck.
____ Ling-Ling pulled her hand back.
____ She saw a snake
____ coiled around the stone.
____ "If I had picked up that stone,
____ the snake would have bitten me.
____ "My lucky cricket saved me."

Resolution

____ "I did save her!" said the cricket.
____ "If I hadn't jumped on her

_____she would have picked up the stone
_____with the snake.
_____Maybe I am lucky
_____after all."

Other ideas recalled, including inferences:

Questions for The Lucky Cricket

1. Where did the story take place?
   Explicit: in a garden

2. At the beginning of the story, why did Ling-Ling keep the cricket she found?
   Explicit: because she thought it would bring her luck

3. Why did Ling-Ling think that the cricket was lucky after she'd seen the crane?
   Implicit: it looked at her for a long time, or it nodded its head at her, or it seemed to communicate with her, or she thought it came to her because of the cricket

4. Why did the cricket want to get away from Ling-Ling?
   Implicit: because he didn't think he was lucky.

5. What did Ling-Ling see when she sat on the bridge?
   Explicit: a goldfish

6. Why did Ling-Ling want to pick up the shiny stone in the water?
   Explicit: she wanted to give it to her grand-mother

7. How did the cricket surprise Ling-Ling when she reached to pick up the stone?
   Implicit: he jumped out of her pocket and landed on her neck

8. Why did the cricket decide at the end that he was lucky after all?
   Implicit: he thought that maybe he was lucky because he had saved her from picking up the snake

Number Correct Explicit: _____

Number Correct Implicit: _____

Total: _____

_____ Independent: 8 correct

_____ Instructional: 6–7 correct

_____ Frustration: 0–5 correct

Level 2

Narrative

Concept Questions:

What is a repairman?

_____

_____

_____ (3-2-1-0)

What is a treasure hunt?

_____

_____

_____ (3-2-1-0)

What is it like inside a refrigerator?

_____

_____

_____ (3-2-1-0)

Score: _____ /9 = _____ %

_____ FAM _____ UNFAM

Prediction:

_____

_____

Father's New Game

It was a cold winter day. Too cold for Mary and Susan to go outside. They wanted something interesting to do. They went to their father and asked if he would take them to a movie. He said, "I'm sorry, girls. Someone is coming to see why the washer isn't working. If you'll play by yourselves for a while, I'll think of a new game for you. But you must promise to stay in your room until I call you." "Okay," said Mary and Susan.

Father wrote notes on pieces of paper and left them around the house. Each note gave a clue as to where to find the next note. Just as the person came to look at the washer, Father called to them. "Mary, Susan, you can come out now!" Then he went into the basement. Mary and Susan came out of their room. They didn't see anything to play with. They thought that their father had forgotten to think of a new game for them to play. Then Susan noticed a piece of paper on the floor. She picked it up and read it aloud. "I'm cold but I give off heat. I'm light when I'm open but dark when I'm closed. What am I? Open me and you'll find the next clue." The girls walked around their house thinking. They came into the kitchen and looked around. "That's it!" yelled Mary. "The refrigerator!" She opened the door and found the next clue taped to the inside of the door. The girls were off again in search for the next clue. After an hour they had found five clues. The person who had fixed the washer was just leaving as Susan found the last clue. It read, "Nice job, girls. Let's go to a movie!" (298 words)

Number of Total Miscues
(Total Accuracy): _____

Number of Meaning-Change Miscues
(Total Acceptability): _____

Total Accuracy		**Total Acceptability**
0–7 miscues	____ Independent	____ 0–7 miscues
8–31 miscues	____ Instructional	____ 8–16 miscues
32+ miscues	____ Frustration	____ 17+ miscues

Rate: $298 \times 60 = 17,880/$ ____ seconds = ____ WPM

Retelling Scoring Sheet for Father's New Game

Setting/Background

____ It was a cold day.
____ Too cold
____ for Mary
____ and Susan
____ to go outside.

Goal

____ They wanted something to do.

Events

____ They went to their father
____ and asked
____ if he would take them
____ to a movie.
____ He said,
____ "I'm sorry.
____ Someone is coming
____ to see
____ why the washer isn't working.
____ I'll think
____ of a game
____ a new game.
____ But you stay
____ in your room
____ until I call you."

____ Father wrote notes
____ on pieces
____ of paper
____ and left them
____ around the house.
____ Each note gave a clue
____ where to find the next note.
____ Father called to them,
____ "You can come out now."
____ Mary
____ and Susan came out
____ of their room.
____ Susan noticed a piece
____ of paper.
____ She read it.
____ They found the next clue
____ in the refrigerator.
____ They found clues
____ five clues.
____ The person who fixed the washer
____ was leaving
____ as Susan found the last clue.

Resolution

____ The last clue
____ read
____ "Nice job,
____ girls.
____ Let's go
____ to a movie."

Other ideas recalled, including inferences:

Level 2

Questions for Father's New Game

1. What kind of day was it?
   Explicit: very cold; winter

2. What did Mary and Susan want?
   Explicit: to go to a movie

3. Why couldn't their father take them to the movie when they asked to go?
   Implicit: their father needed to stay home to wait for someone to come to repair the washer

4. What did their father write in the notes he left them?
   Explicit: clues

5. Why did Mary and Susan think their father had forgotten to think up a new game?
   Implicit: when they came out of their room, they didn't see anything; their dad wasn't there

6. Where did the first clue lead them?
   Explicit: to the refrigerator; if student says, "To the kitchen," ask, "Where in the kitchen?"

7. How did they know it was the refrigerator?
   Implicit: any of the clues—it was cold, but gave off heat; I'm light when I'm opened but dark when I'm closed

8. Why could they go to the movie when they found the last clue?
   Implicit: because the washer was fixed so their father could leave the house

Number Correct Explicit: ____

Number Correct Implicit: ____

Total: ____

____ Independent: 8 correct

____ Instructional: 6–7 correct

____ Frustration: 0–5 correct

Level: Two

Expository

Concept Questions:

How do whales breathe?

_____

_____

_____ (3-2-1-0)

What does "baby animals staying with their mother" mean to you?

_____

_____

_____ (3-2-1-0)

How are baby fish born?

_____

_____

_____ (3-2-1-0)

Score: _____ /9 = _____ %

_____ FAM _____ UNFAM

Prediction:

_____

_____

Whales and Fish

Whales and fish both live in the water, but they are different in many ways. Whales are large animals that live in the water. Even though whales live in the water, they must come to the top of the water to get air. When they come to the top of the water, whales breathe in air through a hole in the top of their heads. At the same time they blow out old air. Whales don't get air like fish. Fish take in air from the water.

Mother whales give birth to live whales. The baby whale must come to the top of the water right away for air. The baby drinks milk from its mother for about a year. Then it finds its own food. Fish have babies in a different way. Most mother fish lay eggs. The babies are born when the eggs hatch. Right after they are born, the baby fish must find their own food.

Whales and fish are alike in some ways too. Whales and fish have flippers on their sides. They also have fins on their tails. Flippers and fins help whales and fish swim. Fins move and push the water away. (197 words)

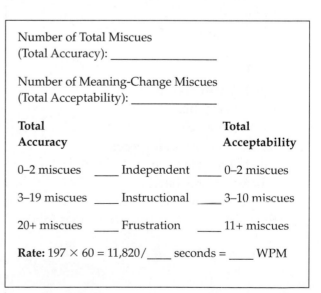

Number of Total Miscues
(Total Accuracy): _____

Number of Meaning-Change Miscues
(Total Acceptability): _____

Total Accuracy		Total Acceptability	
0–2 miscues	____ Independent	____	0–2 miscues
3–19 miscues	____ Instructional	____	3–10 miscues
20+ miscues	____ Frustration	____	11+ miscues

Rate: 197 × 60 = 11,820/____ seconds = ____ WPM

Retelling Scoring Sheet for Whales and Fish

Main Idea

____ Whales

____ and fish both live

____ in the water

____ but they are different

____ in many ways.

Details

____ Whales are large

____ animals.

____ They must come

____ to the top

____ of the water

____ to get air.

____ Whales breathe

____ in air

____ through a hole

____ in the top

____ of their heads.

____ At the same time,

____ they blow out

____ old air.

____ Fish take in air

____ from the water.

____ Mother whales give birth

____ to live whales.

____ The baby whale comes

____ to the top

____ of the water

____ right away

____ for air.

____ The baby drinks milk

____ from its mother

____ for about a year.

____ Most mother fish lay eggs.

____ The babies are born

____ when the eggs hatch.

____ Right after they are born,

____ the baby fish must find their own food.

Main Idea

____ Whales

____ and fish are alike

____ in some ways too.

Details

____ Whales

____ and fish have flippers

____ on their sides.

____ They have fins

____ on their tails.

____ Flippers

____ and fins help whales

____ and fish swim.

____ Fins move

____ and push the water away.

Other ideas recalled, including inferences:

Questions for Whales and Fish

1. What is this passage mainly about?
   Implicit: how whales and fish are alike and different

2. According to the passage, how are whales and fish different?
   Explicit: whales breathe air and fish take in air from the water; whales give birth to live babies and fish lay eggs; baby whales get food from their mother, and baby fish have to get it for themselves

3. According to the passage, name another way that whales and fish are different.
   Explicit: any other of the above answers

4. What part of the whale is like our nose?
   Implicit: the air hole or the hole in the whale's head

5. Why does a baby whale stay with its mother for a year?
   Implicit: it gets food from its mother

6. What part of whales and fish are alike?
   Explicit: fins or flippers

7. Where are fins found on fish and whales?
   Explicit: on the tail

8. Why might a mother fish not know her baby?
   Implicit: the mother does not see the babies when they are born, or the babies hatch from eggs

---

Number Correct Explicit: ____

Number Correct Implicit: ____

Total: ____

____ Independent: 8 correct

____ Instructional: 6–7 correct

____ Frustration: 0–5 correct

Level 2

Level: Two

Expository

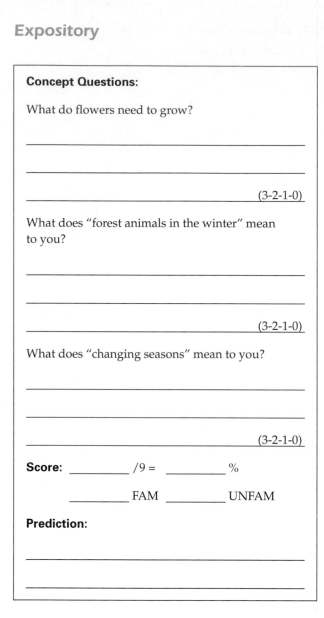

Concept Questions:

What do flowers need to grow?

_____

_____

_____ (3-2-1-0)

What does "forest animals in the winter" mean to you?

_____

_____

_____ (3-2-1-0)

What does "changing seasons" mean to you?

_____

_____

_____ (3-2-1-0)

Score: _____ /9 = _____ %

_____ FAM _____ UNFAM

Prediction:

_____

_____

Seasons

There are four seasons in a year. They are spring, summer, fall, and winter. Each season lasts about three months. Spring is the season when new life begins. The weather becomes warmer. Warm weather, rain, and light make plants grow. Some plants that looked dead during the winter grow again. Tulips are plants that come up every spring.

Summer begins on June 20th for people who live in the United States. June 20th is the longest day of the year for us. We have more sunlight that day than on any other day. Insects come out in summer. One bug that comes out in summer likes to bite. The bite hurts and it itches. Do you know what that bug is? It's the deerfly.

Summer ends and fall begins during September. In fall we continue to get less light from the sun. In the North, leaves begin to die. When they die they turn brown. Then they fall off. Nuts fall from trees. They are saved by squirrels to eat in the winter.

Winter begins just a few days before Christmas. December 21st is the shortest day of the year for us. We have less light that day than on any other day. In winter many animals have to live on food that they stored during the fall. There are no green plants for the animals to eat. Winter ends when spring begins on March 20th. The seasons keep changing. Plant life begins and ends each year. (249 words)

Level: Two

Number of Total Miscues
(Total Accuracy): _____

Number of Meaning-Change Miscues
(Total Acceptability): _____

Total Accuracy			Total Acceptability
0–6 miscues	____ Independent	____	0–6 miscues
7–26 miscues	____ Instructional	____	7–13 miscues
27+ miscues	____ Frustration	____	14+ miscues

Rate: 249 × 60 = 14,940/____ seconds = ____ WPM

Retelling Scoring Sheet for Seasons

Main Idea

____ There are seasons
____ four seasons
____ in a year.

Details

____ They are spring,
____ summer,
____ fall,
____ and winter.

Main Idea

____ Spring is the season
____ when new life begins.

Details

____ The weather becomes warmer.
____ Rain
____ and light make plants grow.
____ Tulips come up
____ every spring.

Main Idea

____ Summer begins
____ on June 20th.

Details

____ June 20th is the longest day
____ of the year.
____ Insects come out
____ in the summer.
____ One bug likes to bite.
____ It's the deerfly.

Main Idea

____ Fall begins
____ during September.

Details

____ We continue to get less light
____ from the sun
____ in the fall.
____ Leaves begin to die.
____ They turn brown.
____ Then they fall off.
____ Nuts are saved
____ by squirrels
____ to eat
____ in the winter.

Main Idea

____ Winter begins
____ a few days
____ before Christmas.

Details

____ December 21st is the shortest day
____ of the year.
____ Animals have to live on food
____ that they stored
____ during the fall.

Other ideas recalled, including inferences:

Questions for Seasons

1. How long does each season usually last?
   Explicit: three months

2. What are the conditions needed for flowers to come up in spring?
   Implicit: warm weather, rain, or light

3. Which day has more sunlight than any other?
   Explicit: June 20th

4. According to your reading, what insect's bite makes you itch?
   Explicit: deerfly

5. How do you know that fall is coming even if the weather is warm?
   Explicit: there is less daylight; the leaves turn brown

6. Why do leaves die in the fall even when the weather is warm?
   Implicit: there is less light

7. About when in September does fall begin?
   Implicit: around September 20th

8. Why do squirrels save nuts for eating in winter?
   Implicit: Food is scarce; there is less food available in the winter.

Number Correct Explicit: ____

Number Correct Implicit: ____

Total: ____

____ Independent: 8 correct

____ Instructional: 6–7 correct

____ Frustration: 0–5 correct

The Trip to the Zoo

The day was bright and sunny. Carlos and Maria jumped out of bed and dressed in a hurry. They didn't want to be late for school today. It was a special day because their classes were going to the zoo. When they got to school, all of the children were waiting outside to get on the bus. When everyone was there, the second and third graders got on the bus and rode to the zoo. On the bus, the children talked about the zoo animals that they liked the best. Joe and Carlos wanted to see the lion, king of the beasts. Maria and Angela wanted to see the chimps. Maria thought they acted a lot like people.

When they got to the zoo, their teachers divided the children into four groups. One teacher, Mr. Lopez, told them if anyone got lost, to go to the ice cream stand. Everyone would meet there at noon. Maria went with the group to the monkey house, where she spent a long time watching the chimps groom each other. She wrote down all the ways that the chimps acted like people. Her notes would help her write a good report of what she liked best at the zoo.

Carlos went with the group to the lion house. He watched the cats pace in front of the glass. Carlos was watching a lion so carefully that he didn't see his group leave. Finally, he noticed that it was very quiet in the lion house. He turned around and didn't see anyone. At first he was worried. Then he remembered what Mr. Lopez had said. He traced his way back to the entrance and found a map. He followed the map to the ice cream stand, just as everyone was meeting there for lunch. Joe smiled and said, "We thought that the lion had you for lunch!"

A Special Birthday for Rosa

Today was the day Rosa had eagerly been waiting for, her birthday! She was very happy but she also felt sad. This would be the first birthday that she would celebrate without all her family around her. The company that Rosa's father worked for had given him a wonderful promotion. But this meant that Rosa, her parents, and her little brother, Jose, had to move to another state. Rosa liked her new home and friends. But, she really wanted to celebrate her birthday with her grandparents, aunts, uncles, and cousins all around her.

They had sent presents but it wouldn't be the same if she couldn't thank them in person. They wouldn't be there to watch her blow out all the candles. And what kind of a birthday would it be without listening to her grandparents' stories about growing up in Italy and Cuba? Also, four people could never sing as loudly or joyfully as her whole family could sing together!

That night, Mama made Rosa's favorite meal. Afterwards, there was a beautiful cake. Mother, Father, and Jose sang "Happy Birthday" while the eight candles glowed. Rosa made a wish, took a deep breath, and blew out all the candles. "I know I won't get what I wished for," she said to herself, "but I'm going to wish for it anyway."

Then it was time for the presents. Rosa's father gave her the first present. It was a videotape. "I think we should play it right now before you open any more presents," her father said. He put the tape into the player. Suddenly, there on the television screen was the rest of Rosa's family smiling and waving and wishing her a a happy birthday. One by one, each person on the tape asked Rosa to open the present they had sent. Her father put the tape on pause while Rosa did this. Then they explained why they had chosen that gift especially for Rosa. After all the presents were unwrapped, her family sang some favorite songs and Rosa, her mother, father, and Jose joined in.

Then, Rosa's grandfather spoke to her. "Rosa, this is a new story, one you have never heard before. I am going to tell it to you as a special birthday gift. It is about my first birthday in this country when I was very lonely for my friends and family. It is about how I met your grandmother." When Grandfather was finished, he and Grandmother blew Rosa a kiss and the tape was finished.

Rosa felt wonderful. It was almost like having her family in the room with her. Rosa hugged her parents and her little brother. "I didn't think I would get my wish but I did," she said. That night, when Mama and Papa came to say goodnight to Rosa, they found her in bed, already asleep, with the videotape next to her. It had been the best birthday ever.

The Friend

Once upon a time there was a boy named Mark. Mark loved to go to the ocean and play his flute. One day he was playing his flute when a school of dolphins swam by. They leaped in the air every 30 seconds. Mark could almost predict when they would leap again. He watched them for a long time because he was so interested in their play. That day he decided that he wanted to learn more about dolphins.

Mark went to the library. The next weekend he took a boat and rowed out about as far as he had seen the dolphins before. He started playing his flute, trying to mimic the pulsed sounds he had heard on tapes of dolphin sounds. He had learned that they make two kinds of pulsed sounds. One kind is called sonar and is used to locate dolphins and objects. The other kind of sound is a burst pulse that tells the emotional state of the dolphin. Mark was trying to mimic sonar. Soon, about 400 yards away, he saw the roll of the dolphins. The boat bounced in the waves as the dolphins came closer. They seemed to be curious about the sounds coming from the boat. Suddenly, the boat tipped sharply and Mark fell out. Somehow he held on to his flute. Mark was a good swimmer, but he was too far from land to swim. The only thing to do was to try to mimic the sound of a dolphin in trouble. Maybe then the dolphins would help him to land. Kicking strongly, he kept himself up above the water. He blew high, burst pulse sounds. Just when he was about to go under water, he felt a push against his leg. Again and again a dolphin pushed him. She managed to keep his face above water as she gently pushed him to shore. Mark couldn't believe what was happening. He got safely to shore, although the boat was never seen again. As he sat on the beach, still shaking from fear, he realized that he had reached his goal. He had surely learned a lot about dolphins that day!

Cats: Lions and Tigers in Your House

House cats, lions, and tigers are part of the same family. When animals are part of the same family, they are alike in many ways. House cats are like lions and tigers in many ways, too. When kittens are first born, they drink milk from their mothers. Lions and tigers drink milk from their mothers, too. When kittens are born, they have claws, just like big cats. Claws are used by lions, tigers, and kittens to help them keep away enemies. As kittens get bigger, they learn to hunt from their mother. House cats hunt in the same way that lions and tigers do. They hide and lie very still. When the animal they are hunting comes close, they jump on it and grab it by the back of the neck. Cats kill other animals by shaking them and breaking their necks.

Lions, tigers, and house cats show when they are afraid in the same ways, too. Their fur puffs up, making them look bigger. They hiss and spit, too. Those are their ways of saying, "I'm afraid, don't come closer."

A cat's tongue has many uses. Because it is rough with little bumps on it, it can be used as a spoon. A cat drinks milk by lapping it. Because of the bumps, the milk stays on the tongue until the cat can swallow it. If you feel the top of a cat's tongue, it is rough. This makes the tongue good for brushing the cat's hair. Lions and tigers clean themselves with their tongues just like house cats do.

Where Do People Live?

People live in different places. Some people live in a city. Others live in the country. Still other people live in between the city and the country. They live in suburbs. Why do people live in these different places?

People live in the city to be near their jobs. Cities have lots of factories, schools, and offices. People work in these buildings. If people don't want to drive a long way to their jobs, they live in the city. There are many other things to do in the city. Cities have museums and zoos. They also have many movie theaters.

People live in the country to be close to their jobs, too. Many people who live in the country are farmers. They plant crops on their land. They may sell their crops or may use them to feed the animals that live on the farm. Farmers raise cows, pigs, and chickens. The main food that these animals eat is grain. There are other things to do in the country. You can find a river to fish in or take walks in the woods. The life in the country is quiet.

People live in between the country and the city. They live in suburbs. Some people think that people who live in the suburbs have the best of both worlds. They live close to their jobs in the city. The suburbs are quieter than the city. They often have many movie theaters, too. It doesn't take as long to go to either the city or the country. The suburbs are more crowded than the country but less crowded than the city. Where people live depends upon what they like most.

Wool: From Sheep to You

Do you have a sweater? Do you know what it is made from? One fiber used to make sweaters is wool. Do you know where wool comes from? It comes from a sheep. However, many things must be done before the wool on a sheep can be woven or knitted to make clothing for you.

First, the wool must be removed from the sheep. People shear the wool off the sheep with electric clippers somewhat like a barber uses when he gives haircuts. Like our hair, the sheep's wool will grow back again. Most sheep are shorn only once a year. After the wool is removed, it must be washed very carefully to get out all the dirt. When the locks of wool dry, they are combed or carded to make all the fibers lie in the same direction. It is somewhat like combing or brushing your hair. Then the wool is formed into fine strands. These can be spun to make yarn. The yarn is knitted or woven into fabric. The fabric is made into clothing.

Yarn can also be used to knit sweaters by hand. Sweaters made from wool are very warm. They help keep you warm even when they are damp. Just think, the sweater you wear on a winter day may once have been on a sheep.

Narrative

Concept Questions:

What is a class trip?

_____

_____

_____ (3-2-1-0)

What does "taking notes" mean to you?

_____

_____

_____ (3-2-1-0)

What does "being by yourself" mean to you?

_____

_____

_____ (3-2-1-0)

Why do people use maps?

_____

_____

_____ (3-2-1-0)

Score: _____ /12 = _____ %

_____ FAM _____ UNFAM

Prediction:

_____

_____

The Trip to the Zoo

The day was bright and sunny. Carlos and Maria jumped out of bed and dressed in a hurry. They didn't want to be late for school today. It was a <u>special</u> day because their classes were going to the zoo. When they got to school, all of the children were waiting outside to get on the bus. When everyone was there, the second and third graders got on the bus and rode to the zoo. On the bus, the children talked about the zoo animals that they liked the best. Joe and Carlos wanted to see the <u>lion</u>, king of the beasts. Maria and Angela wanted to see the chimps. Maria thought they acted a lot like people.

When they got to the zoo, their teachers divided the children into four groups. One teacher, Mr. Lopez, told them if anyone got lost to go to the ice cream stand. Everyone would meet there at noon. Maria went with the group to the monkey house, where she spent a long time watching the chimps groom each other. She wrote down all the ways that the chimps acted like people. Her notes would help her write a good report of what she liked best at the zoo.

Carlos went with the group to the <u>lion</u> house. He watched the cats pace in front of the glass. Carlos was watching a <u>lion</u> so carefully that he didn't see his group leave. Finally, he noticed that it was very quiet in the <u>lion</u> house. He turned around and didn't see anyone. At first he was <u>worried</u>. Then he remembered what Mr. Lopez had said. He traced his way back to the <u>entrance</u> and found a map. He followed the map to the ice cream stand, just as everyone was meeting there for <u>lunch</u>. Joe smiled and said, "We thought that the <u>lion</u> had you for <u>lunch</u>!" (312 words)

Number of Total Miscues
(Total Accuracy): _____

Number of Meaning-Change Miscues
(Total Acceptability): _____

Total Accuracy		**Total Acceptability**
0–7 miscues ____	Independent ____	0–7 miscues
8–32 miscues ____	Instructional ____	8–17 miscues
33+ miscues ____	Frustration ____	18+ miscues

Rate: 312 × 60 = 18,720/____ seconds = ____ WPM

Retelling Scoring Sheet for The Trip to the Zoo

Setting/Background

____ Carlos
____ and Maria jumped
____ out of bed.
____ They didn't want
____ to be late
____ for school.
____ Their classes were going
____ to the zoo.
____ The second
____ and third graders
____ got on the bus
____ and rode
____ to the zoo.
____ They talked

____ about the animals
____ they liked best.

Goal

____ Carlos wanted
____ to see the lion.
____ Maria wanted
____ to see the chimps.

Events

____ Their teacher told them
____ their teacher, Mr. Lopez
____ if anyone got lost
____ to go
____ to the ice cream stand
____ where everyone would meet
____ at noon.
____ Maria went
____ to the monkey house.
____ She wrote down all the ways
____ that chimps acted like people.
____ Her notes would help her
____ write a report.
____ Carlos went
____ to the lion house.

Problem

____ Carlos was watching a lion
____ so carefully
____ he didn't see his group
____ leave.
____ He noticed
____ that it was quiet.
____ He turned around
____ and didn't see anyone.
____ He remembered
____ what Mr. Lopez said.
____ He traced his way
____ to the entrance
____ and found a map.
____ He followed the map
____ to the ice cream stand.

Resolution

___ Everyone was there
___ for lunch.
___ They thought
___ the lion had Carlos
___ for lunch.

Other ideas recalled, including inferences:

Questions for The Trip to the Zoo

1. Why was it a special day for Carlos and Maria?
   Explicit: their classes were going to the zoo

2. What grades were Carlos and Maria in?
   Implicit: second and third

3. What animal did Carlos want to see?
   Explicit: lions

4. Why was Maria watching the chimps so carefully?
   Implicit: so she could write a report for school

5. How did Carlos get separated from his group?
   Explicit: he was watching the lions so carefully he didn't see his group leave

6. What made Carlos realize that his classmates had left the lion house?
   Implicit: it was quiet; he didn't hear any talking; he turned around and no one was there

7. Where did Carlos find the map?
   Explicit: at the zoo entrance

8. Why did Carlos go to get a map from the zoo entrance?
   Implicit: to help him find his way to the ice cream stand

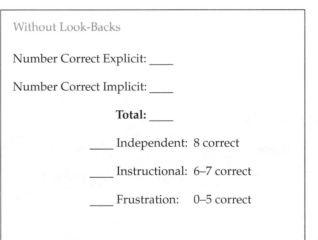

Without Look-Backs

Number Correct Explicit: ____

Number Correct Implicit: ____

Total: ____

____ Independent: 8 correct

____ Instructional: 6–7 correct

____ Frustration: 0–5 correct

With Look-Backs

Number Correct Explicit: ____

Number Correct Implicit: ____

Total: ____

____ Independent: 8 correct

____ Instructional: 6–7 correct

____ Frustration: 0–5 correct

Level: Three

Narrative

Concept Questions:

What does the word "celebration" mean?

_____

_____

_____ (3-2-1-0)

What does it mean for you to miss someone?

_____

_____

_____ (3-2-1-0)

If you are sad, how can someone cheer you up?

_____

_____

_____ (3-2-1-0)

How many candles are on a birthday cake?

_____

_____

_____ (3-2-1-0)

Score: _____ /12 = _____ %

_____ FAM _____ UNFAM

Prediction:

_____

_____

A Special Birthday for Rosa

Today was the day Rosa had eagerly been waiting for, her birthday! She was very happy but she also felt sad. This would be the first birthday that she would celebrate without all her family around her. The company that Rosa's father worked for had given him a wonderful promotion. But this meant that Rosa, her parents, and her little brother, Jose, had to move to another state. Rosa liked her new home and friends. But, she really wanted to celebrate her birthday with her grandparents, aunts, uncles, and cousins all around her.

They had sent presents but it wouldn't be the same if she couldn't thank them in person. They wouldn't be there to watch her blow out all the candles. And what kind of a birthday would it be without listening to her grandparents' stories about growing up in Italy and Cuba? Also, four people could never sing as loudly or joyfully as her whole family could sing together!

That night, Mama made Rosa's favorite meal. Afterwards, there was a beautiful cake. Mother, Father, and Jose sang "Happy Birthday" while the eight candles glowed. Rosa made a wish, took a deep breath and blew out all the candles. "I know I won't get what I wished for," she said to herself, "but I'm going to wish for it anyway."

Then it was time for the presents. Rosa's father gave her the first present. It was a videotape. "I think we should play it right now before you open any more presents," her father said. He put the tape into the player. Suddenly, there on the television screen was the rest of Rosa's family smiling and waving and wishing her a happy birthday. One by one, each person on the tape asked Rosa to open the present they had sent. Her father put the tape on pause while Rosa did this. Then they explained why they had chosen that gift especially for Rosa. After all the presents were unwrapped, her family sang some favorite songs and Rosa, her mother, father, and Jose joined in.

Then, Rosa's grandfather spoke to her. "Rosa, this is a new story, one you have never heard before. I am going to tell it to you as a special birthday gift. It is about my first birthday in this country when I was very lonely for my friends and family. It is about how I met your grandmother." When Grandfather was finished, he and Grandmother blew Rosa a kiss and the tape was finished.

Rosa felt wonderful. It was almost like having her family in the room with her. Rosa hugged her parents and her little brother. "I didn't think I would get my wish but I did," she said. That night, when Mama and Papa came to say goodnight to Rosa, they found her in bed, already asleep, with the videotape next to her. It had been the best birthday ever. (487 words)

Number of Total Miscues
(Total Accuracy): _____

Number of Meaning-Change Miscues
(Total Acceptability): _____

Total Accuracy			**Total Acceptability**
0–9 miscues	____	Independent ____	0–9 miscues
10–48 miscues	____	Instructional ____	10–24 miscues
49+ miscues	____	Frustration ____	25+ miscues

Rate: 487 × 60 = 29,220/ ____ seconds = ____ WPM

Retelling Scoring Sheet for A Special Birthday for Rosa

Setting/Background

____ Today was Rosa's birthday.
____ She was happy
____ but she also felt sad.
____ This would be the first birthday
____ she would celebrate
____ without all her family
____ around her.
____ Her father had been given a promotion.
____ Rosa,
____ her parents,
____ and her brother had to move
____ to another state.

Goal

____ Rosa wanted to celebrate her birthday
____ with her grandparents
____ aunts
____ uncles
____ and cousins around her.

Level: Three

____ They had sent presents
____ but she couldn't thank them in person.
____ They wouldn't watch her blow out candles.
____ She couldn't listen to stories
____ her grandparents' stories
____ about growing up
____ in Italy
____ and Cuba.
____ They wouldn't sing together.

Events

____ Mama made Rosa's favorite meal.
____ Mother,
____ Father,
____ and Jose sang "Happy Birthday."
____ Rosa made a wish.
____ "I know I won't get it,"
____ she said to herself,
____ "but I'm going to wish for it anyway."
____ She blew out all the candles.
____ Rosa's father gave her the first present.
____ It was a videotape.
____ He put the tape into the player.
____ On the television screen
____ was the rest of Rosa's family
____ smiling
____ and waving
____ and wishing her a happy birthday.
____ Each person asked Rosa
____ to open the present they sent.
____ They explained
____ why they chose that gift for Rosa.
____ Her family sang favorite songs
____ and Rosa
____ her mother
____ her father
____ and Jose joined in.
____ Grandfather spoke to Rosa.
____ "This is a new story,
____ one you have never heard before.
____ I am going to tell it
____ as a special birthday gift.
____ It's about my first birthday
____ in this country
____ when I was very lonely.

____ It is about how I met your grandmother."
____ When Grandfather was finished,
____ he
____ and Grandmother blew Rosa a kiss.
____ The tape was finished.

Resolution

____ Rosa felt wonderful.
____ "I didn't think I would get my wish
____ but I did,"
____ she said.
____ When Mama
____ and Papa came to say goodnight,
____ they found Rosa asleep
____ with the videotape next to her.
____ It had been the best birthday ever.

Other ideas recalled, including inferences:

Questions for A Special Birthday for Rosa

1. The story took place on what day?
   Explicit: Rosa's birthday

2. At the beginning of the story what was Rosa's problem?
   Implicit: she would not be celebrating her birthday with her whole family

3. How old was Rosa on this birthday?
   Implicit: eight

4. What did Rosa wish for before she blew out the candles?
   Implicit: that she would be able to spend her birthday with her whole family

5. What was on the videotape?
   Explicit: the rest of Rosa's family wishing her a happy birthday

6. What special birthday gift did her grandfather give her?
   Explicit: he told her a story about when he came to the United States and how he met her grandmother

7. How did the videotape help to solve Rosa's problem?
   Implicit: it brought her family to her, it helped her miss the family less

8. At the end of the story where was the videotape?
   Explicit: in bed beside Rosa

Without Look-Backs

Number Correct Explicit: ____

Number Correct Implicit: ____

Total: ____

____ Independent: 8 correct

____ Instructional: 6–7 correct

____ Frustration: 0–5 correct

With Look-Backs

Number Correct Explicit: ____

Number Correct Implicit: ____

Total: ____

____ Independent: 8 correct

____ Instructional: 6–7 correct

____ Frustration: 0–5 correct

Level 3

Level: Three

Narrative

Concept Questions:

Why do people go to libraries?

_____

_____

_____ (3-2-1-0)

What does "getting animals to come to you" mean to you?

_____

_____

_____ (3-2-1-0)

What can waves do?

_____

_____

_____ (3-2-1-0)

What sounds does a dolphin make?

_____

_____

_____ (3-2-1-0)

Score: _____ /12 = _____ %

_____ FAM _____ UNFAM

Prediction:

_____

_____

The Friend

Once upon a time there was a boy named Mark. Mark loved to go to the ocean and play his flute. One day he was playing his flute when a school of dolphins swam by. They leaped in the air every 30 seconds. Mark could almost predict when they would leap again. He watched them for a long time because he was so interested in their play. That day he decided that he wanted to learn more about dolphins. Mark went to the library.

The next weekend he took a boat and rowed out about as far as he had seen the dolphins before. He started playing his flute, trying to mimic the pulsed sounds he had heard on tapes of dolphin sounds. He had learned that they make two kinds of pulsed sounds. One kind is called sonar and is used to locate dolphins and objects. The other kind of sound is a burst pulse that tells the emotional state of the dolphin. Mark was trying to mimic sonar. Soon, about 400 yards away, he saw the roll of the dolphins. The boat bounced in the waves as the dolphins came closer. They seemed to be curious about the sounds coming from the boat. Suddenly, the boat tipped sharply and Mark fell out. Somehow he held on to his flute. Mark was a good swimmer, but he was too far from land to swim. The only thing to do was to try to mimic the sound of a dolphin in trouble. Maybe then the dolphins would help him to land. Kicking strongly, he kept himself up above the water. He blew high, burst pulse sounds. Just when he was about to go under water, he felt a push against his leg. Again and again a dolphin pushed him. She managed to keep his face above water as she gently pushed him to shore. Mark couldn't believe what was happening. He got safely to shore, although the boat was never seen again. As he sat on the beach, still shaking from fear, he realized that he had reached his goal. He had surely learned a lot about dolphins that day! (357 words)

Number of Total Miscues
(Total Accuracy): _____

Number of Meaning-Change Miscues
(Total Acceptability): _____

Total Accuracy			Total Acceptability
0–8 miscues	____ Independent	____	0–8 miscues
9–37 miscues	____ Instructional	____	9–19 miscues
38+ miscues	____ Frustration	____	20+ miscues

Rate: 357 × 60 = 21,420/____ seconds = ____ WPM

Retelling Scoring Sheet for The Friend

Setting/Background
____ There was a boy
____ named Mark.
____ Mark loved
____ to go
____ to the ocean
____ and play his flute.
____ A school
____ of dolphins swam by.
____ They leaped

____ every 30 seconds.

Goal
____ Mark wanted
____ to learn more
____ about dolphins.

Events
____ Mark went to the library.
____ He took a boat
____ and rowed out
____ where he had seen the dolphins.
____ He played his flute
____ to mimic sounds
____ pulsed sounds
____ of dolphins.
____ One sound is sonar
____ and is used to locate things.
____ Another kind is a pulse
____ burst pulse
____ that tells the emotional state
____ of the dolphin.
____ Mark saw the roll
____ of the dolphins.
____ The boat bounced
____ in the waves
____ as the dolphins came closer.
____ The boat tipped.
____ Mark fell out.
____ He held on to his flute.
____ Mark was a good swimmer
____ but he was too far
____ from land.
____ He tried
____ to mimic the sound
____ of the dolphin
____ in trouble
____ so the dolphin would help him.
____ Kicking
____ strongly
____ he kept himself
____ above water.
____ He blew sounds.
____ A dolphin pushed him
____ to shore.

Level: Three

Resolution

___ He got safely
___ to shore.
___ He realized
___ he had learned a lot
___ about dolphins.

Other ideas recalled, including inferences:

Questions for The Friend

1. What instrument did Mark play?
   Explicit: the flute

2. Where did Mark go to learn more about dolphins?
   Explicit: the library

3. How did Mark learn about the dolphin sounds?
   Implicit: he read about them, he listened to tapes; If student says, "He went to the library," ask, "How did that help him learn about dolphins?"

4. What two kinds of sounds do dolphins make?
   Explicit: sonar, or sounds to locate objects, and burst pulse, or sounds to indicate emotions

5. Why was Mark trying to mimic sonar?
   Implicit: to see if the dolphins would come to him

6. Why did the boat tip over?
   Implicit: the dolphins came close enough to cause waves

7. What did Mark do to save himself?
   Implicit: he tried to make a burst pulse sound like a dolphin in trouble, hoping a dolphin would come to help him. *Note:* If student says, "He kicked strongly," ask "What other thing did Mark do?"

8. How did Mark get to shore?
   Explicit: a dolphin pushed him to shore

Without Look-Backs

Number Correct Explicit: ____

Number Correct Implicit: ____

Total: ____

____ Independent: 8 correct

____ Instructional: 6–7 correct

____ Frustration: 0–5 correct

With Look-Backs

Number Correct Explicit: ____

Number Correct Implicit: ____

Total: ____

____ Independent: 8 correct

____ Instructional: 6–7 correct

____ Frustration: 0–5 correct

Expository

Concept Questions:

What is the cat family?

_____

_____

_____ (3-2-1-0)

How do cats protect themselves?

_____

_____

_____ (3-2-1-0)

What does a cat's tongue look like?

_____

_____

_____ (3-2-1-0)

What are cat sounds?

_____

_____

_____ (3-2-1-0)

Score: _____ /12 = _____ %

_____ FAM _____ UNFAM

Prediction:

_____

_____

Cats: Lions and Tigers in Your House

House cats, lions , and tigers are part of the same family. When animals are part of the same family, they are alike in many ways.

House cats are like lions and tigers in many ways, too. When kittens are first born, they drink milk from their mothers. Lions and tigers drink milk from their mothers, too. When kittens are born, they have claws just like big cats. Claws are used by lions , tigers, and kittens to help them keep away enemies. As kittens get bigger, they learn to hunt from their mother. House cats hunt in the same way that lions and tigers do. They hide and lie very still. When the animal they are hunting comes close, they jump on it and grab it by the back of the neck. Cats kill other animals by shaking them and breaking their necks.

Lions, tigers, and house cats show when they are afraid in the same ways, too. Their fur puffs up, making them look bigger. They hiss and spit, too. Those are their ways of saying, "I'm afraid, don't come closer."

A cat's tongue has many uses. Because it is rough with little bumps on it, it can be used as a spoon. A cat drinks milk by lapping it. Because of the bumps, the milk stays on the tongue until the cat can swallow it. If you feel the top of a cat's tongue, it is rough . This makes the tongue good for brushing the cat's hair. Lions and tigers clean themselves with their tongues just like house cats do. (261 words)

Level: Three

Retelling Scoring Sheet for Cats: Lions and Tigers in Your House

Main Idea

____ Cats,
____ lions,
____ and tigers
____ are part of the same family.
____ They are alike
____ in many ways.

Details

____ When kittens are first born,
____ they drink milk
____ from their mothers.
____ Lions
____ and tigers
____ drink milk
____ from their mothers.
____ Kittens have claws.
____ Lions,
____ tigers,
____ and kittens use claws
____ to keep away enemies.
____ Cats hunt
____ in the same way
____ that lions
____ and tigers do.
____ They jump on the animal

____ and grab it
____ by the neck.
____ Cats kill animals
____ by breaking their necks.
____ When lions,
____ tigers,
____ and cats are afraid,
____ their fur puffs up.
____ They hiss
____ and spit.
____ Because a cat's tongue is rough
____ with bumps,
____ it can be used
____ as a spoon.
____ A cat drinks milk
____ by lapping it.
____ Because of the bumps,
____ the milk stays
____ on the tongue
____ until the cat can swallow it.
____ Lions
____ and tigers clean themselves
____ with their tongues
____ just like cats.

Other ideas recalled, including inferences:

Questions for Cats: Lions and Tigers in Your House

1. What is this passage mostly about?
   Implicit: that cats, lions, and tigers are alike in many ways

2. How are lions, tigers, and cats alike?
   Explicit: any one of the ways presented in the story: milk from their mothers as babies; they have claws; the way they hunt;

the way they show fear; the uses of their tongues

3. What is another way that lions, tigers, and cats are alike?
Explicit: any other of the above responses

4. What is still another way that lions, tigers, and cats are alike?
Explicit: any other of the above responses

5. What does a cat do when it is scared or trapped in a corner?
Implicit: it would hiss, spit, or puff up

6. Why is it important for cats to have claws when they're born?
Implicit: for protection from their enemies

7. Why is the top of a cat's tongue rough?
Implicit: because of the bumps on it, or so it can drink

8. Why doesn't milk fall off a cat's tongue?
Explicit: because of the bumps that make cups on the tongue

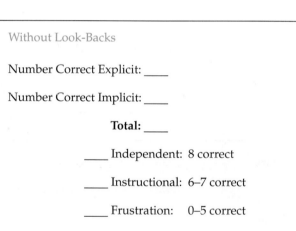

Without Look-Backs

Number Correct Explicit: ____

Number Correct Implicit: ____

        Total: ____

____ Independent: 8 correct

____ Instructional: 6–7 correct

____ Frustration: 0–5 correct

With Look-Backs

Number Correct Explicit: ____

Number Correct Implicit: ____

        Total: ____

____ Independent: 8 correct

____ Instructional: 6–7 correct

____ Frustration: 0–5 correct

Level 3

Level: Three

Expository

Concept Questions:

What does "getting to work" mean to you?

_____

_____

_____ (3-2-1-0)

What does "life in the country" mean to you?

_____

_____

_____ (3-2-1-0)

What do farm animals eat?

_____

_____

_____ (3-2-1-0)

What does "living in the suburbs" mean to you?

_____

_____

_____ (3-2-1-0)

Score: _____ /12 = _____ %

_____ FAM _____ UNFAM

Prediction:

_____

_____

Where Do People Live?

People live in different places. Some people live in a city. Others live in the country. Still other people live in between the city and the country. They live in suburbs. Why do people live in these different places?

People live in the city to be near their jobs. Cities have lots of factories, schools, and offices. People work in these buildings. If people don't want to drive a long way to their jobs, they live in the city. There are many other things to do in the city. Cities have museums and zoos. They also have many movie theaters.

People live in the country to be close to their jobs, too. Many people who live in the country are farmers. They plant crops on their land. They may sell their crops or may use them to feed the animals that live on the farm. Farmers raise cows, pigs, and chickens. The main food that these animals eat is grain. There are other things to do in the country. You can find a river to fish in or take walks in the woods. The life in the country is quiet.

People live in between the country and the city. They live in suburbs. Some people think that people who live in the suburbs have the best of both worlds. They live close to their jobs in the city. The suburbs are quieter than the city. They often have many movie theaters, too. It doesn't take as long to go to either the city or the country. The suburbs are more crowded than the country but less crowded than the city. Where people live depends upon what they like most. (288 words)

Number of Total Miscues
(Total Accuracy): _____

Number of Meaning-Change Miscues
(Total Acceptability): _____

Total Accuracy			**Total Acceptability**
0–7 miscues	____ Independent	____	0–7 miscues
8–30 miscues	____ Instructional	____	8–15 miscues
31+ miscues	____ Frustration	____	16+ miscues

Rate: 288 × 60 = 17,280/____ seconds = ____ WPM

Retelling Scoring Sheet for Where Do People Live?

Main Idea

____ People live
____ in different places.

Details

____ Some people live
____ in the city.
____ Others live
____ in the country.
____ Others live
____ in the suburbs.

Main Idea

____ People live
____ in the city
____ to be near their jobs.

Details

____ Cities have factories,
____ schools,
____ and offices.
____ People work
____ in these buildings.
____ There are many things
____ to do in the city.
____ Cities have museums

____ and zoos.
____ They have theaters
____ movie theaters.

Main Idea

____ People live
____ in the country
____ to be close to their jobs.

Details

____ Many people are farmers.
____ They plant crops.
____ Farmers raise cows,
____ pigs,
____ and chickens.
____ The food that these animals eat
____ is grain.
____ There are other things
____ to do in the country.
____ You can find a river
____ to fish in
____ or take walks
____ in the woods.
____ The life in the country
____ is quiet.

Main Idea

____ Some people think
____ that people who live in the suburbs
____ have the best of both worlds.

Details

____ They live close to their jobs
____ in the city.
____ The suburbs are quieter
____ than the city.
____ The suburbs are more crowded
____ than the country
____ but less crowded
____ than the city.

Other ideas recalled, including inferences:

Level 3

Level: Three

Questions for Where Do People Live?

1. What is this passage mostly about?
   Implicit: why people live where they do

2. Why do people live in the city?
   Explicit: to be near their jobs

3. Why do people want to live close to their jobs?
   Implicit: so they don't have to drive far to work; so they don't have to get up so early to go to work

4. Why would someone who isn't a farmer like to live in the country?
   Implicit: they like the quiet life; they like to fish or take walks; they don't like noise, crowds, etc.

5. What is one thing that the passage says you can do in the country besides farm?
   Explicit: take walks, or fish

6. What crop would be planted by farmers who raise animals?
   Implicit: grain

7. How do the city and suburbs differ?
   Explicit: the suburbs are less crowded than the city or quieter

8. According to the passage, why do people choose different places to live?
   Explicit: it depends on what they like most

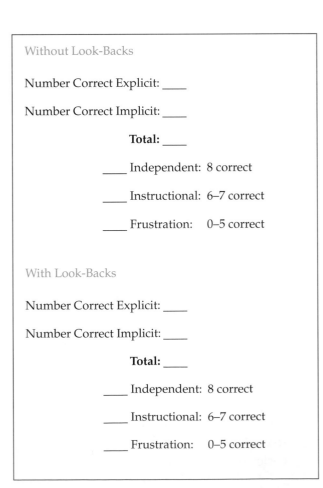

Without Look-Backs

Number Correct Explicit: _____

Number Correct Implicit: _____

Total: _____

_____ Independent: 8 correct

_____ Instructional: 6–7 correct

_____ Frustration: 0–5 correct

With Look-Backs

Number Correct Explicit: _____

Number Correct Implicit: _____

Total: _____

_____ Independent: 8 correct

_____ Instructional: 6–7 correct

_____ Frustration: 0–5 correct

Level 3

Expository

Concept Questions:

What are sheep used for?

_____

_____

_____ (3-2-1-0)

What is wool used for?

_____

_____

_____ (3-2-1-0)

What is yarn used for?

_____

_____

_____ (3-2-1-0)

Why do people get haircuts?

_____

_____

_____ (3-2-1-0)

Score: _____ /12 = _____ %

_____ FAM _____ UNFAM

Prediction:

_____

_____

Wool: From Sheep to You

Do you have a sweater? Do you know what it is made from? One fiber used to make sweaters is wool. Do you know where wool comes from? It comes from a sheep. However, many things must be done before the wool on a sheep can be woven or knitted to make clothing for you.

First, the wool must be removed from the sheep. People shear the wool off the sheep with electric clippers somewhat like a barber uses when he gives haircuts. Like our hair, the sheep's wool will grow back again. Most sheep are shorn only once a year. After the wool is removed, it must be washed very carefully to get out all the dirt. When the locks of wool dry, they are combed or carded to make all the fibers lie in the same direction. It is somewhat like combing or brushing your hair. Then the wool is formed into fine strands. These can be spun to make yarn. The yarn is knitted or woven into fabric. The fabric is made into clothing.

Yarn can also be used to knit sweaters by hand. Sweaters made from wool are very warm. They help keep you warm even when they are damp. Just think, the sweater you wear on a winter day may once have been on a sheep. (221 words)

Level: Three

Number of Total Miscues
(Total Accuracy): _____

Number of Meaning-Change Miscues
(Total Acceptability): _____

Total Accuracy			**Total Acceptability**
0–5 miscues	____	Independent ____	0–5 miscues
6–23 miscues	____	Instructional ____	6–12 miscues
24+ miscues	____	Frustration ____	13+ miscues

Rate: 221 $\times$ 60 = 13,260/____ seconds = ____ WPM

Retelling Scoring Sheet for Wool: From Sheep to You

Main Idea

____ Many things have to be done
____ before wool can be woven
____ or knitted
____ to make clothing.

Details

____ Wool is a fiber
____ used to make sweaters.
____ It comes from a sheep.
____ The wool must be removed
____ from the sheep.
____ People shear the wool
____ off the sheep
____ with clippers
____ electric clippers
____ like a barber uses.
____ The wool will grow back again.
____ Most sheep are shorn
____ once a year.
____ After the wool is removed,
____ it must be washed
____ very carefully
____ to get out the dirt.
____ When the locks are dry,
____ they are combed

____ to make the fibers
____ lie in the same direction.
____ It is like combing
____ or brushing
____ your hair.
____ Then the wool is formed
____ into strands.
____ These can be spun
____ to make yarn.
____ The yarn is knitted
____ or woven into fabric.
____ The fabric is made
____ into clothing
____ and knitted
____ into sweaters.
____ Sweaters made
____ from wool
____ are very warm
____ even when they are damp.

Other ideas recalled, including inferences:

Questions for Wool: From Sheep to You

1. What is this passage mainly about?
   Implicit: how wool is made; what you do to wool in order to use it

2. What is the first step in the making of wool?
   Explicit: cutting it off the sheep

3. What do people use to cut wool off sheep?
   Explicit: electric clippers; electric scissors
   (*electric* must be in the answer)

4. Why can sheep give wool for many years?
   Implicit: because it grows back after it is cut off

5. What is done to the wool after it is washed and dried?
   Explicit: it is combed

6. What happens to wool fibers after they are combed?
   Explicit: the fibers lie in the same direction

7. What two different things can people do with the wool yarn?
   Implicit: knit; weave into fabric; make into clothing

8. Why would it be good to wear a wool sweater out in the snow?
   Implicit: it will keep you warm even when it's damp. *Note:* If the student omits the idea of dampness and says only, "It will keep you warm," ask "Why would it be especially warm in the snow?"

Without Look-Backs

Number Correct Explicit: ____

Number Correct Implicit: ____

Total: ____

____ Independent: 8 correct

____ Instructional: 6–7 correct

____ Frustration: 0–5 correct

With Look-Backs

Number Correct Explicit: ____

Number Correct Implicit: ____

Total: ____

____ Independent: 8 correct

____ Instructional: 6–7 correct

____ Frustration: 0–5 correct

Level 3

Johnny Appleseed

John Chapman was born in 1774 and grew up in Massachusetts. He became a farmer and learned how to grow different kinds of crops and trees. John especially liked to grow and eat apples. Many people were moving west at that time. They were heading for Ohio and Pennsylvania. John knew that apples were a good food for settlers to have. Apple trees were strong and easy to grow. Apples could be eaten raw and they could be cooked in many ways. They could also be dried for later use. So in 1797, John decided to go west. He wanted to plant apple trees for people who would build their new homes there.

John first gathered bags of apple seeds. He got many of his seeds from farmers who squeezed apples to make a drink called cider. Then, in the spring, he left for the western frontier. He planted seeds as he went along. Also, he gave them to people who knew how valuable apple trees were.

John walked many miles in all kinds of weather. He had to cross dangerous rivers and find his way through strange forests. Often he was hungry, cold, and wet. Sometimes he had to hide from unfriendly Indians. His clothes became ragged and torn. He used a sack for a shirt, and he cut out holes for the arms. He wore no shoes. But he never gave up. He guarded his precious seeds and carefully planted them where they had the best chance of growing into strong trees.

John's fame spread. He was nicknamed Johnny Appleseed. New settlers welcomed him and gratefully accepted a gift of apple seeds. Many legends grew up about Johnny Appleseed that were not always true. However, one thing is true. Thanks to Johnny Appleseed, apple trees now grow in parts of America where they once never did.

From *America's History* by B. B. Armbruster, C. L. Mitsakas, and V. R. Rogers, copyright © 1986 by Schoolhouse Press. Reprinted by permission of the publisher.

QRI–3   *Test Materials*

Amelia Earhart

Amelia Earhart was an adventurer and a pioneer in the field of flying. She did things no other woman had ever done before.

During World War I, Earhart worked as a nurse. She cared for pilots who had been hurt in the war. Earhart listened to what they said about flying. She watched planes take off and land. She knew that she, too, must fly.

In 1928, Earhart was the first woman to cross the Atlantic in a plane. But someone else flew the plane. Earhart wanted to be more than just a passenger. She wanted to fly a plane across the ocean herself. For four years, Earhart trained to be a pilot. Then, in 1932, she flew alone across the Atlantic to Ireland. The trip took over fourteen hours.

Flying may seem easy today. However, Earhart faced many dangers. Airplanes had just been invented. They were much smaller than our planes today. Mechanical problems happened quite often. There were also no computers to help her. Flying across the ocean was as frightening as sailing across it had been years before. Earhart knew the dangers she faced. However, she said, "I want to do it because I want to do it. Women must try to do things as men have tried. When they fail, their failure must be a challenge to others."

Earhart planned to fly around the world. She flew more than twenty thousand miles. Then, her plane disappeared somewhere over the huge Pacific Ocean. People searched for a long time. Finally they gave up. Earhart and her plane were never found.

Adapted from *Scott, Foresman Social Studies, Grade 4: Regions of Our Country and Our World* (Glenview, Ill.: Scott, Foresman and Co., 1983), p. 83.

Sequoyah

Sequoyah was a Cherokee Indian who lived in Tennessee in the 1800s. One day he met some Americans who were not Indians. He noticed that they looked at something he had never seen before, large white leaves with black marks on them. It seemed to Sequoyah as if the marks were talking to the people.

Sequoyah decided he would try to create talking leaves for the Cherokee people. He spent all of his time working. He drew his signs and pictures on tree bark. He thought the people would be excited about what he was trying to do, but they were not. Once, when he was away from home, his wife burned the talking leaves. She did not realize they were important, and others in the village agreed.

Sequoyah continued to work on his signs. When he finished, he had eighty-six signs. Now the time had come to test the signs. Sequoyah and his daughter attended a meeting with Cherokee leaders from many villages. Sequoyah was sent out of the lodge. The chiefs gave messages to his daughter. She wrote down whatever they said. Sequoyah was called back into the lodge. He took the paper and read aloud what was written. It was exactly what the chiefs had said. It worked! Now the Cherokee had a written language all their own.

Within months, hundreds of Cherokee knew the new language. Soon the Cherokee nation had a newspaper and many books. Cherokees from different regions could now communicate with one another. Sequoyah became a great hero. He had given the Cherokee a wonderful gift, the written word.

Adapted from *Scott, Foresman Social Studies, Grade 4: Regions of Our Country and Our World* (Glenview, Ill.: Scott, Foresman and Co., 1983), p. 53.

The Busy Beaver

Have you ever heard someone say "busy as a beaver"? Beavers are very busy animals and they are master builders. This furry animal spends its life working and building. As soon as a beaver leaves its family, it has much work to do.

First, the beaver must build a dam. It uses sticks, leaves, and mud to block a stream. The beaver uses its two front teeth to get the sticks. The animal uses its large flat tail to pack mud into place. A pond forms behind the dam. The beaver spends most of its life near this pond.

In the middle of the beaver's pond is a large mound. This mound of mud and twigs is the beaver's lodge or house. The beaver's family is safe in the lodge because it is well hidden. The doorway to the lodge is under the water. After the lodge is built, the beaver still cannot rest. More trees must be cut down to be used as food for the coming winter. Sometimes there will be no more trees around the pond. Then the beaver has to find trees elsewhere. These trees will have to be carried to the pond. The beaver might build canals leading deep into the forest.

All this work changes the land. As trees are cut down, birds, squirrels, and other animals may have to find new homes. Animals that feed on trees lose their food supply. The pond behind the dam floods part of the ground. Animals that used to live there have to move. However, the new environment becomes a home for different kinds of birds, fish, and plants. All this happens because of the very busy beaver.

Adapted from M. R. Cohen, B. J. Del Giorno, J. D. Harlan, A. J. McCormack, and J. R. Staver, *Scott, Foresman Science, Grade 4* (Glenview, Ill.: Scott, Foresman and Co., 1984), p. 287.

Saudi Arabia

Saudi Arabia is a large country. It is about the size of the United States east of the Mississippi River. But it is a country that has not one lake or river!

The capital is a city of both new and old. There are air-conditioned buildings and high-rise apartments. There are also old buildings made of mud brick. Families often sleep on the roofs at night to escape the heat. They don't worry that it will rain. Saudi Arabia has very dry, very hot weather. Where do people find water? They dig wells deep into the earth. The capital, a city of many people, gets water from many of these wells.

Outside the capital lies the world's largest sand desert. Strong winds blow the sand. From the air, the sand dunes look like waves of a great tan ocean. On the ground, the feel of sand covers everything. A few islands of palm trees spring up out of the desert. They mean only one thing, water. These islands of life are the oases of Saudi Arabia, which form around the springs or wells. Many people live near the oases in low mud houses. They plant gardens and orchards and raise camels.

Many groups of people live on the desert itself. They are the Bedouin, who move from place to place in search of food and water for their animals. The Bedouin depend on camels and goats for milk and meat. They use the animals' hair to make rugs and cloth for tents. The Bedouin know no boundaries. The open desert has been their home for generations.

Adapted from *Scott, Foresman Social Studies, Grade 4: Regions of Our Country and Our World* (Glenview, Ill.: Scott, Foresman and Co., 1983), pp. 244–245.

The City of Cahokia

Cahokia was once a city in what is now the state of Illinois. Nobody lives in Cahokia now. There are no buildings. How did people find out about Cahokia?

Cahokia was discovered because of a group of mounds or hills. These hills did not look like regular hills. It seemed that people might have built them.

Archaeologists dug into the hills. They discovered a buried city. They found remains of large buildings. Between the hills, they found many smaller buildings. Some contained small rooms without any windows. In the middle of the buildings was a large open space. A large circle of post holes was found. A thick post fence was around the hills and the houses.

Archaeologists learned about Cahokia by studying all the evidence. Cahokia was a busy city about a thousand years ago. Many of the people were farmers. They probably grew corn, beans, and squash. The city had a strong government. A strong government would be needed to build the hills and the fence. Archaeologists think the circle of holes might have been a huge calendar. It would tell the direction of the sun. The sun told people when to plant and harvest.

The people of Cahokia probably gathered together in large groups. Perhaps they prayed or listened to their leaders. That was what the large open space might have been used for. Cahokia might have had enemies. They built the fence to keep them out.

We don't know everything about Cahokia. However, thanks to archaeologists, we know it is more than a few strange hills.

Adapted from *Scott, Foresman Social Studies, Grade 4: Regions of Our Country and Our World* (Glenview, Ill.: Scott, Foresman and Co., 1983), pp. 22–24.

Narrative

Concept Questions:

Who was Johnny Appleseed?

_____

_____

_____ (3-2-1-0)

Why do people plant fruit trees in certain places?

_____

_____

_____ (3-2-1-0)

Why do people plant apple trees?

_____

_____

_____ (3-2-1-0)

What does "making apple cider" mean to you?

_____

_____

_____ (3-2-1-0)

Score: _____ /12 = _____ %

_____ FAM _____ UNFAM

Prediction:

_____

_____

Johnny Appleseed

John Chapman was born in 1774 and grew up in Massachusetts. He became a farmer and learned how to grow different kinds of crops and trees. John especially liked to grow and eat apples. Many people were moving west at that time. They were heading for Ohio and Pennsylvania. John knew that apples were a good food for settlers to have. Apple trees were strong and easy to grow. Apples could be eaten raw and they could be cooked in many ways. They could also be dried for later use. So in 1797, John decided to go west. He wanted to plant apple trees for people who would build their new homes there.

John first gathered bags of apple seeds. He got many of his seeds from farmers who squeezed apples to make a drink called cider. Then, in the spring, he left for the western frontier. He planted seeds as he went along. Also, he gave them to people who knew how valuable apple trees were.

John walked many miles in all kinds of weather. He had to cross dangerous rivers and find his way through strange forests. Often he was hungry, cold, and wet. Sometimes he had to hide from unfriendly Indians. His clothes became ragged and torn. He used a sack for a shirt, and he cut out holes for the arms. He wore no shoes. But he never gave up. He guarded his precious seeds and carefully planted them where they had the best chance of growing into strong trees.

John's <u>fame</u> spread. He was nicknamed Johnny Appleseed. New <u>settlers</u> welcomed him and gratefully accepted a gift of apple seeds. Many legends grew up about Johnny Appleseed that were not always true. However, one thing is true. Thanks to Johnny Appleseed, apple trees now grow in parts of America where they once never did. (308 words)

From *America's History* by B. B. Armbruster, C. L. Mitsakas, and V. R. Rogers, copyright © 1986 by Schoolhouse Press. Reprinted by permission of the publisher.

Number of Total Miscues
(Total Accuracy): _____

Number of Meaning-Change Miscues
(Total Acceptability): _____

Total Accuracy			**Total Acceptability**
0–7 miscues	____ Independent	____	0–7 miscues
8–32 miscues	____ Instructional	____	8–16 miscues
32+ miscues	____ Frustration	____	17+ miscues

Rate: 308 × 60 = 18,480/____ seconds = ____ WPM

Retelling Scoring Sheet for Johnny Appleseed

Setting/Background

___ John Chapman was born
___ in 1774.
___ He became a farmer
___ and grew crops.
___ John liked
___ to grow

___ and eat apples.
___ People were moving west.
___ Apples were a good food
___ for settlers to have.

Goal

___ John decided
___ to go west.
___ He wanted
___ to plant apple trees.

Events

___ John got many seeds
___ from farmers
___ who squeezed apples
___ to make a drink
___ called cider.
___ He left
___ for the frontier.
___ He planted seeds
___ as he went along.
___ He gave them away.
___ John walked miles.
___ He crossed rivers
___ and went through forests.
___ He was hungry
___ and wet.
___ He had to hide
___ from Indians
___ unfriendly Indians.
___ His clothes were torn.
___ He used a sack
___ for a shirt
___ and he cut out holes
___ for the arms.
___ He wore no shoes.

Resolution

___ John's fame spread.
___ He was nicknamed
___ Johnny Appleseed.
___ Settlers accepted seeds
___ gratefully.
___ Thanks to Johnny Appleseed,
___ apple trees grow

____ in many parts
____ of America.

Other ideas recalled, including inferences:

Questions for Johnny Appleseed

1. What was John Chapman's main goal?
    Implicit: to plant apple trees across the country

2. Why did John choose apples to plant instead of some other fruit?
    Implicit: the trees were easy to grow; the fruit could be used in a lot of ways; he especially liked apples

3. Where did John get most of his seeds?
    Explicit: from farmers or from people who made cider

4. Why would John be able to get so many seeds from cider makers?
    Implicit: cider is a drink and you don't drink seeds; apples have a lot of seeds and you don't use seeds in cider

5. How do we know that John cared about planting apple trees?
    Implicit: he suffered hardships; he guarded the apple seeds carefully

6. How did John get to the many places he visited?
    Explicit: he walked

7. Name one hardship John suffered.
    Explicit: being hungry, cold, wet, lost, in danger from unfriendly Indians

8. Why should we thank Johnny Appleseed?
    Explicit: apple trees now grow in parts of America where they once never did

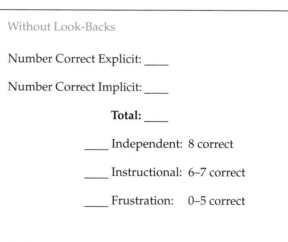

Without Look-Backs

Number Correct Explicit: ____

Number Correct Implicit: ____

Total: ____

____ Independent: 8 correct

____ Instructional: 6–7 correct

____ Frustration: 0–5 correct

With Look-Backs

Number Correct Explicit: ____

Number Correct Implicit: ____

Total: ____

____ Independent: 8 correct

____ Instructional: 6–7 correct

____ Frustration: 0–5 correct

Level 4

Level: Four

Narrative

Amelia Earhart

Amelia Earhart was an <u>adventurer</u> and a pioneer in the field of flying. She did things no other woman had ever done before.

During World War I, Earhart worked as a nurse. She cared for <u>pilots</u> who had been hurt in the war. Earhart listened to what they said about flying. She watched planes take off and land. She knew that she, too, must fly.

In 1928, Earhart was the first woman to cross the Atlantic in a plane. But someone else flew the plane. Earhart wanted to be more than just a <u>passenger</u>. She wanted to fly a plane across the <u>ocean</u> herself. For four years, Earhart trained to be a <u>pilot</u>. Then, in 1932, she flew alone across the Atlantic to Ireland. The trip took over fourteen hours.

Flying may seem easy today. However, Earhart faced many dangers. Airplanes had just been <u>invented</u>. They were much smaller than our planes today. Mechanical problems happened quite often. There were also no computers to help her. Flying across the <u>ocean</u> was as frightening as sailing across it had been years before. Earhart knew the dangers she faced. However, she said, "I want to do it because I want to do it. Women must try to do things as men have tried. When they fail, their failure must be a challenge to others."

Earhart planned to fly around the world. She flew more than twenty thousand miles. Then, her plane disappeared somewhere over

Level: Four

the huge Pacific Ocean. People searched for a long time. Finally they gave up. Earhart and her plane were never found. (263 words)

Adapted from *Scott, Foresman Social Studies, Grade 4: Regions of Our Country and Our World* (Glenview, Ill.: Scott, Foresman and Co., 1983), p. 83.

Number of Total Miscues
(Total Accuracy): _____

Number of Meaning-Change Miscues
(Total Acceptability): _____

Total Accuracy		**Total Acceptability**
0–6 miscues ____	Independent ____	0–6 miscues
7–27 miscues ____	Instructional ____	7–14 miscues
28+ miscues ____	Frustration ____	15+ miscues

Rate: 263 × 60 = 15,780/____ seconds = ____ WPM

Retelling Scoring Sheet for Amelia Earhart

Setting/Background

____ Amelia Earhart was an adventurer.
____ During World War I
____ she was a nurse.
____ She cared for pilots
____ who had been hurt.
____ Earhart watched planes
____ take off
____ and land.

Goal

____ She knew
____ that she must fly.
____ Earhart was the first woman
____ to cross
____ the Atlantic

____ in a plane.
____ Someone else flew the plane.
____ Earhart wanted to be more
____ than a passenger.
____ She wanted
____ to fly a plane
____ across the ocean.

Events

____ Earhart trained
____ to be a pilot.
____ In 1932
____ she flew
____ alone
____ across the Atlantic
____ to Ireland.
____ Earhart faced dangers.
____ Airplanes were smaller.
____ Problems happened often.
____ There were no computers.
____ Earhart said
____ women must try
____ to do things
____ as men have tried.
____ Earhart planned
____ to fly
____ around the world.

Resolution

____ Her plane disappeared
____ over the ocean
____ the Pacific Ocean.
____ People searched
____ for a long time.
____ They gave up.
____ Earhart
____ and her plane were
____ never found.

Other ideas recalled, including inferences:

Level: Four

1. What was Amelia Earhart's main goal?
   Implicit: to fly; to do things that were challenging

2. What was Amelia Earhart doing in a plane when she first crossed the Atlantic?
   Explicit: she was a passenger

3. How long did it take Amelia Earhart when she flew alone across the Atlantic?
   Explicit: over fourteen hours

4. Why would flying *alone* across the Atlantic be an especially dangerous thing to do?
   Implicit: it was a long trip; there was no one to help with problems; there was no one to help her stay awake or give her a break

5. What was one of the dangers of flying in those early days?
   Explicit: small planes; mechanical problems; no computers

6. How do we know Amelia Earhart believed in equal rights for women?
   Implicit: she said women should try to do things just as men have tried

7. What was Amelia Earhart trying to do when her plane disappeared?
   Explicit: fly around the world

8. Why do you think her plane was never found?
   Implicit: probably sank in the ocean; ocean was so big; plane was very small

---

Without Look-Backs

Number Correct Explicit: ____

Number Correct Implicit: ____

Total: ____

____ Independent: 8 correct

____ Instructional: 6–7 correct

____ Frustration: 0–5 correct

With Look-Backs

Number Correct Explicit: ____

Number Correct Implicit: ____

Total: ____

____ Independent: 8 correct

____ Instructional: 6–7 correct

____ Frustration: 0–5 correct

Level 4

Narrative

Concept Questions:

Who was Sequoyah?

_____

_____

_____ (3-2-1-0)

What are alphabets used for?

_____

_____

_____ (3-2-1-0)

Why do people write?

_____

_____

_____ (3-2-1-0)

What does "finishing something that is difficult" mean to you?

_____

_____

_____ (3-2-1-0)

Score: _____ /12 = _____ %

_____ FAM _____ UNFAM

Prediction:

_____

_____

Sequoyah

Sequoyah was a Cherokee Indian who lived in Tennessee in the 1800s. One day he met some Americans who were not Indians.

He noticed that they looked at something he had never seen before, large white leaves with black marks on them. It seemed to Sequoyah as if the marks were talking to the people.

Sequoyah decided he would try to create talking leaves for the Cherokee people. He spent all of his time working. He drew his signs and pictures on tree bark. He thought the people would be excited about what he was trying to do, but they were not. Once, when he was away from home, his wife burned the talking leaves. She did not realize they were important, and others in the village agreed.

Sequoyah continued to work on his signs. When he finished, he had eighty-six signs. Now the time had come to test the signs. Sequoyah and his daughter attended a meeting with Cherokee leaders from many villages. Sequoyah was sent out of the lodge. The chiefs gave messages to his daughter. She wrote down whatever they said. Sequoyah was called back into the lodge. He took the paper and read aloud what was written. It was exactly what the chiefs had said. It worked! Now the Cherokee had a written language all their own.

Within months, hundreds of Cherokee knew the new language. Soon the Cherokee nation had a newspaper and many books.

Cherokees from different regions could now communicate with one another. Sequoyah became a great hero. He had given the Cherokee a wonderful gift, the written word. (266 words)

Adapted from *Scott, Foresman Social Studies, Grade 4: Regions of Our Country and Our World* (Glenville, Ill.: Scott, Foresman and Co., 1983), p. 53.

Number of Total Miscues
(Total Accuracy): _____

Number of Meaning-Change Miscues
(Total Acceptability): _____

Total Accuracy			**Total Acceptability**
0–6 miscues	____ Independent	____	0–6 miscues
7–27 miscues	____ Instructional	____	7–14 miscues
28+ miscues	____ Frustration	____	15+ miscues

Rate: 266 × 60 = 15,960 / ____ seconds = ____ WPM

Retelling Scoring Sheet for Sequoyah

Setting/Background

____ Sequoyah was an Indian
____ a Cherokee Indian.
____ He met some Americans
____ who were not Indians.
____ They looked at leaves
____ large leaves
____ white leaves
____ with marks on them
____ black marks.
____ It seemed to Sequoyah
____ as if the marks were talking
____ to the people.

Goal

____ Sequoyah decided
____ he would create leaves
____ talking leaves
____ for the people
____ the Cherokee people.

Events

____ He drew his signs
____ and pictures
____ on tree bark.
____ When he was away
____ his wife burned the leaves.
____ She did not realize
____ they were important.
____ Sequoyah continued to work.
____ When he finished
____ he had signs.
____ eighty-six signs.
____ The time had come
____ to test the signs.
____ Sequoyah
____ and his daughter attended a meeting
____ with leaders
____ Cherokee leaders.
____ Sequoyah was sent out
____ of the lodge.
____ The chiefs gave messages
____ to his daughter.
____ She wrote down what they said.
____ Sequoyah was called back.
____ He read what was written
____ exactly what the chiefs said.

Resolution

____ The Cherokee had a language
____ a written language
____ all their own.
____ The nation had a newspaper
____ and books.
____ Cherokees could communicate with
____ Cherokees
____ from different regions.

Level 4

___ Sequoyah became a great hero.
___ He gave a gift
___ a wonderful gift
___ to the Cherokee,
___ the written word.

Other ideas recalled, including inferences:

Questions for Sequoyah

1. What was Sequoyah's main goal?
   Implicit: he wanted to make a written language for his people; he wanted to create talking leaves

2. What might have been the objects that Sequoyah thought were large white leaves with black marks?
   Implicit: white paper with black letters/words

3. What did Sequoyah use to draw on?
   Explicit: tree bark

4. Why did Sequoyah's wife burn his signs?
   Explicit: she didn't know they were important

5. How do we know that Sequoyah did not give up easily?
   Implicit: he kept on working even when his signs were burned and others did not agree with him

6. Who tested the signs with Sequoyah and his daughter?
   Explicit: Cherokee chiefs

7. What did the Cherokee nation do with their new language?
   Explicit: make newspapers and books

8. Why was the written word an important gift for the Cherokee?
   Implicit: Cherokees from different regions could now keep in touch

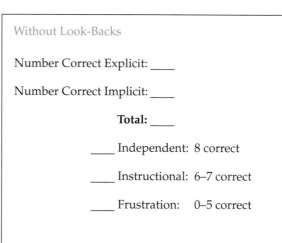

Without Look-Backs

Number Correct Explicit: ____

Number Correct Implicit: ____

Total: ____

___ Independent: 8 correct

___ Instructional: 6–7 correct

___ Frustration: 0–5 correct

With Look-Backs

Number Correct Explicit: ____

Number Correct Implicit: ____

Total: ____

___ Independent: 8 correct

___ Instructional: 6–7 correct

___ Frustration: 0–5 correct

Level 4

Level: Four

Expository

The Busy Beaver

Have you ever heard someone say "busy" as a beaver"? Beavers are very busy animals and they are master builders. This furry animal spends its life working and building. As soon as a beaver leaves its family, it has much work to do.

First, the beaver must build a dam. It uses sticks, leaves, and mud to block a stream. The beaver uses its two front teeth to get the sticks. The animal uses its large flat tail to pack mud into place. A pond forms behind the dam. The beaver spends most of its life near this pond.

In the middle of the beaver's pond is a large mound. This mound of mud and twigs is the beaver's lodge or house. The beaver's family is safe in the lodge because it is well hidden. The doorway to the lodge is under the water. After the lodge is built, the beaver still cannot rest. More trees must be cut down to be used as food for the coming winter. Sometimes there will be no more trees around the pond. Then the beaver has to find trees elsewhere. These trees will have to be carried to the pond. The beaver might build canals leading deep into the forest.

All this work changes the land. As trees are cut down, birds, squirrels, and other animals may have to find new homes. Animals that feed on trees lose their food supply. The pond behind the dam floods part of the ground. Animals that used to live there have to move.

Level: Four

However, the new environment becomes a home for different kinds of birds, fish, and plants. All this happens because of the very <u>busy</u> beaver. (281 words)

Adapted from M. R. Cohen, B. J. Del Giorno, J. D. Harlan, A. J. McCormack, and J. R. Staver, *Scott, Foresman Science, Grade 4* (Glenview, Ill.: Scott, Foresman and Co., 1984), p. 287.

Number of Total Miscues
(Total Accuracy): _____

Number of Meaning-Change Miscues
(Total Acceptability): _____

Total Accuracy			**Total Acceptability**
0–7 miscues	____	Independent ____	0–7 miscues
8–29 miscues	____	Instructional ____	8–15 miscues
30+ miscues	____	Frustration ____	16+ miscues

Rate: 281 × 60 = 16,860/____ seconds = ____ WPM

Retelling Scoring Sheet for The Busy Beaver

Main Idea

____ Have you heard
____ "busy as a beaver"?
____ Beavers are animals
____ busy animals
____ and builders
____ master builders.

Details

____ As soon as a beaver leaves its family,
____ it has much work to do.
____ The beaver builds a dam.
____ It uses sticks,
____ leaves,
____ and mud

____ to block a stream.
____ The beaver uses its teeth
____ its front teeth
____ to get sticks.
____ The animal uses its tail
____ to pack mud.
____ A pond forms
____ behind the dam.
____ The beaver spends its life
____ near the pond.
____ The beaver's home is a mound
____ in the pond.
____ The family is safe
____ because the lodge is well hidden.
____ The doorway
____ to the lodge
____ is under the water.
____ Trees are cut down
____ to be used as food
____ for the winter.
____ Sometimes there will be no trees
____ around the pond.
____ The beaver has to find trees
____ and carry them
____ to the pond.
____ The beaver might build canals.

Main Idea

____ This changes the land.

Details

____ As trees are cut,
____ birds,
____ squirrels,
____ and animals have to find new homes.
____ Animals lose their food supply.
____ The pond floods the land.
____ Animals have to move.
____ A new environment becomes home
____ for different birds
____ and fish.

Other ideas recalled, including inferences:

Questions for The Busy Beaver

1. What is the passage mainly about?
   Implicit: how a beaver keeps busy; what a beaver does

2. According to the passage, what are the beaver's front teeth used for?
   Explicit: to get the sticks

3. Describe the beaver's tail.
   Explicit: large and flat

4. Why does the beaver build a dam?
   Implicit: to make a pond or to make a place for his lodge

5. What is the beaver's lodge or house made of?
   Explicit: mud and sticks

6. Why is the doorway to the beaver's house under the water?
   Implicit: it is safer and more hidden; so enemies can't get in

7. What does the beaver eat during the winter?
   Explicit: trees

8. Why might some people dislike beavers?
   Implicit: they change the land by flooding; they drive out animals; they cut down too many trees

Without Look-Backs

Number Correct Explicit: ____

Number Correct Implicit: ____

Total: ____

____ Independent: 8 correct

____ Instructional: 6–7 correct

____ Frustration: 0–5 correct

With Look-Backs

Number Correct Explicit: ____

Number Correct Implicit: ____

Total: ____

____ Independent: 8 correct

____ Instructional: 6–7 correct

____ Frustration: 0–5 correct

Level 4

Expository

Concept Questions:

What is Saudi Arabia?

_____

_____

_____ (3-2-1-0)

What are problems of living in the desert?

_____

_____

_____ (3-2-1-0)

What does "raising animals in the desert" mean to you?

_____

_____

_____ (3-2-1-0)

What are oases?

_____

_____

_____ (3-2-1-0)

Score: _____ /12 = _____ %

_____ FAM _____ UNFAM

Prediction:

_____

_____

Saudi Arabia

Saudi Arabia is a large country. It is about the size of the United States east of the Mississippi River. But it is a country that has not one lake or river!

The capital is a city of both new and old. There are air-conditioned buildings and high-rise apartments. There are also old buildings made of mud brick. Families often sleep on the roofs at night to escape the heat. They don't worry that it will rain. Saudi Arabia has very dry, very hot weather. Where do people find water? They dig wells deep into the earth. The capital, a city of many people, gets water from many of these wells.

Outside the capital lies the world's largest sand desert. Strong winds blow the sand. From the air, the sand dunes look like waves of a great tan ocean. On the ground, the feel of sand covers everything. A few islands of palm trees spring up out of the desert. They mean only one thing, water. These islands of life are the oases of Saudi Arabia, which form around the springs or wells. Many people live near the oases in low mud houses. They plant gardens and orchards and raise camels.

Many groups of people live on the desert itself. They are the Bedouin, who move from place to place in search of food and water for their animals. The Bedouin depend on camels and goats for milk and meat. They use the animals' hair to make rugs and cloth for tents. The Bedouin know no boundaries. The open

Level: Four

<u>desert</u> has been their home for generations.

(265 words)

Adapted from *Scott, Foresman Social Studies, Grade 4: Regions of Our Country and Our World* (Glenview, Ill.: Scott, Foresman and Co., 1983), p. 244–245.

Number of Total Miscues
(Total Accuracy): _____

Number of Meaning-Change Miscues
(Total Acceptability): _____

Total Accuracy				Total Acceptability
0–6 miscues	____	Independent	____	0–6 miscues
7–27 miscues	____	Instructional	____	7–14 miscues
28+ miscues	____	Frustration	____	15+ miscues

Rate: 265 × 60 = 15,900/____ seconds = ____ WPM

Retelling Scoring Sheet for Saudi Arabia

Main Idea

____ Saudi Arabia is a country
____ a large country.

Details

____ It is the size
____ of the United States
____ east of the Mississippi.
____ It does not have one lake
____ or river.

Main Idea

____ The capital is a city of
____ old
____ and new.

Details

____ There are buildings
____ air-conditioned buildings
____ and apartments
____ high-rise apartments.
____ There are buildings
____ old buildings
____ made of brick
____ mud brick.
____ Families sleep
____ on roofs
____ at night
____ to escape the heat.
____ They don't worry
____ about rain.
____ Saudi Arabia has dry weather
____ and hot weather.
____ People find water
____ by digging wells
____ deep
____ in the earth.

Main Idea

____ Outside the capital
____ is a desert
____ the world's largest desert.

Details

____ Islands are on the desert
____ islands of palm trees.
____ They mean water.
____ They are oases,
____ which form around springs
____ or wells.
____ People live near the oases
____ in houses
____ mud houses.
____ People live on the desert.
____ They are the Bedouin,
____ who move
____ in search of food
____ and water
____ for their animals.
____ The Bedouin depend on camels

____ and goats

____ for milk

____ and meat.

____ They use the animals' hair

____ to make rugs

____ and cloth.

Other ideas recalled, including inferences:

Questions for Saudi Arabia

1. What is this passage mainly about?
   Implicit: how the people of Saudi Arabia live; what Saudi Arabia is like

2. Describe the weather of Saudi Arabia.
   Explicit: very hot and dry

3. Where do the people of Saudi Arabia get water?
   Explicit: from wells and/or springs

4. Why are cities in Saudi Arabia built near wells?
   Implicit: there is little water; they need water

5. What kind of houses would you find by an oasis in Saudi Arabia?
   Explicit: low mud houses

6. What animals do the Bedouin people depend on for meat and milk?
   Explicit: goats and camels

7. Why don't Bedouin live in the cities of Saudi Arabia?
   Implicit: they raise animals; they like to wander

8. Why wouldn't swimming be a popular sport in Saudi Arabia?
   Implicit: there isn't enough water for pools; there are no lakes or rivers

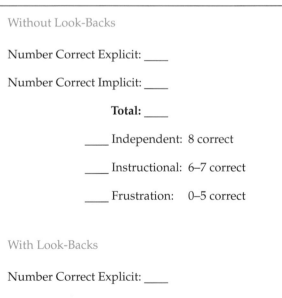

Without Look-Backs

Number Correct Explicit: ____

Number Correct Implicit: ____

Total: ____

____ Independent: 8 correct

____ Instructional: 6–7 correct

____ Frustration: 0–5 correct

With Look-Backs

Number Correct Explicit: ____

Number Correct Implicit: ____

Total: ____

____ Independent: 8 correct

____ Instructional: 6–7 correct

____ Frustration: 0–5 correct

Level: Four

Expository

```
Concept Questions:

What was Cahokia?

_____

_____

_____(3-2-1-0)

What is archaeology?

_____

_____

_____(3-2-1-0)

What are buried cities?

_____

_____

_____(3-2-1-0)

What can remains of long ago tell us?

_____

_____

_____(3-2-1-0)

Score: _____ /12 = _____ %

            _____ FAM _____ UNFAM

Prediction:

_____

_____
```

The City of Cahokia

Cahokia was once a city in what is now the state of Illinois. Nobody lives in Cahokia now.

There are no buildings. How did people find out about Cahokia?

Cahokia was discovered because of a group of mounds or hills. These hills did not look like regular hills. It seemed that people might have built them.

Archaeologists dug into the hills. They discovered a buried city. They found remains of large buildings. Between the hills, they found many smaller buildings. Some contained small rooms without any windows. In the middle of the buildings was a large open space. A large circle of post holes was found. A thick post fence was around the hills and the houses.

Archaeologists learned about Cahokia by studying all the evidence. Cahokia was a busy city about a thousand years ago. Many of the people were farmers. They probably grew corn, beans, and squash. The city had a strong government. A strong government would be needed to build the hills and the fence. Archaeologists think the circle of holes might have been a huge calendar. It would tell the direction of the sun. The sun told people when to plant and harvest.

The people of Cahokia probably gathered together in large groups. Perhaps they prayed or listened to their leaders. That was what the

Level: Four

large open space might have been used for. Cahokia might have had enemies. They built the fence to keep them out.

We don't know everything about Cahokia. However, thanks to archaeologists, we know it is more than a few strange hills. (260 words)

Adapted from *Scott, Foresman Social Studies, Grade 4: Regions of Our Country and Our World* (Glenview, Ill.: Scott, Foresman and Co., 1983), pp. 22–24.

Number of Total Miscues
(Total Accuracy): _____

Number of Meaning-Change Miscues
(Total Acceptability): _____

Total Accuracy			Total Acceptability
0–6 miscues	____ Independent	____	0–6 miscues
7–27 miscues	____ Instructional	____	7–14 miscues
28+ miscues	____ Frustration	____	15+ miscues

Rate: 260 × 60 = 15,600 / ____ seconds = ____ WPM

Retelling Scoring Sheet for The City of Cahokia

Main Idea

____ Cahokia was discovered
____ because of mounds
____ or hills.

Details

____ Cahokia was once a city
____ in Illinois.
____ Nobody lives in Cahokia.
____ The mounds did not look
____ like regular hills.

____ Archaeologists dug
____ into the hills.

Main Idea

____ They discovered a city
____ a buried city.

Details

____ They found remains
____ of buildings.
____ Some contained rooms
____ without windows.
____ In the middle of the buildings
____ they found a space
____ a large space.
____ They found a circle
____ of holes.
____ They found a fence
____ around the hills
____ and houses.

Main Idea

____ Archaeologists learned
____ about Cahokia
____ by studying the evidence.

Details

____ Cahokia was busy
____ a thousand
____ years ago.
____ The people were farmers.
____ They grew corn,
____ beans,
____ and squash.
____ The city had a government
____ a strong government
____ The circle was a calendar.
____ It told the direction
____ of the sun.
____ The sun told people
____ when to plant
____ and harvest.
____ The people gathered together.
____ They prayed
____ or listened to their leaders.

Level: Four

____ That was what the space was for.
____ Cahokia had enemies.
____ They built the fence
____ to keep them out.

Other ideas recalled, including inferences:

Questions for The City of Cahokia

1. What is this passage mainly about?
   Implicit: what the city of Cahokia was like

2. What led to the discovery of Cahokia?
   Explicit: the hills or mounds

3. What was unusual about some of the rooms?
   Implicit: they didn't have windows

4. What did the people of Cahokia probably grow?
   Explicit: corn, beans, or squash

5. How do you think archaeologists knew that the people were farmers?
   Implicit: they probably found remains of tools

6. What do the archaeologists think the huge calendar may have been used for?
   Explicit: to tell the direction of the sun; to tell when to plant and harvest

7. Why did the people build a fence around the city?
   Explicit: to keep out enemies

8. What is the job of an archaeologist?
   Implicit: to study lost cities and people

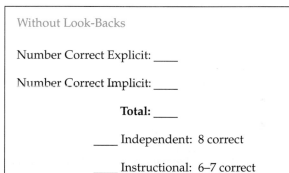

Without Look-Backs

Number Correct Explicit: ____

Number Correct Implicit: ____

Total: ____

____ Independent: 8 correct

____ Instructional: 6–7 correct

____ Frustration: 0–5 correct

With Look-Backs

Number Correct Explicit: ____

Number Correct Implicit: ____

Total: ____

____ Independent: 8 correct

____ Instructional: 6–7 correct

____ Frustration: 0–5 correct

Martin Luther King, Jr.

When Martin Luther King, Jr., was a boy, many laws would not allow black people to go to the same places as whites. Some people thought blacks were not as good as whites. Black children could not attend some schools, and certain restaurants had signs that said "whites only." Blacks could not sit in the front of a bus and, if a bus got crowded, they had to give up their seat to a white person. King did not agree with laws like these, for he believed that all people are equal. He did not think that skin color should keep people apart. Laws separating blacks and whites were unjust, and King decided to protest such laws.

Many people organized to help him. King said that they must protest in a peaceful way. King told his followers to "meet hate with love." In Montgomery, Alabama, Rosa Parks, a black woman, was arrested and fined for not giving up her seat to a white man on a bus. King led the movement to protest this action. Thousands of people refused to ride the buses. The bus companies began to lose money. In time the law was changed. King traveled to many cities. He talked to the people and led them in peaceful marches.

More and more people heard about King's peaceful protests and joined him. King led a march to our center of government, Washington, D.C., to ask that the unjust laws be changed. Finally, the United States Supreme Court agreed with King. The laws separating blacks and whites were changed. King was given the Nobel Peace Prize for his work. Today people still admire King because he fought for justice in a peaceful way. January 15 was named as a national holiday in honor of Martin Luther King, Jr.

From *Holt Social Studies, Our World, Our Regions, and Our History*, edited by JoAnn Cangemi, copyright © 1983 by Holt, Rinehart and Winston, Inc. Reprinted by permission of the publisher.

Christopher Columbus

Christopher Columbus was determined to find an all-water route to the East Indies. Discovering this would bring him fame and fortune. However, Columbus also believed that the world was round. Many people laughed at this idea. They thought the world was flat. Columbus hoped to prove his theory. He would sail west in order to reach the East.

King Ferdinand and Queen Isabella of Spain thought Columbus's idea had merit. However, Spain was fighting a costly war. Columbus had to wait seven long years. Then they gave him money to finance the expedition. It was easy to buy ships and supplies. It was more difficult to find sailors who were willing to join him. Finally, in 1492, he set sail on the uncharted, unexplored Atlantic Ocean. Columbus had ninety sailors and three ships. His ships were the Nina, the Pinta, and the Santa Maria.

After they had been out of sight of land for a month, the sailors became frightened. They did not really believe the earth was round. They were afraid to sail too far to the edge. No one had ever sailed out so far upon the "Sea of Darkness." The sailors talked of mutiny. Columbus tried to convince them that they had nothing to fear. He reminded them of the gold they would get if they finished the voyage, and he told them they would be famous. But still the sailors threatened to take over and turn back.

Just when it seemed they would go no farther, branches and leaves were seen in the water. The sailors felt much better and agreed to continue sailing. Then, on October 12, 1492, the welcome call was heard that land had been sighted. Columbus claimed the new land for Spain and named the inhabitants Indians. He mistakenly thought he had found a new route to the East. In fact, Columbus died believing he had reached the Indies.

Adapted from *The United States and Its Neighbors* by T. M. Helmus, V. E. Arnsdorf, E. A. Toppin, and N. J. G. Pounds. Copyright © 1984 by Silver, Burdett and Ginn, Inc. Used with permission.

Margaret Mead

Margaret Mead had always been interested in the ways of life of people from other lands. When Mead went to college, she took a class in anthropology. This is the study of how different people live. Mead decided to make this her career. She wanted to study primitive people before modern ways of living destroyed their culture.

Mead realized that living with a people is the only effective way to learn about them. She chose a village in Samoa to investigate. Several islands make up Samoa, which is in the Pacific Ocean. Mead worked hard to prepare for Samoa. She studied languages like the Samoan language. She read everything she could about the Samoan people. She read about their food and how they built their homes. She read about their ceremonies, their past history, and their taboos. But she wanted to learn much more.

Finally Mead arrived in Samoa. At first life was difficult for her. She was alone. She was not fluent in the Samoan language. She lived in a house with no walls and no electricity or gas. It had no running water and no bathroom. One day she said to herself, "I can't go on" in Samoan. Then she thought that maybe she could continue after all. Mead became fluent in the Samoan language, and the people soon regarded her as one of the village. She listened to their talk, their jokes, and their gossip. They told her their problems. Mead felt that being a woman assisted her in learning more about the lives of these people. Instead of having to go on hunts with the men, Mead stayed with the women. She observed the children play and learned how food was prepared. She made efforts to get the older people to recount tales of the past.

Mead learned many things from the Samoan people. She always took notes and kept careful records. These notes were used to write her first book, which was called *Coming of Age in Samoa*. It made her famous. Mead spent the rest of her life studying and writing about primitive ways of life that no longer exist today.

Adapted from *The People of Tiegs-Adams: People and Their Heritage* series, Copyright © 1983, by Silver, Burdett and Ginn, Inc. Used with permission.

The Octopus

Some people think of the octopus as a giant creature. They have seen this in science fiction movies. They think the octopus is a mean creature who attacks people and other animals. The octopus is really a shy animal. It is usually quite small.

The octopus has eight arms. Its name tells us this because "octo" means eight. The octopus uses its arms to walk on the ocean floor. Its arms are also used to capture crabs. Crabs are its favorite food. The octopus bites into the crab with its strong beak. This sends poison into the crab's body.

The octopus protects itself in three ways. First, when frightened, the octopus can push water from its body in a powerful stream. This action pushes the octopus forward very rapidly. This allows it to escape.

Second, the body of the octopus has a special sac or pouch that holds a dark, ink-like fluid. When an enemy comes close, the octopus squirts some of this fluid. It then swims away. All that the predator sees is a dark cloud in the water where the octopus was. Meanwhile, the octopus has escaped.

Finally, the octopus's body changes color when the octopus is excited or frightened. Suppose an octopus sees a crab. Patches of pink, purple, or blue will appear on the octopus's skin. Suppose the octopus sees an enemy. The octopus will completely change color. Then it seems to disappear into the background of its hiding place. It is hard for the predator to find the octopus.

Adapted from M. R. Cohen, B. J. Del Giorno, J. D. Harlan, A. J. McCormack, and J. R. Staver, *Scott, Foresman Science, Grade 5* (Glenview, Ill.: Scott, Foresman and Co., 1984), p. 31.

Getting Rid of Trash

In the past, when people wanted to get rid of their trash, they just threw it out. Sometimes they threw it into the streets or alleys, and sometimes they packed it into a wagon and dumped it near the edge of town. Open dumping caused many problems. The trash was ugly and often smelled. It attracted rats and other animals that carried diseases.

Over the years, people have changed the way they get rid of trash. Now trash is often crushed and put in open places. A layer of trash is dumped and smashed down. Then it is covered with dirt. Another layer of trash is dumped and covered with dirt. This way of getting rid of trash is called landfill. Buildings can be built on landfill.

Burning trash is another way of getting rid of it; however, this often adds to air pollution. Today we have new furnaces for burning trash that are called incinerators. These new incinerators have scrubbers on their chimneys that cut down on air pollution. The new incinerators also gather some of the heat let off by burning trash. This energy can be used to heat homes and businesses.

There is another way of dealing with trash. It is recycling or changing waste products so they can be used again. We can do this with paper, glass, or aluminum. Glass can be crushed, melted down, and then made into new jars and bottles. This cuts down on the amount of trash. It also takes less energy to recycle glass and cans than to make new ones.

Adapted from M. R. Cohen, B. J. Del Giorno, J. D. Harlan, A. J. McCormack, and J. R. Staver, *Scott, Foresman Science, Grade 5* (Glenview, Ill.: Scott, Foresman and Co., 1984), pp. 374–376.

Laser Light

Scientists have found a new kind of light. This light is called laser light. Lasers are being used in medicine, industry, and science research.

How is laser light different from other kinds of light? White light actually contains all the colors of the rainbow. And the "red" light in a traffic signal contains red light of many different wavelengths. But the waves of laser light are all the same wavelength. So the light from a laser is one pure color. Another difference between laser light and other light is that a laser makes a thin beam of light that travels only in one direction. Finally, the waves of laser light are all lined up. Because the waves of laser light are the same length, travel in one direction, and all line up, a beam of laser light can be very powerful. A laser beam can even drill holes in metal. A lens focuses the laser beam to hit the point where the hole is to be drilled.

Laser light is useful in many ways. Laser beams can be used to carry radio and telephone messages. Lasers can even prevent some people from going blind. A person's eye is often damaged in an accident. Doctors use laser beams to reattach the retina. Lasers can be used to burn out tumors without a lot of bleeding. Lasers are also used to cut cloth for clothes. Every year new uses for laser light are being discovered. This new light in our life will continue to help us in many ways.

Adapted from M. R. Cohen, B. J. Del Giorno, J. D. Harlan, A. J. McCormack, and J. R. Staver, *Scott, Foresman Science, Grade 5* (Glenview, Ill.: Scott, Foresman and Co., 1984), p. 289.

Narrative

Concept Questions:

Who was Martin Luther King?

_____

_____

_____ (3-2-1-0)

What is racism?

_____

_____

_____ (3-2-1-0)

What is Washington, D.C.?

_____

_____

_____ (3-2-1-0)

What does "equal rights for blacks" mean to you?

_____

_____

_____ (3-2-1-0)

Score: _____ /12 = _____ %

_____ FAM _____ UNFAM

Prediction:

_____

_____

Martin Luther King, Jr.

When Martin Luther King, Jr., was a boy, many laws would not allow black people to go to the same places as whites. Some people thought blacks were not as good as whites. Black children could not attend some schools, and certain restaurants had signs that said "whites only." Blacks could not sit in the front of a bus and, if a bus got crowded, they had to give up their seat to a white person. King did not agree with laws like these, for he believed that all people are equal. He did not think that skin color should keep people apart. Laws separating blacks and whites were unjust, and King decided to protest such laws.

Many people organized to help him. King said that they must protest in a peaceful way. King told his followers to "meet hate with love." In Montgomery, Alabama, Rosa Parks, a black woman, was arrested and fined for not giving up her seat to a white man on a bus. King led the movement to protest this action. Thousands of people refused to ride the buses. The bus companies began to lose money. In time the law was changed. King traveled to many cities. He talked to the people and led them in peaceful marches.

More and more people heard about King's peaceful protests and joined him. King led a march to our center of government, Washington, D.C., to ask that the unjust laws be changed. Finally, the United States Supreme Court agreed with King. The laws separating blacks and whites were changed. King was given the Nobel Peace Prize for his work. Today people still admire King because he fought for justice in a peaceful way. January 15 was named as a national holiday in honor of Martin Luther King, Jr. (297 words)

From *Holt Social Studies, Our World, Our Regions, and Our History*, edited by JoAnn Cangemi, copyright © 1983 by Holt, Rinehart and Winston, Inc. Reprinted by permission of the publisher.

Number of Total Miscues
(Total Accuracy): _____

Number of Meaning-Change Miscues
(Total Acceptability): _____

Total Accuracy			Total Acceptability
0–7 miscues	____ Independent	____	0–7 miscues
8–31 miscues	____ Instructional	____	8–16 miscues
32+ miscues	____ Frustration	____	17+ miscues

Rate: 297 × 60 = 17,820/ ____ seconds = ____ WPM

Retelling Scoring Sheet for Martin Luther King, Jr.

Setting/Background

____ When Martin Luther King, Jr., was a boy,
____ laws would not allow blacks
____ to go to the same places
____ as whites.
____ People thought
____ blacks weren't as good
____ as whites.
____ Black children could not attend some schools.
____ Certain restaurants had signs

____ that said
____ "whites only."
____ Blacks could not sit
____ in front
____ of a bus.
____ If the bus got crowded,
____ they had to give up their seat
____ to a white.

Goal

____ King did not agree
____ with these laws.
____ He believed
____ that all people are equal.
____ He decided
____ to protest these laws.

Events

____ King said
____ they must protest
____ in a peaceful way.
____ In Alabama
____ Rosa Parks was arrested
____ for not giving up her seat
____ to a white man.
____ King led a movement
____ to protest this action.
____ Thousands refused
____ to ride the buses.
____ The bus company lost money.
____ The law was changed.
____ King led a march
____ to our center of government,
____ Washington, D.C.,
____ to ask
____ that the laws be changed
____ the unjust laws.

Resolution

____ The Supreme Court agreed.
____ The laws were changed
____ laws separating blacks and whites.
____ King was given a prize
____ the Nobel Peace Prize
____ for his work.

Level 5

___ People still admire King.
___ January 15 was named
___ as a holiday
___ a national holiday
___ in honor of King.

Other ideas recalled, including references:

Questions for Martin Luther King, Jr.

1. What was Martin Luther King's main goal?
   Implicit: he wanted equality for black people

2. Why had people made laws separating blacks and whites?
   Implicit: they thought blacks were not as good as whites

3. In some cities, what did blacks have to do on a crowded bus?
   Explicit: give up their seat to a white person

4. Why was Rosa Parks arrested?
   Explicit: she refused to give up her seat

5. What did many people do to protest Rosa Parks's arrest?
   Explicit: they refused to ride the buses

6. What happened when people refused to ride the buses?
   Implicit: the law was changed. If the student says, "The bus companies lost money," ask "What happened because of that?"

7. Why was Washington, D.C., an important place to protest unjust laws?
   Implicit: it is where the president and government officials are, so they would see the protest

8. Name one way in which Martin Luther King was honored for his work.
   Explicit: the Nobel Peace Prize; or the national holiday

Without Look-Backs

Number Correct Explicit: ____

Number Correct Implicit: ____

Total: ____

____ Independent: 8 correct

____ Instructional: 6–7 correct

____ Frustration: 0–5 correct

With Look-Backs

Number Correct Explicit: ____

Number Correct Implicit: ____

Total: ____

____ Independent: 8 correct

____ Instructional: 6–7 correct

____ Frustration: 0–5 correct

Narrative

Concept Questions:

Who was Christopher Columbus?

_____

_____

_____ (3-2-1-0)

What did Christopher Columbus want to prove?

_____

_____

_____ (3-2-1-0)

What does "sea voyages of long ago" mean to you?

_____

_____

_____ (3-2-1-0)

Why are we called Americans?

_____

_____

_____ (3-2-1-0)

Score: _____ /12 = _____ %

_____ FAM _____ UNFAM

Prediction:

_____

_____

Christopher Columbus

Christopher Columbus was determined to find an all-water route to the East Indies. Discovering this would bring him fame and fortune. However, Columbus also believed that the world was round. Many people laughed at this idea. They thought the world was flat. Columbus hoped to prove his theory. He would sail west in order to reach the East.

King Ferdinand and Queen Isabella of Spain thought Columbus's idea had merit. However, Spain was fighting a costly war. Columbus had to wait seven long years. Then they gave him money to finance the expedition. It was easy to buy ships and supplies. It was more difficult to find sailors who were willing to join him. Finally, in 1492, he set sail on the uncharted, unexplored Atlantic Ocean. Columbus had ninety sailors and three ships. His ships were the Nina, the Pinta, and the Santa Maria.

After they had been out of sight of land for a month, the sailors became frightened. They did not really believe the earth was round. They were afraid to sail too far to the edge. No one had ever sailed out so far upon the "Sea of Darkness." The sailors talked of mutiny. Columbus tried to convince them that they had nothing to fear. He reminded them of the gold they would get if they finished the voyage, and he told them they would be famous. But still the sailors threatened to take over and turn back.

Level 5

Level: Five

Just when it seemed they would go no farther, branches and leaves were seen in the water. The <u>sailors</u> felt much better and agreed to <u>continue</u> sailing. Then, on October 12, 1492, the welcome call was heard that land had been sighted. Columbus claimed the new land for Spain and named the inhabitants Indians. He mistakenly thought he had found a new route to the East. In fact, Columbus died believing he had reached the Indies. (317 words)

Adapted from *The United States and Its Neighbors* by T. M. Helmus, V. E. Arnsdorf, E. A. Toppin, and N. J. G. Pounds. © Copyright 1984 by Silver, Burdett and Ginn, Inc. Used with permission.

Number of Total Miscues
(Total Accuracy): _____

Number of Meaning-Change Miscues
(Total Acceptability): _____

Total Accuracy		**Total Acceptability**
0–7 miscues ____ Independent		____ 0–7 miscues
8–33 miscues ____ Instructional		____ 8–17 miscues
34+ miscues ____ Frustration		____ 18+ miscues

Rate: 317 × 60 = 19,020/____ seconds = ____ WPM

Retelling Scoring Sheet for Christopher Columbus

Setting/Background

____ Columbus believed
____ that the world was round.
____ People thought
____ the world was flat.
____ Columbus hoped
____ to prove his theory.

Goal

____ Columbus was determined
____ to find a route
____ an all-water route
____ to the Indies.
____ He would sail west
____ to reach the East.

Events

____ Spain was fighting a war.
____ Columbus had to wait
____ for years.
____ Then King Ferdinand
____ and Queen Isabella gave him money.
____ It was easy
____ to buy ships
____ and supplies.
____ It was difficult
____ to find sailors.
____ In 1492
____ he set sail.
____ Columbus had sailors
____ Ninety sailors and ships,
____ three ships,
____ the Nina,
____ the Pinta,
____ and the Santa Maria.
____ The sailors were afraid
____ to sail too far
____ to the edge.
____ Columbus tried to convince them
____ that they had nothing to fear.
____ Columbus reminded them
____ of the gold
____ they would get.
____ He told them
____ they would be famous.
____ But the sailors threatened
____ to take over
____ and turn back.
____ Just when it seemed

____ they would go no farther,
____ branches
____ and leaves were seen
____ in the water.
____ The sailors felt better
____ and agreed
____ to continue.

Resolution

____ Land was sighted.
____ Columbus claimed the land
____ for Spain.
____ He named the inhabitants
____ Indians.
____ Columbus died
____ believing
____ he had reached the Indies.

Other ideas recalled, including inferences:

Questions for Christopher Columbus

1. What was Christopher Columbus's main goal?
   Implicit: to prove the world was round; to sail west to get to the East Indies

2. How long did Christopher Columbus have to wait before he got the money from the king and queen of Spain?
   Explicit: seven years

3. Why was it more difficult to get sailors than ships and supplies?
   Implicit: people did not believe the world was round; the Atlantic was uncharted and unknown. If student says, "Sailors were afraid," ask, "Why?"

4. Why did the text say the sailors became frightened after being out of sight of land for a month?
   Explicit: they didn't believe the earth was round and they didn't want to sail close to the edge

5. Why did many people of that time call the Atlantic Ocean a "Sea of Darkness"?
   Implicit: no one knew much about it; they thought they would die if they sailed too far

6. How did Christopher Columbus try to convince the sailors to continue the voyage?
   Explicit: he said there was nothing to fear; he said they would be rich and famous

7. What did the sailors see that made them agree to continue sailing?
   Explicit: branches and leaves in the water

8. Why did Christopher Columbus name the inhabitants of the new lands Indians?
   Implicit: he thought he had reached the Indies

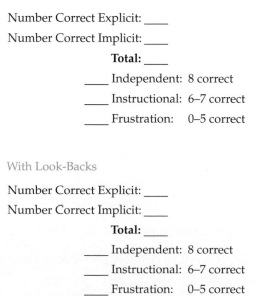

Without Look-Backs

Number Correct Explicit: ____
Number Correct Implicit: ____
          Total: ____
          ____ Independent: 8 correct
          ____ Instructional: 6–7 correct
          ____ Frustration: 0–5 correct

With Look-Backs

Number Correct Explicit: ____
Number Correct Implicit: ____
          Total: ____
          ____ Independent: 8 correct
          ____ Instructional: 6–7 correct
          ____ Frustration: 0–5 correct

Narrative

Concept Questions:

Who was Margaret Mead?

_____

_____

_____ (3-2-1-0)

How do we learn about different people?

_____

_____

_____ (3-2-1-0)

What are primitive people?

_____

_____

_____ (3-2-1-0)

What are problems learning a new language?

_____

_____

_____ (3-2-1-0)

Score: _____ /12 = _____ %

_____ FAM _____ UNFAM

Prediction:

_____

_____

Margaret Mead

Margaret Mead had always been interested in the ways of life of people from other lands. When Mead went to college, she took a class in anthropology. This is the study of how different people live. Mead decided to make this her career. She wanted to study primitive people before modern ways of living destroyed their culture.

Mead realized that living with a people is the only effective way to learn about them. She chose a village in Samoa to investigate. Several islands make up Samoa, which is in the Pacific Ocean. Mead worked hard to prepare for Samoa. She studied languages like the Samoan language. She read everything she could about the Samoan people. She read about their food and how they built their homes. She read about their ceremonies, their past history, and their taboos. But she wanted to learn much more.

Finally Mead arrived in Samoa. At first life was difficult for her. She was alone. She was not fluent in the Samoan language. She lived in a house with no walls and no electricity or gas. It had no running water and no bathroom. One day she said to herself, "I can't go on" in Samoan. Then she thought that maybe she could <u>continue</u> after all. Mead became fluent in the Samoan language, and the people soon regarded her as one of the village. She listened to their talk, their jokes, and their gossip. They told her their problems. Mead felt that being a woman assisted her in learning more about the lives of these people. Instead of having to go on hunts with the men, Mead stayed with the women. She observed the children play and learned how food was prepared. She made efforts to get the older people to recount tales of the past.

Mead learned many things from the Samoan people. She always took notes and kept careful records. These notes were used to write her first book, which was called *Coming of Age in Samoa*. It made her famous. Mead spent the rest of her life studying and writing about primitive ways of life that no longer exist today. (357 words)

Adapted from *The People of Tiegs-Adams: People and Their Heritage* series, © Copyright 1983 by Silver, Burdett and Ginn, Inc. Used with permission.

Number of Total Miscues
(Total Accuracy): _____

Number of Meaning-Change Miscues
(Total Acceptability): _____

Total Accuracy			**Total Acceptability**
0–5 miscues	____ Independent	____	0–8 miscues
9–37 miscues	____ Instructional	____	9–19 miscues
38+ miscues	____ Frustration	____	20+ miscues

Rate: 357 × 60 = 21,420/____ seconds = ____ WPM

Retelling Scoring Sheet for Margaret Mead

Background/Setting

____ When Margaret Mead went to college,
____ she took a class
____ in anthropology.
____ She decided to make this her career.

Goal

____ She wanted to study people
____ primitive people.
____ She chose a village
____ in Samoa
____ to investigate.
____ Islands make up Samoa,
____ which is in the Pacific Ocean.

Events

____ Margaret Mead studied languages
____ like the Samoan language.
____ She read everything she could
____ about the Samoan people.
____ She read
____ about their food
____ and how they built their homes.
____ She arrived in Samoa.
____ Life was difficult.
____ She lived
____ in a house
____ with no walls
____ with no electricity.
____ She said,
____ "I can't go on"
____ in Samoan.
____ Then she thought
____ that she could continue.
____ The people regarded her
____ as one of the village.
____ She listened
____ to their jokes,
____ their gossip.
____ Instead of having to go
____ on hunts
____ with the men,

Level: Five

____ Margaret Mead stayed
____ with the women.
____ She observed the children
____ play
____ and learned
____ how food was prepared.

Resolutions

____ She wrote a book
____ called *Coming of Age in Samoa.*
____ It made her famous.

Other ideas recalled, including inferences:

Questions for Margaret Mead

1. What was Margaret Mead's main goal?
   Implicit: to study primitive people

2. What people did Margaret Mead choose to investigate?
   Explicit: people in Samoa

3. Name one thing Margaret Mead read about to prepare her for Samoa.
   Explicit: homes; food; ceremonies; Samoa's history; taboos; the Samoan language

4. Give one reason why life in Samoa was difficult at first.
   Explicit: she was alone; there were no walls, electricity, running water, or bathroom; she was not fluent in the language

5. What made Margaret Mead decide she would be able to stay in Samoa?
   Implicit: when she talked to herself in Samoan and realized she knew the language

6. Why was Margaret Mead able to learn a lot about the family life of the Samoans?
   Implicit: she stayed with the women and children; the women and children talked to her

7. Why did Margaret Mead want to hear the stories of the Samoans' past?
   Implicit: she wanted to learn as much about them as she could

8. What did Margaret Mead do with the notes and records she kept?
   Explicit: she wrote a book

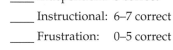

Without Look-Backs

Number Correct Explicit: ____
Number Correct Implicit: ____
         Total: ____
____ Independent: 8 correct
____ Instructional: 6–7 correct
____ Frustration: 0–5 correct

With Look-Backs

Number Correct Explicit: ____
Number Correct Implicit: ____
         Total: ____
____ Independent: 8 correct
____ Instructional: 6–7 correct
____ Frustration: 0–5 correct

Expository

Concept Questions:

What is an octopus?

_____

_____

_____ (3-2-1-0)

Why does an animal attack another animal?

_____

_____

_____ (3-2-1-0)

What are animal defenses?

_____

_____

_____ (3-2-1-0)

What is animal camouflage?

_____

_____

_____ (3-2-1-0)

Score: _____ /12 = _____ %

_____ FAM _____ UNFAM

Prediction:

_____

_____

The Octopus

Some people think of the octopus as a <u>giant</u> <u>creature</u>. They have seen this in science fiction movies. They think the octopus is a mean <u>creature</u> who attacks people and other animals. The octopus is really a shy animal. It is usually quite small.

The octopus has eight arms. Its name tells us this because "octo" means eight. The octopus uses its arms to walk on the ocean floor. Its arms are also used to capture crabs. Crabs are its favorite food. The octopus bites into the crab with its strong beak. This sends <u>poison</u> into the crab's body.

The octopus protects itself in three ways. First, when frightened, the octopus can push water from its body in a powerful stream. This action pushes the octopus forward very rapidly. This allows it to escape.

Second, the body of the octopus has a special sac or pouch that holds a dark, ink-like fluid. When an enemy comes close, the octopus squirts some of this fluid. It then swims away. All that the predator sees is a dark cloud in the water where the octopus was. Meanwhile, the octopus has escaped.

Finally, the octopus's body changes color when the octopus is excited or frightened. Suppose an octopus sees a crab. Patches of pink, purple, or blue will appear on the octopus's skin. Suppose the octopus sees an enemy. The octopus will completely change color. Then it

Level: Five

seems to disappear into the background of its hiding place. It is hard for the predator to find the octopus. (254 words)

Adapted from M. R. Cohen, B. J. Del Giorno, J. D. Harlan, A. J. McCormack, and J. R. Staver, *Scott, Foresman Science, Grade 5* (Glenview, Ill.: Scott, Foresman and Co., 1984), p. 31.

Number of Total Miscues
(Total Accuracy): _____

Number of Meaning-Change Miscues
(Total Acceptability): _____

Total Accuracy		**Total Acceptability**
0–6 miscues ____	Independent ____	0–6 miscues
7–26 miscues ____	Instructional ____	7–13 miscues
27+ miscues ____	Frustration ____	14+ miscues

Rate: 254 × 60 = 21,240/____ seconds = ____ WPM

Retelling Scoring Sheet for The Octopus

Main Idea

____ Some people think
____ the octopus is a giant creature
____ and a mean creature.
____ They have seen this
____ in movies
____ science fiction movies.
____ The octopus is shy
____ and small.

Details

____ The octopus has eight arms.
____ Octo means "eight."
____ It uses its arms
____ to walk
____ and capture crabs.

____ Crabs are its food
____ its favorite food.
____ The octopus bites
____ into the crab.
____ This sends poison
____ into the crab's body.
____ The octopus protects itself
____ in three ways.
____ First,
____ when frightened,
____ the octopus can push water
____ from its body.
____ This action pushes the octopus
____ forward
____ very rapidly.
____ This allows it
____ to escape.
____ Second,
____ the octopus has a sac
____ that holds a liquid
____ an ink-like liquid.
____ When an enemy comes close,
____ the octopus squirts fluid.
____ It swims away.
____ The predator sees a cloud
____ a dark cloud.
____ The octopus has escaped.
____ Finally,
____ the octopus changes color
____ when it is excited
____ or scared.
____ Suppose the octopus sees a crab.
____ Pink patches,
____ purple patches,
____ or blue patches
____ appear.
____ If the octopus sees an enemy,
____ the octopus will change color
____ completely.
____ It seems to disappear
____ into the background.

Other ideas recalled, including inferences:

Questions for The Octopus

1. What is this passage mainly about?
   Implicit: what the octopus is like; how it behaves

2. What is the favorite food of the octopus?
   Explicit: crabs

3. How does the octopus move forward very rapidly when it is frightened?
   Explicit: it pushes water from its body

4. What does the ink-like fluid do to the water?
   Explicit: it changes it into a dark cloud

5. What is one color that an octopus can change to?
   Explicit: pink, purple, or blue

6. Why doesn't an octopus completely change color when it sees a crab?
   Implicit: it is excited, not frightened

7. What color does an octopus probably become when it sees an enemy?
   Implicit: a dark blue or brown or black; it camouflages itself with the background

8. Why might the shy octopus attack another creature?
   Implicit: for food

Without Look-Backs

Number Correct Explicit: _____

Number Correct Implicit: _____

Total: _____

_____ Independent: 8 correct

_____ Instructional: 6–7 correct

_____ Frustration: 0–5 correct

With Look-Backs

Number Correct Explicit: _____

Number Correct Implicit: _____

Total: _____

_____ Independent: 8 correct

_____ Instructional: 6–7 correct

_____ Frustration: 0–5 correct

Level 5

Level: Five

Expository

Concept Questions:

What does "getting rid of trash" mean to you?

_____

_____

_____ (3-2-1-0)

What are the purposes of recycling?

_____

_____

_____ (3-2-1-0)

What happens after products are recycled?

_____

_____

_____ (3-2-1-0)

What is landfill?

_____

_____

_____ (3-2-1-0)

Score: _____ /12 = _____ %

_____ FAM _____ UNFAM

Prediction:

_____

_____

Getting Rid of Trash

In the past, when people wanted to get rid of their trash, they just threw it out. Sometimes they threw it into the streets or alleys, and sometimes they packed it into a wagon and dumped it near the edge of town. Open dumping caused many problems. The trash was ugly and often smelled. It attracted rats and other animals that carried diseases.

Over the years, people have changed the way they get rid of trash. Now trash is often crushed and put in open places. A layer of trash is dumped and smashed down. Then it is covered with dirt. Another layer of trash is dumped and covered with dirt. This way of getting rid of trash is called landfill. Buildings can be built on landfill.

Burning trash is another way of getting rid of it; however, this often adds to air pollution. Today we have new furnaces for burning trash that are called incinerators. These new incinerators have scrubbers on their chimneys that cut down on air pollution. The new incinerators also gather some of the heat let off by burning trash. This energy can be used to heat homes and businesses.

There is another way of dealing with trash. It is recycling or changing waste products so they can be used again. We can do this with paper, glass, or aluminum . Glass can be crushed, melted down, and then made into new jars and bottles. This cuts down on the amount of trash. It also takes less energy to recycle glass and cans than to make new ones. (261 words)

Level: Five

Adapted from M. R. Cohen, B. J. Del Giorno, J. D. Harlan, A. J. McCormack, and J. R. Staver, *Scott, Foresman Science, Grade 5* (Glenview, Ill.: Scott, Foresman and Co., 1984), pp. 374–376.

Number of Total Miscues
(Total Accuracy): _____

Number of Meaning-Change Miscues
(Total Acceptability): _____ _____

Total Accuracy				Total Acceptability
0–6 miscues	____	Independent	____	0–6 miscues
7–27 miscues	____	Instructional	____	7–14 miscues
28+ miscues	____	Frustration	____	15+ miscues

Rate: 261 × 60 = 15,660/____ seconds = ____ WPM

Retelling Scoring Sheet for Getting Rid of Trash

Main Idea

____ In the past,
____ when people got rid of trash,
____ they threw it out.

Details

____ They threw it
____ into streets
____ or alleys
____ or dumped it
____ near the edge
____ of town.
____ Dumping caused problems.
____ The trash was ugly
____ and smelled.
____ It attracted rats
____ and animals carrying diseases.

Main Idea

____ A way of getting rid of trash
____ is landfill.

Details

____ Trash is crushed
____ and put in open places.
____ A layer is dumped
____ and smashed down.
____ It is covered
____ with dirt.
____ Another layer of trash is dumped
____ and covered
____ with dirt.
____ Buildings can be built on landfill.

Main Idea

____ Burning is another way
____ of getting rid of trash.

Details

____ This added to pollution.
____ Furnaces burn trash.
____ They are called incinerators.
____ They have scrubbers
____ to cut down pollution.
____ They gather heat.
____ This energy can heat homes
____ and businesses.

Main Idea

____ Recycling gets rid of trash.

Details

____ We do this with paper,
____ glass,
____ and aluminum.
____ Glass can be melted
____ and made into jars
____ and bottles.
____ It takes less energy
____ to recycle glass
____ and cans
____ than to make new ones.

Other ideas recalled, including inferences:

Level: Five

Questions for Getting Rid of Trash

1. What is this passage mainly about?
   Implicit: different ways to get rid of trash

2. What was one problem caused by open dumping?
   Explicit: bad smells, diseased animals, ugly sights

3. Why is trash crushed before it is placed in a landfill?
   Implicit: it takes up less space/land

4. Landfills get rid of trash. What other use do they have?
   Implicit: you can build on them

5. What is put on incinerator chimneys to cut down on pollution?
   Explicit: scrubbers

6. What can the heat let off by burning trash be used for?
   Explicit: heating homes and businesses

7. Name one product that can be recycled.
   Explicit: glass; paper; aluminum

8. Why might recycled cans and bottles be cheaper than new ones?
   Implicit: used less energy so they probably cost less

Without Look-Backs

Number Correct Explicit: ____

Number Correct Implicit: ____

         Total: ____

____ Independent: 8 correct

____ Instructional: 6–7 correct

____ Frustration: 0–5 correct

With Look-Backs

Number Correct Explicit: ____

Number Correct Implicit: ____

         Total: ____

____ Independent: 8 correct

____ Instructional: 6–7 correct

____ Frustration: 0–5 correct

Expository

Concept Questions:

What is laser light?

_____

_____

_____ (3-2-1-0)

What are things that light can go through?

_____

_____

_____ (3-2-1-0)

Why does bleeding stop?

_____

_____

_____ (3-2-1-0)

What do artists make?

_____

_____

_____ (3-2-1-0)

Score: _____ /12 = _____ %

_____ FAM _____ UNFAM

Prediction:

_____

_____

Laser Light

Scientists have found a new kind of light. This light is called laser light. Lasers are being used in medicine, industry, and science research.

How is laser light different from other kinds of light? White light actually contains all the colors of the rainbow. And the "red" light in a traffic signal contains red light of many different wavelengths. But the waves of laser light are all the same wavelength. So the light from a laser is one pure color. Another difference between laser light and other light is that a laser makes a thin beam of light that travels only in one direction. Finally, the waves of laser light are all lined up. Because the waves of laser light are the same length, travel in one direction, and all line up, a beam of laser light can be very powerful. A laser beam can even drill holes in metal. A lens focuses the laser beam to hit the point where the hole is to be drilled.

Laser light is useful in many ways. Laser beams can be used to carry radio and telephone messages. Lasers can even prevent some people from going blind. A person's eye is often damaged in an accident. Doctors use laser beams to reattach the retina. Lasers can be used to burn out tumors without a lot of bleeding. Lasers are also used to cut cloth for clothes. Every year new uses for laser light are being discovered. This new light in our life will continue to help us in many ways. (257 words)

Level: Five

Adapted from M. R. Cohen, B. J. Del Giorno, J. D. Harlan, A. J. McCormack, and J. R. Staver, *Scott, Foresman Science, Grade 5* (Glenview, Ill.: Scott, Foresman and Co., 1984), p. 289.

Number of Total Miscues
(Total Accuracy): _____

Number of Meaning-Change Miscues
(Total Acceptability): _____

Total Accuracy			**Total Acceptability**
0–6 miscues	____	Independent	____ 0–6 miscues
7–26 miscues	____	Instructional	____ 7–14 miscues
27+ miscues	____	Frustration	____ 15+ miscues

Rate: $257 \times 60 = 15{,}420/$____ seconds = ____ WPM

Retelling Scoring Sheet for Laser Light

Main Idea

____ Scientists have found a new kind
____ of light
____ called laser light.

Details

____ Lasers are used in medicine,
____ industry,
____ and science.

Main Idea

____ Laser light is different
____ from other kinds of light.

Details

____ White light
____ contains all the colors
____ of the rainbow.
____ "Red" light
____ in a traffic signal
____ contains different wavelengths.
____ Waves of laser light

____ are the same wavelength.
____ Laser light is one color.
____ A laser makes a beam
____ that travels
____ in one direction.
____ Waves of laser light are lined up.
____ A laser beam is very powerful.
____ It can drill holes
____ in metal.

Main Idea

____ Laser light is useful
____ in many ways.

Details

____ Laser beams carry
____ radio
____ and telephone messages.
____ They can prevent blindness.
____ They can reattach a retina
____ or burn out tumors
____ without a lot of bleeding.
____ Lasers cut cloth.
____ Every year
____ new uses
____ are being discovered.

Other ideas recalled, including inferences:

Questions for Laser Light

1. What is this passage mainly about?
   Implicit: how laser light works; how laser light is used

2. What colors are contained in white light?
   Explicit: all the colors of the rainbow

3. In what direction do the waves of laser light travel, compared to other types of light?
   Explicit: in one direction; they all go the same way

4. If a laser beam hits a solid object, what happens to the object?
   Implicit: a hole is made in it

5. What is used to focus the laser beam so that it strikes a certain point?
   Explicit: a lens

6. What kinds of messages can laser beams carry?
   Explicit: telephone or radio

7. Why would laser surgery be safer than surgery that uses a knife?
   Implicit: there would be less bleeding

8. How might a sculptor use laser light?
   Implicit: to sculpt metal or stone or wood

Without Look-Backs

Number Correct Explicit: ____

Number Correct Implicit: ____

Total: ____

____ Independent: 8 correct

____ Instructional: 6–7 correct

____ Frustration: 0–5 correct

With Look-Backs

Number Correct Explicit: ____

Number Correct Implicit: ____

Total: ____

____ Independent: 8 correct

____ Instructional: 6–7 correct

____ Frustration: 0–5 correct

Pele

Pele was born in the South American country of Brazil. He lived in a small village and his family was very poor. But Pele had a dream. He wanted to become a professional soccer player. He could not afford a soccer ball so he fashioned one. He took an old sock, stuffed it with newspapers, and sewed it together with string. It was a poor substitute, but it was better than nothing. Pele and his friends formed their own team. They did not have enough money to purchase shoes, but that did not stop them. They played barefoot and became known as the "barefoot team."

Pele and his friends saved their money, and eventually the team was able to get a regular ball and shoes. Pele discovered that the ball could be better controlled when he wore shoes. Pele and his team practiced continuously. They soon began playing older and more established teams from the big cities. The team began to win most of its games. Pele was the star of the team. People thought this was amazing because he was only eleven years old!

Pele's skill at soccer came to the attention of influential people, and when he was fifteen, he was signed by the Santos team. Pele led the Santos team to many championships. He also led the Brazilian national team to three world championships. Pele also holds many records and has scored over twelve hundred goals in his career as a professional player.

Pele decided to retire in 1974. Then he changed his mind and came to the United States, where he joined the New York Cosmos. Soccer had not been very popular in the United States up to this point, but Pele's presence had a dramatic effect. Crowds at games doubled and tripled as people came to see the famous and exciting Pele. Games began to be shown on television. Soccer gained in popularity and many children in the United States began to play soccer. Soccer is now one of the most popular sports in the United States, due in part to the dream of a young boy in Brazil.

From *Holt Social Studies, Our World, Our Regions, and Our History*, edited by JoAnn Cangemi, copyright © 1983 by Holt, Rinehart and Winston, Inc. Reprinted by permission of the publisher.

Abraham Lincoln

When Abraham Lincoln was nineteen years old, he visited the city of New Orleans. He saw things he would never forget. He saw black people being sold in slave markets. They were chained together and treated like animals. Lincoln watched little children being sold to strangers and taken away from their parents. Lincoln was heartbroken and these memories stayed with him for the rest of his life. Although slavery was allowed in many states of the Union, Lincoln believed that it was wrong and he was not afraid to say so.

In 1858, Lincoln ran for the United States Senate against Stephen Douglas. There was much talk about slavery. Should the owning of slaves be allowed in new states that were just coming into the Union? Douglas said that the decision to own slaves was up to each individual person. Lincoln said that slavery must not be allowed to spread because it was wrong. But he knew that it would not be easy to end slavery in those states that had allowed it for so many years. Lincoln believed it was important to keep the United States strong. He felt that slavery weakened the country. In one speech, he said the country could not last half slave and half free. He said, "A house divided against itself cannot stand." Lincoln lost the election to the Senate, but he became well known for his views. In 1860 he ran for president of the United States.

The slave states opposed Lincoln as president. They did not want to abolish slavery. They threatened to leave the Union if Lincoln was elected. When he became president, the slave states carried out their threat. A terrible war broke out between the northern and southern states. At times, members of the same family were fighting against one another.

In 1863, Lincoln gave an order called the Emancipation Proclamation, which ended slavery. The war finally ended two years later. The southern states once more became part of the Union, but slavery was no longer allowed. No more would little children be torn from their parents and sold to strangers. Abraham Lincoln had achieved his goal.

Andrew Carnegie

Andrew Carnegie was the son of Scottish immigrants. One of his first jobs was as a messenger boy. He earned $2.50 a week! At the age of eighteen, Carnegie got a job on the Pennsylvania Railroad. He soon realized that iron was not a good construction material for the railroad. Iron rails tended to crack and often had to be replaced. The weight of a train weakened iron bridges. Carnegie felt that steel would be a stronger building material. He decided to find ways to increase the production of steel.

Carnegie carefully saved his money and used it to become part owner of a small iron company. Eventually he acquired the ownership of several more companies. But making steel was slow and costly. Then Carnegie learned about the Bessemer process. Using this method, steel could be made quickly and on a large scale. Carnegie decided to risk all. He built a huge steel mill. He bought iron and coal mines as well as ships and trains for transport. By 1900, three million tons of steel were produced by Carnegie's mills each year, and his fortune was worth two hundred and fifty million.

Carnegie accomplished his dream, that of increasing steel production, and, in doing so, he developed and shaped the United States steel industry. In 1901, at the peak of his career, Carnegie sold his business and retired. He then spent much of his time and money in helping others and started more than two thousand libraries in the United States and around the world. Carnegie can truly be called the Man of Steel.

From *Holt Social Studies, Our World, Our Regions, and Our History,* edited by JoAnn Cangemi, copyright © 1983 by Holt, Rinehart and Winston, Inc. Reprinted by permission of the publisher.

Computers

Computers are machines that help solve problems, but they can't do anything without directions from humans. People give computers information. Then they tell them what to do with it. Computers cannot come up with any new information, but they can save much work and time.

For example, you could store all the information in the phone book in a computer's memory. Then you could ask the computer to tell you all the names of people living on one single street. If you lived in a big city, it might take days or even weeks for you to come up with all the names. But the computer could do it in seconds!

The first computers were huge. One filled a whole floor of a large office building. The machines were very costly. Only big industries could buy them. But because computers could save so much time, other businesses wanted them. So scientists found a way to make computers smaller and cheaper by inventing chips. Chips made it possible to store more information in less space.

Today a computer can fit on your lap. Computers are still shrinking in size and price. More businesses use them. Hospitals use them to keep track of billing. Stores use them to make checkouts easier and faster. Families use computers too. Many students have computers at home that help them with their homework. Computer games are very popular. A computer can help to keep track of a family's expenses. Someday every family may have a home computer.

Adapted from M. R. Cohen, B. J. Del Giorno, J. D. Harlan, A. J. McCormack, and J. R. Staver, *Scott, Foresman Science, Grade 5* (Glenview, Ill.: Scott, Foresman and Co., 1984), pp. 348–349.

Predicting Earthquakes

Some scientists think that certain animals know when an earthquake is coming. They sense the earthquake days or hours before it happens. In some cases, animal behavior has predicted a coming earthquake.

Before the Chinese earthquake in February of 1975, people noted animals doing strange things. Birds suddenly flew away. They would not return to their nests. Chickens refused to enter their coops. Rats ran around bumping into things. Well-trained police dogs howled and would not obey their masters. They kept sniffing the ground.

What might these animals know that we do not? Perhaps they can sense some of the changes that happen in the earth before an earthquake. Certain animals might hear low booms that come before an earthquake. Perhaps they can smell certain gases that escape from the earth.

Scientists wanted to study the possible connection between animal behavior and earthquakes. They set up a project in California. It ran for three years. Over a thousand volunteers took part. The volunteers watched animals and called the project every day to report on their actions. During the project at least thirteen earthquakes were recorded. Some were bigger than others. The volunteers saw an unusually high amount of strange behavior before seven of the earthquakes. Someday we may use animals to warn people of an earthquake. If this happens, we can thank the efforts of scientists and volunteers around the world.

Adapted from M. R. Cohen, B. J. Del Giorno, J. D. Harlan, A. J. McCormack, and J. R. Staver, *Scott, Foresman Science, Grade 4* (Glenview, Ill.: Scott, Foresman and Co., 1984), p. 99.

Ultrasound

Some medical research uses sounds that you cannot hear. The word ultrasonic is used to describe sounds with very high frequencies. Ultrasonic sounds range from twenty thousand to more than a billion vibrations per second. These sounds are too high for humans to hear. But dogs and other animals can hear them.

Scientists have found many uses for ultrasonic sounds. For example, doctors use ultrasound to study the health of babies before they are born. Ultrasonic sounds can be sent through the mother's abdomen. The waves reflect off the baby's body into a microphone that picks up these waves. The reflected sounds can be made into a picture and shown on a television screen.

The ultrasonic wave patterns show some of the health problems a baby might have. Heart problems and slow growth can be detected. The doctors can use this information to plan ahead for what the baby might need as soon as it is born. Doctors can also use this method to tell the mother if she is expecting twins or triplets.

Many industrial uses of ultrasonics have also been found. Some factories use ultrasonic waves to look for hidden cracks in metals. Such waves can be used to find gas and oil deposits underground. Paint and homogenized milk can be mixed by ultrasonic waves. Dentists can even clean your teeth with these waves. This unheard sound has become a useful tool in many areas of medicine, industry, and science research.

Adapted from M. R. Cohen, B. J. Del Giorno, J. D. Harlan, A. J. McCormack, and J. R. Staver, *Scott, Foresman Science, Grade 5* (Glenview, Ill.: Scott, Foresman and Co., 1984), p. 239.

Narrative

Concept Questions:

Who is Pele?

_____

_____

_____ (3-2-1-0)

What is soccer?

_____

_____

_____ (3-2-1-0)

What are professional athletes?

_____

_____

_____ (3-2-1-0)

Why do some sports become popular?

_____

_____

_____ (3-2-1-0)

Score: _____ /12 = _____ %

_____ FAM _____ UNFAM

Prediction:

_____

_____

Pele

Pele was born in the South American country of Brazil. He lived in a small village and his family was very poor. But Pele had a dream.

He wanted to become a professional soccer player. He could not afford a soccer ball so he fashioned one. He took an old sock, stuffed it with newspapers, and sewed it together with string. It was a poor substitute, but it was better than nothing. Pele and his friends formed their own team. They did not have enough money to purchase shoes, but that did not stop them. They played barefoot and became known as the "barefoot team."

Pele and his friends saved their money, and eventually the team was able to get a regular ball and shoes. Pele discovered that the ball could be better controlled when he wore shoes. Pele and his team practiced continuously. They soon began playing older and more established teams from the big cities. The team began to win most of its games. Pele was the star of the team. People thought this was amazing because he was only eleven years old!

Pele's skill at soccer came to the attention of influential people, and when he was fifteen, he was signed by the Santos team. Pele led the Santos team to many championships. He also led the Brazilian national team to three world championships. Pele also holds many records and has scored over twelve hundred goals in his career as a professional player.

Level: Six

Pele decided to retire in 1974. Then he changed his mind and came to the United States, where he joined the New York Cosmos. Soccer had not been very popular in the United States up to this point, but Pele's presence had a dramatic effect. Crowds at games doubled and tripled as people came to see the famous and exciting Pele. Games began to be shown on television. Soccer gained in popularity and many children in the United States began to play soccer. Soccer is now one of the most popular sports in the United States, due in part to the dream of a young boy in Brazil. (351 words)

From *Holt Social Studies, Our World, Our Regions, and Our History*, edited by JoAnn Cangemi, copyright © 1983 by Holt, Rinehart and Winston, Inc. Reprinted by permission of the publisher.

Number of Total Miscues
(Total Accuracy): _____

Number of Meaning-Change Miscues
(Total Acceptability): _____

Total Accuracy		Total Acceptability	
0–8 miscues	____ Independent	____	0–8 miscues
9–36 miscues	____ Instructional	____	9–19 miscues
37+ miscues	____ Frustration	____	20+ miscues

Rate: 351 × 60 − 21,060/____ seconds = ____ WPM

Retelling Scoring Sheet for Pele

Setting/Background

____ Pele was born
____ in Brazil.
____ Pele's family was poor.

Goal

____ Pele had a dream.
____ He wanted
____ to become a soccer player
____ a professional player.

Events

____ He could not afford a ball.
____ He fashioned a ball.
____ He took a sock
____ and stuffed it
____ with newspapers
____ and sewed it together
____ with string.
____ Pele
____ and his friends formed a team
____ their own team.
____ They did not have enough money
____ to purchase shoes.
____ They played barefoot
____ and became known
____ as the "barefoot team."
____ Pele
____ and his friends saved their money,
____ and eventually
____ the team was able
____ to get a ball
____ a regular ball
____ and shoes.
____ Pele discovered
____ that the ball could be controlled
____ better
____ when he wore shoes.
____ They began
____ to play teams
____ from big cities
____ and to win games

Level: Six

____ most of their games.
____ Pele was the star.
____ He was only eleven.
____ He was signed
____ by the Santos team.

Resolution

____ Pele led the team
____ to championships.
____ He led the team
____ the Brazilian team
____ to championships
____ world championships.
____ Pele held many records.
____ Pele decided
____ to retire
____ in 1974.
____ Then he changed his mind
____ and came to the United States,
____ where he joined the Cosmos
____ the New York Cosmos.
____ Pele's presence had an effect.
____ Crowds doubled
____ and tripled
____ and people came
____ to see Pele.
____ Soccer gained
____ in popularity.
____ Soccer is now one
____ of the most popular sports
____ in the United States

Other ideas recalled, including inferences:

Questions for Pele

1. What was Pele's main goal?
   Implicit: to become a professional soccer player

2. What did Pele use to make a soccer ball?
   Explicit: an old sock, string, and newspaper

3. What was Pele's team called when they had no shoes?
   Explicit: the barefoot team

4. Why did the purchase of shoes affect the number of games won by Pele's team?
   Implicit: they played better because they could control the ball more effectively

5. Why was it amazing that Pele became a star at the age of eleven?
   Implicit: he was very young to be playing so well against older and more established teams from the big cities

6. How old was Pele when he was signed by a professional soccer team?
   Explicit: fifteen

7. What American team did Pele join?
   Explicit: New York Cosmos

8. How did Pele's presence help to make soccer popular in the United States?
   Implicit: people came to see Pele and grew to like the game itself

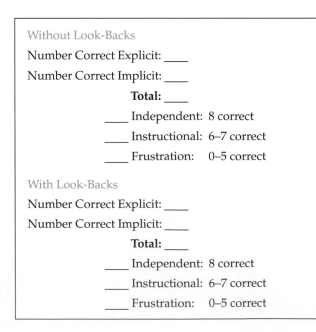

Without Look-Backs

Number Correct Explicit: ____

Number Correct Implicit: ____

      Total: ____

      ____ Independent: 8 correct

      ____ Instructional: 6–7 correct

      ____ Frustration: 0–5 correct

With Look-Backs

Number Correct Explicit: ____

Number Correct Implicit: ____

      Total: ____

      ____ Independent: 8 correct

      ____ Instructional: 6–7 correct

      ____ Frustration: 0–5 correct

Narrative

Concept Questions:

Who was Abraham Lincoln?

_____

_____

_____ (3-2-1-0)

What are the evils of slavery?

_____

_____

_____ (3-2-1-0)

Why was the Civil War fought?

_____

_____

_____ (3-2-1-0)

What were the results of the Civil War?

_____

_____

_____ (3-2-1-0)

Score: _____ /12 = _____ %

_____ FAM _____ UNFAM

Prediction:

_____

_____

Abraham Lincoln

When Abraham Lincoln was nineteen years old, he visited the city of New Orleans. He saw things he would never forget. He saw black people being sold in slave markets. They were chained together and treated like animals. Lincoln watched little children being sold to strangers and taken away from their parents. Lincoln was heartbroken and these memories stayed with him for the rest of his life. Although slavery was allowed in many states of the Union, Lincoln believed that it was wrong and he was not afraid to say so.

In 1858, Lincoln ran for the United States Senate against Stephen Douglas. There was much talk about slavery. Should the owning of slaves be allowed in new states that were just coming into the Union? Douglas said that the decision to own slaves was up to each individual person. Lincoln said that slavery must not be allowed to spread because it was wrong. But he knew that it would not be easy to end slavery in those states that had allowed it for so many years. Lincoln believed that it was important to keep the United States strong. He felt that slavery weakened the country. In one speech, he said the country could not last half slave and half free. He said, "A house divided against itself cannot stand." Lincoln lost the election to the Senate, but he became well known for his views. In 1860 he ran for president of the United States.

Level: Six

The slave states opposed Lincoln as president. They did not want to <u>abolish</u> <u>slavery</u>. They threatened to leave the Union if Lincoln was elected. When he became president, the slave states carried out their threat. A terrible war broke out between the northern and southern states. At times, members of the same family were fighting against one another.

In 1863, Lincoln gave an order called the Emancipation Proclamation, which ended <u>slavery</u>. The war finally ended two years later. The southern states once more became part of the Union, but <u>slavery</u> was no longer allowed. No more would little children be torn from their parents and sold to strangers. Abraham Lincoln had achieved his goal. (358 words)

Number of Total Miscues
(Total Accuracy): _____

Number of Meaning-Change Miscues
(Total Acceptability): _____

Total Accuracy			**Total Acceptability**
0–8 miscues	____ Independent	____	0–8 miscues
9–37 miscues	____ Instructional	____	9–19 miscues
38+ miscues	____ Frustration	____	20+ miscues

Rate: 358 × 60 = 21,480/____ seconds = ____ WPM

Retelling Scoring Sheet for Abraham Lincoln

Setting/Background

____ When Abraham Lincoln was nineteen,
____ he visited the city
____ of New Orleans.
____ He saw things
____ he would never forget.
____ He saw black people
____ being sold
____ in slave markets.
____ They were chained together
____ and treated like animals.
____ Lincoln watched children
____ being sold
____ to strangers
____ and taken away
____ from their parents.

Goal

____ Lincoln believed
____ that slavery was wrong.
____ He was not afraid
____ to say so.

Events

____ Lincoln ran
____ for the Senate
____ against Stephen Douglas.
____ Lincoln said
____ that slavery must not spread.
____ He felt
____ that slavery weakened the country.
____ Lincoln lost the election
____ to the Senate.
____ He ran
____ for president.
____ The slave states opposed Lincoln.
____ They did not want
____ to abolish slavery.
____ They threatened
____ to leave the union
____ if Lincoln was elected.
____ When Lincoln became president,

____ a war broke out

____ a war between the states.

Resolution

____ Lincoln gave an order

____ called the Emancipation Proclamation,

____ which ended slavery.

____ The war ended.

____ The southern states became part

____ of the Union

____ but slavery was not allowed.

____ Abraham Lincoln had achieved his goal.

Other ideas recalled, including inferences:

Questions for Abraham Lincoln

1. What was Abraham Lincoln's main goal?
   Implicit: to end slavery in the United States

2. Name one thing that Abraham Lincoln saw in the slave markets of New Orleans.
   Explicit: blacks chained together; blacks treated like animals; blacks being sold; children being separated from parents; children being sold to strangers

3. How did the sights of the slave market influence Abraham Lincoln's later life?
   Implicit: he was against slavery and fought to end it; it made him sick and he wanted to stop it

4. What office did Abraham Lincoln run for against Douglas?
   Explicit: he ran for the U.S. Senate

5. What did the southern states threaten to do if Abraham Lincoln was elected president?
   Explicit: leave the Union

6. Why did the southern states oppose Abraham Lincoln as president?
   Implicit: he was against slavery and he would fight to end it in their states

7. How did Abraham Lincoln's prediction that "A house divided against itself cannot stand" come true?
   Implicit: the war between the states broke out

8. What did the Emancipation Proclamation do?
   Explicit: it ended slavery

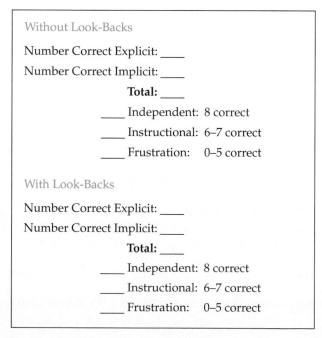

Without Look-Backs

Number Correct Explicit: ____

Number Correct Implicit: ____

        Total: ____

    ____ Independent: 8 correct

    ____ Instructional: 6–7 correct

    ____ Frustration: 0–5 correct

With Look-Backs

Number Correct Explicit: ____

Number Correct Implicit: ____

        Total: ____

    ____ Independent: 8 correct

    ____ Instructional: 6–7 correct

    ____ Frustration: 0–5 correct

Narrative

Concept Questions:

Who was Andrew Carnegie?

_____

_____

_____ (3-2-1-0)

What are the characteristics of steel?

_____

_____

_____ (3-2-1-0)

How is steel made?

_____

_____

_____ (3-2-1-0)

How do companies make a profit?

_____

_____

_____ (3-2-1-0)

Score: _____ /12 = _____ %

_____ FAM _____ UNFAM

Prediction:

_____

_____

Andrew Carnegie

Andrew Carnegie was the son of Scottish immigrants. One of his first jobs was as a messenger boy. He earned $2.50 a week! At the age of eighteen, Carnegie got a job on the Pennsylvania Railroad. He soon realized that iron was not a good construction material for the railroad. Iron rails tended to crack and often had to be replaced. The weight of a train weakened iron bridges. Carnegie felt that steel would be a stronger building material. He decided to find ways to increase the production of steel.

Carnegie carefully saved his money and used it to become part owner of a small iron company. Eventually he acquired the ownership of several more companies. But making steel was slow and costly. Then Carnegie learned about the Bessemer process. Using this method, steel could be made quickly and on a large scale. Carnegie decided to risk all. He built a huge steel mill. He bought iron and coal mines as well as ships and trains for transport. By 1900, three million tons of steel were produced by Carnegie's mills each year, and his fortune was worth two hundred and fifty million.

Carnegie accomplished his dream, that of increasing steel production, and, in doing so, he developed and shaped the United States steel industry. In 1901, at the peak of his career, Carnegie sold his business and retired. He then spent much of his time and money in helping others and started more than two thousand libraries in the United States and around the world. Carnegie can truly be called the Man of Steel. (264 words)

From *Holt Social Studies, Our World, Our Regions, and Our History*, edited by JoAnn Cangemi, copyright © 1983 by Holt, Rinehart and Winston, Inc. Reprinted by permission of the publisher.

Number of Total Miscues
(Total Accuracy): _____

Number of Meaning-Change Miscues
(Total Acceptability): _____

Total Accuracy			**Total Acceptability**
0–6 miscues	____ Independent	____	0–6 miscues
7–27 miscues	____ Instructional	____	7–14 miscues
28+ miscues	____ Frustration	____	15+ miscues

Rate: 264 × 60 = 15,840/____ seconds = ____ WPM

Retelling Scoring Sheet for Andrew Carnegie

Setting/Background

____ Andrew Carnegie was the son
____ of immigrants
____ Scottish immigrants.
____ One of his jobs
____ first jobs
____ was as a messenger boy.
____ He earned $2.50
____ a week.
____ At the age of eighteen
____ Carnegie got a job
____ on the railroad.

____ He realized
____ that iron was not a good material
____ for the railroad.
____ Rails cracked
____ iron rails.
____ The weight of the train
____ weakened bridges
____ iron bridges.

Goal

____ Carnegie felt
____ steel would be stronger.
____ He decided
____ to find ways
____ to increase steel production.

Events

____ Carnegie saved his money.
____ He became the owner
____ of a company
____ an iron company.
____ He acquired the ownership
____ of more companies.
____ Making steel was
____ slow
____ and costly.
____ Carnegie learned
____ about the Bessemer process.
____ Steel could be made
____ quickly.
____ Carnegie decided
____ to risk all.
____ He built a steel mill.
____ He bought mines,
____ ships,
____ and trains.
____ By 1900
____ his fortune was worth millions.

Resolution

____ Carnegie accomplished his dream
____ of increasing steel production.
____ He developed the steel industry
____ in the United States.
____ He sold his business

____ and retired.
____ He helped others
____ and started libraries.
____ He can be called the Man of Steel.

Other ideas recalled, including references:

Questions for Andrew Carnegie

1. What was Carnegie's main goal?
   Implicit: to make steel faster and cheaper

2. What was one of Andrew Carnegie's first jobs?
   Explicit: messenger boy

3. Why would using steel as construction material make railroads safer?
   Implicit: bridges and rails would be stronger

4. What was the first business that Andrew Carnegie bought?
   Explicit: an iron company

5. Why wasn't steel used a lot for construction?
   Implicit: it was slow to make and cost a lot

6. Why did Andrew Carnegie buy ships and trains?
   Explicit: to transport iron and coal

7. Why did the Bessemer process of making steel make Andrew Carnegie's fortune?
   Implicit: he could make more steel with less cost

8. During his retirement, what did Andrew Carnegie start?
   Explicit: libraries

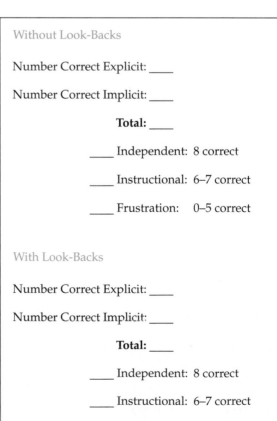

Without Look-Backs

Number Correct Explicit: ____

Number Correct Implicit: ____

   Total: ____

   ____ Independent: 8 correct

   ____ Instructional: 6–7 correct

   ____ Frustration: 0–5 correct

With Look-Backs

Number Correct Explicit: ____

Number Correct Implicit: ____

   Total: ____

   ____ Independent: 8 correct

   ____ Instructional: 6–7 correct

   ____ Frustration: 0–5 correct

Expository

Concept Questions:

What are uses of computers?

_____

_____

_____ (3-2-1-0)

What does "changes in computers" mean to you?

_____

_____

_____ (3-2-1-0)

What is computer input?

_____

_____

_____ (3-2-1-0)

What is a computer chip?

_____

_____

_____ (3-2-1-0)

Score: _____ /12 = _____ %

_____ FAM _____ UNFAM

Prediction:

_____

_____

Computers

Computers are machines that help solve problems, but they can't do anything without directions from humans. People give comput-ers information. Then they tell them what to do with it. Computers cannot come up with any new information, but they can save much work and time.

For example, you could store all the infor-mation in the phone book in a computer's memory. Then you could ask the computer to tell you all the names of people living on one single street. If you lived in a big city, it might take days or even weeks for you to come up with all the names. But the computer could do it in seconds!

The first computers were huge. One filled a whole floor of a large office building. The machines were very costly. Only big industries could buy them. But because computers could save so much time, other businesses wanted them. So scientists found a way to make com-puters smaller and cheaper by inventing chips. Chips made it possible to store more informa-tion in less space.

Today a computer can fit on your lap. Computers are still shrinking in size and price. More businesses use them. Hospitals use them to keep track of billing. Stores use them to make checkouts easier and faster. Families use computers too. Many students have computers at home that help them with their homework.

Level: Six

Computer games are very popular. A computer can help to keep track of a family's expenses. Someday every family may have a home computer. (254 words)

Adapted from M. R. Cohen, B. J. Del Giorno, J. D. Harlan, A. J. McCormack, and J. R. Staver, *Scott, Foresman Science, Grade 5* (Glenview, Ill.: Scott, Foresman and Co., 1984), pp. 348–349.

Number of Total Miscues
(Total Accuracy): _____

Number of Meaning-Change Miscues
(Total Acceptability): _____

Total Accuracy			**Total Acceptability**
0–6 miscues	____	Independent	____ 0–6 miscues
7–26 miscues	____	Instructional	____ 7–13 miscues
27+ miscues	____	Frustration	____ 14+ miscues

Rate: 254 × 60 = 15,240/____ seconds = ____ WPM

Retelling Scoring Sheet for Computers

Main Idea

____ Computers are machines
____ that solve problems
____ and save work
____ and time.

Details

____ Computers can't do anything
____ without directions
____ from humans.
____ You can store the information
____ in the phone book
____ in the computer.
____ The computer could tell you
____ the names
____ of people living

____ on one street.
____ It might take days
____ for you to come up
____ with the names.
____ A computer can do it
____ in seconds.

Main Idea

____ The first computers were huge.

Details

____ One filled a whole floor
____ of a building.
____ The machines were costly.
____ Only industries
____ big industries
____ could buy them.
____ But because computers could save
____ so much time,
____ other businesses wanted them.
____ Scientists found a way
____ to make computers
____ smaller
____ and cheaper
____ by inventing chips.
____ Chips made it possible
____ to store information
____ in less space.

Main Idea

____ Computers are shrinking
____ in size
____ and price.

Details

____ Computers can fit
____ on your lap
____ More businesses use them.
____ Hospitals use them.
____ Stores use them.
____ Families use computers
____ to help
____ with homework.
____ Computer games
____ are popular.

____ Someday
____ every family may have a computer.

Other ideas recalled, including inferences:

Questions for Computers

1. What is this passage mainly about?
   Implicit: how computers have changed

2. Why might a computer arrive at a wrong answer to a problem?
   Implicit: it was given the wrong information

3. Why were big businesses the only ones who could afford the first computers?
   Explicit: they cost so much

4. What did scientists invent that made computers smaller?
   Explicit: the computer chip

5. Why would businesses want a smaller computer?
   Implicit: it would take less space and/or cost less

6. Why are computers still getting smaller and cheaper?
   Implicit: the chips are more efficient; the chips store more information

7. According to the passage, how do stores use computers?
   Explicit: they help with checkout

8. According to the passage, what is one way that a family might use a computer?
   Explicit: homework; games; to keep track of expenses

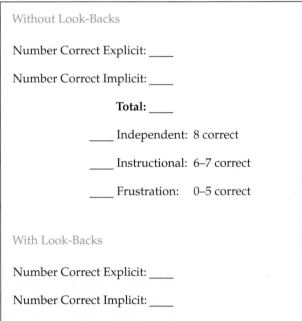

Without Look-Backs

Number Correct Explicit: ____

Number Correct Implicit: ____

Total: ____

____ Independent: 8 correct

____ Instructional: 6–7 correct

____ Frustration: 0–5 correct

With Look-Backs

Number Correct Explicit: ____

Number Correct Implicit: ____

Total: ____

____ Independent: 8 correct

____ Instructional: 6–7 correct

____ Frustration: 0–5 correct

Expository

Concept Questions:

What are earthquakes?

_____

_____

_____ (3-2-1-0)

What does "sizes of earthquakes" mean to you?

_____

_____

_____ (3-2-1-0)

Where are places where earthquakes happen?

_____

_____

_____ (3-2-1-0)

What are things that animals can sense but humans can't?

_____

_____

_____ (3-2-1-0)

Score: _____ /12 = _____ %

_____ FAM _____ UNFAM

Prediction:

_____

_____

Predicting Earthquakes

Some scientists think that certain animals know when an earthquake is coming. They sense the earthquake days or hours before it happens. In some cases, animal behavior has predicted a coming earthquake.

Before the Chinese earthquake in February of 1975, people noted animals doing strange things. Birds suddenly flew away. They would not return to their nests. Chickens refused to enter their coops. Rats ran around bumping into things. Well-trained police dogs howled and would not obey their masters. They kept sniffing the ground.

What might these animals know that we do not? Perhaps they can sense some of the changes that happen in the earth before an earthquake. Certain animals might hear low booms that come before an earthquake. Perhaps they can smell certain gases that escape from the earth.

Scientists wanted to study the possible connection between animal behavior and earthquakes. They set up a project in California. It ran for three years. Over a thousand volunteers took part. The volunteers watched animals and called the project every day to report on their actions. During the project at least thirteen earthquakes were recorded. Some were bigger than others. The volunteers saw an unusually high amount of strange behavior before seven of the earthquakes. Someday we may use animals to warn people of an earthquake. If this happens, we can thank the efforts of scientists and volunteers around the world. (231 words)

Adapted from M. R. Cohen, B. J. Del Giorno, J. D. Harlan, A. J. McCormack, and J. R. Staver, *Scott, Foresman Science, Grade 4* (Glenview, Ill.: Scott, Foresman and Co., 1984), p. 99.

Number of Total Miscues
(Total Accuracy): _____

Number of Meaning-Change Miscues
(Total Acceptability): _____

Total Accuracy		**Total Acceptability**
0–5 miscues	____ Independent ____	0–5 miscues
6–24 miscues	____ Instructional ____	6–12 miscues
25+ miscues	____ Frustration ____	13+ miscues

Rate: $231 \times 60 = 13,860/$____ seconds = ____ WPM

Retelling Scoring Sheet for Predicting Earthquakes

Main Idea

____ Scientists think
____ that animals know
____ when an earthquake is coming.

Details

____ Animal behavior
____ has predicted an earthquake.
____ Before the earthquake
____ the Chinese earthquake
____ of 1975,
____ people noted animals
____ doing strange things.
____ Birds flew away
____ and would not return
____ to their nests.

____ Chickens would not enter their coops.
____ Rats ran around
____ bumping into things.
____ Dogs howled
____ police dogs
____ and would not obey their masters.
____ They kept sniffing
____ the ground.

Main Idea

____ What might these animals know?

Details

____ They might sense changes
____ that happen
____ in the earth.
____ They might hear booms
____ low booms.
____ They might smell certain gases
____ that escape
____ from the earth.

Main Idea

____ Scientists wanted
____ to study the connection
____ between animal behavior
____ and earthquakes.

Details

____ They set up a project
____ in California.
____ It ran
____ for years
____ three years.
____ They watched animals
____ and reported their actions.
____ Earthquakes
____ thirteen earthquakes
____ were recorded.
____ Volunteers saw
____ strange behavior
____ before seven
____ of the earthquakes.
____ Someday
____ we may use animals

Level: Six

___ to warn people
___ of an earthquake.
___ If this happens
___ we can thank the efforts
___ of scientists
___ and volunteers.

Other ideas recalled, including inferences:

Questions for Predicting Earthquakes

1. What is this passage mainly about?
   Implicit: how animals may be able to predict earthquakes

2. How did chickens behave before the Chinese earthquake?
   Explicit: they wouldn't enter their coops

3. What might animals hear before an earthquake?
   Explicit: low booms

4. Why might dogs sniff the ground before an earthquake?
   Implicit: they may smell escaping gases

5. What did the California project volunteers observe?
   Explicit: animals; animal actions; animal behaviors

6. How many earthquakes were predicted by the animals during the California project?
   Explicit: seven

7. Why didn't the animals in the California project show strange behavior before all the earthquakes?
   Implicit: some earthquakes were not big enough

8. Why was California a good state for an earthquake project?
   Implicit: they have a lot of earthquakes

Without Look-Backs

Number Correct Explicit: ____

Number Correct Implicit: ____

Total: ____

____ Independent: 8 correct

____ Instructional: 6–7 correct

____ Frustration: 0–5 correct

With Look-Backs

Number Correct Explicit: ____

Number Correct Implicit: ____

Total: ____

____ Independent: 8 correct

____ Instructional: 6–7 correct

____ Frustration: 0–5 correct

Level: Six

Expository

Ultrasound

Some medical research uses sounds that you cannot hear. The word ultrasonic is used to describe sounds with very high frequencies. Ultrasonic sounds range from twenty thousand to more than a billion vibrations per second. These sounds are too high for humans to hear. But dogs and other animals can hear them.

Scientists have found many uses for ultrasonic sounds. For example, doctors use ultrasound to study the health of babies before they are born. Ultrasonic sounds can be sent through the mother's abdomen. The waves reflect off the baby's body into a microphone that picks up these waves. The reflected sounds can be made into a picture and shown on a television screen.

The ultrasonic wave patterns show some of the health problems a baby might have. Heart problems and slow growth can be detected. The doctors can use this information to plan ahead for what the baby might need as soon as it is born. Doctors can also use this method to tell the mother if she is expecting twins or triplets.

Many industrial uses of ultrasonics have also been found. Some factories use ultrasonic waves to look for hidden cracks in metals. Such waves can be used to find gas and oil deposits underground. Paint and homogenized milk can be mixed by ultrasonic waves. Dentists

Level 6

can even clean your teeth with these waves. This unheard sound has become a useful tool in many areas of medicine, industry, and science research. (242 words)

Adapted from M. R. Cohen, B. J. Del Giorno, J. D. Harlan, A. J. McCormack, and J. R. Staver, *Scott, Foresman Science, Grade 5* (Glenview, Ill.: Scott, Foresman and Co., 1984), p. 239.

Number of Total Miscues
(Total Accuracy): _____

Number of Meaning-Change Miscues
(Total Acceptability): _____

Total Accuracy			Total Acceptability
0–6 miscues	____	Independent	____ 0–6 miscues
7–25 miscues	____	Instructional	____ 7–13 miscues
26+ miscues	____	Frustration	____ 14+ miscues

Rate: 242 × 60 = 14,520/____ seconds = ____ WPM

Retelling Scoring Sheet for Ultrasound

Main Idea

____ Ultrasonic is used to describe sounds
____ with very high frequencies.

Details

____ These sounds are too high
____ for humans to hear.
____ But dogs
____ and other animals can hear them.

Main Idea

____ Scientists have found many uses
____ for ultrasonic sounds.

Details

____ Doctors use ultrasound
____ to study the health

____ of babies
____ before they are born.
____ Ultrasonic sounds can be sent
____ through the abdomen
____ the mother's abdomen.
____ The ultrasonic patterns show some of the
____ problems
____ a baby might have.
____ Heart problems
____ and slow growth can be detected.
____ Doctors can use this method
____ to tell the mother
____ if she is expecting twins
____ or triplets.

Main Idea

____ Industrial uses of ultrasonics have been
____ found.

Details

____ Factories use ultrasonic waves
____ to look for cracks
____ in metals.
____ Such waves can be used
____ to find gas
____ and oil
____ underground.
____ Paint
____ and milk
____ can be mixed
____ by ultrasound.
____ Dentists can clean your teeth
____ with these waves.
____ This sound has become a tool
____ this unheard sound
____ a useful tool
____ in many areas
____ of medicine,
____ industry,
____ and science.

Other ideas recalled, including inferences:

Questions for Ultrasound

1. What is this passage mainly about?
   Implicit: how ultrasound is used

2. What kinds of frequencies do ultrasounds have?
   Explicit: very high ones

3. Why can't humans hear ultrasounds?
   Explicit: they are too high

4. How is animal hearing different from human hearing?
   Implicit: animals can hear higher frequencies

5. What possible health problems of an unborn baby can a doctor see by using ultrasound?
   Explicit: heart problems or slow growth

6. Why is it important for doctors to use ultrasound with unborn babies?
   Implicit: the doctors can plan ahead

7. How does the paint industry use ultrasound?
   Explicit: to mix paint

8. How could ultrasound be used to discover if a bridge is sound?
   Implicit: it could locate hidden cracks

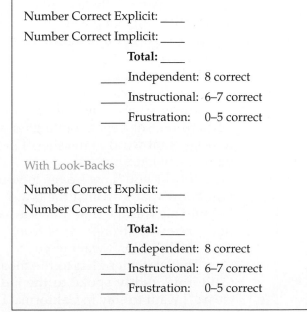

Without Look-Backs

Number Correct Explicit: ____

Number Correct Implicit: ____

 Total: ____

____ Independent: 8 correct

____ Instructional: 6–7 correct

____ Frustration: 0–5 correct

With Look-Backs

Number Correct Explicit: ____

Number Correct Implicit: ____

 Total: ____

____ Independent: 8 correct

____ Instructional: 6–7 correct

____ Frustration: 0–5 correct

Biddy Mason

Sometimes it seemed they would never stop traveling. First there had been the long trip to Utah. All day Biddy had walked along behind the wagons, tending the cattle. For months they walked, getting farther and farther from Mississippi. It was a hard trip, especially for her children. But what could Biddy do? She was born a slave. She was a slave today. Her master told her to walk across the plains and she did it.

They had stayed in Utah only one year. Then word came of a new settlement in southern California. Robert Smith decided to go. Again the wagons were packed. Again they began the long days of walking.

Biddy had plenty of time for thinking along the way. What she mostly thought about was freedom. As a child she had never known a black person who wasn't a slave. Oh, she heard about them, about the ones who escaped to the North. But it was so hard to imagine!

Then came the trip west. Things were different here. She had seen families, *black families,* traveling west with their own wagons! Just think of it! They planned to find their own land, start their own farms, or find work in the towns. Biddy had thought about them for days.

Biddy looked down at her bare feet. They were tired and sore and covered with dust. "These feet walked every mile from Mississippi," she thought. "And they remembered every step. They have walked for Mr. Smith and his family. They have walked after his crops and his wagons and his cattle. But someday these feet are going to walk for me. Someday these feet will walk me to freedom. I'm sure of it."

A few days later, the tired travelers arrived at San Bernardino, California. It was a lovely place. It was their new home.

There were many reasons to enjoy living in California in 1852. The climate was pleasant. The land was good. The air was fresh and warm. Cities were booming. Everywhere there was a sense of promise and excitement.

The most important thing for Biddy was the promise of freedom. She had heard people talking. The new state of California did not permit slavery, they said. By law, all people here were free. Biddy looked again at her dusty traveling feet. "Soon," she said to herself, "soon."

Three years passed. Life was pretty good, but Mr. Smith must have loved traveling. Even this beautiful settlement could not hold him. He decided to move again, this time to Texas. The wagons were loaded and made ready to go.

Biddy knew she had to act. As soon as the wagons left San Bernardino, she began looking for an opportunity. She found one. Somehow she sent word to the sheriff in Los Angeles. He stopped the wagons before they left California.

"I hear you have slaves in your party," said the sheriff. "I suppose you know that's against the law. Is it true?" Biddy came forward. In all her life this was the first time she had ever spoken to a white sheriff. Still her voice was strong. "It is true," she said. "Mr. Smith is taking us to Texas and we don't want to go."

That statement led to the most important slavery trial in southern California. Biddy spoke to the judge, and her words were strong and clear: "I want to stay in California. I want to be free."

The judge sided with Biddy. He scolded Mr. Smith for breaking the law. He gave all the slaves their freedom.

Biddy gathered up her children and said, "We are moving once more, but it won't be very far. We are going to Los Angeles, and this time," she said looking at her tired feet, "I am walking for me!"

She started her new life by taking as her full name Biddy Mason. She went to work as a nurse and a housekeeper. Before long she had saved enough money to buy a house. Soon she bought other property too. Biddy Mason was a good businesswoman. She became one of the wealthiest blacks in Los Angeles.

She shared that wealth with others. She gave land to build schools and hospitals and nursing homes. She supported the education of black children and helped people in need. Biddy Mason had come a long way from that slave's cabin in Mississippi. She still remembered the walking. And she made sure she helped others along their way. (750 words)

Malcolm X

It was because of my letters that I happened to stumble upon starting to acquire some kind of homemade education.

I became increasingly frustrated at not being able to express what I wanted to convey in letters that I wrote, especially those to Mr. Elijah Muhammad. In the street, I had been the most articulate hustler out there. I had commanded attention when I said something. But now, trying to write simple English, I not only wasn't articulate, I wasn't even functional. How would I sound writing in slang, the way I would *say* it, something such as, "Look, daddy, let me pull your coat about a cat, Elijah Muhammad."

Many who today hear me somewhere in person, or on television, or those who read something I've said, will think I went to school far beyond the eighth grade. This impression is due entirely to my prison studies.

It had really begun back in the Charlestown Prison, when Bimbi first made me feel envy of his stock of knowledge. Bimbi had always taken charge of any conversation he was in, and I had tried to emulate him. But every book I picked up had few sentences which didn't contain anywhere from one to nearly all of the words that might as well have been in Chinese. When I just skipped those words, of course, I really ended up with little idea of what the book said. So I had come to the Norfolk Prison Colony still going through only book-reading motions. Pretty soon, I would have quit even these motions, unless I had received the motivation that I did.

I saw that the best thing I could do was get hold of a dictionary to study, to learn some words. I was lucky enough to reason also that I should try to improve my penmanship. It was sad. I couldn't even write in a straight line. It was both ideas together that moved me to request a dictionary along with some tablets and pencils from the Norfolk Prison Colony school.

I spent two days just riffling uncertainly through the dictionary's pages. I'd never realized so many words existed! I didn't know *which* words I needed to learn. Finally, just to start some kind of action, I began copying.

In my slow, painstaking, ragged handwriting, I copied into my tablet everything printed on that first page, down to the punctuation marks.

I believe it took me a day. Then, aloud, I read back to myself everything I'd written on the tablet. Over and over, aloud, to myself, I read my own handwriting.

I woke up the next morning, thinking about those words, immensely proud to realize that not only had I written so much at one time, but I'd written words that I never knew were in the world. Moreover, with a little effort, I also could remember what many of these words meant. I reviewed the words whose meanings I didn't remember. Funny thing, from the dictionary first page right now, that "aardvark" springs to my mind. The dictionary had a picture of it, a long-tailed, long-eared, burrowing African mammal, which lives off termites caught by sticking out its tongue as an anteater does for ants.

I was so fascinated that I went on. I copied the dictionary's next page. And the same experience came when I studied that. With every succeeding page, I also learned of people and places and events from history. Actually, the dictionary is like a miniature encyclopedia. Finally, the dictionary's A section had filled a whole tablet—and I went on to the B's. That was the way I started copying what eventually became the entire dictionary. It went a lot faster after so much practice helped me to pick up handwriting speed. Between what I wrote in my tablet, and writing letters, during the rest of my time in prison I would guess I wrote a million words.

I suppose it was inevitable that as my word-base broadened, I could for the first time pick up a book and read and now begin to understand what the book was saying. Anyone who has read a great deal can imagine the new world that opened. Let me tell you something: from then until I left that prison, in every free moment I had, if I was not reading in the library, I was reading on my bunk. You couldn't have gotten me out of books with a wedge. Between Mr. Muhammad's teachings, my correspondence, my visitors, usually Ella and Reginald, and my reading of books, months passed without my even thinking about being imprisoned. In fact, up to then, I never had been so truly free in my life. (786 words)

Lewis and Clark

In April 1803, President Thomas Jefferson purchased the entire area of Louisiana from France. The territory stretched from the Mississippi River to the middle of the Rocky Mountains, but no one was really sure where the Mississippi River started or where exactly the Rocky Mountains were located. Meriwether Lewis and William Clark were commissioned by Jefferson to find answers to some of the many questions that people had regarding the new purchase. They were to explore the area and describe the land and its human and animal inhabitants.

Lewis and Clark departed in May 1804 with forty-three men and sufficient supplies for two years. They paddled up the Missouri River in canoes and halted with the coming of winter. They became acquainted with a sixteen-year-old Indian woman and adopted her as their primary guide. Her name was Sacajawea, which means Bird Woman. When the ice melted, they continued on their journey. All along the way, Lewis and Clark drew maps and diagrams and recorded what they observed in meticulous detail. They encountered Indian leaders, told them about the United States, and presented them with medals and American flags from the president. They acquired knowledge about soil and weather conditions and investigated fur trading possibilities. After seven months of difficult travel, they reached the Rocky Mountains.

Thanks to Sacajawea's influence, Lewis and Clark obtained horses from the Indians. Their intention was to cross the Rockies with the Pacific Ocean as their final destination. The weather grew cold, the food became scarce, and the mountains seemed endless. When they finally arrived at the ocean, Clark wrote in his journal, "The ocean is in view! Oh, what joy!" When the expedition finally returned home over two years after they began their journey, they were awarded a tumultuous welcome. People had long since given them up for dead. That welcome was well deserved. During the long and arduous voyage, Lewis and Clark had accomplished an outstanding feat in describing the land, the rivers, and the Indian inhabitants. They had proven that there was a way to reach the Pacific and had opened a huge new area for settlement and trade. Many other Americans would soon follow in their footsteps.

Adapted from L. J. Buggey, G. A. Danzer, C. L. Mitsakos, and C. F. Risinger, *America! America!* (Glenview, Ill.: Scott, Foresman and Co., 1982), pp. 267–269.

Ferdinand Magellan

In the early sixteenth century, a Portuguese noble, soldier, and sailor named Ferdinand Magellan performed what has been designated the greatest single human achievement on the sea. Magellan had spent long years in Asia, and he often gazed across the wide expanse of the Pacific Ocean and asked himself a question. "How far away from here are the lands discovered by Columbus? If I sailed to the New World, could I find a passage to the Pacific Ocean and the rich Spice Islands?" Magellan hoped to find answers to his questions as well as obtain a large cargo of rare and costly spices. When the Portuguese king refused to assist him, he turned to Spain for help.

In 1519, Magellan sailed from Spain with five ships and a crew of almost three hundred sailors. He navigated the Atlantic and when he reached the New World, he followed the coast of South America until he found the straits that connected the two oceans. It took Magellan thirty-eight days to sail through the stormy straits to the Pacific Ocean, and during that difficult time, one ship was wrecked and one headed back to Spain. Once in the Pacific Ocean, Magellan turned north and traveled for months without sighting land.

The voyage was filled with extreme hardship. At one point several resentful Spanish captains initiated a rebellion against their Portuguese admiral. Magellan defeated the rebels and left two of them on shore to die. Several times the ships ran low on supplies, and with little food and water, the sailors begged to turn back, but Magellan would not allow this. At one point he declared that they would continue the voyage even if they had to eat the leather rigging of the ships. Disease and starvation claimed many of the crew but, mindful of the fate of the earlier rebels, no one opposed Magellan's will.

Magellan finally reached the islands of the Pacific, but he was unfortunately killed in a skirmish with some natives. One of his ships became unseaworthy and the other was wrecked. The remaining vessel with only seventeen of the original crew members sailed west through the Indian Ocean and around the southern tip of Africa. When they limped into a Spanish port, they had been gone three years! Although Magellan did not live to see the conclusion of the voyage, he and his crew accomplished what no one had ever done before. They had circumnavigated, or sailed around, the world. Magellan would never know that he had proved what Columbus had correctly predicted, that the lands of the East could be reached by sailing west.

Adapted from L. J. Buggey, G. A. Danzer, C. L. Mitsakos, and C. F. Risinger, *America! America!* (Glenview, Ill.: Scott, Foresman and Co., 1982), pp. 83–86.

Fireworks

Most of us have seen beautiful fireworks. They are often used on the Fourth of July, Labor Day, or other holidays. Around the world, firecrackers, Roman candles, cherry bombs, and rockets are used to celebrate many important events. Royal weddings, military victories, important births, peace treaties, and religious holidays have all been causes for setting off fireworks. Fireworks are also used just for fun. Their sound, color, and sparkle have charmed people for centuries.

Chemicals in Fireworks

Fireworks were probably invented in China about seven hundred years ago. A mixture of saltpeter, sulfur, and carbon was found to be useful for two quite different purposes: gunpowder and fireworks. Since then, these two uses of explosives have developed at the same time. A Roman candle is not much different from a small bomb. An explosion sends the rocket into the air and then makes it blow apart. Powdered metals catch fire and cause the sparks and flames. Metallic compounds add color to the sparks. Sodium compounds produce a yellow color. Calcium compounds make red. Green comes from barium and blue-green from copper. Ammonium compounds change the shades of these colors, and sulfur makes the colors more brilliant.

Dangers of Fireworks

Because fireworks are so dangerous, they are not allowed in many parts of the United States. Every year fireworks used without careful supervision hurt both children and adults, some very seriously. People do not understand how fast fireworks explode after the fuse is lit. They also do not realize the force of the explosion. Putting on a huge fireworks display is a dangerous job, even for those who know what they are doing. Timing is crucial, as is knowing how far apart to place the various kinds of fireworks used. A rocket may not explode when it is expected to, or it may not shoot as far into the sky as it should. Fireworks may be fun, but they are a dangerous kind of fun.

Adapted from T. Cooney, J. Pasachoff, and N. Pasachoff, *Physical Science* (Glenview, Ill.: Scott, Foresman and Co., 1984), p. 269.

Life Cycles of Stars

Stars have life cycles, just like humans. In fact, a star is born, changes, and then dies. In contrast to the human life cycle that lasts about 75 years, the life cycle of a typical star is measured in billions of years.

Every star in the sky is at a different stage in its life cycle. Some stars are relatively young, while others are near the end of their existence. The sun is about halfway through its 10-billion-year-long life cycle.

Birth of a Star

The space between stars is not entirely empty. In some places, there are great clouds of gas and dust. Each of these clouds is a nebula. A nebula is where stars are born.

The element hydrogen makes up most of a nebula. Helium and a sprinkling of dust are also present. The particles in a nebula are spread very thin. In fact, the particles are a million times less dense than the particles in the air you breathe. However, because nebulae are very large, they contain enormous amounts of matter.

Gravity causes matter to be attracted to other matter. Therefore, as a nebula travels though space, it collects more dust and gas. The clouds become packed tighter and tighter, as gravity pulls it all together. Whenever matter is packed in this way, it heats up. An especially dense part of the nebula may form a hot, spinning ball of matter. Such a ball of hot matter is called a *protostar*.

A protostar doesn't yet shine by ordinary light, but it does give off infrared energy. Scientists identify protostars within nebulae by using infrared telescopes. A protostar eventually becomes hot enough for nuclear fusion to take place in its core. When nuclear fusion produces great amounts of energy, a star comes to life.

Life of a Low-Mass Star

Stars begin their life cycle with different masses. A star's mass determines how long its life cycle will last and how it will die. Stars with a mass less than five times that of the sun are called low-mass stars. Most stars are in this group.

A low-mass star begins its life cycle as a main-sequence star. Over a period of billions of years, its supply of hydrogen is slowly changed by nuclear fusion into helium. During this time, the star changes very little.

Red Giant Stage. As the hydrogen in the core of a low-mass star is used up, the core starts to collapse. The core of the star becomes denser and hotter. The increased temperature causes another kind of nuclear reaction. Helium is converted to carbon. This nuclear reaction gives off great amounts of energy, causing the star to expand. It becomes a red giant.

The red giant stage in a star's life is relatively short. The sun will be a main-sequence star for a total of 10 billion years. But the sun will be a red giant for only about 500 million years.

Dwarf Stage. Eventually, most of the helium in a red giant's core is changed into carbon. Nuclear fusion slows. The star cools, and gravity makes it collapse inward. The matter making up the star is squeezed together very tightly, and the star becomes a white dwarf.

A typical white dwarf is about the size of Earth. But its matter is far denser than any matter on Earth. Eventually, the star becomes a burned-out black chunk of very dense matter that gives off no visible light. Then it is called a black dwarf.

Adapted from *Science Insights: Exploring Earth and Science* by M. D. Spezio, M. Linner-Luebe, M. Lisowski, G. Skoog, and B. Sparks. © 1996 by Addison-Wesley Publishing Company, Inc. Used by permission.

Literature

Concept Questions:

What is a biography?

_____

_____

_____ (3-2-1-0)

What is slavery?

_____

_____

_____ (3-2-1-0)

What does it mean to be courageous?

_____

_____

_____ (3-2-1-0)

What is a settlement?

_____

_____

_____ (3-2-1-0)

Score: _____ /12 = _____ %

_____ FAM _____ UNFAM

Prediction:

_____

_____

Biddy Mason

Sometimes it seemed they would never stop traveling. First there had been the long trip to Utah. All day Biddy had walked along behind the wagons, tending the cattle. For months they walked, getting farther and farther from Mississippi. It was a hard trip, especially for her children. But what could Biddy do? She was born a slave. She was a slave today. Her master told her to walk across the plains and she did it.

They had stayed in Utah only one year. Then word came of a new settlement in southern California. Robert Smith decided to go. Again the wagons were packed. Again they began the long days of walking.

Biddy had plenty of time for thinking along the way. What she mostly thought about was freedom. As a child she had never known a black person who wasn't a slave. Oh, she heard about them, about the ones who escaped to the North. But it was so hard to imagine!

Then came the trip west. Things were different here. She had seen families, *black families*, traveling west with their own wagons! Just think of it! They planned to find their own land, start their own farms, or find work in the towns. Biddy had thought about them for days.

Biddy looked down at her bare feet. They were tired and sore and covered with dust. "These feet walked every mile from Mississippi," she thought. "And they remembered

Level: Upper Middle School

every step. They have walked for Mr. Smith and his family. They have walked after his crops and his wagons and his cattle. But someday these feet are going to walk for me. Someday these feet will walk me to freedom. I'm sure of it."

A few days later, the tired travelers arrived at San Bernardino, California. It was a lovely place. It was their new home.

There were many reasons to enjoy living in California in 1852. The climate was pleasant. The land was good. The air was fresh and warm. Cities were booming. Everywhere there was a sense of promise and excitement.

The most important thing for Biddy was the promise of freedom. She had heard people talking. The new state of California did not permit slavery, they said. By law, all people here were free. Biddy looked again at her dusty traveling feet. "Soon," she said to herself, "soon."

Three years passed. Life was pretty good, but Mr. Smith must have loved traveling. Even this beautiful settlement could not hold him. He decided to move again, this time to Texas. The wagons were loaded and made ready to go.

Biddy knew she had to act. As soon as the wagons left San Bernardino, she began looking for an opportunity. She found one. Somehow she sent word to the sheriff in Los Angeles. He stopped the wagons before they left California.

"I hear you have slaves in your party," said the sheriff. "I suppose you know that's against the law. Is it true?" Biddy came forward. In all her life this was the first time she had ever spoken to a white sheriff. Still her voice was strong. "It is true," she said. "Mr. Smith is taking us to Texas and we don't want to go."

That statement led to the most important slavery trial in southern California. Biddy spoke to the judge, and her words were strong and clear: "I want to stay in California. I want to be free."

The judge sided with Biddy. He scolded Mr. Smith for breaking the law. He gave all the slaves their freedom.

Biddy gathered up her children and said, "We are moving once more, but it won't be very far. We are going to Los Angeles, and this time," she said looking at her tired feet, "I am walking for me!"

She started her new life by taking as her full name Biddy Mason. She went to work as a nurse and a housekeeper. Before long she had saved enough money to buy a house. Soon she bought other property too. Biddy Mason was a good businesswoman. She became one of the wealthiest blacks in Los Angeles.

She shared that wealth with others. She gave land to build schools and hospitals and nursing homes. She supported the education of black children and helped people in need. Biddy Mason had come a long way from that slave's cabin in Mississippi. She still <u>remembered</u> the walking. And she made sure she helped others along their way. (750 words)

"Biddy Mason" from *Black Heroes of the Wild West* by Ruth Pelz. Copyright © 1990 by Open Hand Publishing, Inc. Reprinted by permission of Open Hand Publishing, Inc.

Number of Total Miscues
(Total Accuracy): _____

Number of Meaning-Change Miscues
(Total Acceptability): _____

Total Accuracy		Total Acceptability	
0–15 miscues	____ Independent ____	0–15 miscues	
16–75 miscues	____ Instructional ____	16–37 miscues	
76+ miscues	____ Frustration ____	38+ miscues	

Rate: 750 × 60 = 45,000 / ____ seconds = ____ WPM

Retelling Scoring Sheet for Biddy Mason

Setting/Background

____ Biddy walked
____ behind the wagons.
____ She was a slave.
____ Her master told her to walk
____ and she did it.
____ Word came
____ of a settlement

____ in California.
____ Robert Smith decided to go.

Goal

____ Biddy thought about freedom.
____ She had never known a black person
____ who wasn't a slave.
____ On the trip west,
____ she saw black families
____ traveling west
____ planning to find land
____ and start farms.
____ Her feet were tired.
____ "They have walked for Mr. Smith,
____ but someday
____ they are going to walk for me
____ to freedom!"

Events

____ They arrived in California.
____ Biddy heard people talking.
____ California did not permit slavery.
____ Mr. Smith decided to move again.
____ The wagons were packed.

Goal

____ Biddy knew
____ she had to act.
____ She sent word
____ to the sheriff
____ in Los Angeles.

Events

____ He stopped the wagons.
____ "I hear you have slaves.
____ Is it true?"
____ Biddy came forward.
____ Her voice was strong.
____ "It is true.
____ We don't want to go."
____ Her statement led to a trial.
____ Biddy spoke to the judge.
____ "I want to stay in California."
____ The judge sided with Biddy.

Level: Upper Middle School

___ He scolded Mr. Smith
___ for breaking the law.
___ The judge gave the slaves
___ their freedom.
___ Biddy gathered her children.
___ "We are moving
___ to Los Angeles.
___ I am walking for me."

Resolution

___ She went to work
___ as a nurse
___ and housekeeper.
___ She saved money.
___ She bought property.
___ She was a good businesswoman.
___ She became one of the wealthiest blacks.
___ She shared her wealth.
___ She gave land for schools
___ and hospitals
___ and nursing homes.
___ She helped people
___ in need.

Other ideas recalled, including summary
statements and inferences:

Questions for Biddy Mason

1. What is this selection mainly about?
   Implicit: how a slave gained freedom

2. What did Biddy think about while she was
   walking from state to state?
   Explicit: freedom

3. What did Biddy see on the trip west that
   was different from anything she had
   ever seen before? *Explicit:* black families
   traveling west with their own wagons and
   planning to start their own farms

4. What was special about California in the
   1850s?
   Explicit: California did not permit slavery
   and one of the following: the climate was
   good, cities were booming, there was a
   sense of promise and excitement

5. Why did Biddy need to act quickly when
   Mr. Smith decided to move to Texas?
   Implicit: when they left California, she
   would lose her chance of being freed

6. What two events happened when the Los Angeles sheriff stopped Mr. Smith's wagons?
Explicit: the sheriff asked if there were slaves *and* Biddy spoke up saying she didn't want to go to Texas

7. What was the outcome of the trial?
Explicit: the slaves were freed

8. What did Biddy mean when she told her children that they were going to Los Angeles but that this time, her feet were walking for her?
Implicit: she was walking as a free person going where she wanted to go

9. Give two examples of Biddy's behavior that indicate that she was a courageous person.
Implicit: she took risks such as speaking up to the sheriff *or* she told the judge she wanted to stay in California *or* she became a successful businesswoman

10. Why do you think the author chose to write a biography of Biddy Mason?
Implicit: because Biddy went from slavery to success *or* she helped others in need *or* her life could be an inspiration to others

Without Look-Backs

Number Correct Explicit: ____

Number Correct Implicit: ____

        Total: ____

____ Independent: 9–10 correct

____ Instructional: 7–8 correct

____ Frustration: 6 or less correct

With Look-Backs

Number Correct Explicit: ____

Number Correct Implicit: ____

        Total: ____

____ Independent: 9–10 correct

____ Instructional: 7–8 correct

____ Frustration: 6 or less correct

Level: Upper Middle School

Literature

Concept Questions:

What is an autobiography?

_____

_____

_____ (3-2-1-0)

Who was Malcolm X?

_____

_____

_____ (3-2-1-0)

What does the word "articulate" mean?

_____

_____

_____ (3-2-1-0)

What does it mean to emulate someone?

_____

_____

_____ (3-2-1-0)

Score: _____ /12 = _____ %

_____ FAM _____ UNFAM

Prediction:

_____

_____

Malcolm X

It was because of my letters that I happened to stumble upon starting to acquire some kind of homemade education.

I became increasingly frustrated at not being able to express what I wanted to convey in letters that I wrote, especially those to Mr. Elijah Muhammad. In the street, I had been the most articulate hustler out there. I had commanded attention when I said something. But now, trying to write simple English, I not only wasn't articulate, I wasn't even functional. How would I sound writing in slang, the way I would *say* it, something such as, "Look, daddy, let me pull your coat about a cat, Elijah Muhammad."

Many who today hear me somewhere in person, or on television, or those who read something I've said, will think I went to school far beyond the eighth grade. This impression is due entirely to my prison studies.

It had really begun back in the Charlestown Prison, when Bimbi first made me feel envy of his stock of knowledge. Bimbi had always taken charge of any conversation he was in, and I had tried to emulate him. But every book I picked up had few sentences which didn't contain anywhere from one to nearly all of the words that might as well have been in Chinese. When I just skipped those words, of course, I really ended up with little idea of what the book said. So I had come to the Norfolk Prison Colony still going through only book-reading motions. Pretty soon, I would have quit even these motions, unless I had received the motivation that I did.

I saw that the best thing I could do was get hold of a dictionary to study, to learn some words. I was lucky enough to reason also that I should try to improve my penmanship. It was sad. I couldn't even write in a straight line. It was both ideas together that moved me to request a dictionary along with some tablets and pencils from the Norfolk Prison Colony school.

I spent two days just riffling uncertainly through the dictionary's pages. I'd never realized so many words existed! I didn't know *which* words I needed to learn. Finally, just to start some kind of action, I began copying.

In my slow, painstaking, ragged handwriting, I copied into my tablet everything printed on that first page, down to the punctuation marks.

I believe it took me a day. Then, aloud, I read back to myself everything I'd written on the tablet. Over and over, aloud, to myself, I read my own handwriting.

I woke up the next morning, thinking about those words, immensely proud to realize that not only had I written so much at one time, but I'd written words that I never knew were in the world. Moreover, with a little effort, I also could remember what many of these words meant. I reviewed the words whose meanings I didn't remember. Funny thing, from the dictionary first page right now, that "aardvark" springs to my mind. The dictionary had a picture of it, a long-tailed, long-eared, burrowing African mammal, which lives off termites caught by sticking out its tongue as an anteater does for ants.

I was so fascinated that I went on. I copied the dictionary's next page. And the same experience came when I studied that. With every succeeding page, I also learned of people and places and events from history. Actually, the dictionary is like a miniature encyclopedia. Finally, the dictionary's A section had filled a whole tablet—and I went on to the B's. That was the way I started copying what eventually became the entire dictionary. It went a lot faster after so much practice helped me to pick up handwriting speed. Between what I wrote in my tablet, and writing letters, during the rest of my time in prison I would guess I wrote a million words.

I suppose it was inevitable that as my word-base broadened, I could for the first time pick up a book and read and now begin to understand what the book was saying. Anyone who has read a great deal can imagine the new world that opened. Let me tell you something: from then until I left that prison, in every free moment I had, if I was not reading in the library, I was reading on my bunk. You couldn't have gotten me out of books with a wedge. Between Mr. Muhammad's teachings, my correspondence, my visitors, usually Ella and Reginald, and my reading of books, months passed without my even thinking about being imprisoned. In fact, up to then, I never had been so truly free in my life. (786 words)

From *The Autobiography of Malcolm X* by Malcolm X with the assistance of Alex Haley. Copyright © 1964 by Alex Haley and Malcolm X. Copyright (c) 1965 by Alex Haley and Betty Shabazz. Reprinted by permission of Random House, Inc.

Number of Total Miscues
(Total Accuracy): _____

Number of Meaning-Change Miscues
(Total Acceptability): _____

Total Accuracy				**Total Acceptability**
0–16 miscues	____	Independent	____	0–16 miscues
17–79 miscues	____	Instructional	____	17–39 miscues
80+ miscues	____	Frustration	____	40+ miscues

Rate: 786 × 60 = 47,160/____ seconds = ____ WPM

Retelling Scoring Sheet for Malcolm X

Goal

____ I became frustrated
____ at not being able to express myself

____ in letters.
____ I had been a hustler
____ a most articulate hustler.
____ But trying to write English,
____ I wasn't functional.
____ Today
____ people think I went to school
____ beyond eighth grade.
____ This impression is due to my prison studies.

Setting/Background

____ It began in prison
____ where Bimbi made me envious
____ of his knowledge.
____ He took charge of conversation.
____ I tried to emulate him.
____ I had little idea
____ of what a book said.

Events

____ I got hold of a dictionary
____ to study some words.
____ I reasoned
____ that I should improve my penmanship.
____ I couldn't write in a straight line.
____ I requested a dictionary
____ along with tablets
____ and pencils.
____ I spent two days
____ rifling through the pages.
____ I never realized
____ that so many words existed.
____ I began copying
____ in my slow handwriting.
____ I copied the first page.
____ It took me a day.
____ I read back to myself
____ everything I'd written
____ over and over.
____ I woke up the next morning
____ immensely proud.
____ I could remember
____ what the words meant.
____ I reviewed the words

____ whose meanings I didn't remember.
____ I copied the next page.
____ With every page,
____ I learned of people,
____ places,
____ and events.
____ I copied the entire dictionary.
____ It went a lot faster
____ after practice helped me
____ pick up handwriting speed.
____ Between what I wrote
____ and writing letters
____ I wrote a million words.

Resolution

____ As my word-base broadened,
____ I could pick up a book
____ and understand it.
____ From then until I left prison,
____ I spent every free moment
____ reading.
____ I had never been so free
____ in my life.

Other ideas recalled, including summary statements and inferences:

Questions for Malcolm X

1. What was this selection mostly about?
   Implicit: how Malcolm X got an education in prison by reading *or* how Malcolm X improved his reading and writing by studying in prison

2. How did Malcolm X describe his early writing abilities?
   Explicit: he couldn't express what he wanted to say *or* the writing wasn't even functional

3. Why did Malcolm X decide he should learn to write better?
   Explicit: he couldn't express his ideas clearly in writing, especially in letters to Elijah Muhammad

4. Before he went to prison, what was the highest grade of formal schooling that Malcolm X had completed?
   Implicit: eighth grade

Level: Upper Middle School

5. Before Malcolm X improved his reading skills, what did he do when he was reading and came to words that he didn't know?
Explicit: he skipped them

6. How did Malcolm X begin his informal, prison-based education?
Explicit: by reading and copying the dictionary

7. What evidence do we have that Malcolm X was highly motivated to improve his vocabulary?
Implicit: he copied the entire first page of the dictionary and read it over and over *or* he copied the entire dictionary

8. In addition to the meanings of many words, what else improved as Malcolm X copied the dictionary?
Explicit: his knowledge of people, places, and events from history *or* his handwriting speed

9. What kept Malcolm X motivated to continue his study of the dictionary?
Implicit: He was proud when he had copied the first page and learned many new words *or* he could remember many of the words he had copied *or* he could read with understanding

10. Why did Malcolm X say, "I had never been so truly free in my life" even though he was in prison at the time?
Implicit: because he was learning so much *or* he loved reading

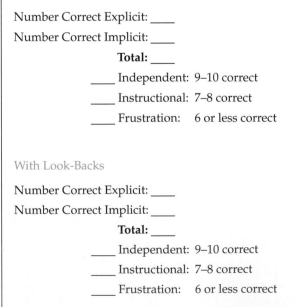

Without Look-Backs

Number Correct Explicit: ____

Number Correct Implicit: ____

     Total: ____

____ Independent: 9–10 correct

____ Instructional: 7–8 correct

____ Frustration: 6 or less correct

With Look-Backs

Number Correct Explicit: ____

Number Correct Implicit: ____

     Total: ____

____ Independent: 9–10 correct

____ Instructional: 7–8 correct

____ Frustration: 6 or less correct

Level: Upper Middle School

Upper Middle School

Social Studies

Concept Questions:

Who were Lewis and Clark?

_____

_____

_____ (3-2-1-0)

What does "exploring new territory" mean to you?

_____

_____

_____ (3-2-1-0)

What are reasons for giving gifts to strangers?

_____

_____

_____ (3-2-1-0)

Why do people use maps?

_____

_____

_____ (3-2-1-0)

Score: _____ /12 = _____ %

_____ FAM _____ UNFAM

Prediction:

_____

_____

Lewis and Clark

In April 1803, President Thomas Jefferson purchased the entire area of Louisiana from France. The territory stretched from the Mississippi River to the middle of the Rocky Mountains, but no one was really sure where the Mississippi River started or where exactly the Rocky Mountains were located. Meriwether Lewis and William Clark were commissioned by Jefferson to find answers to some of the many questions that people had regarding the new purchase. They were to explore the area and describe the land and its human and animal inhabitants.

Lewis and Clark departed in May 1804 with forty-three men and sufficient supplies for two years. They paddled up the Missouri River in canoes and halted with the coming of winter. They became acquainted with a sixteen-year-old Indian woman and adopted her as their primary guide. Her name was Sacajawea, which means Bird Woman. When the ice melted, they continued on their journey. All along the way, Lewis and Clark drew maps and diagrams and recorded what they observed in meticulous detail. They encountered Indian leaders, told them about the United States, and presented them with medals and American flags from the president. They acquired knowledge about soil and weather conditions and investigated fur trading possibilities. After seven months of difficult travel, they reached the Rocky Mountains.

Thanks to Sacajawea's influence, Lewis and Clark obtained horses from the Indians. Their intention was to cross the Rockies with the Pacific Ocean as their final destination. The weather grew cold, the food became scarce, and the mountains seemed endless. When they finally arrived at the ocean, Clark wrote in his journal, "The ocean is in view! Oh what joy!" When the expedition finally returned home over two years after they began their journey, they were awarded a <u>tumultuous</u> welcome. People had long since given them up for dead. That welcome was well deserved. During the long and <u>arduous</u> voyage, Lewis and Clark had accomplished an outstanding feat in describing the land, the rivers, and the Indian inhabitants. They had proven that there was a way to reach the Pacific and had opened a huge new area for settlement and trade. Many other Americans would soon follow in their footsteps. (368 words)

Adapted from L. J. Buggey, G. A. Danzer, C. L. Mitsakos, and C. F. Risinger, *America! America!* (Glenview, Ill.: Scott, Foresman and Co., 1982), pp. 267–269.

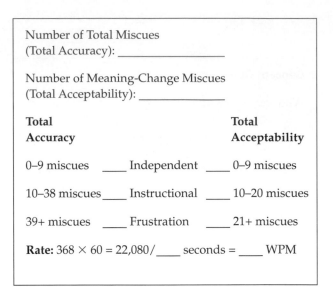

Number of Total Miscues
(Total Accuracy): _____

Number of Meaning-Change Miscues
(Total Acceptability): _____

Total Accuracy		**Total Acceptability**
0–9 miscues ____	Independent ____	0–9 miscues
10–38 miscues ____	Instructional ____	10–20 miscues
39+ miscues ____	Frustration ____	21+ miscues

Rate: $368 \times 60 = 22,080/$ ____ seconds = ____ WPM

Retelling Scoring Sheet for Lewis and Clark

Background/Setting

____ In 1803,
____ Thomas Jefferson purchased Louisiana
____ from France.
____ The territory stretched
____ from the Mississippi River
____ to the middle
____ of the Rocky Mountains.
____ No one knew
____ where the Mississippi River started or
____ where the Rocky Mountains were.
____ Jefferson commissioned Meriwether Lewis
____ and William Clark
____ to find answers to questions
____ about the new purchase.

Goal

____ They were to explore the area
____ and describe the land
____ and its human inhabitants
____ and animal inhabitants.

Events

____ Lewis
____ and Clark departed

____ with men

____ forty-three men

____ and supplies

____ for years

____ two years.

____ They paddled

____ up the Missouri River.

____ They became acquainted

____ with a woman

____ a sixteen-year-old woman

____ an Indian woman

____ and adopted her

____ as their guide

____ primary guide.

____ Her name was Sacajawea,

____ which means Bird Woman.

____ They drew maps.

____ They encountered leaders

____ Indian leaders

____ and presented them with medals.

____ They acquired knowledge

____ about soil,

____ weather,

____ and trading

____ fur trading.

____ They reached the Rocky Mountains.

____ They obtained horses

____ from the Indians.

____ Their intention was to cross the Rockies.

____ The Pacific Ocean was their destination.

____ The weather grew cold.

____ Food became scarce,

____ and the mountains seemed endless.

____ They finally arrived at the ocean.

____ Clark wrote

____ in his journal,

____ "The ocean is in view!

____ Oh, what joy."

Resolution

____ When the expedition returned,

____ they were awarded a welcome

____ a tumultuous welcome.

____ People had given them up

____ for dead.

____ They had accomplished a feat

____ an outstanding feat.

____ They had opened an area

____ a huge area

____ for settlement

____ and trade.

____ Americans

____ would follow

____ in their footsteps.

Other ideas recalled, including summary statements and inferences:

Questions for Lewis and Clark

1. What was the main goal of Meriwether Lewis and William Clark?
   Implicit: to explore the new territory

2. Name one of the boundaries of the new Louisiana territory.
   Explicit: Mississippi River and/or Rocky Mountains

3. In this selection, what tells us that Lewis and Clark expected to be gone a long time?
   Implicit: they carried supplies for two years

4. Whom did Lewis and Clark adopt as their primary guide?
   Explicit: an Indian woman, Sacajawea; Bird Woman

Level: Upper Middle School

5. What did Lewis and Clark give to the Indians they met?
   Explicit: American flags and/or medals from the president

6. Why would the president of the United States want Lewis and Clark to give these special items to the Indians?
   Implicit: the Indians now lived in territory owned by the United States; he wanted friendly relations with the Indians

7. What body of water was their final destination?
   Explicit: Pacific Ocean

8. What hardships did they suffer crossing the Rocky Mountains?
   Explicit: cold and scarce food

9. Why would Clark be so happy to see the Pacific Ocean?
   Implicit: it represented the end of the journey; they had suffered so many hardships crossing the Rockies

10. How did the journey of Lewis and Clark make it easier for the settlers who would follow?
    Implicit: there were maps to follow; they knew what to expect

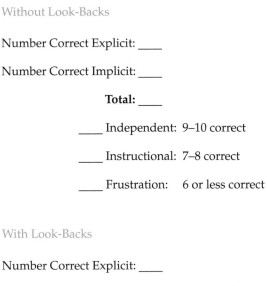

Without Look-Backs

Number Correct Explicit: ____

Number Correct Implicit: ____

Total: ____

____ Independent: 9–10 correct

____ Instructional: 7–8 correct

____ Frustration: 6 or less correct

With Look-Backs

Number Correct Explicit: ____

Number Correct Implicit: ____

Total: ____

____ Independent: 9–10 correct

____ Instructional: 7–8 correct

____ Frustration: 6 or less correct

Social Studies

Concept Questions:

Who was Ferdinand Magellan?

_____

_____

_____ (3-2-1-0)

What is circumnavigation?

_____

_____

_____ (3-2-1-0)

Why do countries support exploration?

_____

_____

_____ (3-2-1-0)

What are reasons for rebelling against authority?

_____

_____

_____ (3-2-1-0)

Score: _____ /12 = _____ %

_____ FAM _____ UNFAM

Prediction:

_____

_____

Ferdinand Magellan

In the early sixteenth century, a Portuguese noble, soldier, and sailor named Ferdinand Magellan performed what has been designated the greatest single human achievement on the sea. Magellan had spent long years in Asia and he often gazed across the wide expanse of the Pacific Ocean and asked himself a question. "How far away from here are the lands discovered by Columbus? If I sailed to the New World, could I find a passage to the Pacific Ocean and the rich Spice Islands?" Magellan hoped to find answers to his questions as well as obtain a large cargo of rare and costly spices. When the Portuguese king refused to assist him, he turned to Spain for help.

In 1519, Magellan sailed from Spain with five ships and a crew of almost three hundred sailors. He navigated the Atlantic and when he reached the New World, he followed the coast of South America until he found the straits that connected the two oceans. It took Magellan thirty-eight days to sail through the stormy straits to the Pacific Ocean, and during that difficult time, one ship was wrecked and one headed back to Spain. Once in the Pacific Ocean, Magellan turned north and traveled for months without sighting land.

The voyage was filled with extreme hardship. At one point several resentful Spanish captains initiated a rebellion against their Portuguese admiral. Magellan defeated the

Level: Upper Middle School

rebels and left two of them on shore to die. Several times the ships ran low on supplies, and with little food and water, the sailors begged to turn back, but Magellan would not allow this. At one point he declared that they would continue the voyage even if they had to eat the leather rigging of the ships. Disease and starvation claimed many of the crew but, mindful of the fate of the earlier rebels, no one opposed Magellan's will.

Magellan finally reached the islands of the Pacific, but he was unfortunately killed in a skirmish with some natives. One of his ships became unseaworthy and the other was wrecked. The remaining vessel with only seventeen of the original crew members sailed west through the Indian Ocean and around the southern tip of Africa. When they limped into a Spanish port, they had been gone three years! Although Magellan did not live to see the conclusion of the voyage, he and his crew accomplished what no one had ever done before. They had circumnavigated, or sailed around, the world. Magellan would never know that he had proved what Columbus had correctly predicted, that the lands of the East could be reached by sailing west. (436 words)

Adapted from L. J. Buggey, G. A. Danzer, C. L. Mitsakos, and C. F. Risinger, *America! America!* (Glenview, Ill.: Scott, Foresman and Co., 1982), pp. 83–86.

Number of Total Miscues
(Total Accuracy): _____

Number of Meaning-Change Miscues
(Total Acceptability): _____

Total Accuracy		Total Acceptability
0–10 miscues ____	Independent ____	0–10 miscues
11–45 miscues ____	Instructional ____	11–23 miscues
46+ miscues ____	Frustration ____	24+ miscues

Rate: 436 × 60 = 26,160/____ seconds = ____ WPM

Retelling Scoring Sheet for Ferdinand Magellan

Setting/Background
____ In the sixteenth century
____ a Portuguese sailor
____ named Ferdinand Magellan
____ performed a great achievement
____ on the sea.

Goal
____ Magellan asked,
____ "If I sailed
____ to the New World,
____ could I find a passage
____ to the Pacific Ocean
____ and the Spice Islands?"

Events
____ When the Portuguese king refused
____ to help him,
____ he turned to Spain
____ for help.
____ Magellan sailed
____ from Spain

Level: Upper Middle School

____ with ships
____ five ships
____ and a crew
____ of sailors
____ three hundred sailors.
____ He navigated the Atlantic
____ and followed the coast
____ of South America
____ until he found the straits
____ that connected the two oceans.
____ It took days
____ thirty-eight days
____ to sail through the straits
____ to the Pacific Ocean.
____ One ship was wrecked
____ and one headed back.
____ The voyage was filled
____ with hardship.
____ Several captains initiated a rebellion
____ against their admiral.
____ Magellan defeated the rebels
____ and left two
____ on shore
____ to die.
____ The ships ran low
____ on supplies
____ with little food
____ and water.
____ The sailors begged
____ to turn back,
____ but Magellan would not allow this.
____ He said
____ they would continue the voyage
____ if they had to eat the rigging
____ the leather rigging.
____ Disease
____ and starvation claimed many.

Resolution

____ Magellan reached islands
____ in the Pacific,
____ but he was killed
____ in a skirmish
____ with natives.
____ One ship became unseaworthy

____ and the other was wrecked.
____ The remaining ship sailed
____ around the tip
____ of Africa
____ with seventeen
____ of the original crew.
____ When they limped
____ into port
____ Spanish port,
____ they had been gone
____ for years
____ three years.
____ Magellan had sailed around the world.
____ He had proved
____ that the East could be reached
____ by sailing west.

Other ideas recalled, including summary statements and inferences:

Questions for Ferdinand Magellan

1. What was Ferdinand Magellan's main goal?
   Implicit: to reach the Pacific by sailing west through the Atlantic

2. What kind of cargo did Ferdinand Magellan hope to find on his journey?
   Explicit: rich spices

3. Why do you think Spain was interested in helping Magellan with his venture?
   Implicit: they wanted a route to the Spice Islands; they wanted the cargo of spices

Level: Upper Middle School

4. How long did it take Ferdinand Magellan to sail through the straits connecting the Atlantic and Pacific?
   Explicit: thirty-eight days

5. Why did the Spanish captains rebel against Ferdinand Magellan?
   Implicit: the hardship; they resented him; he was not Spanish

6. What did Ferdinand Magellan do to the rebels?
   Explicit: defeated them and left two to die

7. What did Ferdinand Magellan say they would eat before they would turn back?
   Explicit: the leather rigging

8. Why did Ferdinand Magellan's crew continue on the journey despite all of the problems and hardships?
   Implicit: they knew what had happened to the rebels; they hoped to get rich

9. How did Ferdinand Magellan die?
   Explicit: he was killed in a battle with some natives

10. How did Ferdinand Magellan prove beyond a doubt that the earth was round?
    Implicit: he and his crew circumnavigated or sailed around it

---

Without Look-Backs

Number Correct Explicit: ____

Number Correct Implicit: ____

Total: ____

____ Independent: 9–10 correct

____ Instructional: 7–8 correct

____ Frustration: 6 or less correct

With Look-Backs

Number Correct Explicit: ____

Number Correct Implicit: ____

Total: ____

____ Independent: 9–10 correct

____ Instructional: 7–8 correct

____ Frustration: 6 or less correct

Science

Concept Questions:

What are fireworks?

_____

_____

_____ (3-2-1-0)

What does making fireworks mean?

_____

_____

_____ (3-2-1-0)

What makes colors in fireworks?

_____

_____

_____ (3-2-1-0)

What are dangers of fireworks?

_____

_____

_____ (3-2-1-0)

Score: _____ /12 = _____ %

_____ FAM _____ UNFAM

Prediction:

_____

_____

Fireworks

Most of us have seen beautiful fireworks. They are often used on the Fourth of July, Labor Day, or other holidays. Around the world, firecrackers, Roman candles, cherry bombs, and rockets are used to celebrate many important events. Royal weddings, military victories, important births, peace treaties, and religious holidays have all been causes for setting off fireworks. Fireworks are also used just for fun. Their sound, color, and sparkle have charmed people for centuries.

Chemicals in Fireworks

Fireworks were probably invented in China about seven hundred years ago. A mixture of saltpeter, sulfur, and carbon was found to be useful for two quite different purposes: gunpowder and fireworks. Since then, these two uses of explosives have developed at the same time. A Roman candle is not much different from a small bomb. An explosion sends the rocket into the air and then makes it blow apart. Powdered metals catch fire and cause the sparks and flames. Metallic compounds add color to the sparks. Sodium compounds produce a yellow color. Calcium compounds make red. Green comes from barium and blue-green from copper. Ammonium compounds change the shades of these colors, and sulfur makes the colors more brilliant.

Level: Upper Middle School

Dangers of Fireworks

Because fireworks are so dangerous, they are not allowed in many parts of the United States. Every year fireworks used without careful supervision hurt both children and adults, some very seriously. People do not understand how fast fireworks explode after the fuse is lit. They also do not realize the force of the explosion. Putting on a huge fireworks display is a dangerous job, even for those who know what they are doing. Timing is <u>crucial</u>, as is knowing how far apart to place the various kinds of fireworks used. A rocket may not explode when it is expected to, or it may not shoot as far into the sky as it should. Fireworks may be fun, but they are a dangerous kind of fun. (318 words)

Adapted from T. Cooney, J. Pasachoff, and N. Pasachoff, *Physical Science* (Glenview, Ill.: Scott, Foresman and Co., 1984), p. 269.

Number of Total Miscues
(Total Accuracy): _____

Number of Meaning-Change Miscues
(Total Acceptability): _____

Total Accuracy		Total Acceptability
0–7 miscues	____ Independent	____ 0–7 miscues
8–33 miscues	____ Instructional	____ 8–17 miscues
34+ miscues	____ Frustration	____ 18+ miscues

Rate: $318 \times 60 = 19{,}080/$____ seconds = ____ WPM

Retelling Scoring Sheet for Fireworks

Main Idea

____ Fireworks are used to celebrate events
____ important events.

Details

____ They are used
____ on the Fourth of July
____ and Labor Day.
____ Weddings,
____ military victories,
____ births,
____ peace treaties,
____ and holidays
____ have been causes
____ for fireworks.

Main Idea

____ Fireworks are made
____ of chemicals.

Details

____ A mixture
____ of saltpeter,
____ sulfur,
____ and carbon
____ was used for gunpowder
____ and fireworks.
____ A Roman candle
____ is like a bomb
____ a small bomb.
____ An explosion sends the rocket
____ into the air
____ and blows it apart.
____ Powdered
____ metals cause sparks.
____ Metallic
____ compounds add color.
____ Sodium
____ compounds produce color
____ yellow color.
____ Calcium
____ compounds make red.
____ Green comes from barium

____ and blue-green from copper.

Main Idea

____ Fireworks are dangerous.

Details

____ They are not allowed
____ in parts of the United States
____ Fireworks hurt children
____ and adults
____ some very seriously.
____ People do not understand
____ how fast
____ fireworks explode.
____ Putting on a display
____ is a dangerous job
____ even for those who know
____ what they are doing.
____ Timing is crucial.
____ Fireworks may be fun
____ but they are dangerous.

Other ideas recalled, including summary statements and inferences:

Questions for Fireworks

1. What is this selection mainly about?
   Implicit: how fireworks are made; what they are used for; their dangers

2. What is one kind of firework mentioned in the selection?
   Explicit: firecrackers; Roman candles; cherry bombs; rockets

3. What is one special event mentioned in the article that is celebrated by fireworks?
   Explicit: holidays (Fourth of July, Labor Day); royal weddings; military victories; peace treaties; important births; religious holidays

4. How are gunpowder and fireworks alike?
   Implicit: share the same ingredients; can injure people; both are explosives

5. Name one ingredient shared by gunpowder and fireworks.
   Explicit: saltpeter; sulfur; carbon

Level: Upper Middle School

6. Why would the color of calcium compounds be especially useful for Fourth of July fireworks?
   Implicit: they make the color red; red is a color in our flag

7. What do ammonium compounds do to the color of fireworks?
   Explicit: change the shades of the colors

8. Why are fireworks not allowed in some parts of the United States?
   Explicit: they are so dangerous

9. Why do you think many fireworks injuries occur to the hands?
   Implicit: people hold the fireworks too long because they don't realize how fast they can explode

10. What specific dangers might be faced by those who design and set off holiday fireworks displays?
    Implicit: one may ignite those nearby, and too many may explode at one time

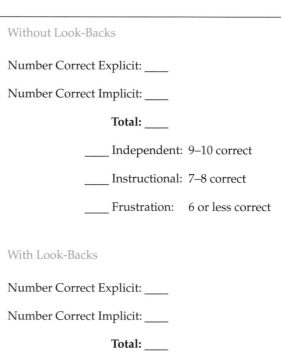

Without Look-Backs

Number Correct Explicit: ____

Number Correct Implicit: ____

Total: ____

____ Independent: 9–10 correct

____ Instructional: 7–8 correct

____ Frustration: 6 or less correct

With Look-Backs

Number Correct Explicit: ____

Number Correct Implicit: ____

Total: ____

____ Independent: 9–10 correct

____ Instructional: 7–8 correct

____ Frustration: 6 or less correct

Science

Concept Questions:

What are stars made of?

_____

_____

_____ (3-2-1-0)

How do stars change over time?

_____

_____

_____ (3-2-1-0)

What is gravity?

_____

_____

_____ (3-2-1-0)

What is mass?

_____

_____

_____ (3-2-1-0)

What do nuclear reactions produce?

_____

_____

_____ (3-2-1-0)

Score: _____ /15 = _____ %

_____ FAM _____ UNFAM

Prediction:

_____

_____

Life Cycles of Stars

Stars have life cycles, just like humans. In fact, a star is born, changes, and then dies. In contrast to the human life cycle that lasts about 75 years, the life cycle of a typical star is measured in billions of years.

Every star in the sky is at a different stage in its life cycle. Some stars are relatively young, while others are near the end of their existence. The sun is about halfway through its 10-billion-year-long life cycle.

Birth of a Star

The space between stars is not entirely empty. In some places, there are great clouds of gas and dust. Each of these clouds is a nebula. A nebula is where stars are born.

The element hydrogen makes up most of a nebula. Helium and a sprinkling of dust are also present. The particles in a nebula are spread very thin. In fact, the particles are a million times less dense than the particles in the air you breathe. However, because nebulae are very large, they contain enormous amounts of matter.

Gravity causes matter to be attracted to other matter. Therefore, as a nebula travels though space, it collects more dust and gas. The clouds become packed tighter and tighter,

Upper Middle School

as gravity pulls it all together. Whenever matter is packed in this way, it heats up. An especially dense part of the nebula may form a hot, spinning ball of matter. Such a ball of hot matter is called a *protostar*.

A protostar doesn't yet shine by ordinary light, but it does give off infrared energy. Scientists identify protostars within nebulae by using infrared telescopes. A protostar eventually becomes hot enough for nuclear fusion to take place in its core. When nuclear fusion produces great amounts of energy, a star comes to life.

Life of a Low-Mass Star

Stars begin their life cycle with different masses. A star's mass determines how long its life cycle will last and how it will die. Stars with a mass less than five times that of the sun are called low-mass stars. Most stars are in this group.

A low-mass star begins its life cycle as a main-sequence star. Over a period of billions of years, its supply of hydrogen is slowly changed by nuclear fusion into helium. During this time, the star changes very little.

Red Giant Stage. As the hydrogen in the core of a low-mass star is used up, the core starts to collapse. The core of the star becomes denser and hotter. The increased temperature causes another kind of nuclear reaction. Helium is converted to carbon. This nuclear reaction gives off great amounts of energy, causing the star to expand. It becomes a red giant.

The red giant stage in a star's life is relatively short. The sun will be a main-sequence star for a total of 10 billion years. But the sun will be a red giant for only about 500 million years.

Dwarf Stage. Eventually, most of the helium in a red giant's core is changed into carbon. Nuclear fusion slows. The star cools, and gravity makes it collapse inward. The matter making up the star is squeezed together very tightly, and the star becomes a white dwarf.

A typical white dwarf is about the size of Earth. But its matter is far denser than any matter on Earth. Eventually, the star becomes a burned-out black chunk of very dense matter that gives off no visible light. Then it is called a black dwarf. (583 words)

Adapted from *Science Insights: Exploring Earth and Science* by M. D. Spezio, M. Linner-Luebe, M. Lisowski, G. Skoog, and B. Sparks. © 1996 by Addison-Wesley Publishing Company, Inc. Used by permission.

Level: Upper Middle School

Number of Total Miscues
(Total Accuracy): _____

Number of Meaning-Change Miscues
(Total Acceptability): _____

Total Accuracy			**Total Acceptability**
0–12 miscues	____ Independent	____	0–12 miscues
13–58 miscues	____ Instructional	____	13–29 miscues
59+ miscues	____ Frustration	____	59+ miscues

Rate: 583 × 60 = 34,980/____ seconds = ____ WPM

Retelling Scoring Sheet for Life Cycles of Stars

Main Idea

____ Stars have life cycles.

Details

____ A star is born,

____ changes,

____ and dies.

____ The life cycle is measured

____ in billions of years.

____ Every star is at a different stage.

Main Idea

____ A star is born.

Details

____ There are clouds

____ of gas

____ and dust.

____ Each cloud is a nebula.

____ A nebula is where stars are born.

____ Hydrogen,

____ helium,

____ and dust are in the nebula.

____ As the nebula travels

____ through space,

____ it collects more dust

____ and gases.

____ The cloud becomes packed

____ as gravity pulls it together.

____ A part of the nebula may form a ball

____ a hot ball

____ of matter.

____ This is called a protostar.

____ Scientists identify protostars

____ by using infrared telescopes.

____ When the protostar becomes hot enough,

____ nuclear fusion takes place.

____ A star comes to life.

Main Idea

____ Life of a low-mass star.

Details

____ Low-mass stars have a mass

____ five time less

____ than the sun.

____ A star's mass determines its life cycle.

____ The cycle begins

____ as a main-sequence star.

____ Hydrogen is changed into helium.

____ The star changes very little.

Main Idea

____ The red giant stage

Details

____ As the hydrogen is used up,

____ the core collapses.

____ The core becomes denser

____ and hotter.

____ Helium is converted into carbon.

____ The star expands.

____ The red giant stage is short.

Main Idea

____ The dwarf stage

Details

____ Fusion slows.

____ The star cools.

____ Gravity makes it collapse inward.

Level: Upper Middle School

____ Matter is squeezed together.
____ The star becomes a white dwarf.
____ A dwarf is the size of Earth.
____ Eventually,
____ the star becomes a chunk
____ a black chunk
____ a burned-out chunk
____ and gives off no visible light.
____ It is called a black dwarf.

Other ideas recalled, including summary statements and inferences:

Questions for Life Cycles of Stars

1. What is this passage mainly about?
   Implicit: the life cycle of stars

2. What is a nebula?
   Explicit: a cloud of gas and dust

3. Why do nebulae collect more dust and gas as they move through space?
   Implicit: gravity causes dust to be attracted to other dust

4. What is a protostar?
   Explicit: a dense, hot part of the nebula

5. If a protostar doesn't give off light, how do scientists know it exists?
   Implicit: it gives off infrared energy, which can be detected using infrared telescopes

6. What is the final action that causes a protostar to become a star?

Implicit: the core becomes so hot that nuclear fusion occurs and produces great amounts of energy

7. What determines how long a star will live?
   Explicit: its mass

8. What causes all life cycle changes in a star?
   Implicit: nuclear reactions

9. What series of events causes a star to go into the red giant stage?
   Explicit: the core collapses when hydrogen is used up; it becomes denser and hotter; another kind of nuclear reaction occurs and the star expands

10. What is the stage in which the star becomes a chunk of dense matter that gives off no visible light?
    Explicit: black dwarf stage

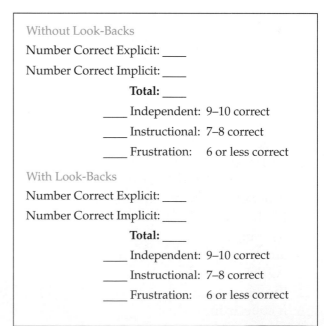

Without Look-Backs
Number Correct Explicit: ____
Number Correct Implicit: ____
            Total: ____
        ____ Independent: 9–10 correct
        ____ Instructional: 7–8 correct
        ____ Frustration: 6 or less correct

With Look-Backs
Number Correct Explicit: ____
Number Correct Implicit: ____
            Total: ____
        ____ Independent: 9–10 correct
        ____ Instructional: 7–8 correct
        ____ Frustration: 6 or less correct

Where the Ashes Are—Part 1

"Wake up, wake up!" my mother shouted. "We've got to get out of here! How can you sleep through all this?" She pulled the covers off me, handed me my clothes, and rushed out of the room.

"Wait!" I cried out, throwing off my pajamas. One leg in and one out of my dark blue school trousers, I stumbled over to my sister Dieu-Ha's room. My mother was yelling, "Are you deaf? Get out! We're going downstairs!"

It was five in the morning. Explosions and gunfire echoed through the high-ceilinged rooms of the government guesthouse. Arched corridors surrounded the twenty bedrooms on the second floor of the massive French-style mansion. My parents had taken the master suite at the end of the hall while my two sisters and I had large rooms next to one another. We had arrived at the end of January 1968, two days before the lunar New Year. Our family were the only guests in the building. Rather than having us stay at my grandfather's small house, my father felt we would be safer at the guesthouse, where extra platoons of local soldiers had been assigned to protect him. He also preferred the guesthouse because it was built along the bank of the river in Hue, the old imperial city, and away from the town's noisy center. The nearby train station was defunct, since the war had disrupted all but a few railway lines.

For many years my father had been working for the government of South Vietnam. Assigned to central Vietnam as a civilian deputy to the military governor, he was based in Da Nang, a coastal town just over an hour's drive from Hue. He sent us to visit his parents there regularly, especially at holidays. He came along on this holiday visit—for the lunar New Year, Tet, in 1968.

Although my father had been warned about a possible escalation in the fighting, he said to my mother: "There's a ceasefire. It's New Year's. We'll be safe." But he abandoned his plan to drive and instead arranged for a flight to Hue. We'd landed at the Phu Bai airport in midafternoon.

The road into town had been taken over by an endless convoy of tanks and army trucks transporting U.S. soldiers, most likely toward Khe Sanh, an American base that had been under siege for several months. Along with a few other civilian cars, small trucks, and innumerable motorcycles, we inched our way toward Hue. I kept looking out the car window, glimpsing rice fields here and there. Mostly, though, the view was blocked by the olive green steel of tanks and trucks.

My mother sought to distract us. "You kids are going to be spoiled this year. I bet your grandparents will have lots of treats for you. But I want you to behave."

Settled in at the guesthouse, on the second night of our stay my mother and sisters and I fell asleep just after twelve, insulated by its thick walls and heavy curtains. Endless rounds of firecrackers went off as the people of Hue celebrated the arrival of Tet. No one knew that along with the Year of the Monkey, the dreaded Viet Cong soldiers had also arrived. No one could tell when the firecrackers stopped and the gunfire began.

Dieu-Ha and I followed my mother into my other sister's room. Dieu-Quynh hid herself under a pile of blankets. Ma shook her. "Come on, we're going downstairs!" As she started to rifle through Dieu-Quynh's drawers, grabbing clothes for her to change into, she said to Dieu-Ha and me, "Go see if your father's downstairs. and stay with him!"

We rushed down the corridors toward the double staircase. Its marble steps formed a half-circle framed by an intricately carved banister. A bullet shattered a porthole as we skipped down the steps. Dieu-Ha screamed. Pieces of glass and marble flew by. We raced past the elephant tusks in the huge vestibule and toward the reception hall. A chilly wind blew through the huge room. Someone had opened the drapes and shutters of the dozens of windows rising from knee level to ten feet above my head, each framing a view of the River of Perfume, Song Hu'o'ng.

"Where the Ashes Are" by Nguyen Qui Duc, from *Literature and Integrated Studies*, © 1997 by Scott, Foresman and Company. Reprinted by permission of author.

In the somber light I could make out dark foliage swaying by the riverbank as a coat of morning mist rose above the water. Nature paints winter scenes in Hue in shades of gray, but this morning I could see rapid bursts of orange and red fire coming from behind the bushes. A flare shot out from the far distance. Exploding with a thud, it hung from a small parachute and cast a brilliant midday light over a large area of the river as it floated down. Rockets exploded across the burning sky and fell to the ground in rapid succession. Deafened, Dieu-Ha and I dove behind an antique cabinet at the end of the room. My father had been nowhere in sight. **STOP**

That night he had stayed up late to read a French book that contrasted two warriors: North Vietnam's famed general Vo Nguyen Giap and William Westmoreland, commander of the U.S. ground troops in South Vietnam. Just before four o'clock Cha (father in Vietnamese) had left his bed and gone up to the rooftop terrace, where he marveled at the red and green tracers flying across the sky like shooting stars. Despite his interest in the generals, he had little understanding of the role of flares and tracers as tools of warfare. They were simply a beautiful sight as they burst over the night sky. **STOP**

"Your father's still up there. Been on that roof an hour! He'll get killed!" Ma wailed as she came down the staircase. Seeing the open windows, she took us into a chamber behind the reception room. "Where's Dieu-Quynh?" she exclaimed. "She was just on the stairs with me!"

In the midst of the gunfire and explosions, my sister had gone back to bed—a mad thing to, since bullets were now flying indoors. By 1968, however, most of what Dieu-Quynh did was irrational. For four years she had been showing signs of mental illness. Ordering Dieu-Ha and me to sit still, my mother dashed back upstairs. A bullet came through Dieu-Quynh's room, hitting the lamp on her bedstand. Sparks flew in all directions. Ma grabbed my older sister by the wrist and led her downstairs, calling out to my father all the while. **STOP**

"We shouldn't worry too much," he said in his usual unruffled tone when he entered the room a few minutes later. When he had finally left the roof, he went downstairs to look for the butler, then into an office off the living room. "I called the provincial office; they say the fighting is far away."

"Look out the windows!" my mother shot back.

"I did," Cha replied, still calm and composed. Our soldiers are still at their posts." From the rooftop he had been able to see men in green surrounding the guesthouse. **STOP**

We gathered together, crouching on the floor. No one spoke. My father glanced at the spacious desk and heavy armchairs, hoping to hide behind the furniture until the gunfire died down.

Between explosions came the sound of someone knocking at the front door. My parents put out their arms. We sat still. The pounding grew louder. After a moment of hesitation, Ma stood up. "It's our soldiers," she declared. "Come on!" My sisters followed her through the reception area to the vestibule. As my father and I reached the door to the reception room, we heard her scream. **STOP**

My father led me back to the office in the back, locking the door behind him as quietly as possible. We went to the desk, and I held his hand as we lowered ourselves behind it. My father didn't know what else to do. Spotting a steel safe in the corner of the room, he went over to open it, then without a word closed it again. Not even a nine-year-old boy could fit inside. **STOP**

"I have a young son in the house," my mother was explaining to the intruders in the vestibule, Viet Cong soldiers in olive green uniforms. They wore no insignia or badges that showed affiliation or rank. Whether because of the darkness or distance, his poor eyesight, or his unfamiliarity with military matters, my father had mistaken them for our own Southern Republican Army troops.

One of the soldiers now threatened to shoot anyone still hiding in the house. "Tell us where everyone is and you'll be safe, sister," he assured my mother. Please don't hurt us, please!" she begged. "Just let me go find my son." **STOP**

Cha groped behind the heavy dark green drapes along the office wall, where a set of double doors opened onto a hallway. We tiptoed through the hail to the doors that led outside. My father motioned me out first, then carefully closed the doors behind him. I ran down the steps and turned toward the hedges that separated the guesthouse grounds from the riverbank. "Hey, boy!" someone cried. I turned. A Viet Cong soldier sitting cross-legged pointed his rifle at me. I ran back to my father.

Back in the hallway inside the house, Cha quietly approached each door to the offices surrounding the reception area. A gun muzzle protruded from one, and we backed off. The doorway to yet another office also had a gun muzzle poking out from it. There was no escape. **STOP**

Out in the courtyard it was still dark. Dozens of people in nightclothes shivered in the early morning dampness. Slowly the soldiers separated families from one another. The guesthouse was to be used as a temporary holding center. More people were brought into the courtyard. A disheveled Frenchman of about thirty entered the area barefooted, a trench coat thrown on over his pajamas. Hands clasped together, he tried to explain his situation to two Viet Cong soldiers. "De Gaulle, Ho Chi Minh, amis," he kept saying. "Friends."

The two Viet Cong waved him away. One of them shouted, "Khong biet tieng dtiu!" They did not speak any foreign languages. **STOP**

"They're regular soldiers," my father whispered to a man next to him, whose crisp white shirt was tucked into pajama trousers. "Such a strong northern accent."

"You're right," the man whispered back. "The way they call everybody 'Sister' and 'Brother' is strange." The men and women before us were not part of the so-called National Liberation Front within South Viet Nam. Ho Chi Minh was now sending in troops from the North for an outright offensive, a full invasion. **STOP**

In the confusion our family took refuge in a small temple just off the grounds of the guesthouse. Searching through his wallet, my father took out all his business cards and hid them under a mat. "Just say you're a teacher," whispered my mother.

He never had the chance. When a Viet Cong woman found us in the temple a little more than an hour later, she jabbed her index finger into his chest. "You, Brother, I know who you are," she said. "The Party and the Revolution will be generous to all those willing to confess their crimes against the People." **STOP**

"The Party" could only be the Communist party headquartered in Ha Noi. The enemy's arm had now reached into the heart of Hue. "Don't lie!" the woman continued. Putting her finger up to my father's nose, she said, "Brother, we know—you're the general staying in this house. Such opulence." We'll take care of you. **STOP**

We lost track of the time as the soldiers sorted out all the people gathered in front of the guesthouse. At last, however, they accepted my father's protestations that he was not a general but a government functionary. He and the other men were taken inside the mansion. Women and children were sent to a neighboring building, down into a long rectangular basement with extremely thick walls and a single narrow door at one end. The rocket explosions had ceased, but the sound of gunfire continued. We had become accustomed to it and no longer jumped at the bursts from automatic weapons. Ten families followed each other below ground. I ended up leading the way into the darkness. **STOP**

"Go to the far end. Go!" my mother urged me, and made sure that Dieu-Quynh stayed with us. She knew that, on capturing a town, the Communists would use residents as workers to support military operations. Women would be sent to look for food, or nurse the wounded. If not required to take up arms themselves, men would have to gather the wounded and the dead. Dieu-Quynh, a tall girl of eighteen, was at risk of being drafted for such service. Turning to the family behind her, my mother explained. "My daughter is ill. A big girl, but not all that wise." It was an explanation she would feel compelled to repeat often in the next days. I finally settled for a spot below a minuscule window with iron bars. In the damp, cavernous basement, the tiny hole let in a faint ray of the light that signaled the first day of the Year of the Monkey. **STOP**

Throughout that day and most of the next night the adults carried on a whispered debate, trying to make sense out of what had happened. "They can't win," the guesthouse chauffeur pronounced. "I bet they'll retreat soon. The Americans will bomb, and our troops will rescue us in a few days." My mother listened dispassionately. She sighed often and refused to eat any of the food the family next to us offered. Busy with their prisoners in the mansion, the soldiers left us alone. **STOP**

In our second day of captivity, a female voice shouted into the basement. "Mrs. Dai! Is there a Mrs. Dai down there?" My mother picked her way toward the door. "Your husband's up in the house. He wants to see you," the voice announced. My mother went up alone, warning me to keep my sister Dieu-Quynh from wandering out. During the night, Dieu-Quynh had been difficult, continually demanding hot water. For the last year or so she had been obsessed with matters of hygiene, compulsively washing her hands as well as any household utensils before she would use them. Finally realizing that this was a luxury, she now sat silent and withdrawn. I asked Dieu-Ha to stay with her, then went to sit at the door to wait for my mother. **STOP**

The guns had gone quiet at some point without anyone noticing. More soldiers had arrived in the compound and were now setting up a crude hospital. A stretched-out army poncho served as an awning, sheltering three bamboo cots that had been shoved together. The soldiers put a mat of woven branches and leaves on top of the cots, enlarging the surface to accommodate five wounded men. Looking like pallbearers carrying a white porcelain coffin, three young men and a woman in civilian clothes brought in an ancient French bathtub. They filled the tub half full of water, warning us not to use it. No one seemed to be in charge, yet a lot of orders were being issued. Sitting by the door of the basement, I watched the men and women from the North while waiting for my mother. **STOP**

"What are you doing here?" she asked when she returned, roughing up my hair. "We're going up to see your father in a while." She did not sound excited. After checking on my sisters, she set about looking for food for my father.

"Ma, what are they going to do with him?" I asked. I repeated the question again and again, but my mother would only shake her head; finally she responded, "Oh, he'll be all right. They said all he needed was a few days of re-education. They're taking him somewhere, but he'll be back."

Taken where? Would we be rescued first? Would they let him go? I didn't think she knew the answers to my questions. I tugged at her sleeve. "Ma, what's 're-education'?" She glanced at the wounded Viet Cong lying beneath the poncho. "It's like school, that's all. Now help me with this pot." **STOP**

Spoiled since her youth by household servants, my mother had rarely gone near a kitchen. Now she was cooking a big pot of rice she had secured from a woman in the basement. The Viet Cong had set up a few clay burners and gave us some coal. Other than the rice, there was nothing to cook. We ate it with pickled leeks and cucumber, which normally accompanied fancier foods during Tet. The rice tasted of the river water my mother had used to cook it in. The Viet Cong had allowed her only a small amount of water from the bathtub to take to my father. She was happy to have cleaner water for him to drink—until she tasted it. It smelled of Mercurochrome, the red disinfectant common in Viet Nam. The soldiers had used the water to wash the wounds of injured men, then poured back unused portions, now laced with Mercurochrome. She found a tiny bit of tea to steep in the water and packed some rice into a big bowl for my father. **STOP**

I sensed that my father was happy to see us, but his face showed no such emotion. He took the woven basket Ma handed him, which contained a towel, two T-shirts, and a pair of pants she had found on her previous trip to the guesthouse to see him. "There's no need—you will be well provided for," a Viet Cong cadre said. "You'll be in re-education for just a short time. Now that the region is liberated, you'll be allowed to come back soon."

In the big hall across from the master suite, my father kept caressing my head. I couldn't think of much to say. Some prisoners crouched along the wall, watching us. Others were curled up on the floor like shrimps. My mother gave my father the bowl of rice and the tea. I waited to see if he could taste the Mercurochrome, but I couldn't tell from his expression. **STOP**

I glanced around my parents' bedroom. It had been turned upside down. The book my father had been reading about Giap and Westmoreland still lay by his bed. My mother's jewelry and toilet case had had a hole gashed through it with a crude knife.

"Your mother will take you over to your grandparents' in a few days," Cha said. "I'll be back after a time."

Later, sometime past midnight, Communist soldiers took my father and a dozen other men away. Standing on a stool with my mother at my side, I watched through the tiny basement window. A rope was hooked through my father's elbows and tied behind his back, while his wrists were bound together in front of his chest. He was also tied to the man in front of him. It would be sixteen years before I saw him again. **STOP**

World War I, also known as the Great War, drew in not only the major powers of Europe, but those of America and Asia as well. Many economic and political factors caused the war. Newly industrialized nations competed with one another for trade and markets for their goods. Also, the urge for national power and independence from other nations came from old and new powers. When a new nation tried to increase its power by building a strong military, an older nation perceived the new nation as a threat to its power. Such tensions led to the division of Europe into two groups for security: one composed of Britain, France, and Russia, the other of Austria, Hungary, and Germany.

Although the factors discussed above caused the war, the final breaking point was a local conflict between Austria and Serbia, a tiny kingdom in southeastern Europe. Serbia, supported by Russia, wanted to unite with the Serbs living in the Austro-Hungarian Empire and create a Greater Serbia. Austria, supported by Germany, did not want Serbia cutting into its empire. The war officially started in August of 1914, after the assassination of the Austrian heir to the throne, who was visiting Sarajevo, near Serbia's border. The assassin was a young man with connections to the military intelligence branch of the Serbian government. Austria's attempt to punish Serbia drew Russia and its allies Britain and France into a war against Austria–Hungary and Germany. The map below illustrates the geographical location of the countries in Europe and surrounding regions in 1914.

The War Raged on Two Fronts

Germany hoped to defeat France by striking quickly through Belgium and, therefore, to minimize the danger of a two-front war. The highly trained German troops nearly reached Paris before the French stopped them. However, the Russians aided France by suddenly attacking Germany on its eastern front, and Germany sent troops from western Europe to face the attack. With the German forces diminished, the French were able to force the weakened Germans back. The war in the west became a stalemate with neither side able to achieve a victory. As a result, both sides sought new allies to help them gain victory, and the war became a world war as Japan, Italy, Portugal, Rumania, and other countries joined Britain, France, and Russia. Germany and Austria–Hungary drew in Bulgaria and the Ottoman Empire, which included Turkey.

On the eastern front Russia kept part of the German army busy. Although Russia fought valiantly, it had not been prepared for war and thus was unable to defeat the Germans. Russian defeats led to a revolution that toppled the tsar of Russia. In late 1917 the new leader of Russia, Lenin, offered to make peace with Germany. As part of the treaty agreement, Germany gained coal mines and oil fields from Russia, which gave Germany power to fuel its army. More important, it allowed the war to be fought on only one front—the western front.

The United States entered the war when Germany began attacking American ships that were taking supplies to Britain and France. U.S. President Woodrow Wilson warned the Germans to stop the attacks, and for a while they did. But they announced an unrestricted submarine warfare after the British blockade shut off supplies to Germany. The final event that caused the United States to join the Allies was the interception of a telegram from the German foreign secretary to Mexico asking Mexico to ally itself with Germany and help fight the United States Germany promised Mexico financial aid and the recovery of Texas, New Mexico, and Arizona when the Allies were defeated.

Adapted from *History and Life* by T. W. Wallbank, A. Schrier, D. Maier, and P. Gutierrez-Smith. © 1993 by Scott, Foresman and Company, Inc. Used by permission.

In the fall of 1918, German military leaders realized they could not win. One by one Germany's allies quit. **STOP** On November 3, German sailors mutinied at Kiel, a city and port in northwest Germany. Four days later a revolution broke out in Germany. A republic was founded, and the kaiser fled to Holland. **STOP**

Leaders of the new German government agreed to an armistice, which is an agreement to stop fighting. **STOP** They asked that the peace settlement be based on President Wilson's Fourteen Points, which he had described in a speech to Congress in 1918. The Fourteen Points outlined the president's ideas for solving the problems that led to the war. Wilson wanted an end to secret agreements, freedom of the seas in peace and war, the reduction of armaments, the right of nationality groups to form their own nations, and an association of nations to keep the peace. In other speeches Wilson called for a negotiated peace with reasonable demands made on the losers. The Allies agreed to model the peace settlement on the Fourteen Points. **STOP**

Early in the morning of November 11, 1918, the war ended. In a railroad car in the Compiègne Forest in northern France, two German delegates met Allied officials to sign the armistice. The guns were silent.

The Victors Tried to Build a Lasting Peace

No previous war had caused such widespread horror. **STOP** More than 10 million troops were killed in battle, and 20 million more were wounded. Thirteen million civilians died from war-related famine, disease, and injuries. The cost of the war was estimated at more than $350 billion. Destruction was everywhere. **STOP**

Three Leaders Dominated the Paris Peace Conference

After the armistice had been signed, the Allied nations met in Paris to discuss peace terms. Contrary to Wilson's wishes, the defeated countries were not allowed to send representatives to the peace conference. Thus, the so-called Big Three dominated the meeting: President Wilson; David Lloyd George, prime minister of Great Britain; and Georges Clemenceau, premier of France. **STOP** At the conference Wilson pushed his Fourteen Points. Above all, he wanted to see a League of Nations, an international association established to keep the peace. To get the others to agree, however, he had to make compromises. **STOP**

Georges Clemenceau, known as the "Old Tiger," had led France during the darkest hours of the war. He wanted Germany to pay war damages because almost all of the fighting on the western front had been on French soil. Most of all he insisted that France be made safe from attack by Germany in the future. He wanted German power destroyed even at the cost of permanently taking much of Germany's western territories from her. Clemenceau placed little faith in Wilson's proposed "League of Nations." **STOP**

Lloyd George in turn wanted Germany's colonies for Britain. He also wanted the German navy destroyed. During the peace talks, he mediated between the idealism of Wilson and the severe terms of Clemenceau. **STOP** In the resulting compromise, Wilson gave in on many details and agreed to form an alliance with Britain and France against future German attacks. Clemenceau and Lloyd George agreed to make the creation of the League of Nations part of the peace agreement, which was called the Versailles Treaty. **STOP**

Adapted from *History and Life* by T. W. Wallbank, A. Schrier, D. Maier, and P. Gutierrez-Smith. © 1993 by Scott, Foresman and Company, Inc. Used by permission.

Germany Lost Territory and Wealth in Its Defeat

When the German delegation arrived to sign the Versailles Treaty, they found its terms harsher than they had expected. The Germans were outraged at the war-guilt clause, which placed the entire blame for the war on Germany and its allies. They were also dismayed that many of Wilson's Fourteen Points were missing or had been weakened by changes. The first delegates from Germany refused to sign the treaty. To avoid further attacks by Allied soldiers, however, a second German delegation signed it on June 28, 1919. Even though Germany signed the treaty, there was strong resentment over its harsh terms. **STOP**

In the treaty, France won back the provinces of Alsace and Lorraine, lost to Germany in the late 1800's. The German territory west of the Rhine River, called the Rhineland, was to become a buffer zone between the two enemies. It was to be occupied by Allied troops for at least 15 years. France was also given the rich coal mines of the Saar, located on the French–German border. But after 15 years, the Saarlanders could vote to have their region go back to the German government or remain under the French. In 1935 they voted to become part of Germany again. **STOP**

In the treaty the Allies required that Germany repay much of the cost of the war, or make reparations. They wanted an immediate payment of $5 billion in cash. Two years later they billed Germany for $32 billion, plus interest. The treaty reduced German military power and permitted Germany an army of no more than 100,000 men. The navy was allowed only six warships, some other vessels, and no submarines or military airplanes. The Germans were not alone in thinking such peace terms were unjust. Even David Lloyd George doubted the justice of the Versailles Treaty. President Wilson hoped that his dream, the League of Nations, could correct the unjust treaty later. **STOP**

New Independent Nations Were Formed

Four empires had fallen apart in the course of World War I: the German, the Austro-Hungarian, the Ottoman, and the Russian. Based partly on secret agreements made during the war, the Allies drew up treaties to divide the territory. The map on the next page shows how the empires were divided up. The western portion of the old Russian Empire lost to Germany during the war was reorganized. Finland, Latvia, Lithuania, and Estonia emerged from this territory, and part of this area was used to create Poland. **STOP**

The defeated Austro-Hungarian Empire was also divided into several new countries: Austria, Hungary, Czechoslovakia, and Yugoslavia. The creation of the new countries helped fulfill one of Wilson's Fourteen Points, the right of self-determination, or the right of people to form their own nations. **STOP**

The Ottoman Empire too was divided up. Syria, Iraq, Trans-Jordan, and Palestine were created from the Ottoman Empire. They became mandates, lands given to certain nations to develop. Syria was ruled by France, the other three by Britain. These mandates were promised independence at a future time. **STOP**

Redrawing the map of Europe, however, brought some new groups under foreign control. There were social, cultural, and language implications of this foreign control. For example, Austrians living in the southwestern part of the old Austro-Hungarian Empire came under the rule of Italy. Other German-speaking Austrians were placed under Czechoslovakian rule.

One of the biggest problems was the newly independent Poland, created from the Polish-language provinces of prewar Austria–Hungary, Germany, and Russia. The treaty's authors gave Poland some territory in eastern Germany known as the Polish Corridor. The Polish Corridor and other areas would prove to be problems in the future because they contained many ethnic minorities. Some Germans lived in the new Polish Corridor, and to complicate matters, many Hungarians also came under Romanian control. Few of these peoples were happy about the changes, and their discontent was a dangerous sign for the future. **STOP**

Adapted from *History and Life* by T. W. Wallbank, A. Schrier, D. Maier, and P. Gutierrez-Smith.
© 1993 by Scott, Foresman and Company, Inc. Used by permission.

Similarities and Differences Between Viruses and Cells

If you ever had a cold or the flu, you probably hosted viruses. A virus is an infectious agent made up of a core of nucleic acid and a protein coat. Viruses are not cells. Unlike plant and animal cells, a virus package does not have a nucleus, a membrane, or cellular organelles such as ribosomes, mitochondria, or chloroplasts. Although viruses are not cells, they do have organized structural parts.

Compared to even the smallest cell, a virus is tiny. The virus that causes polio, for example, measures only 20 nanometers in diameter. One nanometer is one billionth of a meter. At that size, 3000 polioviruses could line up across the period at the end of this sentence.

All viruses have at least two parts: a protective protein coat and a core of nucleic acid. The protein coat around the core of the nucleic acid is called a capsid. Depending on the virus, the capsid may consist of one or several kinds of protein. The capsid protects the viral nucleic acid core from its environment.

In cells, DNA is the hereditary material. Some viruses also contain DNA, while other viruses contain only RNA. In viruses containing RNA, the RNA functions as the hereditary material.

Compared to a cell, a virus has a relatively simple existence. Viruses do not eat, respire, or respond to environmental changes as cells do. It should not surprise you, therefore, to learn that viruses have fewer genes

An Influenza Virus

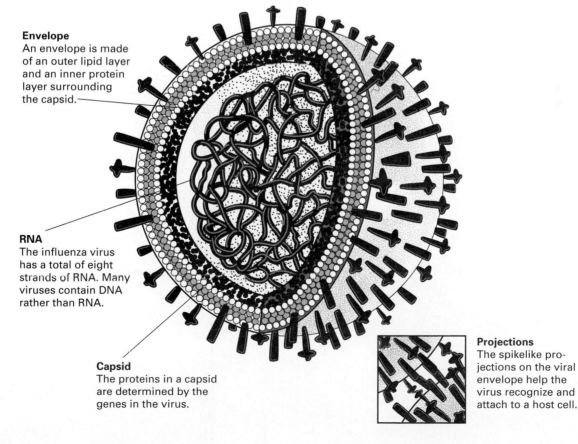

Envelope
An envelope is made of an outer lipid layer and an inner protein layer surrounding the capsid.

RNA
The influenza virus has a total of eight strands of RNA. Many viruses contain DNA rather than RNA.

Capsid
The proteins in a capsid are determined by the genes in the virus.

Projections
The spikelike projections on the viral envelope help the virus recognize and attach to a host cell.

than cells have. While a human cell may contain about 100,000 genes and a bacterial cell about 1000, a virus may contain only 5 genes.

In the figure on the previous page, you can see the parts of an influenza virus: a core of RNA, a surrounding capsid, and an outer covering called an envelope. An envelope is an additional protective coating usually made up of lipids, proteins, and carbohydrates. Envelopes are found only in viruses that infect animal cells. An envelope has spike-like projections that recognize and bind to complementary sites on the membrane of the cell being infected. Think about how a prickly burr sticks to objects.

From *Biology: The Web of Life* by Eric Strauss and Marylin Lisowski. © 1998 by Addison Wesley Longman, Inc. Used by permission.

Characteristics of Viruses—Part 2

Viral Replication: Ticking Time Bombs

Viruses do not reproduce, they replicate. **STOP** Reproduction, which is characteristic of living things, involves cell division. Replication does not involve cell division. **STOP** Viruses cannot replicate on their own. In order to replicate, viruses require a host. **STOP** A host is an organism that shelters and nourishes something. Living cells host viruses. These host cells provide all the materials that viruses need to copy themselves. **STOP**

When it enters a host cell, a virus may immediately begin to replicate, or it may remain relatively inactive. **STOP** The viral replication process that rapidly kills a host cell is called the lytic cycle. You can follow the lytic cycle in the figure below. **STOP** The lytic cycle begins when a virus invades a host cell and begins to replicate immediately, producing many new viruses. **STOP** Eventually, the host cell lyses, or breaks apart, releasing the newly made viruses. The new viruses may then enter other cells and repeat the cycle.

As a child you may have had chicken pox, which is caused by a virus. While you were ill, most of the viruses were in the lytic cycle. Because your cells were being destroyed by the chicken pox virus, you showed symptoms of the disease. **STOP**

Lytic Cycle

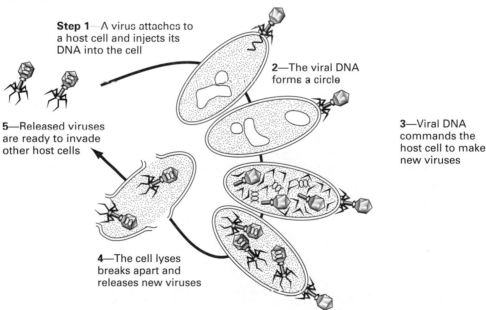

Step 1—A virus attaches to a host cell and injects its DNA into the cell

2—The viral DNA forms a circle

3—Viral DNA commands the host cell to make new viruses

4—The cell lyses breaks apart and releases new viruses

5—Released viruses are ready to invade other host cells

Sometimes a virus does not start the lytic cycle immediately. Instead the virus enters the lysogenic cycle. The lysogenic cycle is a type of replication in which a virus does not immediately kill a host cell. The lysogenic cycle in a bacteria cell is shown on the right side of the figure on the next page. **STOP**

Lysogenic Cycle

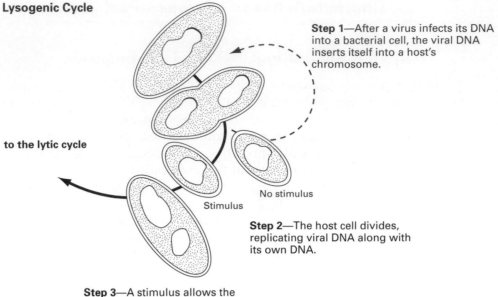

Step 1—After a virus infects its DNA into a bacterial cell, the viral DNA inserts itself into a host's chromosome.

to the lytic cycle

No stimulus

Stimulus

Step 2—The host cell divides, replicating viral DNA along with its own DNA.

Step 3—A stimulus allows the viral DNA to separate from the cell's chromosome and enter the lytic cycle. Without a stimulus, the viral DNA stays in the cell's chromosome.

During the lysogenic cycle, viral DNA inserts itself into a host cell's chromosome. A viral DNA segment that is inserted in a bacterial chromosome is called a prophage. A host cell carrying a prophage may divide many times. The prophage is replicated every time the host cell's chromosome replicates. **STOP**

Some prophages remain in the lysogenic cycle indefinitely. Usually, however, some type of environmental stimulus eventually results in the separation of a prophage from the chromosome of its host cell. The viral DNA then enters the lytic cycle. The virus that causes cold sores in humans can go through the lysogenic cycle, for example. Cold sores erupt when these viruses enter the lytic cycle. **STOP**

From *Biology: The Web of Life* by Eric Strauss and Marylin Lisowski. © 1998 by Addison Wesley Longman, Inc. Used by permission.

Diversity of Viruses: An Unending Supply

Classifying viruses is difficult because they are so diverse. As a result, biologists have developed several different ways of organizing viruses. Sometimes they are organized by shape, sometimes by the host they infect. Viruses may also be classified according to the way they function inside a cell. **STOP**

Shape. The arrangement of proteins in capsids determines the shape of the viruses.

Host. Viruses can be organized according to the type of host they infect. There are animal viruses, plant viruses, and bacterial viruses. Viruses that infect only bacterial cells are referred to as bacteriophages.

Many but not all viruses invade only a specific type of organism. For example, the virus that causes polio replicates only inside human host cells. The virus that causes rabies infects only the cells of a particular animal species, such as dogs and humans. **STOP**

You may wonder how viruses can be so specific. Earlier you learned that capsids and envelopes contain specific proteins. Receptor sites on host cells also contain specific proteins. If the outer proteins in a virus do not fit with the outer proteins of a cell, the virus will not attach to the cell. Without attachment, the viral nucleic acid cannot enter the host cell to replicate. **STOP**

Function. Some viruses, such as retroviruses, can also be classified based on how they function in a host. A retrovirus is a virus that contains an RNA code that replicates by first transcribing its RNA into DNA. The prefix "retro-" means "reverse." What do you think might work in reverse in this group of viruses? **STOP**

Most viruses and all organisms make RNA from DNA in the process of transcription. Retroviruses are able to make nucleic acids in reverse order from the usual process. In retroviruses DNA is made from RNA. As you can see in the figure on the next page, retroviruses have an enzyme called reverse transcriptase, which transcribes viral RNA into viral DNA inside the host cell. You can study the figure to better understand the replication of a human immunodeficiency virus (HIV). The retrovirus causes acquired immunodeficiency syndrome (AIDS). **STOP**

Retroviruses include tumor-producing viruses as well as HIV. Tumor-producing retroviruses and HIV follow a similar invasion pattern. Many tumor-producing viruses, however, enter the lysogenic cycle after Step 3 in the figure. Tumors do not immediately appear, but the virual DNA replicates along with the host cell DNA. Eventually many host cells will contain tumor-producing viral DNA. Using what you have learned about the lysogenic cycle, you can probably predict what will happen eventually. **STOP**

Nonviral particles. Scientists have discovered two infectious agents that have simpler structures than viruses: viroids and prions. A viroid is

The Retrovirus

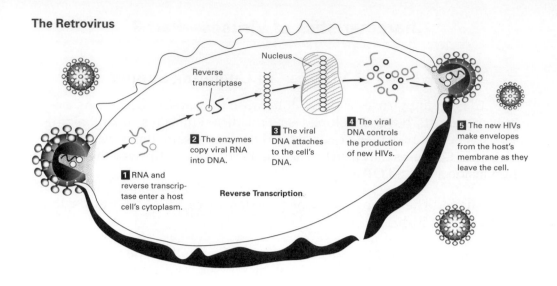

1 RNA and reverse transcriptase enter a host cell's cytoplasm.

2 The enzymes copy viral RNA into DNA.

3 The viral DNA attaches to the cell's DNA.

4 The viral DNA controls the production of new HIVs.

5 The new HIVs make envelopes from the host's membrane as they leave the cell.

Reverse Transcription

a single strand of pure RNA. Viroids cause plant diseases. For example, viroids have killed many coconut palm trees in the Philippines. Other viroids affect the health of crops such as potatoes and tomatoes. Unlike viruses, viroids do not have capsids protecting their nucleic acids. **STOP**

A prion is a protein molecule that can cause disease in animals. Prions are the only known infectious agents that do not contain DNA or RNA but can, nonetheless, spread throughout an organism. A prion causes a fatal disease called scrapie in sheep. Prions have also been found in the brains of cows that died from the so-called mad cow disease. Other prions are found in humans who suffer from kuru or Creutzfeldt-Jakob disease. Both of these diseases affect the central nervous system. A cure has not yet been found for diseases caused by viroids or prions. **STOP**

From *Biology: The Web of Life* by Eric Strauss and Marylin Lisowski. © 1998 by Addison Wesley Longman, Inc. Used by permission.

Literature

Concept Questions:

Tell me what you know about the country of Vietnam.

_____

_____

_____ (3-2-1-0)

What does "civilian" mean?

_____

_____

_____ (3-2-1-0)

What does "escalation" mean?

_____

_____

_____ (3-2-1-0)

What does "convoy" mean?

_____

_____

_____ (3-2-1-0)

What is a ceasefire?

_____

_____

_____ (3-2-1-0)

Score: _____ /15 = _____ %

_____ FAM _____ UNFAM

Where the Ashes Are—Part 1

"Wake up, wake up!" my mother shouted. "We've got to get out of here! How can you sleep through all this?" She pulled the covers off me, handed me my clothes, and rushed out of the room.

"Wait!" I cried out, throwing off my pajamas. One leg in and one out of my dark blue school trousers, I stumbled over to my sister Dieu-Ha's room. My mother was yelling, "Are you deaf? Get out! We're going downstairs!"

It was five in the morning. Explosions and gunfire echoed through the high-ceilinged rooms of the government guesthouse. Arched corridors surrounded the twenty bedrooms on the second floor of the massive French-style mansion. My parents had taken the master suite at the end of the hall while my two sisters and I had large rooms next to one another. We had arrived at the end of January 1968, two days before the lunar New Year. Our family were the only guests in the building. Rather than having us stay at my grandfather's small house, my father felt we would be safer at the guesthouse, where extra platoons of local soldiers had been assigned to protect him. He also preferred the guesthouse because it was built along the bank of the river in Hue, the old imperial city, and away from the town's noisy center. The nearby train station was defunct, since the war had disrupted all but a few railway lines.

For many years my father had been working for the government of South Vietnam. Assigned to central Vietnam as a civilian deputy to the military governor, he was based in Da Nang, a coastal town just over an hour's drive from Hue. He sent us to visit his parents there regularly, especially at holidays. He came along on this holiday visit—for the lunar New Year, Tet, in 1968.

Although my father had been warned about a possible escalation in the fighting, he said to my mother: "There's a ceasefire. It's New Year's. We'll be safe." But he abandoned his plan to drive and instead arranged for a flight to Hue. We'd landed at the Phu Bai airport in midafternoon.

The road into town had been taken over by an endless convoy of tanks and army trucks transporting U.S. soldiers, most likely toward Khe Sanh, an American base that had been under siege for several months. Along with a few other civilian cars, small trucks, and innumerable motorcycles, we inched our way toward Hue. I kept looking out the car window, glimpsing rice fields here and there. Mostly, though, the view was blocked by the olive green steel of tanks and trucks.

My mother sought to distract us. "You kids are going to be spoiled this year. I bet your grandparents will have lots of treats for you. But I want you to behave."

Settled in at the guesthouse, on the second night of our stay my mother and sisters and I fell asleep just after twelve, insulated by its thick walls and heavy curtains. Endless rounds of firecrackers went off as the people of Hue celebrated the arrival of Tet. No one knew that along with the Year of the Monkey, the dreaded Viet Cong soldiers had also arrived. No one could tell when the firecrackers stopped and the gunfire began.

Dieu-Ha and I followed my mother into my other sister's room. Dieu-Quynh hid herself under a pile of blankets. Ma shook her. "Come on, we're going downstairs!" As she started to rifle through Dieu-Quynh's drawers, grabbing clothes for her to change into, she said to Dieu-Ha and me, "Go see if your father's downstairs. and stay with him!"

We rushed down the corridors toward the double staircase. Its marble steps formed a half-circle framed by an intricately carved banister. A bullet shattered a porthole as we skipped down the steps. Dieu-Ha screamed. Pieces of glass and marble flew by. We raced past the elephant tusks in the huge vestibule and toward the reception hall. A chilly wind blew through the huge room. Someone had opened the drapes and shutters of the dozens of windows rising from knee level to ten feet above my head, each framing a view of the River of Perfume, Song Hu'o'ng.

"Where the Ashes Are" by Nguyen Qui Duc, from *Literature and Integrated Studies*, © 1997 by Scott, Foresman and Company. Reprinted by permission of author.

Retelling Scoring Sheet for Where the Ashes Are—Part 1

Setting/Background

____ "Wake up,"
____ my mother shouted.
____ Explosions and gunfire echoed
____ through the rooms
____ of the government guesthouse.
____ It was two days
____ before the New Year.
____ Rather than stay at grandfather's house,
____ my father felt
____ we would be safer
____ where soldiers
____ had been assigned
____ to protect him.
____ My father worked for the government
____ of South Vietnam
____ as a civilian deputy
____ to the governor.

Goal

____ He sent us to visit his parents.

Events

____ Although my father had been warned
____ about a possible escalation
____ in the fighting,
____ he said,
____ "There's a ceasefire.
____ It's New Year's.
____ We'll be safe."
____ The road into town had been taken over
____ by a convoy of tanks
____ and trucks
____ transporting soldiers
____ U.S. soldiers.
____ In the guesthouse,
____ my mother,
____ my sisters,
____ and I fell asleep.
____ Firecrackers went off
____ as people celebrated the New Year.
____ No one knew
____ that along with the Year of the Monkey,
____ the soldiers had arrived
____ the Viet Cong soldiers.
____ No one could tell
____ when the firecrackers stopped
____ and the gunfire began.
____ A bullet shattered a porthole
____ as we skipped down the steps.

Other ideas recalled, including summary statements and inferences:

High School

Level: High School

Questions for Where the Ashes Are—Part 1

1. What is the story mostly about so far?
   Implicit: a family in Vietnam who are visiting relatives for the New Year and get involved in a battle or attack

2. When did the story take place?
   Explicit: January 1968 (The reader should remember both the month and the year.)

3. Describe what the road into Hue looked like from the car as the family drove into town.
   Explicit: tanks; army trucks; U.S. soldiers; cars; small trucks; motorcycles; rice fields (Accept any three descriptions.)

4. Why did the mother try to distract the children from the view out of the car window?
   Implicit: she was afraid that the army trucks and tanks would scare the children

5. Who do you think wrote *Where the Ashes Are*?
   Implicit: one of the children (If the reader gives the author's name, ask who that was in the story.)

6. During the family's trip to Hue, why did the father choose to stay at the guesthouse instead of at the grandfather's house?
   Explicit: he thought it would be safer there because extra soldiers had been assigned to protect him, *or* it was built on the bank of a river, *or* it was away from the town's noisy center

7. Describe the guesthouse.
   Explicit: it was large; it had high-ceilinged rooms; arched corridors; twenty bedrooms; thick walls; heavy curtains; a double staircase; marble steps; a carved banister; elephant tusks; a huge vestibule; a reception hall; and windows over ten feet (Because the author uses detail to evoke imagery, the reader should be able to describe at least three features of the guesthouse.)

8. What was father's position within the government of South Vietnam?
   Explicit: he was a civilian deputy to the military governor or he worked for the government. (The most important idea is that he worked for the South Vietnam government as a civilian and was not part of the military.)

9. Give two reasons why the family went on this trip despite the possibility of increased fighting?
   Implicit: they usually went during the holidays, *or* the father believed they would be safe, *or* they visited their grandparents a lot

10. Why weren't the children afraid to go to sleep on the evening before the New Year despite all the loud noise?
    Implicit: there were so many firecrackers going off that they couldn't tell gunfire and fireworks apart, *or* they thought all the noise was fireworks, *or* they didn't really hear it because of the insulated walls and heavy curtains.

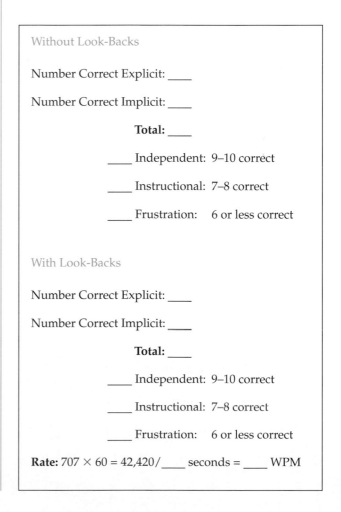

Without Look-Backs

Number Correct Explicit: ____

Number Correct Implicit: ____

Total: ____

____ Independent: 9–10 correct

____ Instructional: 7–8 correct

____ Frustration: 6 or less correct

With Look-Backs

Number Correct Explicit: ____

Number Correct Implicit: ____

Total: ____

____ Independent: 9–10 correct

____ Instructional: 7–8 correct

____ Frustration: 6 or less correct

Rate: 707 × 60 = 42,420/____ seconds = ____ WPM

High School

Literature

Concept Questions:

What does the word "marveled" mean?

_____

_____

_____ (3-2-1-0)

What is an invasion?

_____

_____

_____ (3-2-1-0)

What are tracers used for?

_____

_____

_____ (3-2-1-0)

What does the word "opulence" mean?

_____

_____

_____ (3-2-1-0)

Score: _____ /12 = _____ %

_____ FAM _____ UNFAM

Where the Ashes Are—Part 2

I am going to demonstrate a process called a think-aloud. When you are reading and come to the word STOP in the text, I will ask you to tell me what you are thinking about. Then I will tell you what I am thinking about. The purpose for this is to show you many different kinds of thinking that can go on during reading. At the end of the section, I will ask you to retell what you remember and then I will ask you questions. When you read the final section of text, I will ask you to do a think-aloud alone while reading.

In the somber light I could make out dark foliage swaying by the riverbank as a coat of morning mist rose above the water. Nature paints winter scenes in Hue in shades of gray, but this morning I could see rapid bursts of orange and red fire coming from behind the bushes. A flare shot out from the far distance. Exploding with a thud, it hung from a small parachute and cast a brilliant midday light over a large area of the river as it floated down. Rockets exploded across the burning sky and fell to the ground in rapid succession. Deafened, Dieu-Ha and I dove behind an antique cabinet at the end of the room. My father had been nowhere in sight. **STOP.** *I know what a flare is but I didn't know that flares were connected to parachutes. (Reporting prior knowledge)*

That night he had stayed up late to read a French book that contrasted two warriors: North Vietnam's famed general Vo Nguyen

Giap and William Westmoreland, commander of the U.S. ground troops in South Vietnam. Just before four o'clock Cha [father in Vietnamese] had left his bed and gone up to the rooftop terrace, where he marveled at the red and green tracers flying across the sky like shooting stars. Despite his interest in the generals, he had little understanding of the role of flares and tracers as tools of warfare. They were simply a beautiful sight as they burst over the night sky. **STOP** *Father was interested in warfare but I don't think watching it from a roof is too smart. (Making new meaning)*

"Your father's still up there. Been on that roof an hour! He'll get killed!" Ma wailed as she came down the staircase. Seeing the open windows, she took us into a chamber behind the reception room. "Where's Dieu-Quynh?" she exclaimed. "She was just on the stairs with me!"

In the midst of the gunfire and explosions, my sister had gone back to bed—a mad thing to do, since bullets were now flying indoors. By 1968, however, most of what Dieu-Quynh did was irrational. For four years she had been showing signs of mental illness. Ordering Dieu-Ha and me to sit still, my mother dashed back upstairs. A bullet came through Dieu-Quynh's room, hitting the lamp on her bed-

stand. Sparks flew in all directions. Ma grabbed my older sister by the wrist and led her downstairs, calling out to my father all the while. **STOP** *I wonder what caused her mental illness. Could it have been the war? (Questioning)*

"We shouldn't worry too much," he said in his usual unruffled tone when he entered the room a few minutes later. When he had finally left the roof, he went downstairs to look for the butler, then into an office off the living room. "I called the provincial office; they say the fighting is far away."

"Look out the windows!" my mother shot back.

"I did," Cha replied, still calm and composed. "Our soldiers are still at their posts." From the rooftop he had been able to see men in green surrounding the guesthouse. **STOP**. *If there is a lot of gunfire and stuff, a few soldiers aren't going to help much. I've seen a lot of war movies. (Reporting prior knowledge)*

We gathered together, crouching on the floor. No one spoke. My father glanced at the spacious desk and heavy armchairs, hoping to hide behind the furniture until the gunfire died down.

Between explosions came the sound of someone knocking at the front door. My parents put out their arms. We sat still. The pounding grew louder. After a moment of hesitation, Ma stood up. "It's our soldiers," she declared. "Come on!" My sisters followed her through the reception area to the vestibule. As my father and I reached the door to the reception room, we heard her scream. **STOP** *I bet it was enemy soldiers at the door, not their soldiers (Making new meaning)*

My father led me back to the office in the back, locking the door behind him as quietly as possible. We went to the desk, and I held his hand as we lowered ourselves behind it. My father didn't know what else to do. Spotting a steel safe in the corner of the room, he went over to open it, then without a word closed it again. Not even a nine-year-old boy could fit inside. **STOP** *He is trying to find a place to hide his son; he must be worried. (Making new meaning)*

"I have a young son in the house," my mother was explaining to the intruders in the vestibule, Viet Cong soldiers in olive green uniforms. They wore no insignia or badges that showed affiliation or rank. Whether because of the darkness or distance, his poor eyesight, or his unfamiliarity with military matters, my father had mistaken them for our own Southern Republican Army troops.

One of the soldiers now threatened to shoot anyone still hiding in the house. "Tell us where everyone is and you'll be safe, Sister," he assured my mother. "Please, please don't hurt us, please!" she begged. "Just let me go find my son." **STOP** *I really don't understand why she told the soldiers her son was in the house. Wouldn't she want to keep him hid or give him a chance to get away? (Noting understanding)*

Cha groped behind the heavy dark green drapes along the office wall, where a set of double doors opened onto a hallway. We tiptoed through the hall to the doors that led outside. My father motioned me out first, then carefully closed the doors behind him. I ran down the steps and turned toward the hedges that separated the guesthouse grounds from the riverbank. "Hey, boy!" someone cried. I turned. A Viet Cong soldier sitting cross-legged pointed his rifle at me. I ran back to my father.

Back in the hallway inside the house, Cha quietly approached each door to the offices surrounding the reception area. A gun muzzle protruded from one, and we backed off. The doorway to yet another office also had a gun muzzle poking out from it. There was no escape. **STOP** *The son tried to escape to the river but* *a soldier cut him off so he and his dad returned to the house and there were guns pointing from the office doors. (Summarizing or paraphrasing)*

Out in the courtyard it was still dark. Dozens of people in nightclothes shivered in the early morning dampness. Slowly the soldiers separated families from one another. The guesthouse was to be used as a temporary holding center. More people were brought into the courtyard. A disheveled Frenchman of about thirty entered the area barefooted, a trench coat thrown on over his pajamas. Hands clasped together, he tried to explain his situation to two Viet Cong soldiers. "De Gaulle, Ho Chi Minh, amis," he kept saying. "Friends."

The two Viet Cong waved him away. One of them shouted, "Khong biet tieng dtiu!" They did not speak any foreign languages. **STOP** *Where did all those people in the courtyard come from? I thought the family were the only ones in the guesthouse. (Questioning)*

"They're regular soldiers," my father whispered to a man next to him, whose crisp white shirt was tucked into pajama trousers. "Such a strong northern accent."

"You're right," the man whispered back. "The way they call everybody 'Sister' and 'Brother' is strange." The men and women before us were not part of the so-called National Liberation Front within South Vietnam. Ho Chi Minh was now sending in troops from the North for an outright offensive, a full invasion. **STOP** *I think that it is pretty important that a full invasion is starting. (Making new meaning)*

In the confusion our family took refuge in a small temple just off the grounds of the guesthouse. Searching through his wallet, my father took out all his business cards and hid them under a mat. "Just say you're a teacher," whispered my mother.

He never had the chance. When a Viet Cong woman found us in the temple a little more than an hour later, she jabbed her index finger into his chest. "You, Brother, I know who you are," she said. "The Party and the Revolution will be generous to all those willing to confess their crimes against the People." **STOP** *I would be absolutely terrified at this point. These soldiers are not friendly and think the father has committed crimes. (Identifying personally)*

"The Party" could only be the Communist party headquartered in Ha Noi. The enemy's arm had now reached into the heart of Hue. "Don't lie!" the woman continued. Putting her finger up to my father's nose, she said, "Brother, we know—you're the general staying in this house. Such opulence. We'll take care of you." **STOP** *Now I understand. They think he is a* *general because he was staying at the guesthouse.*

(Noting understanding)

"Where the Ashes Are" by Nguyen Qui Duc, from *Literature and Integrated Studies*, © 1997 by Scott, Foresman and Company. Reprinted by permission of author.

Retelling Scoring Sheet for Where the Ashes Are—Part 2

Setting/Background

____ Cha had gone to the roof

____ where he marveled at the tracers.

____ He had little understanding

____ of the roles of flares

____ and tracers.

____ My sister (Dieu-Quynh) had gone back to bed.

____ She had been showing signs of mental illness.

Goal

____ Ma grabbed my sister

____ and led her downstairs

____ calling out to my father.

Events

____ "Our soldiers are still at their posts,"

____ Cha said.

____ Between explosions

____ came the sound

____ of someone knocking

____ at the door.

____ "It's our soldiers,"

____ Ma declared.

____ "Come on."

____ We heard her scream.

Goal

____ My father led me back

____ to the office.

____ We lowered ourselves

____ behind the desk.

Events

____ "I have a young son

____ in the house,"

____ my mother was explaining

____ to the Viet Cong soldiers.

____ My father had mistaken them

____ for our own troops.

____ One of the soldiers threatened

____ to shoot anyone

____ still hiding

____ in the house.

____ My father motioned me outside.

____ A soldier pointed his rifle at me.

____ I ran back.

____ There was no escape.

Setting/Background

____ Out in the courtyard

____ dozens of people shivered.

Goal

____ The soldiers separated families.

Events

____ The guesthouse was a holding center.

____ Ho Chi Minh was sending in troops

____ for an invasion.

____ Our family took refuge

____ in a temple.

____ My father took his business cards

____ and hid them.

____ "Just say you're a teacher,"

____ whispered my mother.

____ A Viet Cong woman found us

____ "I know who you are,"

____ she said.

____ "The Party will be generous

____ to those who confess their crimes."

____ The party could only be the

____ Communist Party.

____ "We know you're the general

____ staying in this house."

Other ideas recalled, including summary statements and inferences:

Questions for Where the Ashes Are—Part 2

1. What is this segment of the story mostly about?
   Implicit: how the family is captured by soldiers

2. Describe how the river looked in the early morning light.
   Explicit: foliage was swaying on the bank, *or* mist rose from the water, *or* orange and red fire came from behind the bushes

3. What was the content of the book that the father was reading late at night?
   Explicit: it contrasted two warriors or generals

4. What was the father watching on the roof?
   Explicit: flares or tracers or rockets (If the reader says "explosions," ask what caused the explosions.)

5. What evidence does the author present that tells us that the father doesn't know much about war?
   Implicit: he didn't understand the role of flares and tracers, *or* he stayed on the roof to watch the war, *or* he didn't recognize enemy troops, *or* he thought the war was far away even though bullets were coming in the guesthouse

6. Describe Cha's personality.
   Implicit: he was calm *or* he doesn't easily get excited or worried

7. Who do you now think is the author of the story?
   Implicit: the young son

8. What did Cha try to do with his son?
   Explicit: he tried to escape

9. What happened to prevent their escape?
   Explicit: they were cut off by soldiers with guns

10. Why did the Viet Cong soldier think that Cha was a general?
    Implicit: because he was staying at the guest-house and she figured that only an army general could stay at such a grand place

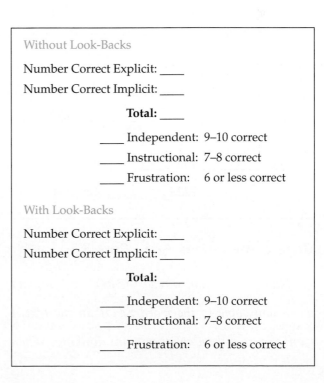

Without Look-Backs

Number Correct Explicit: ____
Number Correct Implicit: ____

     Total: ____

    ____ Independent: 9–10 correct
    ____ Instructional: 7–8 correct
    ____ Frustration: 6 or less correct

With Look-Backs

Number Correct Explicit: ____
Number Correct Implicit: ____

     Total: ____

    ____ Independent: 9–10 correct
    ____ Instructional: 7–8 correct
    ____ Frustration: 6 or less correct

Literature

Concept Questions:

What does "captivity" mean?

_____

_____

_____ (3-2-1-0)

What does "liberated" mean?

_____

_____

_____ (3-2-1-0)

What is a disinfectant?

_____

_____

_____ (3-2-1-0)

What do you think "re-education" means in the context of this story?

_____

_____

_____ (3-2-1-0)

Score: _____ /12 = _____ %

_____ FAM _____ UNFAM

Where the Ashes Are—Part 3

Now I want you to read the next section, and when you come to the word STOP in the text, I want you to tell me what you are thinking. When you have finished reading, I will ask you to tell me what you remember and then I will ask you questions.

We lost track of the time as the soldiers sorted out all the people gathered in front of the guesthouse. At last, however, they accepted my father's <u>protestations</u> that he was not a general but a government functionary. He and the other men were taken inside the mansion. Women and children were sent to a neighboring building, down into a long rectangular basement with extremely thick walls and a single narrow door at one end. The rocket explosions had ceased, but the sound of gunfire continued. We had become accustomed to it and no longer jumped at the bursts from automatic weapons. Ten families followed each other below ground. I ended up leading the way into the darkness. **STOP**

_____

_____

_____

_____

_____

"Go to the far end. Go!" my mother urged me, and made sure that Dieu-Quynh stayed with us. She knew that, on capturing a town, the Communists would use residents as workers to support military operations. Women would be sent to look for food, or nurse the wounded. If not required to take up arms themselves, men would have to gather the wounded and the dead. Dieu-Quynh, a tall girl of eighteen, was at risk of being drafted for such service. Turning to the family behind her, my mother explained. "My daughter is ill. A big girl, but not all that wise." It was an explanation she would feel compelled to repeat often in the next days. I finally settled for a spot below a minuscule window with iron bars. In the damp, cavernous basement, the tiny hole let in a faint ray of the light that signaled the first day of the Year of the Monkey. **STOP**

_____

_____

_____

_____

_____

Throughout that day and most of the next night the adults carried on a whispered debate, trying to make sense out of what had happened. "They can't win," the guesthouse chauffeur pronounced. "I bet they'll retreat soon. The Americans will bomb, and our troops will rescue us in a few days." My mother listened dispassionately. She sighed often and refused to eat any of the food the family next to

us offered. Busy with their prisoners in the mansion, the soldiers left us alone. **STOP**

_____

_____

_____

_____

_____

In our second day of captivity, a female voice shouted into the basement. "Mrs. Dai! Is there a Mrs. Dai down there?" My mother picked her way toward the door. "Your husband's up in the house. He wants to see you," the voice announced. My mother went up alone, warning me to keep my sister Dieu-Quynh from wandering out. During the night, Dieu-Quynh had been difficult, continually demanding hot water. For the last year or so she had been obsessed with matters of hygiene, compulsively washing her hands as well as any household utensils before she would use them. Finally realizing that this was a luxury, she now sat silent and withdrawn. I asked Dieu-Ha to stay with her, then went to sit at the door to wait for my mother. **STOP**

_____

_____

_____

_____

_____

The guns had gone quiet at some point without anyone noticing. More soldiers had arrived in the compound and were now setting up a crude hospital. A stretched-out army poncho served as an awning, sheltering three bamboo cots that had been shoved together. The soldiers put a mat of woven branches and leaves on top of the cots, enlarging the surface to accommodate five wounded men. Looking like pallbearers carrying a white porcelain coffin, three young men and a woman in civilian clothes brought in an ancient French bathtub. They filled the tub half full of water, warning us not to use it. No one seemed to be in charge, yet a lot of orders were being issued. Sitting by the door of the basement, I watched the men and women from the North while waiting for my mother. **STOP**

_____

_____

_____

_____

"What are you doing here?" she asked when she returned, roughing up my hair. "We're going up to see your father in a while." She did not sound excited. After checking on my sisters, she set about looking for food for my father. "Ma, what are they going to do with him?" I asked. I repeated the question again and again, but my mother would only shake her head; finally she responded, "Oh, he'll be all right. They said all he needed was a few days of re-education. They're taking him somewhere, but he'll be back."

Taken where? Would we be rescued first? Would they let him go? I didn't think she knew the answers to my questions. I tugged at her sleeve. "Ma, what's 're-education'?"

She glanced at the wounded Viet Cong lying beneath the poncho. "It's like school, that's all. Now help me with this pot." **STOP**

_____

_____

_____

_____

Spoiled since her youth by household servants, my mother had rarely gone near a kitchen. Now she was cooking a big pot of rice she had secured from a woman in the basement. The Viet Cong had set up a few clay burners and gave us some coal. Other than the rice, there was nothing to cook. We ate it with pickled leeks and cucumber, which normally accompanied fancier foods during Tet. The rice tasted of the river water my mother had used to cook it in. The Viet Cong had allowed her only a small amount of water from the bathtub to take to my father. She was happy to have cleaner water for him to drink—until she tasted it. It smelled of Mercurochrome, the red disinfectant common in Vietnam. The soldiers had used the water to wash the wounds of injured men, then poured back unused portions, now laced with Mercurochrome. She found a tiny bit of tea to steep in the water and packed some rice into a big bowl for my father. **STOP**

_____

_____

_____

_____

_____

I sensed that my father was happy to see us, but his face showed no such emotion. He took the woven basket Ma handed him, which contained a towel, two T-shirts, and a pair of pants she had found on her previous trip to the guesthouse to see him. "There's no need—you will be well provided for," a Viet Cong cadre said. "You'll be in re-education for just a short time. Now that the region is liberated, you'll be allowed to come back soon."

In the big hall across from the master suite, my father kept caressing my head. I couldn't think of much to say. Some prisoners crouched along the wall, watching us. Others were curled up on the floor like shrimps. My mother gave my father the bowl of rice and the tea. I waited to see if he could taste the Mercurochrome, but I couldn't tell from his expression. **STOP**

_____

_____

_____

_____

_____

I glanced around my parents' bedroom. It had been turned upside down. The book my father had been reading about Giap and Westmoreland still lay by his bed. My mother's jewelry and toilet case had had a hole gashed through it with a crude knife.

"Your mother will take you over to your grandparents' in a few days," Cha said. "I'll be back after a time."

Later, sometime past midnight, Communist soldiers took my father and a dozen other men away. Standing on a stool with my mother at my side, I watched through the tiny basement window. A rope was hooked through my father's elbows and tied behind his back, while his wrists were bound together in front of his chest. He was also tied to the man in front of him. It would be sixteen years before I saw him

again. **STOP**

_____

_____

_____

_____

_____

_____

"Where the Ashes Are" by Nguyen Qui Duc, from *Literature and Integrated Studies*, © 1997 by Scott, Foresman and Company. Reprinted by permission of author.

Retelling Scoring Sheet for Where the Ashes Are—Part 3

Setting/Background

____ They accepted my father's protestations
____ that he was not a general.

Goal

____ He and the other men were taken
____ inside the mansion.
____ Women and children were sent
____ into a basement.

Events

____ I led the way.
____ Mother knew that
____ women would be sent
____ to look for food
____ or nurse the wounded.
____ Men would have to gather the wounded
____ and the dead.
____ Dieu-Quynh was at risk
____ of being drafted for this.
____ "My daughter is ill,"
____ mother explained.
____ The soldiers left us alone.
____ "Your husband wants to see you,"
____ a voice announced.

____ My mother went up alone.
____ She returned.

Goal

____ "We're going to see your father
____ in a while."

Events

____ "What are they going to do to him?"
____ I asked.
____ "Oh, he'll be all right.
____ They said
____ all he needed was re-education.
____ They're taking him somewhere,
____ but he'll be back."
____ "What's re-education?"
____ "It's like school."
____ Ma was happy
____ to have water
____ for my father to drink
____ until she tasted it.
____ It smelled
____ of Mercurochrome.
____ The soldiers had used the water
____ to wash the wounds
____ of men
____ and then poured back portions
____ now laced with Mercurochrome.
____ My father was happy to see us,
____ but his face showed no such emotion.
____ I glanced around my parents' bedroom.
____ It had been turned upside down.

Resolution

____ Sometime past midnight,
____ soldiers took my father away
____ with other men.
____ A rope was hooked through his elbows
____ and tied behind his back
____ while his wrists were bound together
____ in front of his chest.
____ He was also tied to the man
____ in front of him.
____ It would be years
____ sixteen years

___ before I saw him again.

Other ideas recalled, including summary statements and inferences:

Questions for Where the Ashes Are Part—3

1. What was this section of the story about?
   Implicit: the capture of the family and/or the separation of the father from the rest of the family

2. Describe the basement where the mother and children were kept.
   Explicit: it was rectangular; it had thick walls; a single narrow door; a tiny window with bars; it was damp (The reader should remember at least two of the details.)

3. Why didn't the family jump anymore when they heard gunfire?
   Explicit: they had gotten used to it

4. Why did the mother feel it necessary to protect the daughter, Dieu-Quynh?
   Implicit: this daughter was suffering from a mental disorder

5. Describe the hospital that the soldiers were setting up.
   Explicit: it was crude; it had a poncho as an awning; there were three cots, branches and leaves were put on the cots; there was an old bathtub filled with water (The reader should remember at least two of these details.)

6. Why was it unusual for Mrs. Dai to be cooking?
   Implicit: she had been spoiled as a youth by having servants, so she had rarely been near a kitchen

7. What did it mean that the father had to have "re-education"?
   Implicit: he had to learn to think like the Viet Cong

High School

8. What did the mother bring to the father to eat and drink?
   Explicit: rice and tea made from water with a red disinfectant in it

9. Where was the family going to stay after the father left?
   Explicit: at their grandparents' house

10. Where do you think Cha went at the end of the story, and why?
    Implicit: to prison or to a work camp, because he was tied up and being forced to go (To get full credit the reader should give a reason for the answer.)

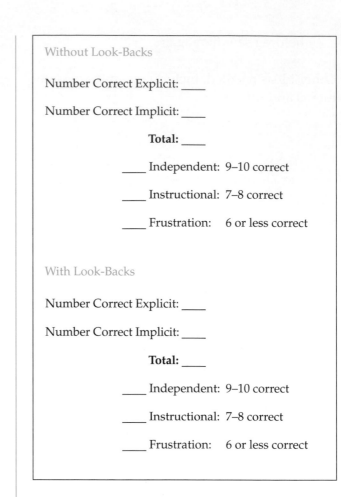

Without Look-Backs

Number Correct Explicit: ____

Number Correct Implicit: ____

                          Total: ____

____ Independent: 9–10 correct

____ Instructional: 7–8 correct

____ Frustration: 6 or less correct

With Look-Backs

Number Correct Explicit: ____

Number Correct Implicit: ____

                          Total: ____

____ Independent: 9–10 correct

____ Instructional: 7–8 correct

____ Frustration: 6 or less correct

Think-Aloud Summary

Think-Aloud Statements That Indicate Understanding

Paraphrasing/Summarizing   ____

Making New Meaning   ____

Questioning That Indicates Understanding   ____

Noting Understanding   ____

Reporting Prior Knowledge   ____

Identifying Personally   ____

Think-Aloud Statements That Indicate Lack of Understanding

Questioning That Indicates Lack of Understanding   ____

Noting Lack of Understanding   ____

Social Studies

Concept Questions:

What are some causes of wars?

_____

_____

_____ (3-2-1-0)

What were the causes of World War I?

_____

_____

_____ (3-2-1-0)

What does "interception" mean?

_____

_____

_____ (3-2-1-0)

What does "unrestricted" mean?

_____

_____

_____ (3-2-1-0)

Score: _____ /12 = _____ %

_____ FAM _____ UNFAM

World War I—Part 1

World War I, also known as the Great War, drew in not only the major powers of Europe, but those of America and Asia as well. Many economic and political factors caused the war. Newly industrialized nations competed with one another for trade and markets for their goods. Also, the urge for national power and independence from other nations came from old and new powers. When a new nation tried to increase its power by building a strong military, an older nation perceived the new nation as a threat to its power. Such tensions led to the division of Europe into two groups for security: one composed of Britain, France, and Russia, the other of Austria, Hungary, and Germany.

Although the factors discussed above caused the war, the final breaking point was a local conflict between Austria and Serbia, a tiny kingdom in southeastern Europe. Serbia, supported by Russia, wanted to unite with the Serbs living in the Austro-Hungarian Empire and create a Greater Serbia. Austria, supported by Germany, did not want Serbia cutting into its empire. The war officially started in August of 1914, after the assassination of the Austrian heir to the throne, who was visiting Sarajevo, near Serbia's border. The assassin was a young man with connections to the military intelligence branch of the Serbian government. Austria's attempt to punish Serbia drew Russia and its allies Britain and France into a war against Austria–Hungary and Germany. The map obelow illustrates the geographical location of the countries in Europe and surrounding regions in 1914.

High School

The War Raged on Two Fronts

Germany hoped to defeat France by striking quickly through Belgium and, therefore, to minimize the danger of a two-front war. The highly trained German troops nearly reached Paris before the French stopped them. However, the Russians aided France by suddenly attacking Germany on its eastern front, and Germany sent troops from western Europe to face the attack. With the German forces diminished, the French were able to force the weakened Germans back. The war in the west became a stalemate with neither side able to achieve a victory. As a result, both sides sought new allies to help them gain victory, and the war became a world war as Japan, Italy, Portugal, Rumania, and other countries joined Britain, France, and Russia. Germany and Austria–Hungary drew in Bulgaria and the Ottoman Empire, which included Turkey.

On the eastern front Russia kept part of the German army busy. Although Russia fought valiantly, it had not been prepared for war and thus was unable to defeat the Germans. Russian defeats led to a revolution that toppled the tsar of Russia. In late 1917 the new leader of Russia, Lenin, offered to make peace with Germany. As part of the treaty agreement, Germany gained coal mines and oil fields from Russia, which gave Germany power to fuel its army. More important, it allowed the war to be fought on only one front—the western front.

The United States entered the war when Germany began attacking American ships that were taking supplies to Britain and France. U.S. President Woodrow Wilson warned the Germans to stop the attacks, and for a while they did. But they announced an unrestricted submarine warfare after the British blockade shut off supplies to Germany. The final event that caused the United States to join the Allies was the interception of a telegram from the German foreign secretary to Mexico asking Mexico to ally itself with Germany and help fight the United States Germany promised Mexico financial aid and the recovery of Texas, New Mexico, and Arizona when the Allies were defeated.

Adapted from *History and Life* by T. W. Wallbank, A. Schrier, D. Maier, and P. Gutierrez-Smith. © 1993 by Scott, Foresman and Company, Inc. Used by permission.

Level: High School

Main Idea

____ Many economic
____ and political factors
____ caused World War I.

Details

____ Nations competed
____ for trade
____ and markets
____ and power.
____ Such tensions led to two groups:
____ one composed of Britain,
____ France,
____ and Russia,
____ the other of Austria,
____ Hungary,
____ and Germany.

Main Idea

____ The breaking point was a conflict
____ between Austria and Serbia.

Details

____ The war officially started
____ after the assassination of the heir
____ to the Austrian throne.
____ Austria attempted
____ to punish Serbia
____ and drew Russia
____ and its allies
____ Britain
____ and France into a war
____ against Austria–Hungary
____ and Germany.

Main Idea

____ The war raged on two fronts.

Details

____ Germany hoped to defeat France
____ and almost reached Paris
____ before the French stopped them.

____ The Russians aided France
____ and attacked Germany
____ on the eastern front.
____ The war became a stalemate
____ with neither side achieving victory.
____ Russian defeats led to a revolution
____ that toppled the tsar.
____ Lenin offered to make peace
____ with Germany.
____ It allowed the war
____ to be fought on one front
____ the western front.

Main Idea

____ The United States entered the war

Details

____ when Germany began attacking
____ American ships
____ that were taking supplies
____ to Britain
____ and France.
____ The final event was the interception
____ of a telegram
____ from Germany
____ asking Mexico
____ to ally with Germany
____ and fight the United States
____ Germany promised Mexico
____ financial aid
____ and the recovery of Texas,
____ New Mexico,
____ and Arizona.

Other ideas recalled, including summary statements and inferences:

Questions for World War I—Part 1

1. What is this passage mostly about?
   Implicit: how and why World War I started
   (If the student says only World War I, ask
   "What about WWI?")

2. What two types of factors caused the war?
   Explicit: economic and political (The reader
   should remember both of these.)

3. How did the rise of new powers cause the
   War?
   Implicit: when a new country tried to build
   its military, old countries perceived the
   new nation as a threat to their power

4. Name one set of countries in Europe and
   the surrounding regions that grouped together for security reasons in 1914.
   Explicit: Britain, France, and Russia *or* Austria, Hungary, and Germany (The reader
   should remember all three countries in one
   set.)

5. What event finally triggered the war?
   Explicit: the assassination of the Austrian
   heir to the throne by a Serbian *or* by a man
   with ties to the military intelligence branch
   of the Serbian government

6. Why do you think that Germany wanted
   to avoid fighting a war on two fronts?
   Implicit: so its resources wouldn't be divided

7. How did the defeat of Russia on the western front help Germany?
   Explicit: Germany gained oil fields and coal
   mines that gave fuel to its army, *or* it allowed
   the war to be fought on only one front so all
   their armies could be unified there

8. Why did Germany attack U.S. ships?
   Implicit: because U.S. ships were taking
   supplies to Britain and France, who were
   part of the Allies

9. What final event caused the United States
   to join the Allies?
   Explicit: the interception of a telegram from
   Germany to Mexico asking Mexico to ally
   itself with Germany and help fight the
   United States.

10. Why might Mexico have wanted to join
    Germany?
    Implicit: Mexico was promised financial aid
    from Germany, *or* it was promised it
    would get part of its original territory
    back—Texas, New Mexico, and Arizona

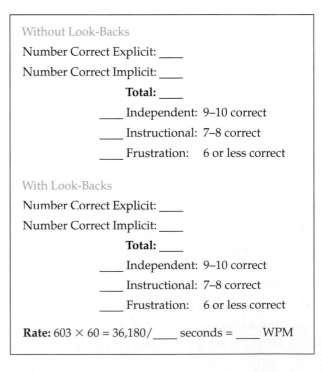

Without Look-Backs

Number Correct Explicit: ____

Number Correct Implicit: ____

        Total: ____

    ____ Independent: 9–10 correct

    ____ Instructional: 7–8 correct

    ____ Frustration: 6 or less correct

With Look-Backs

Number Correct Explicit: ____

Number Correct Implicit: ____

        Total: ____

    ____ Independent: 9–10 correct

    ____ Instructional: 7–8 correct

    ____ Frustration: 6 or less correct

Rate: $603 \times 60 = 36,180/$____ seconds = ____ WPM

Level: High School

Social Studies

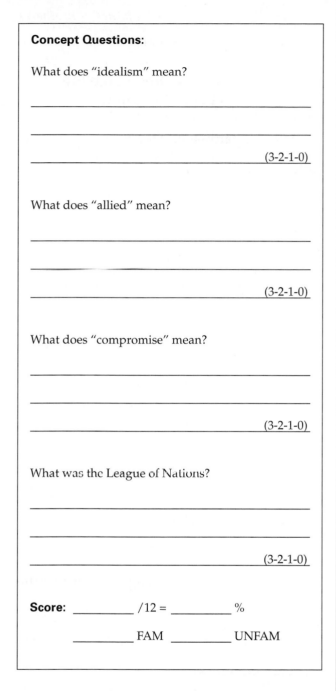

Concept Questions:

What does "idealism" mean?

_____

_____

_____ (3-2-1-0)

What does "allied" mean?

_____

_____

_____ (3-2-1-0)

What does "compromise" mean?

_____

_____

_____ (3-2-1-0)

What was the League of Nations?

_____

_____

_____ (3-2-1-0)

Score: _____ /12 = _____ %

_____ FAM _____ UNFAM

World War I—Part 2

I am going to demonstrate a process called a think-aloud. When you are reading and come to the word **STOP** *in the text, I will ask you what you're thinking, and then I will tell you what I'm thinking. The purpose for this is to show you many different kinds of thinking that can go on during reading. At the end of the text I will ask you to retell what you remember, and then I'll ask you questions. When you read the final section of text, I'll ask you to do a think-aloud alone while reading.*

In the fall of 1918, German military leaders realized they could not win. One by one Germany's allies quit. **STOP** *I wonder if the allies quitting was the reason that Germany knew they couldn't win. If the allies had stayed with them, would they have continued the war?* (Questioning) On November 3, German sailors mutinied at Kiel, a city and port in northwest Germany. Four days later a revolution broke out in Germany. A republic was founded, and the kaiser fled to Holland. **STOP** *The revolution was probably the biggest and most important reason that Germany quit; it was like the people of Germany said "enough."* (Making new meaning)

Leaders of the new German government agreed to an <u>armistice</u>, which is an agreement to stop fighting. **STOP** *Now I understand what an armistice is. It comes first and then they make a treaty.* (Noting understanding) They asked that the peace settlement be based on President Wilson's Fourteen Points, which he had described in a speech to Congress in 1918. The

Fourteen Points outlined the president's ideas for solving the problems that led to the war. Wilson wanted an end to secret agreements, freedom of the seas in peace and war, the reduction of armaments, the right of nationality groups to form their own nations, and an association of nations to keep the peace. In other speeches Wilson called for a negotiated peace with reasonable demands made on the losers. The Allies agreed to model the peace settlement on the Fourteen Points. **STOP** *I know something about Wilson and his Fourteen Points and I thought they were good ideas. (Reporting prior knowledge)*

Early in the morning of November 11, 1918, the war ended. In a railroad car in the Compiègne Forest in northern France, two German delegates met Allied officials to sign the armistice. The guns were silent.

The Victors Tried to Build a Lasting Peace

No previous war had caused such widespread horror. **STOP** *Why did this war cause such horror? (Questioning)* More than 10 million troops were killed in battle, and 20 million more were wounded. Thirteen million civilians died from war-related famine, disease, and injuries. The cost of the war was estimated at more than $350 billion. Destruction was everywhere. **STOP** *It doesn't seem to me that anything is worth all that. If I had lost a father or brother, I would be very angry. (Identifying personally)*

Three Leaders Dominated the Paris Peace Conference

After the armistice had been signed, the Allied nations met in Paris to discuss peace terms. Contrary to Wilson's wishes, the defeated countries were not allowed to send representatives to the peace conference. Thus, the so-called Big Three dominated the meeting: President Wilson; David Lloyd George, prime minister of Great Britain; and Georges Clemenceau, premier of France. **STOP** *I am confused here. I thought that both parties worked on a treaty, but Germany is not even represented. (Noting understanding)* At the conference Wilson pushed his Fourteen Points. Above all, he wanted to see a League of Nations, an international association established to keep the peace. To get the others to agree, however, he had to make compromises. **STOP** *Compromises aren't always easy because you don't get everything you want. (Making new meaning)*

Georges Clemenceau, known as the "Old Tiger," had led France during the darkest hours of the war. He wanted Germany to pay war damages because almost all of the fighting on the western front had been on French soil.

Level: High School

Most of all he insisted that France be made safe from attack by Germany in the future. He wanted German power destroyed even at the cost of permanently taking much of Germany's western territories from her. Clemenceau placed little faith in Wilson's proposed "League of Nations." **STOP** *So France wanted to really get even. The name "Tiger" fits him. (Making new meaning)*

Lloyd George in turn wanted Germany's colonies for Britain. He also wanted the German navy destroyed. During the peace talks, he <u>mediated</u> between the <u>idealism</u> of Wilson and the severe terms of Clemenceau. **STOP** *Well, England wanted colonies and they wanted to destroy the navy. So Lloyd George was a kind of mediator. (Summarizing or paraphrasing)* In the resulting compromise, Wilson gave in on many details and agreed to form an <u>alliance</u> with Britain and France against future German attacks. Clemenceau and Lloyd George agreed to make the creation of the League of Nations part of the peace agreement, which was called the Versailles Treaty. **STOP** *I didn't know that Wilson agreed to form a future alliance with England and France as part of the treaty. I thought we were just naturally allies anyway. (Reporting prior knowledge)*

Adapted from *History and Life* by T. W. Wallbank, A. Schrier, D. Maier, and P. Gutierrez-Smith. © 1993 by Scott, Foresman and Company, Inc. Used by permission.

Retelling Scoring Sheet for World War I—Part 2

Main Idea

____ In the fall of 1918,
____ German leaders realized
____ they could not win.

Details

____ Their allies quit.
____ A revolution broke out
____ in Germany.
____ A republic was founded
____ and the kaiser fled.
____ Germany agreed to an armistice.
____ Germany asked
____ that the peace settlement be based
____ on President Wilson's Fourteen Points.

Main Idea

____ The Fourteen Points outlined ideas
____ for solving the problems
____ that led to the war.

Details

____ Wilson wanted
____ to end secret agreements,
____ freedom of the seas,
____ the rejection of armaments,
____ the right of nationality groups
____ to form their own nations,
____ and an association of nations
____ to keep the peace.

Main Idea

____ The war ended
____ on November 11,
____ 1918.

Details

___ No war in previous history
___ had caused such widespread horror.
___ More than 10 million
___ troops were killed,
___ and 20 million
___ were wounded.
___ Destruction was everywhere.

Main Idea

___ The Allied nations met
___ to discuss peace terms.

Details

___ Three leaders
___ dominated the peace conference,
___ President Wilson,
___ David Lloyd George
___ of Great Britain,
___ and Georges Clemenceau
___ of France.
___ The defeated nations
___ were not allowed
___ to send representatives.
___ Wilson wanted
___ to establish a League of Nations
___ to keep the peace.
___ Clemenceau wanted Germany
___ to pay war damages
___ because most of the fighting
___ had been on French soil.
___ He insisted that France be made safe
___ from attack by Germany
___ in the future.
___ He wanted German power destroyed.
___ Lloyd George wanted
___ Germany's colonies for Britain
___ and the German navy destroyed.

Main Idea

___ The Big Three compromised.

Details

___ Wilson agreed to form an alliance
___ with Britain

___ and France.
___ Clemenceau
___ and Lloyd George
___ agreed to the League of Nations
___ as part of the Versailles Treaty.

Other ideas recalled, including summary statements and inferences:

Questions for World War I—Part 2

1. What was this passage mostly about?
   Implicit: how the peace agreement was determined at the Paris Peace Conference

2. What happened on November 11, 1918?
   Explicit: World War I ended *or* the armistice was signed

3. Name one important point in Wilson's 14-point plan for solving the problems that caused the War.
   Explicit: any one of the following: a reduction in armaments, negotiated peace with reasonable demands on the losers of the war, freedom of the seas in peace and war, an end to secret agreements, right of nationality groups to form their own nations, establishment of a peace-keeping association

4. Name another important point in Wilson's plan.
   Explicit: any of the above not given as an answer to Question 3

5. Who attended the Paris Peace Conference?
   Explicit: President Wilson; David Lloyd George, prime minister of Great Britain; and Georges Clemenceau, premier of France (The reader can give either a name, such as Clemenceau, or the position, premier of France, but both are not required.)

6. Why could President Wilson be considered an idealist?
   Implicit: he thought that the League of Nations would keep permanent peace (If the reader says he or she does not know what an idealist is, define the term and then see whether the reader can answer the question.)

7. What did France's leader demand for France in the peace negotiations?
   Explicit: that France be made safe from German attack *or* that Germany pay war damages

8. How was the Paris Peace Conference a compromise among the United States, Britain, and France?
   Implicit: each country wanted something out of the agreement, and each had to give up something

9. Which of the Fourteen points was most important to President Wilson, and how do you know?
   Implicit: the establishment of an international peace association, the League of Nations, because Wilson was willing to compromise a lot for it

10. Why would it have been appropriate for Germany to give money to France, but not the United States?
    Implicit: most of the fighting in the west had been on French soil, so they had sustained damages to their country, whereas the United States did not

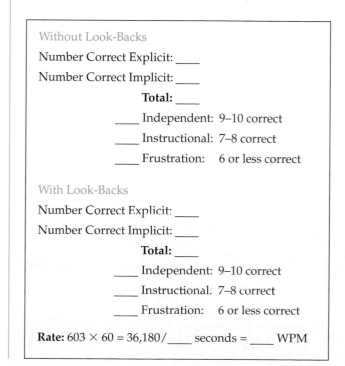

Without Look-Backs

Number Correct Explicit: ____

Number Correct Implicit: ____

    Total: ____

    ____ Independent: 9–10 correct

    ____ Instructional: 7–8 correct

    ____ Frustration: 6 or less correct

With Look-Backs

Number Correct Explicit: ____

Number Correct Implicit: ____

    Total: ____

    ____ Independent: 9–10 correct

    ____ Instructional: 7–8 correct

    ____ Frustration: 6 or less correct

Rate: $603 \times 60 = 36{,}180/$____ seconds = ____ WPM

Social Studies

Concept Questions:

What happens to a country that loses a war?

_____

_____

_____ (3-2-1-0)

What is a treaty?

_____

_____

_____ (3-2-1-0)

What are reparations?

_____

_____

_____ (3-2-1-0)

What are ethnic minorities?

_____

_____

_____ (3-2-1-0)

Score: _____ /12 = _____ %

_____ FAM _____ UNFAM

World War I—Part 3

Now I want you to read the next section and when you come to the word **STOP** *in the text, I want you to tell me what you are thinking. When you are done reading, I will ask you to tell me what you remember and then I will ask you questions.*

Germany Lost Territory and Wealth in Its Defeat

When the German delegation arrived to sign the Versailles Treaty, they found its terms harsher than they had expected. The Germans were outraged at the war-guilt clause, which placed the entire blame for the war on Germany and its allies. They were also dismayed that many of Wilson's Fourteen Points were missing or had been weakened by changes. The first delegates from Germany refused to sign the treaty. To avoid further attacks by Allied soldiers, however, a second German delegation signed it on June 28, 1919. Even though Germany signed the treaty, there was strong resentment over its harsh terms. **STOP**

_____

_____

_____

_____

_____

In the treaty, France won back the provinces of Alsace and Lorraine, lost to Germany in the late 1800's. The German territory west of the Rhine River, called the Rhineland, was to become a buffer zone between the two enemies. It was to be occupied by Allied troops for at least 15 years. France was also given the rich coal mines of the Saar, located on the French–German border. But after 15 years, the Saarlanders could vote to have their region go back to the German government or remain under the French. In 1935 they voted to become part of Germany again. **STOP**

_____

_____

_____

_____

_____

In the treaty the Allies required that Germany repay much of the cost of the war, or make reparations. They wanted an immediate payment of $5 billion in cash. Two years later they billed Germany for $32 billion, plus interest. The treaty reduced German military power and permitted Germany an army of no more than 100,000 men. The navy was allowed only six warships, some other vessels, and no submarines or military airplanes. The Germans were not alone in thinking such peace terms were unjust. Even David Lloyd George doubted the justice of the Versailles Treaty. President Wilson hoped that his dream, the

League of Nations, could correct the unjust treaty later. **STOP**

_____

_____

_____

_____

_____

New Independent Nations Were Formed

Four empires had fallen apart in the course of World War I: the German, the Austro-Hungarian, the Ottoman, and the Russian. Based partly on secret agreements made during the war, the Allies drew up treaties to divide the territory. The map on the next page shows how the empires were divided up. The western portion of the old Russian Empire lost to Germany during the war was reorganized. Finland, Latvia, Lithuania, and Estonia emerged from this territory, and part of this area was used to create Poland. **STOP**

_____

_____

_____

_____

_____

The defeated Austro-Hungarian Empire was also divided into several new countries: Austria, Hungary, Czechoslovakia, and Yugoslavia. The creation of the new countries helped fulfill one of Wilson's Fourteen Points, the right of self-determination, or the right of people to form their own nations. **STOP**

_____

_____

_____

_____

_____

The Ottoman Empire too was divided up. Syria, Iraq, Trans-Jordan, and Palestine were created from the Ottoman Empire. They became <u>mandates</u>, lands given to certain nations to develop. Syria was ruled by France, the other three by Britain. These mandates were promised independence at a future time. **STOP**

_____

_____

_____

_____

_____

Redrawing the map of Europe, however, brought some new groups under foreign control. There were social, cultural, and language implications of this foreign control. For exam-

ple, Austrians living in the southwestern part of the old Austro-Hungarian Empire came under the rule of Italy. Other German-speaking Austrians were placed under Czechoslovakian rule.

One of the biggest problems was the newly independent Poland, created from the Polish-language provinces of prewar Austria–Hungary, Germany, and Russia. The treaty's authors gave Poland some territory in eastern Germany known as the Polish Corridor. The Polish Corridor and other areas would prove to be problems in the future because they contained many ethnic minorities. Some Germans lived in the new Polish Corridor, and to complicate matters, many Hungarians also came under Romanian control. Few of these peoples were happy about the changes, and their discontent was a dangerous sign for the future. **STOP**

_____

_____

_____

_____

_____

Adapted from _History and Life_ by T. W. Wallbank, A. Schrier, D. Maier, and P. Gutierrez-Smith. © 1993 by Scott, Foresman and Company, Inc. Used by permission.

Retelling Scoring Sheet for
World War I—Part 3

Main Idea

____ The German delegation found the terms
____ of the treaty
____ harsher than they expected.

Details

____ The Germans were outraged
____ at the war-guilt clause,
____ which placed the entire blame
____ for the war
____ on Germany.
____ They refused
____ to sign the treaty.
____ A second delegation
____ signed it.
____ There was resentment
____ over its terms.

Main Idea

____ Germany lost territory,
____ wealth,
____ and power.

Details

____ France won back the provinces
____ of Alsace and Lorraine.
____ The Rhineland became a buffer zone.
____ France was given the coal mines
____ of the Saar.
____ Germany had to repay the cost
____ of the war,
____ or make reparations.
____ The treaty reduced military power.
____ The navy was allowed
____ only six warships
____ and no submarines
____ or airplanes.

Main Idea

____ New nations were formed.

Details

____ Empires had fallen apart,
____ four empires:
____ the German,
____ the Austro-Hungarian,
____ the Ottoman,
____ and the Russian.
____ The allies divided the territory.
____ Part of Russia was reorganized into
____ Finland,
____ Latvia,
____ Lithuania,
____ Estonia,
____ and Poland.
____ The Austro-Hungarian Empire was
____ divided into Austria,
____ Hungary,
____ Czechoslovakia,
____ and Yugoslavia.
____ The Ottoman Empire was divided
____ into Syria,
____ Iraq,
____ Trans-Jordan,
____ and Palestine.
____ They became mandates,
____ lands given to nations
____ to develop.
____ The treaty gave German territory
____ to Poland
____ known as the Polish Corridor.
____ Few people were happy
____ about the changes,
____ and their discontent was a sign
____ a dangerous sign
____ for the future.

Other ideas recalled, including summary statements and inferences:

Questions for World War I—Part 3

1. What is this passage mostly about?
   Implicit: how the empires were divided up after the war

2. Why didn't the Germans want to sign the Versailles Treaty?
   Implicit: the terms were too harsh, *or* they were entirely blamed for the war, *or* many of Wilson's Fourteen points were missing or weakened

3. What would have happened if Germany hadn't signed the treaty?
   Implicit: the Allies would have attacked Germany

4. What did France gain as a result of the treaty?
   Explicit: provinces of Alsace and Lorraine *or* the rich coal mines of the Saar

5. Why did France benefit only temporarily when it was given the rich coal mines of the Saar?
   Implicit: after 15 years the Saarlanders voted to become a part of Germany again

6. How was Germany weakened after the war? *Implicit:* it lost money, military power, and land (The reader should offer at least two of the three points.)

7. What happened to the land that Russia had lost to Germany?
Explicit: it was reorganized into five new nations: Poland, Finland, Latvia, Lithuania, and Estonia (The reader should recall at least two of these countries.)

8. How was the Austro-Hungarian empire divided up?
Explicit: into Austria, Hungary, Czechoslovakia, and Yugoslavia (The reader should remember at least two of these countries.)

9. What is the right of self-determination?
Explicit: the right of peoples to form their own nations

10. What caused the problems in the Polish Corridor?
Explicit: ethnic minorities weren't happy about living under one government

---

Without Look-Backs

Number Correct Explicit: ____

Number Correct Implicit: ____

Total: ____

____ Independent: 9–10 correct

____ Instructional: 7–8 correct

____ Frustration: 6 or less correct

With Look-Backs

Number Correct Explicit: ____

Number Correct Implicit: ____

Total: ____

____ Independent: 9–10 correct

____ Instructional: 7–8 correct

____ Frustration: 6 or less correct

Think-Aloud Summary

Think-Aloud Statements That Indicate Understanding

Paraphrasing/Summarizing ____

Making New Meaning ____

Questioning That Indicates Understanding ____

Noting Understanding ____

Reporting Prior Knowledge ____

Identifying Personally ____

Think-Aloud Statements That Indicate Lack of Understanding

Questioning That Indicates Lack of Understanding ____

Noting Lack of Understanding ____

Concept Questions:

What is a virus?

_____

_____

_____ (3-2-1-0)

What is DNA?

_____

_____

_____ (3-2-1-0)

What does "infectious" mean?

_____

_____

_____ (3-2-1-0)

What is a membrane?

_____

_____

_____ (3-2-1-0)

Score: _____ /12 = _____ %

_____ FAM _____ UNFAM

Similarities and Differences Between Viruses and Cells

If you ever had a cold or the flu, you probably hosted viruses. A virus is an infectious agent made up of a core of nucleic acid and a protein coat. Viruses are not cells. Unlike plant and animal cells, a virus package does not have a nucleus, a membrane, or cellular organelles such as ribosomes, mitochondria, or chloroplasts. Although viruses are not cells, they do have organized structural parts.

Compared to even the smallest cell, a virus is tiny. The virus that causes polio, for example, measures only 20 nanometers in diameter. One nanometer is one billionth of a meter. At that size, 3000 polioviruses could line up across the period at the end of this sentence.

All viruses have at least two parts: a protective protein coat and a core of nucleic acid. The protein coat around the core of the nucleic acid is called a capsid. Depending on the virus, the capsid may consist of one or several kinds of protein. The capsid protects the viral nucleic acid core from its environment.

In cells, DNA is the hereditary material. Some viruses also contain DNA, while other viruses contain only RNA. In viruses containing RNA, the RNA functions as the hereditary material.

Compared to a cell, a virus has a relatively simple existence. Viruses do not eat, respire, or respond to environmental changes as cells do. It should not surprise you, therefore, to learn that viruses have fewer genes than cells have. While a human cell may contain about 100,000 genes and a bacterial cell about 1000, a virus may contain only 5 genes.

In the figure on the previous page, you can see the parts of an influenza virus: a core of RNA, a surrounding capsid, and an outer covering called an envelope. An envelope is an additional protective coating usually made up of lipids, proteins, and carbohydrates. Envelopes are found only in viruses that infect animal cells. An envelope has spike-like projections that recognize and bind to complementary sites on the membrane of the cell being infected. Think about how a prickly burr sticks to objects.

From *Biology: The Web of Life* by Eric Strauss and Marylin Lisowski. © 1998 by Addison Wesley Longman, Inc. Used by permission.

Retelling Scoring Sheet for Characteristics of Viruses—Part 1

Main Idea

____ There are similarities

____ and differences
____ between viruses
____ and cells.

Details

____ A virus is an agent
____ an infectious agent
____ made up of a core
____ of nucleic acid
____ and a protein coat.
____ Viruses are not cells.
____ A virus does not have a nucleus,
____ a membrane,
____ or organelles.

Main Idea

____ A virus is tiny.

Details

____ 3000 polioviruses
____ could line up
____ across the period
____ at the end of a sentence.

Main Idea

____ All viruses have two parts.

Details

____ A virus has a protein coat
____ and a core
____ of nucleic acid
____ The coat is called a capsid.
____ The capsid protects the core.

Main Idea

____ Some viruses contain DNA,
____ while other viruses contain only RNA.

Details

____ In cells
____ DNA is the hereditary material.
____ In viruses
____ RNA is the hereditary material.

Level: High School

Main Idea

____ A virus has a simple existence.

Details

____ Viruses do not eat,
____ respire,
____ or respond
____ to changes.
____ Viruses contain fewer genes
____ than a human cell.
____ A human cell has 100,000 genes
____ and a virus has 5 genes.

Other ideas recalled, including summary statements and inferences:

Questions for Characteristics of Viruses—Part 1

1. What is this section mainly about?
   Implicit: it describes what a virus is *and* how it is different from a cell

2. What are the two parts of a virus?
   Explicit: a core of acid (nucleic not required) *and* a protein (or protective) coat

3. What is the function of the protein coat of the virus?
   Explicit: it protects the core of acid

4. Why isn't a virus a cell?
   Implicit: it doesn't have a nucleus or a membrane or organelles (Ribosomes, mitochondria, and chloroplasts are not required.)

5. If a virus contains both DNA and RNA, which functions as the hereditary material?
   Explicit: RNA

6. What determines the proteins in a capsid?
   Explicit from figure: genes in the virus

7. How is the envelope of the influenza virus different from the capsid?
   Implicit: it is an additional protective coating outside of the virus

8. What types of viruses have envelopes?
   Explicit: viruses that infect animal cells

9. How does the envelope of the virus help the virus infect a cell?
   Implicit: its projections bind to complementary sites on the cell membrane

10. How does the text suggest that the existence of a virus is less complex than that of a cell?
    Implicit: viruses have fewer genes *or* their genetic makeup is less complex *or* they don't do as many things as cells do (That they don't respire or eat is correct but not required.)

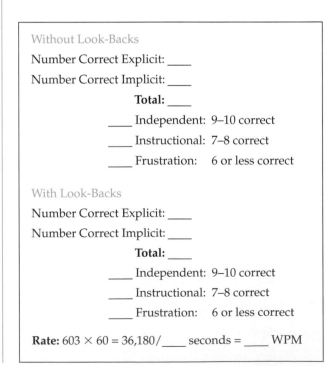

Without Look-Backs

Number Correct Explicit: ____

Number Correct Implicit: ____

        Total: ____

    ____ Independent: 9–10 correct

    ____ Instructional: 7–8 correct

    ____ Frustration: 6 or less correct

With Look-Backs

Number Correct Explicit: ____

Number Correct Implicit: ____

        Total: ____

    ____ Independent: 9–10 correct

    ____ Instructional: 7–8 correct

    ____ Frustration: 6 or less correct

Rate: $603 \times 60 = 36{,}180/$____ seconds = ____ WPM

Science

Concept Questions:

What does it mean to reproduce?

_____

_____

_____ (3-2-1-0)

What is a parasite?

_____

_____

_____ (3-2-1-0)

What does it mean to replicate?

_____

_____

_____ (3-2-1-0)

What is a chromosome?

_____

_____

_____ (3-2-1-0)

Score: _____ /12 = _____ %

_____ FAM _____ UNFAM

Characteristics of Viruses—Part 2

I am going to demonstrate a process called a think-aloud. When you are reading and come to the word **STOP** *in the text, I will ask you to tell me what you are thinking about. Then I will tell you what I am thinking about. The purpose for this is to show you many different kinds of thinking that can go on during reading. At the end of the section, I will ask you to retell what you remember, and then I will ask you questions. When you read the final section of text, I will ask you to do a think-aloud alone while reading.*

Viral Replication: Ticking Time Bombs

Viruses do not reproduce, they replicate. **STOP** *I'm wondering what is the difference? (Questioning)* Reproduction, which is characteristic of living things, involves cell division. Replication does not involve cell division. **STOP** *Well, they answered my question. (Noting understanding)* Viruses cannot replicate on their own. In order to replicate, viruses require a host. **STOP** *I remember learning about a host in science. (Reporting prior knowledge)* A host is an organism that shelters and nourishes something. Living cells host viruses. These host cells provide all the materials that viruses need to copy themselves. **STOP** *So the viruses feed off the host sort of like a parasite. (Making new meaning)*

When it enters a host cell, a virus may immediately begin to replicate, or it may remain relatively inactive. **STOP** *We probably have a lot of those inactive viruses in our body and don't know about them. (Making new meaning)* The viral replication process that rapidly kills a host cell is called the lytic cycle. You can follow the lytic cycle in the figure below. **STOP** *I am getting confused. I hope the figure helps me. (Noting understanding)* The lytic cycle begins when a virus invades a host cell and begins to replicate immediately, producing many new viruses. **STOP** *The virus gets into a cell and begins to replicate. (Summarizing or paraphrasing)* Eventually, the host cell lyses, or breaks apart, releasing the newly made viruses. The new viruses may then enter other cells and repeat the cycle.

As a child you may have had chicken pox, which is caused by a virus. While you were ill, most of the viruses were in the lytic cycle. Because your cells were being destroyed by the chicken pox virus, you showed symptoms of the disease. **STOP** *I remember when I had the chicken pox. I was miserable (Identifying personally)*

Sometimes a virus does not start the lytic cycle immediately. Instead the virus enters the lysogenic cycle. The lysogenic cycle is a type of replication in which a virus does not immediately kill a host cell. The lysogenic cycle in a bac-

teria cell is shown on the right side of the figure on the next page. **STOP** *The figure shows both kinds of cycles. The lytic cycle has five steps and the lysogenic has three. (Summarizing or paraphrasing)*

During the lysogenic cycle, viral DNA inserts itself into a host cell's chromosome. A viral DNA segment that is inserted in a bacterial chromosome is called a prophage. A host cell carrying a prophage may divide many times. The prophage is replicated every time the host cell's chromosome replicates. **STOP** *I get the idea of the prophage (Noting understanding)*

Some prophages remain in the lysogenic cycle indefinitely. Usually, however, some type of environmental stimulus eventually results in the separation of a prophage from the chromosome of its host cell. The viral DNA then enters the lytic cycle. The virus that causes cold sores in humans can go through the lysogenic cycle, for example. Cold sores erupt when these viruses enter the lytic cycle. **STOP** *I heard this on television that cold sores were caused by a virus. (Reporting prior knowledge)*

Retelling Scoring Sheet for Characteristics of Viruses—Part 2

Main Idea

____ Viruses do not reproduce.
____ They replicate.

Details

____ Viruses cannot replicate
on their own.
____ Viruses require a host.
____ A host is an organism
____ that shelters
____ and nourishes something.
____ Living cells host viruses.

Main Idea

____ The replication process
____ that kills the host cell
____ is called the lytic cycle.

Details

____ When a virus enters a cell,
____ it may replicate immediately
____ or it may remain inactive.
____ The lytic cycle begins
____ when a virus invades a cell
____ and replicates immediately,
____ producing new viruses.
____ The host cell breaks apart,
____ releasing the new viruses.
____ The new viruses enter other cells
____ and repeat the cycle.
____ Chicken pox is caused by a virus.
____ When you were ill,
____ most of the viruses were in the lytic cycle.

Main Idea

____ Some viruses do not start the cycle
____ immediately.

Details

____ The virus enters the cycle
____ the lysogenic cycle.
____ The virus does not kill the host cell

____ immediately.
____ DNA insets itself
____ into a chromosome
____ of the host cell.
____ This segment is called a prophage.
____ A cell carrying a prophage
____ may divide many times.
____ The prophage is replicated
____ every time.
____ An environmental stimulus results
____ in the separation of the prophage
____ from the chromosome.
____ DNA then enters the lytic cycle.
____ Cold sores erupt
____ when the virus enters the lytic cycle.

Other ideas recalled, including summary statements and inferences:

Questions for Characteristics of Viruses—Part 2

1. What is this passage mostly about?
   Implicit: the two cycles of viral replication

2. How does a virus increase in number?
   Explicit: it replicates

3. What does a virus need to replicate?
   Explicit: a host

High School

4. How is replication different from reproduction?
   Explicit: reproduction requires cell division, and replication does not

5. What is the major difference between the lytic cycle and the lysogenic cycle?
   Implicit: in the lytic cycle, the virus immediately begins to replicate and kill the host cell, whereas in the lysogenic cycle, it doesn't kill the host cell

6. If a virus enters your body but you show no symptoms of a disease, what cycle is the virus in? *Implicit:* the lysogenic cycle

7. In the lytic cycle, what role does DNA play in replication?
   Implicit: it tells the cell to replicate or make new viruses *or* it carries the information necessary for replication

8. If a cell's viral DNA separates from the cell's chromosome, what can we conclude?
   Implicit: a stimulus has prompted it *or* the lytic cycle will begin soon

9. When a cold sore erupts, what cycle is the virus in?
   Explicit: the lytic cycle

10. What happens to a prophage when the host cell divides?
    Explicit: the prophage is replicated each time

Without Look-Backs

Number Correct Explicit: ____

Number Correct Implicit: ____

         Total: ____

____ Independent: 9–10 correct

____ Instructional: 7–8 correct

____ Frustration: 6 or less correct

With Look-Backs

Number Correct Explicit: ____

Number Correct Implicit: ____

         Total: ____

____ Independent: 9–10 correct

____ Instructional: 7–8 correct

____ Frustration: 6 or less correct

Science

Concept Questions:

What does it mean to classify something?

_____

_____

_____ (3-2-1-0)

What does it mean to invade something?)

_____

_____

_____ (3-2-1-0)

What does the prefix "retro" mean?

_____

_____

_____ (3-2-1-0)

What is an enzyme?

_____

_____

_____ (3-2-1-0)

Score: _____ /12 = _____ %

_____ FAM _____ UNFAM

Characteristics of Viruses—Part 3

Now I want you to read the next section, and when you come to the word **STOP** *in the text, I want you to tell me what you are thinking. When*

you have finished reading, I will ask you to tell me what you remember, and then I will ask you questions.

Diversity of Viruses: An Unending Supply

Classifying viruses is difficult because they are so diverse. As a result, biologists have developed several different ways of organizing viruses. Sometimes they are organized by shape, sometimes by the host they infect. Viruses may also be classified according to the way they function inside a cell. **STOP**

_____

_____

_____

_____

_____

Shape. The arrangement of proteins in capsids determines the shape of the viruses.

Host. Viruses can be organized according to the type of host they infect. There are animal viruses, plant viruses, and bacterial viruses. Viruses that infect only bacterial cells are referred to as bacteriophages.

Many but not all viruses invade only a specific type of organism. For example, the virus that causes polio replicates only inside human host cells. The virus that causes rabies infects only the cells of a particular animal species, such as dogs and humans. **STOP**

_____

_____

_____

_____

_____

You may wonder how viruses can be so specific. Earlier you learned that capsids and envelopes contain specific proteins. Receptor sites on host cells also contain specific proteins. If the outer proteins in a virus do not fit with the outer proteins of a cell, the virus will not attach to the cell. Without attachment, the viral nucleic acid cannot enter the host cell to replicate. **STOP**

_____

_____

_____

_____

Function. Some viruses, such as retroviruses, can also be classified based on how they function in a host. A retrovirus is a virus that contains an RNA code that replicates by first transcribing its RNA into DNA. The prefix "retro" means "reverse." What do you think might work in reverse in this group of viruses?

STOP

_____

_____

_____

_____

Most viruses and all organisms make RNA from DNA in the process of transcription. Retroviruses are able to make nucleic acids in reverse order from the usual process. In retroviruses DNA is made from RNA. As you can see in the figure on the next page, retroviruses have an enzyme called reverse transcriptase, which transcribes viral RNA into viral DNA inside the host cell. You can study the figure to better understand the replication of a human immunodeficiency virus (HIV). The retrovirus causes acquired immunodeficiency syndrome (AIDS). **STOP**

_____

_____

_____

_____

_____

Retroviruses include tumor-producing viruses as well as HIV. Tumor-producing retroviruses and HIV follow a similar invasion pattern. Many tumor-producing viruses, however, enter the lysogenic cycle after Step 3 in the figure. Tumors do not immediately appear, but the viral DNA replicates along with the host cell DNA. Eventually many host cells will contain tumor-producing viral DNA. Using what you have learned about the lysogenic cycle, you can probably predict what will happen eventually. **STOP**

_____

_____

_____

_____

_____

Nonviral particles. Scientists have discovered two infectious agents that have simpler structures than viruses: viroids and prions. A viroid is a single strand of pure RNA. Viroids cause plant diseases. For example, viroids have killed many coconut palm trees in the Philippines. Other viroids affect the health of crops such as potatoes and tomatoes. Unlike viruses, viroids do not have capsids protecting their nucleic acids. **STOP**

_____

_____

_____

_____

_____

A prion is a protein molecule that can cause disease in animals. Prions are the only known infectious agents that do not contain DNA or RNA but can, nonetheless, spread throughout an organism. A prion causes a fatal disease called scrapie in sheep. Prions have also been found in the brains of cows that died from the so-called mad cow disease. Other prions are found in humans who suffer from kuru or Creutzfeldt-Jakob disease. Both of these diseases affect the central nervous system. A cure has not yet been found for diseases caused by viroids or prions. **STOP**

_____

_____

_____

_____

_____

_____

From *Biology: The Web of Life* by Eric Strauss and Marylin Lisowski. © 1998 by Addison Wesley Longman, Inc. Used by permission.

Retelling Scoring Sheet for Characteristics of Viruses—Part 3

Main Idea

____ Classifying viruses is difficult
____ because they are so diverse.

Details

____ They are organized by shape,

____ by the host they infect,

____ and according to the way

____ they function in a cell.

____ There are animal viruses,

____ plant viruses,

____ and bacterial viruses.

____ Many viruses invade only a specific type

____ of organism.

Main Idea

____ Some viruses are classified as retro-
viruses.

Details

____ A retrovirus is a virus

____ that contains an RNA code.

____ It replicates

____ by transcribing the RNA

____ into DNA.

____ Retroviruses include HIV

____ and tumor-producing viruses.

Main Idea

____ Two agents have simpler structures

____ than viruses:

____ viroids

____ and prions.

Details

____ A viroid is a strand

____ of RNA.

____ Viroids cause plant diseases.

____ A prion is a molecule

____ that can cause disease in animals.

____ Prions have been found in cows

____ that died from mad cow disease.

____ Prions have been found in humans

____ who have nervous system diseases.

____ A cure has not been found

____ for diseases

____ caused by viroids

____ or prions.

Other ideas recalled, including summary statements and inferences:

Questions for Characteristics of Viruses—Part 3

1. What are the major topics included in this section?
   Implicit: any two of the following: how viruses are classified, retroviruses, and nonviral particles

2. Name three ways in which viruses are classified.
   Explicit: by shape, host, and the way they function

3. What is necessary for the virus to attach to a host?
   Explicit: the outer proteins must match

4. What is a retrovirus?
   Explicit: a virus that replicates by first transcribing its RNA into DNA

5. How do retroviruses and other viruses differ?
   Implicit: regular viruses make RNA from DNA

6. What enzyme is necessary for HIV to replicate?
   Explicit in figure: reverse transcriptase

7. What are the two types of illnesses caused by a retrovirus?
   Explicit: AIDS and tumors. (Cancer is acceptable.)

8. What happens when tumor-producing viral DNA goes into the lytic cycle?
   Implicit: tumors are produced

9. If a person is found to be HIV positive but shows no symptoms of AIDS, what cycle is the HIV virus in?
   Implicit: the lysogenic cycle

10. How are viroids and prions alike, and how are they different?
    Implicit: they are both infectious agents, and no cure has been found for the diseases they produce but viroids cause plant diseases and prions cause animal diseases (Answer should include one likeness and one difference.)

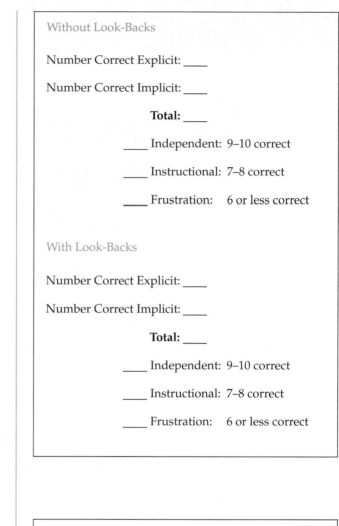

Without Look-Backs

Number Correct Explicit: ____

Number Correct Implicit: ____

Total: ____

____ Independent: 9–10 correct

____ Instructional: 7–8 correct

____ Frustration: 6 or less correct

With Look-Backs

Number Correct Explicit: ____

Number Correct Implicit: ____

Total: ____

____ Independent: 9–10 correct

____ Instructional: 7–8 correct

____ Frustration: 6 or less correct

Think-Aloud Summary

Think-Aloud Statements That Indicate Understanding

Paraphrasing/Summarizing ____

Making New Meaning ____

Questioning That Indicates Understanding ____

Noting Understanding ____

Reporting Prior Knowledge ____

Identifying Personally ____

Think-Aloud Statements That Indicate Lack of Understanding

Questioning That Indicates Lack of Understanding ____

Noting Lack of Understanding ____

16

Technical Development of the Qualitative Reading Inventory–3

This section describes our rationale for the development of the *QRI–3*. The rationale includes our initial decisions in designing the instrument, as well as information we obtained from piloting and decisions made as a result of pilot data. This section is divided into three parts. The first part includes the purposes for the pilot and a description of the children who formed our pilot sample. The second part describes a rationale for the development of each part of the *QRI–3* and presents the results of data analyses supporting our decisions. This section provides validity data for sections of the test. The third part discusses the reliability and validity data for the overall test.

The Pilot

The piloting for the third edition of the *QRI* was focused on **three objectives**:

1. Users had indicated a need for additional passages at the pre-primer through third grade levels, so we developed both pictured and non-pictured text at these levels. We piloted these texts to evaluate them for clarity and to determine their difficulty compared to passages from past editions of the *QRI*.
2. We added new passages at the upper middle school level and divided them into three content areas: literature, science, and social studies. We built in a look-back procedure to allow examiners to distinguish students' comprehension of the text from their memory of it. Piloting of the *QRI–II* and *QRI–3* indicated that this was an excellent diagnostic option.
3. We developed a high school level assessment system that included segments of chapters (including maps or figures) from high school history and biology texts and a long autobiography from a high school English literature text. Thus the texts were chosen from the same three content areas as the upper middle school texts. For administration purposes the texts were divided into three segments. The first segment is administered exactly like all other passages on the *QRI*. However, on the second segment a think-aloud procedure is modeled in addition to the typical *QRI* procedures. On the third segment of text, the student is asked to think aloud at predetermined stop points. This procedure provides a glimpse into the student's thinking process.

In addition to these major objectives, we rephrased or rewrote some of the questions and provided additional correct answers to questions that continued to cause students difficulty. Finally, we assessed the reliability and validity of new passages.

The sample reported here consists of those children who received the new passages. The analyses reported throughout this section are based on the sample described here unless otherwise noted. We felt it unnecessary to redo all of the statistical analyses presented in the original version of the *QRI*. However, we report new data whenever we had at least ten students read a particular selection. To make this section as concise as possible, we are not repeating the original *QRI* piloting information.

The current sample comprised 267 children in first through ninth grade from seven schools and one university clinic. Table 16.1 presents demographic data on this sample. Three schools were private: two inner-city (Milwaukee) and one small town, and four were public schools in Milwaukee. One of the inner-city private schools is a K–8 private school not religiously affiliated that enrolled over 250 African-American or Hispanic children. The other inner-city private school is a K–8 Catholic school with families from African-American, Hispanic, Caucasian, and East Asian origin. Families choose the schools through Milwaukee's Choice Program. This program allows low-income

TABLE 16.1

Subjects in the *QRI–3* Pilot Sample According to Grade, Gender, and Percent Below Average on Standardized Tests

Grade	Number	Percent Male	Percent Female	Percent Below Average*
1	4	75	25	100
2	79	47	53	87
3	53	47	53	83
4	16	48	52	100
8	43	36	64	23

*Below 50th percentile or below state standard of proficiency

families to send their children to private schools. Both of these inner-city schools were involved in Marquette University's Literacy Project (Leslie & Allen, 1999). In addition, one of the public schools was also involved in the Literacy Project. It was a K–5 inner-city school with a racial mix of African-American, Caucasian, Hispanic, and East Asian families. The percentage of children in these schools who qualified for free or reduced-cost lunch ranged from 75% to 90%. The population of children from the university clinic is primarily suburban and Caucasian.

The other schools involved with the piloting were two K–8 public schools, two K–8 private schools, and one private high school. The parents of all eighth graders in these schools were solicited to involve their students in the study. Forty-two eighth graders were tested on the upper middle and high school texts: 62% were African-American, 33% were Caucasian, 2% were Hispanic, and 2% were Arabic. Seventy-eight percent of the eighth grade sample were students who scored proficient or above on the Wisconsin State Assessment System (*Terra Nova*, published by McGraw-Hill) taken in spring 1999. We chose this group to examine whether performance on our high school passages was correlated with scores on the WSAS. Details of this study will be presented under the section entitled "Development of the High School Passages."

In contrast to the eighth grade sample, our elementary grade sample is more heavily weighted with children of below-average reading ability. This is the sample on which the *QRI* is most frequently used, so it seems appropriate.

We have conducted a variety of analyses, and we have used the results to document our decisions in scoring and interpreting the *QRI–3*. The results of these analyses are presented within each of the following sections, which describe the development of the instrument.

Development of the Word-Identification Tests

The words selected for the word-identification test came from the 53 passages on the *QRI–3*. We used this procedure to facilitate direct comparison between words read in isolation and in context. This is particularly valuable for beginning readers, who may "recognize" words in context that they are unable to recognize on word lists.

We chose words from each passage that were representative of the difficulty of words at that readability level. We estimated word frequency from the Standard Frequency Index in the Carroll, Davies, and Richman *Word Frequency Book* (1971). The average frequency of the lists was determined using the Standard Frequency Index (SFI). The average SFI of each word list is presented in Table 16.2.

TABLE 16.2

Mean Standard Frequency Index for Word Lists

Pre-primer	Primer	First	Second	Third	Fourth	Fifth	Sixth	MS	HS
74.78	70.50	66.24	59.80	56.67	54.16	50.43	47.08	41.02	34.82

Analysis of the Word-List Data

1. Which is more predictive of contextual reading: words correct or words correct and automatic? We compared the total number of words on each word list that subjects read correctly to the total number that they read correctly and within one second (automatically). Students at all levels read an average of one or two more words correctly than automatically. For children reading at less than a third grade level, we found that the number of words read *correctly and automatically* was more highly correlated with word-recognition accuracy and reading rate in context than was the total number of words read correctly. It should be recognized that the number of words read correctly and automatically and the total read correctly are highly correlated (significant at all levels, and $r = .73+$ at all levels). Thus, although we find automaticity of word recognition in isolation to be more highly correlated with word recognition accuracy and reading rate, persons using simple number correct will certainly see a relationship between performance on the word lists and word recognition and reading rate in context.

2. What is the relationship between word identification in isolation and word identification in context? An examination of the correlations between word identification on the word lists and in the context of the passages indicated significant correlations for seven out of the eleven pre-primer through first grade passages. Thus word identification on word lists predicted word identification in context at these levels. However, there were several first graders who could read most of the words on the primer word list and who could read the pre-primer passages with above 90% accuracy, but whose oral reading accuracy scores on the primer passages were around 80%. Remember that the words on the lists are a high-frequency sample of those found in the passages. Thus, beyond these high-frequency words, these first graders did not have a large enough word-recognition vocabulary to read very accurately in context. Although they could read the pre-primer passages, which were short and predictable texts (some with pictures), they were unable to read the longer primer passages with or without pictures. These observations provide support for inclusion of the pre-primer passages.

At second grade level and above, the relationship between word identification and oral reading accuracy in context was not significant. This was probably because of a high word-identification ability in context on the part of most of the children reading those passages and also because, as the readability level of the passage increased, fewer students read the passages orally, reducing the number on which the correlations were based.

It appears that when students are beginning readers, defined as reading at instruction levels from pre-primer through first grade, word identification in isolation is significantly correlated with accuracy in oral reading. Thus for users assessing children within these ranges, the word lists provide useful information about the level of passages with which to begin assessment. If the examiner is unaware of the approximate range of the student's reading ability, the word lists provide a quick estimate. (See Section 7 for our recommendations of where to start depending on the grade level of the student.)

3. Are the word lists of increasing difficulty? This question was addressed by examining how students of different instructional levels performed on word lists below, above, or at their instructional levels. For example, the analyses examined performance on first grade lists by students whose overall instructional levels were primer, first grade, and second grade. It is important to note that their performance on the word lists is not used to judge their instructional levels. The analyses compared the number of words read *correctly and automatically* with the total correct as a function of the level of the word list. In all analyses, the number of words read decreased on both measures (automatic and total correct) as the level of the list increased, relative to the students' instructional levels. For the eighth graders, the high school list was more difficult than the upper middle school list ($p < .01$). The average number of words read correctly on the word list at the students' instructional levels was 16 (80%). This figure corresponds to figures cited by McCracken (1966).

Development of the Prior-Knowledge Assessment Tasks

Identification of Concepts

We chose the concepts, which were phrased as questions, for the conceptual-questions task on the basis of their relationship to the comprehension questions. Chrystal (1991) examined the predictive validity of the understanding of concepts that were necessary to answer implicit comprehension questions. She examined the correlation between these concepts and comprehension of two second grade and two fifth grade texts. She found that concepts chosen because of their relationship to implicit questions correlated more highly with comprehension than did the original *QRI* concepts. Furthermore, concepts scored in relation to information found in the passage predicted as well for Native American as for Caucasian students. Therefore, in developing the *QRI–II* and the *QRI–3*, the authors (Leslie and Caldwell) and two master's degree students in reading independently chose concepts the understanding of which appeared necessary to answer implicit questions on each passage. For example, consider the first grade passage "The Bear and the Rabbit." The last question, a difficult one for many young readers, is "Why did the bear and the rabbit become friends?" We felt that in order to answer that question, using the clues in the passage, children needed to know that one reason why people become friends is shared interests (in this particular case, their love of music). Thus we chose the concept question "What makes a friend?" After the four of us independently chose concepts, we met to examine the consistency of our selection. We were pleased to discover that in over 90% of the cases, we chose the same concepts. Often our wording was different, so we negotiated what we thought would be the best wording, and final decisions were made after piloting.

Instructions

The instructions for the concepts, phrases, and questions were examined in piloting and in a study by Leslie and Cooper (1993). The more precise definition-type instructions (see Section 8) resulted in slightly higher concept scores at all levels studied (i.e., the second, third, fourth, and sixth grade reading levels) although in all cases the differences were not statistically significant at the .05 level. Interestingly, in all cases the *p* values were between .052 and .07, suggesting a consistent marginal relationship. More important, in Leslie and Cooper (1993) the concept scores of sixth graders who received the more precise definition-type instructions were significantly correlated with retelling and comprehension of narrative text, whereas the concept scores of students receiving the standard free-association instructions were not statistically significantly correlated with retelling or comprehension. A follow-up analysis of these correlations found that students who received definition-type instructions gave more 3-point and 0-point responses, whereas students who received the free-association instructions gave more 1-point responses. It appears that the definition-type instructions tapped more directly into what students knew or didn't know about the concepts, phrases, and questions. For this reason the *QRI–II* contains direct, precise questions about the concepts.

1. Does prior knowledge measured by concept questions or by prediction predict comprehension? We correlated the total conceptual-knowledge question score, with comprehension, as measured by retelling and questions. We also correlated the prediction scores with retelling and answers to comprehension questions. We examined the results on passages at all levels in which the number of students who had read the passages was greater than or equal to 10.

The results support a developmental view of reading acquisition. At the pre-primer and primer levels, prior-knowledge measures were not related to retelling or comprehension. At these levels, the children's word-recognition ability and use of picture cues supported comprehension. At the first and second grade levels, retelling was predicted by either conceptual-knowledge scores or prediction scores. At third grade, retelling of narrative text was predicted by prediction scores, whereas on expository text, retelling and comprehension were predicted by conceptual-knowledge scores. At fourth grade level, retelling of narrative text was predicted by conceptual-knowledge scores, as were retelling and comprehension of expository text. Leslie and Cooper (1993) found that conceptual-knowledge scores were correlated with retelling and comprehension of narrative text but that prediction scores correlated with retelling and comprehension of expository text. Our study of the upper middle school and high school texts showed strong evidence of the relationship between prior knowledge and comprehension. Prior knowledge was significantly correlated with comprehension or retelling of all six upper middle school texts, with the average $r = .60$. At the high school level, prior knowledge correlated significantly with retelling, inferences generated during retelling, or comprehension assess with and without look-backs *on all texts* with an average $r = .57$.

In summary, at first grade level and above, either conceptual knowledge or prediction was significantly correlated with some form of comprehension, either retelling, inferences generated during retelling, comprehension without access to text, and/or comprehension with look-backs. These significant correlations are more consistently found as the density of the conceptual load in the texts increases. An examination of the materials on the *QRI–3* and in textbooks illustrates how this increase is noticeable in third grade materials and continues throughout the grades. In the high school texts, students are expected to learn many new concepts and vocabulary in a single chapter.

The results on the prediction task in general indicated that children reading at the third grade level and higher could use the title of the passage and the concepts, phrases, and questions to make overall predictions of passage content that correlated significantly with retelling or answers to comprehension questions. Specifically, at the third grade level, prediction correlated significantly (range of correlations was .70 to .84) with comprehension, as measured by retelling, on four out of six passages. At sixth grade, prediction was significantly correlated with retelling (.55) and comprehension (.57) of the three expository texts. On the upper middle school texts, prediction was related to retelling and comprehension only on the Magellan text. Concept measures were the better predictors of comprehension on the upper middle school texts.

2. Do prior-knowledge measures predict comprehension better on narrative or on expository texts? In contrast to the results of Valencia and Stallman (1989), we did not consistently find that prior knowledge, measured by either our concept tasks or predictions, correlated more highly on expository than on narrative text. Only at sixth grade level did we find that prediction consistently correlated with retelling and comprehension of expository text but not narrative text (Leslie & Cooper, 1993).

3. Is knowledge or general reading ability more predictive of comprehension? We had National Curve Equivalence (NCE) scores from Total Reading Composite scores on the California Achievement Test for all first, second, and fourth graders from one private school. An examination of the correlation among NCE, conceptual-knowledge scores, and retelling or comprehension found that on all the measures where conceptual-knowledge scores were correlated with either retelling or comprehension, NCE never added to the prediction. However, at the fourth grade level, there were two occasions in which NCE correlated with comprehension while conceptual-knowledge scores did not, and one occasion in which NCE correlated with retelling but conceptual-knowledge scores correlated with comprehension. At no other passage level did NCE correlate with retelling or comprehension.

Our study of eighth graders compared the predictive validity of conceptual-knowledge scores and the Wisconsin Student Assessment System Reading Subscale scores to retelling, inferences generated during retelling and comprehension (with and without look-backs). First we examined the simple correlations among conceptual knowledge, WSAS-Reading, and measures of comprehension. If either conceptual knowledge or the WSAS-Reading score was correlated with a measure of comprehension, then partial correlations were computed. On the six middle school texts, prior knowledge was the best predictor of one or more comprehension measures. However, on "Biddy Mason," WSAS-Reading scores predicted comprehension with look-backs even after the conceptual-knowledge score was entered.

The high school passages were analyzed in three separate sections because each had a different conceptual-knowledge score. On the literature selection, "Where the Ashes Are," conceptual-knowledge predicted the number of inferences made during retelling on the three sections. WSAS-Reading score was correlated only with inference generation on the third section, and when the conceptual-knowledge score was controlled for, the WSAS score was no longer significantly correlated with the number of inferences generated. On Parts 1 and 2 of "World War I," conceptual-knowledge scores and WSAS-Reading correlated with comprehension that included look-backs. When conceptual-knowledge scores were entered, WSAS-Reading remained a significant predictor of comprehension with look-backs. Only conceptual-knowledge scores correlated with retelling on the third section. On Part 1 of the biology text, "Characteristics of Viruses," only conceptual knowledge correlated with retelling, but both conceptual knowledge and WSAS Reading were correlated with comprehension (without look-backs). When conceptual-knowledge scores were entered, WSAS-Reading did not significantly predict comprehension. On Part 2, only conceptual knowledge predicted retelling, and on Part 3, only WSAS-Science predicted comprehension with and without look-backs.

In summary, prior knowledge of concepts contained in passages predicted passage comprehension more frequently than did a general measure of reading achievement. This finding illustrates the value of measuring conceptual knowledge in reading assessment.

How Much Prior Knowledge Is Enough? We conducted discriminant function analyses on all passages that showed significant correlations between the total-concept scores and the total-comprehension score to determine what concept score best discriminated instructional level comprehension (70%+) from frustration level comprehension (< 70% comprehension). The concept score that best predicted the cut-off score was obtained from the classification function coefficients. The average concept score across the passages was 55% (range 40%–66%, with 70% between 50% and 60%). The average score is a bit higher for the *QRI-II* than for the first edition of the *QRI*. This is because our new instructions generate somewhat higher scores on the conceptual-knowledge task.

Development of the Measures of Comprehension

We have three measures of comprehension: a retelling measure where the student is required to retell what s/he remembers from the passage; explicit questions (those where the answer is stated explicitly in the passage); and implicit questions (where an inference must be made in order to answer the question). We have included both a retelling measure of comprehension and a question measure, because research has indicated that the two are not measuring the same aspects of comprehension (Miller & Leslie, unpublished; Taft & Leslie, 1985). A retelling measure allows one to examine how the memory for the text is structured. Although we do not provide a qualitative score based on the sequence of retelling, the more the student's retelling sequence conforms to the structure of the narrative, the greater the recall. Retelling indicates how the child organized the information, and it may divulge inferences made during comprehension. Questions, on the other hand, contain information that may drive the inferencing process, acting as scaffolds. Questions remain the primary vehicle for assessing comprehension in the classroom (Durkin, 1978–79; *Becoming a Nation of Readers*, 1985). We included explicit and implicit questions in order to tap both kinds of comprehension (Pearson & Johnson, 1978). We chose not to include a third type of question, scriptally implicit (Pearson & Johnson, 1978), because we felt that it assessed prior knowledge (Taft & Leslie, 1985), which was measured on the conceptual-questions test.

The authors designed the questions. Those from narrative texts were designed to tap the most important information in the story. According to story grammars, the goal of the main character (protagonist) is the focus around which all other information is interpreted. Therefore, in all narratives one question asked for the goal of the protagonist. The other questions were designed to tap important information to enable the student to make a coherent representation of the text. That is, a detail was questioned if it was an important detail in the story, but not if it was unimportant. In expository text of third grade readability and above, the first question always asked for the implicit main idea of the passage. Again, the other questions were written to tap understanding of important information contained in the exposition. In each case the authors read each passage and questions and categorized the questions into explicit/implicit categories. If the authors disagreed as to whether an answer was explicitly or implicitly stated in the passage, the question was rewritten or dropped.

The passage dependency of questions on the expositional passages was of concern, particularly at the pre-primer, primer, and first grade levels. In order to determine the percentage of children who could answer the questions correctly without having read the passage, fifteen first and second grade poor readers were read the questions from two passages: "Living and Not Living" (primer) and "What You Eat" (first). These passages were chosen because their questions seemed most likely to be passage-independent. We chose this sample of children because it comprised the type of children for whom the QRI was intended. On the basis of the results, we changed three questions on "Living and Not Living." Despite kindergarten instruction on food groups, the children were unable to answer the questions on "What You Eat" without reading the passage. We must acknowledge that high-achieving students are more likely to have knowledge that they can use to answer questions on expositional passages. Thus, if a school used the QRI–3 to place high-achieving students, the students would be more likely to be able to answer questions correctly without reading the expository passages. However, a comparison of the ability of these students to retell the passage with their ability to answer questions might identify what the student was able to recall independently of the information provided by questions.

One author conducted all the propositional analyses (Clark & Clark, 1977) necessary for scoring the retellings. Another judge propositionally analyzed a sample of nine passages. The interjudge reliability of the propositions identified on a passage was .98+ on the passages. After more than twenty subjects had read each passage below the high school level, the percentage of readers recalling each proposition on a passage was calculated. A map of each text following the story map format for narratives, and a main idea that supported detail structure for exposition, was constructed. Each map was designed on the basis of (1) theoretical considerations of importance and (2) empirical evidence from students that these propositions were recalled with some frequency. First, one of the QRI authors would design a map based on the elements of a story for the narrative passages (such as setting, goal, events, resolution) and, based on main idea, supporting details for expository passages. Then the frequency with which students recalled these propositions would be examined. Usually, propositions recalled by more than 20% of the students were placed on the map. However, there were details that many students recalled that were not important to the overall message of the passage but were interesting to the students. For example, on the Margaret Mead passage, 32% of the students recalled that "in the village in Samoa she lived in a house with no running water or bathroom." Also, there were ideas that were theoretically important but were not recalled by the students. For example, in the passage on Andrew Carnegie, students did not recall that "Carnegie accomplished his dream." This was part of the resolution of the narrative and was considered important, so this proposition was placed on the map. Similarly, on the passage on ultrasound, one main idea was that industrial uses of ultrasonics have been found, but in recall students omitted the detail that "factories use ultrasonic waves." We also put this proposition on the map. Thus the maps are our best judgment of important propositions and those recalled by the students. After we designed the maps, a research assistant rescored all the retelling. Propositions that students frequently recalled but that were not on the map were added.

At the high school level an additional procedure was added. We gave the texts to high school teachers of the relevant content (e.g., English teachers read the literature texts), and asked them to underline the segments of text that they thought were important for students to remember. Then they were asked to reread the texts and underline (in a different color) the segments that they thought students would remember after one reading. If a segment of text was underlined by 50% or more of the teachers, it was put on the high school retelling map. If over 20% of students recalled a segment that the teachers had not marked, it was added to the map. Although this did not occur frequently, there were details that over 20% of students remembered that teachers did not believe were important. Thus the maps were a combination of teachers' judgments of important propositions and students' memory of text.

1. Is retelling different in narrative and expository text? The student's retelling is evaluated in comparison to the ideas listed on the passage maps, plus appropriate inferences. Our data suggest that the amount of retelling is related to the type of text. The mean retelling of narrative texts ranged from 17% to 41%, whereas the mean retelling of expository texts ranged from 13% to 31%. The superior retelling of narrative texts was found from pre-primer through fourth grade reading levels. Differences have also been found among sixth grade average (Leslie & Cooper, 1993) and below-average readers (Leslie, unpublished). On the upper middle school texts, retelling was higher on the literature texts than on the social studies or science texts.

At the high school level, we analyzed retelling for each segment of text and compared it to the same segment in the other content areas. Overall, the proportion of propositions recalled was very low. In the face of the longer texts, students resorted to a gist retelling. When Parts 1 of "Where the Ashes Are," "World War I," and "Characteristics of Viruses" were compared, there were no significant differences in retelling. However, on Part 2, retelling was significantly higher on "Ashes" and "World War I" than on "Viruses," $p < .05$. On Part 3, recall of the "World War I" text decreased markedly and was significantly lower than that of the "Viruses" or "Ashes" text. An examination of the third section of "World War I" explains these results. It is a description of how the countries were reorganized after the war. Countries are listed and the new name for them given. Unless a student had great familiarity with these countries, recall would be very unlikely. It is interesting to note that these data were gathered at the time of the Serbian conflict in spring of 1999. Although the parallels between World War I and current events were not lost on our students, few names of the countries were familiar, so main ideas were recalled but not details. In summary, the high school results indicate that the retelling of high school text is more dependent on the content *within* the text than on differences across content areas.

2. What is the relationship between retelling and comprehension as measured by questions? Correlations between retelling scores (number of propositions retold that are on the retelling scoring sheet plus relevant inferences) and total number of questions correctly answered were examined on all passages with n of 10 or larger. The number of statistically significant correlations ranged across readability levels. At the pre-primer level, two out of the three correlations were significant. In "Just Like Mom," the print basically describes the actions in the pictures. There was no significant correlation between retelling and comprehension on "Just Like Mom." The non-pictured pre-primer story, "Lost and Found," is a predictable sequence of goal-directed events. There was a significant correlation, $r (25) = .61, p < .01$, between retelling and comprehension on "Lost and Found." The expository pictured passage, "People at Work," also showed a significant correlation between retelling and comprehension, $r (28) = .60, p < .01$. At primer, no correlations were statistically significant on the two passages with n greater than or equal to 10. At first grade level, one out of four, and at second grade level, two out of four, were significant. At third and fourth grade levels, three out of six correlations were significant. At fifth and sixth grade levels, one out of two correlations were significant.

At the upper middle and high school levels, there were significant correlations between retelling and comprehension with and without look-backs on *all* texts except for "Fireworks." There were an equal number of significant correlations between retelling and comprehension with, and comprehension without, look-backs. In addition, there were five times where the number of inferences made during retelling was also significantly correlated with exact retelling, and two additional times where inference generation was correlated with comprehension with look-backs.

The upper middle and high school texts demonstrate a strong relationship between what is retold and comprehension assessed by questions. At the lower levels there were no consistent patterns by which to explain the differential results. We have concluded that retelling and comprehension share some of the same processes but that there are also different processes at work. Characteristics of the text may influence whether retelling and comprehension are significantly correlated. For young readers reading other than predictable text, the relationship between retelling and comprehension is not consistently strong. Many children have not been asked to retell what they have read, yet they are familiar with the question format. They probably have a less-well-developed schema for narrative or expository text and thus cannot organize a retelling. As children spend more time reading and listening to stories, they build a schema for text (narrative and expository), and retelling and comprehension share more common properties. This is evident at the high school level, where retelling and comprehension are consistently significantly correlated. If a student at this level cannot form a coherent text representation, then retelling and comprehension suffer.

3. What is the relationship between explicit and implicit comprehension? Because there are only four or five explicit questions and zero, two, four, or five implicit questions, depending upon the level of the passages, any conclusion about a child's ability to answer these types of questions based on the administration of a single passage is unwarranted. In order to address this question with more reliable data, we examined the correlation between explicit and implicit comprehension on data from pairs of passages. In the *QRI–3* there are passages of the same type (i.e., narrative, expository) at each level above pre-primer. We collapsed data from students who read more than one of each type and examined the correlation between explicit and implicit comprehension. The correlations were significant on three of the five narrative passage sets from second grade through sixth grade, but on only one of the five sets of expository passages. Only one of the correlations was greater than .60. Based on the standard error of measurement on explicit and implicit questions on two passages (that is, eight of each type of question), if a student answered three to four explicit questions and only one or no implicit questions correctly on *two or more passages at his or her instructional level in familiar text*, then the difference is of diagnostic significance. This figure was determined by considering the standard error of measurement of these questions. The standard error of measurement of the difference between two scores is roughly equal to the square root of the sum of the squared standard errors of both tests (Thorndike & Hagen, 1977, p. 100).

4. What are the effects of look-backs? We examined the effects of having students look back in text to find answers to questions that they had not answered correctly. In the case of explicit questions, all they had to do was find the answer. In the case of implicit questions, they had to find text clues to support their answers. When we had beginning readers do this, we found that most of them could not skim to find answers but rather chose to re-read the entire passage. Because that was not the purpose of the look-backs, we discontinued that aspect of our pilot. However, we found that students with instructional levels at or above third grade could do this readily. At third grade instructional level, children engaging in look-backs ($n = 13$) increased their explicit and implicit comprehension by an average of one item ($p <$ .001). At fourth grade instructional level, children who looked back ($n = 16$) increased their explicit comprehension by 1.25 items ($p < .001$) and their implicit comprehension by .78 item ($p < .01$). At sixth grade instructional level, students ($n = 51$) increased their explicit comprehension by 1.5 items ($p < .001$), and their implicit comprehension by 1.3 items ($p < .001$).

At the upper middle and high school levels, the differences between total comprehension and comprehension with look-backs remained high. Table 16.3 presents mean comprehension with and without look-backs on the high school texts. The greatest gains came on explicit questions, where the smallest gain was 1.5 items and the largest was 3.5 items with mean gain = 2.36 (out of five questions). On implicit questions the gain from look-backs ranged from .5 item to 2.67 items with mean gain = 1.48.

Note the increase in students' abilities to use look-backs to improve comprehension as they increase in reading ability. This increase could be because of the growing awareness of question type and strategies to find answers to different types of questions (Raphael, 1986). Of course, the real challenge is the use of text clues to answer implicit questions. Sixth and eighth grade average and above-average readers demonstrated that they could do this very well.

In summary, we recommend that examiners use look-backs with children of third grade instructional level and above to determine whether students can use look-backs to improve their overall memory and comprehension of text. Look-backs help to distinguish between what is remembered after a

TABLE 16.3

Means and Standard Deviation of Proportion Comprehension With and Without Look-Backs on High School Passages

Content	Comprehension	
	Without Look-Backs	With Look-Backs
Literature		
"Where the Ashes Are" ($n = 16$)		
Section 1	.41	.84
	(.20)	(.15)
Section 2	.47	.76
	(.22)	(.21)
Section 3	.62	.82
	(.20)	(.11)
Social Studies		
"World War I" ($n = 15$)		
Section 1	.31	.76
	(.22)	(.22)
Section 2	.37	.81
	(.26)	(.15)
Section 3	.44	.93
	(.25)	(.08))
Science		
"Characteristics of Viruses" ($n = 19$)		
Section 1	.22	.75
	(.17)	(.17)
Section 2	.38	.81
	(.18)	(.11)
Section 3	.18	.70
	(.16)	(.17)

single reading and what is understood with text access. Although informal reading inventories have historically not allowed access to text, students in upper elementary through high school classrooms are rarely expected to read a text once and answer questions of the difficulty of those on the *QRI–3*. The finding that eighth grade WSAS scores more frequently correlated with comprehension with look-backs than with comprehension without text access at the high school level suggests that **comprehension with look-backs should be the score used to determine the instructional level on the *QRI–3* at the high school level.**

Development of the Think-Aloud Procedure

Research with high school and college students indicates that students' think-alouds (TALs) provide access to what students do when they face difficulties in text. This view of strategic processing could provide teachers with ideas for instructional intervention for students experiencing difficulty with high school texts. For these reasons, the authors decided to examine whether a think-aloud procedure would enhance the diagnostic utility of the *QRI–3*. Because we suspected that most students would not know what a think-aloud was, we decided to model for them the type of TALs found in the literature. Thus, on the second section of each high school text, we inserted STOPs into the text and provided examples of TALs for the examiners to read to the students. We included eleven different types of TALs gleaned from the research literature (Pressley & Afflerbach, 1995). After reading Part 2, students were asked to retell it and were asked questions, just as on Part 1. Finally, on Part 3, students were asked to think aloud when they came to STOPs in the text.

All eighth grade students were first administered the middle school and high school word lists comprised of words from the texts at these respective levels. Then the student was asked which content area they would prefer to read: literature, social studies, or science. The examiner then chose one of the two upper middle school texts from the content area chosen by the student (e.g., "Biddy Mason" or "Malcolm X" in literature). The student's prior knowledge of concepts related to the text was assessed; then the student read silently, retold what he or she remembered from the text, and answered questions. If the student could not answer some questions correctly, then, after all questions were asked, the student was asked to look back in the text to find the answers. If the student's comprehension including look-backs was 70% or higher, the high school text in the same content area was given to the student to read. Part 1 was administered in exactly the same way as the upper middle school texts. Part 2 included the modeled TALs, and Part 3 included students' TALs.

Analysis of Think-Aloud Results. First, as expected, no student was familiar with the TAL procedure. Analyses of the TAL results were guided by the following questions: How do students respond to the TAL procedure? Do they engage seriously when asked to tell us what they are thinking? Do the think-alouds generated by students fall into the eleven categories found by past research, and are these categories predictive of comprehension on that segment of text? Finally, are the comprehension scores and TALs correlated to general reading ability as measured by an external measure of reading comprehension?

The numbers of statements or questions generated as a result of this think-aloud (TAL) request were classified into eleven categories chosen from the research literature (Pressley & Afflerbach, 1995). Three categories occurred most frequently: paraphrasing or summarizing what was understood, making new meaning by generating inferences, and asking questions. These three types of TALs accounted for over 50% of the total TALs made in each content-area text. There were also some differences in TALs across content areas. For example, on the high school science text, "Characteristics of Viruses," students made relatively more comments about their lack of understanding of what they'd read, reporting 25% of the time either that they didn't understand something or that what they'd read conflicted with their prior knowledge. Generation of such TALs was less frequent on the high school history text (14%) and was rare on the literature text (5%).

Classification of TALs. We divided the eleven TAL categories into two classifications based on whether the statement indicated that students understood the text or not. The statement categories that indicated understanding were stating a match with prior knowledge, stating understanding, making new meaning, paraphrasing/summarizing, identifying personally, making a judgment, using text structure, predicting, and asking questions that indicated an understanding of what was read. The TAL statements or questions that indicated lack of understanding were reporting a conflict with prior knowledge, stating lack of understanding, and asking questions that indicated a lack of understanding.

Three sets of analyses were conducted to validate this classification system. First we examined correlations between the number of TALs that represented understanding and the number that represented lack of understanding. If these categories reflect the theoretical premise used to design them, then there should be a negative correlation between the number of statements representing Understanding [U] and the number representing Lack of Understanding [Lack]. Significant negative correlations were found in all content areas: Literature [r (18) $= -.76$], History [r (17) $= -.72$], and Science [r ($-.67$)], all $p < .01$. These findings indicate that the greater the number of think-alouds that represent an understanding of text, the less the number of TALs generated by the student indicating a lack of understanding of text. This finding indicates that students were not simply responding to a request from the examiner to say *something* when they encountered the word STOP in text. Rather, the significant negative correlations between these classifications of TALs can be interpreted as validity evidence for the Understanding vs. Lack of Understanding classification.

Next, we examined the correlation between the number of U-TALs and measures of comprehension on that segment of text in which the TALs occurred. Theoretically, TALs indicating understanding should correlate positively with comprehension as measured by exact retelling, inferences made during retelling, comprehension without look-backs, and/or total comprehension including look-backs. Support for U-TALs was found on "Where the Ashes Are," where the number of U-TALs correlated significantly with the total comprehension score that included look-backs [r (18) $= .60, p <$ .01]. Specifically, the more that students paraphrased/summarized during their TAL, the more inferences they made during retelling [r (18) $= .46, p <$ .05] and the greater their total comprehension of the third section of the text [$r = .50, p < .02$].

On the history text, the overall number of U-TALs was not correlated with any measure of comprehension; however, the more U-TALs that were making new meaning, the more the student retold of Part 3 [r (17) $= .40, p < .06$]. The same results were found on the biology text, where the greater the number of U-TALs that were making new meaning, the more inferences the student generated during retelling of Part 3, [r (18) $= .43, p < .05$].

External Validity of U-TALs. The same pattern of results appeared when the numbers of U-TALs were correlated with the WSAS Reading Score for eighth graders. Only on the high school literature text, "Where the Ashes

Are," was the number of U-TALs significantly correlated with WSAS-Reading [r (18) = .51, $p < .05$].

In summary, U-TALs, especially those that were students' attempts to paraphrase or summarize what was read, and their attempts at making new meaning through inferencing were correlated with retelling, inferences during retelling, or comprehension with look-backs. These results are encouraging because most of the TAL literature does not attempt to correlate TALs with comprehension. We believed that although think-alouds are interesting in their own right, to justify their inclusion on the *QRI–3* it is necessary to establish a relationship between TALs and some measure of comprehension. At this point we *tentatively* conclude that TALs generated by eighth grade average and above-average readers can provide a valid window to their comprehension process. However, more research is needed on the relationship between TALs and various measures of comprehension.

Development of the Passages

Although there is debate about the utility of readability formulas for judging the comprehensibility of text (Davison & Kantor, 1982), we needed some indication that our texts were of increasing difficulty prior to empirical validation. Thus we estimated the difficulty of our passages through an examination of the difficulty of vocabulary as measured by word frequency or number of syllables and average sentence length. Although we agree that these factors do not, in and of themselves, *cause* reading difficulties, they are good *indices* of difficulty (Klare, 1974–1975).

At the pre-primer level we used the most frequent word list in the *Word Frequency Book* (Carroll, Davies & Richman, 1971), and the Harris-Jacobson formula (Harris & Sipay, 1985). Above the pre-primer level we used three or four formulae to measure the readability levels of all passages. For primer-level passages, we used the Spache Readability Formula (Spache, 1974), Harris-Jacobson (Harris & Sipay, 1985), and Wheeler and Smith formula (1954) to estimate level. We used agreement between two of the three formulae to estimate level. Passages at the first through third grade were estimated through the Spache Readability Formula (Spache, 1974), Harris-Jacobson (Harris & Sipay, 1985), Fry Readability Graph (Fry, 1977), and Wheeler and Smith formula (1954). The Fry and Wheeler-Smith were estimated by the computer program, "Readability Estimator" (Hardy & Jerman, 1985). We used agreement between three of the four formulae, using one standard error of measurement, to estimate level. Because the Wheeler-Smith formula counts the number of syllables per word and the Fry formula determines readability using average number of syllables per word and average sentence length, these two were in agreement most often. The Spache and Harris-Jacobson use average sentence length; they also look for the particular word on their word lists. Thus, content-area materials that contain less familiar words would sometimes be considered more difficult using the Spache and Harris-Jacobson formulae. This was a problem on the first grade passage, "What You Eat," and the third grade passage, "Wool: From Sheep to You," where two formulae estimated the passages at one level and the other formulae at one level higher.

For passages at the fourth grade through sixth grade level, we estimated readability levels using the Dale-Chall formula (1948) and Fry Readability Graph (1977) through the use of the computer program, "Readability Estimator" (Hardy & Jerman, 1985). The Harris-Jacobson was calculated by hand. We used agreement on two of the three formulae to estimate level. We modified the Dale-Chall formula according to the following criteria: if a key concept contained in the title of the passage was repeated throughout the passage and was not on the Dale list, we counted it only once (we did not count repetitions as unfamiliar words). If a word that was not on the Dale list was defined in the text, we did not count it as an unfamiliar word *after its initial appearance*. These modifications are the same as those recommended for use with the Harris-Jacobson. With these modifications of the formula, the Dale-Chall and the Fry Index were the most similar in their estimate of the readability of the passages. On most of the passages, all three formulae agreed; when discrepancies existed, all were within one grade level of the other formulae.

Development of Pre-primer Through Third-Grade Passages

In addition to including the pre-primer through third grade passages from the *QRI-II*, we developed five new passages at the request of our users. The third edition includes two new pre-primer passages with rhyming words at the end of the sentence. One passage has pictures; the other does not. These passages were predictable texts in several ways: rhyming pattern (e.g., rain/train), sentence structure (e.g., I can . . . I can . . . , and repeated words (e.g., can, like, play, go). We chose to include such texts at the pre-primer level because of the influence of rhyme (and its orthographic equivalent, rime) on children's word recognition (Bradley & Bryant, 1985; Gaskins, Downer, Anderson, Cunningham, Gaskins & Schommer, 1988; Leslie & Calhoon, 1995). Although we don't believe in altering text with decodable words simply for the sake of including such words, we do believe that quality literature exists that includes *some* rhyming words (Allen, 1998). Given the importance of rhyme for early reading acquisition (Maclean, Bryant & Bradley, 1987) we thought including passages with rhyming words would allow a user to determine whether a child could use such patterns to assist word recognition.

We decided to include both narrative and expository text, and both pictured and non-pictured passages, at the pre-primer level through the second grade level to allow users to compare students' abilities with a variety of text types with and without pictures. To determine concepts that were familiar to children reading at these levels, we examined basal readers, children's literature, and content-area (science and social studies) textbooks. We took ideas for content of the passages from these books and other children's books, and we used the length of passages included in basal readers and children's literature at the primer and first grade levels to guide the length of our passages. Our passages are purposely longer than the passages on most inventories to provide enough content to assess comprehension without asking questions on unimportant information.

A comparison of word-recognition accuracy in pictured vs. non-pictured narratives revealed that the narrative with pictures, "Just Like Mom," was read more accurately than the narrative without pictures, "Lost and Found," whether total accuracy (means = 90% vs. 83%), $F (1, 11) = 11.92, p < .005$, or acceptable accuracy (means = 92% vs. 86%), $F (1, 11) = 6.75, p < .05$ was measured. However, there were no statistically significant differences in retelling (means = 38% vs. 25%) or comprehension (means = 63% vs. 73%). It appears that the lower word-recognition accuracy on "Lost and Found" did not interfere with general comprehension of the story. The accuracy percentages on these pre-primer stories suggest that word-recognition accuracy below 90% can be associated with instructional-level comprehension at pre-primer level.

A comparison between the pre-primer narrative and expository pictured passages revealed a higher total word accuracy on the narrative text (means = 90.5% vs. 78.14%), $F (1, 13) = 14.60, p < .01$, higher acceptable accuracy on the narrative text (means = 92.14% vs. 80.57%), $F (1, 13) = 13.02, p < .01$, and higher reading rates (means = 31.50 wpm vs. 24.93 wpm), F (1, 13) = 13.07, $p < .01$. In addition, retelling of the narrative text was higher than that of the expository text (means = 40% vs. 15%), F (1,14) = 14.13, $p < .01$, despite higher conceptual-knowledge scores on the expository text (means = 56% vs. 74%), F (1, 14) = 7.30, $p < .05$. The differences in comprehension favored narrative text (means = 53% vs. 32%), although the differences were not statistically significant, F (1, 14) = 3.47, $p < .08$.

In summary, the pictured pre-primer narrative text was easier for children to read and retell than the pictured expository text, in spite of their having higher conceptual-knowledge scores on the expository text. It was the experience of one of the authors (LL) that the pictures on the expository text did not facilitate word identification as readily as the pictures on the narrative text. This difference allows for examination of children's reading ability in different contexts.

In addition to the pictured passages from the *QRI-II*, the new passages at primer, first grade, and second grade levels included pictures because the vast majority of books that children read contain pictures. At these levels, pictures were designed to support the *ideas* in text rather than word identification. These texts were also longer than those at the pre-primer level, so children could not read the text by reading the pictures, as was possible with one story at the pre-primer level.

In conclusion, the role of pictures depends on several factors. At the pre-primer level, pictures helped children "read" words that they were not able to read otherwise. Above that level, pictures did not provide as much word-recognition support but, rather, assisted retelling or comprehension.

Development of Fourth Through Sixth Grade Passages

The fourth grade through sixth grade passages were taken from social studies and science materials published by Scott, Foresman and Company; Silver Burdett & Ginn; and Holt, Rinehart and Winston, Inc. We made minor changes in order to improve their coherence.

Development of the Upper Middle School and High School Passages

Three content areas were chosen to represent upper middle school and high school texts: literature, social studies, and science. At the upper middle school level, two passages were selected from each content area. At the high school level, one topic was chosen and three selections of similar length were designed. In the history and biology textbooks, maps or figures accompanied the texts. Preliminary testing indicated that these visual aids were confusing to college students, so we attempted to make the aids clearer. All four figures in the biology text were simplified by removing any unnecessary information. In the original text, the second and third figures were combined into one that stretched across two pages. Because we were unable to format like that, and to improve clarity, we made them two figures.

The literature passages came from two levels of *Literature and Integrated Studies* (Scott, Foresman, 1997). The high school history passage came from *History and Life* (Scott, Foresman, 1993). Three texts were continued from the *QRI-II*: "Lewis and Clark" and "Ferdinand Magellan" represented upper middle school social studies, and "Fireworks" represented upper middle school science. The middle school science passage, "Life Cycles of Stars," came from *Science Insights: Exploring Earth* (Addison Wesley Longman, 1999), and the high school science text, "Characteristics of Viruses" came from *Biology and the Web of Life* (Addison Wesley Longman, 1998).

The readability levels of the selections were estimated through the use of three formulas: Dale-Chall (1948), Fry (1977), and Flesch-Kincaid. The readability estimates varied widely, so the modal values were used to estimate levels. The modal readability level of the upper middle school texts fell in the range of grades 7–8. The modal value of the high school passages was 9–10 for social studies and science, but only 7–8 for literature. As you will see below, the empirical validation of the difficulty of the high school literature text suggests otherwise.

Empirical Validation

1. Are the passages of increasing difficulty? We assessed the difficulty of passages by comparing the performances of students reading passages of increasing readability. Specifically, we conducted multivariate analyses of variance with readability as the within-subjects factor and with total comprehension, retelling, and reading rate as the dependent measures. Also, we designated total oral reading accuracy and acceptable accuracy as dependent measures in analyses through sixth grade. We conducted separate analyses for different text types (narrative and expository) because data indicated differences in comprehension among these text types (see page 430 for a discussion of these results). We conducted sets of analyses on adjacent levels, which we will refer to as PP-P, P–1, 1–2, 2–3, 3–4, 4–5, 5–6, 6– upper middle school, and upper middle vs. high school.

Our results showed significant differences at each level. On P–1 narratives, we found differences on all measures: total comprehension, retelling, rate, total oral reading accuracy, and acceptable accuracy. In all cases, students performed better on the lower level passages. On the P-PP, P–1 expository passages, we found differences illustrating the greater difficulty of the first-level passages on all measures except rate. On the 1–2 narratives, total oral reading accuracy, acceptable accuracy, and comprehension of first-level passages were higher than on second level. We found no significant differences on exposition, where only eight students had read first- and second-level expository passages. Mean differences illustrated that second level was harder than first.

On the 2–3 narratives, total oral reading accuracy and total comprehension were significantly higher on second-level material. We found no differences on exposition, where only ten students had read second and third grade expository passages. On the 3–4 narratives, comprehension, retelling, and rate were higher on third than fourth, although total or acceptable miscues did not differ. Thus, although the students could decode the texts equally well, they read the fourth grade narratives more slowly and retold them and comprehended them less well. On the 3–4 expository passages, we found significant differences on all dependent measures.

On the 4–5 narratives, comprehension of fourth grade passages was higher than of fifth grade passages. There were no other significant differences. Again, although the students could decode these materials similarly, they comprehended the fourth grade materials better. On the 4–5 exposition, total oral reading accuracy, acceptable accuracy, and comprehension were higher on fourth than on fifth grade materials. On the 5–6 narrative and expository passages, we found no significant differences. Means illustrated higher comprehension on fifth than on sixth ($p < .10$).

On the 6 and upper middle school narratives, comprehension and total retelling were higher on the 6 than on the upper middle school passages. On the exposition for these levels, comprehension was significantly higher on the sixth grade passages.

When we compared the upper middle school texts to the high school texts, we found the upper middle school texts to be easier to comprehend both with and without look-backs than the high school texts. Specifically, the comprehension scores on "Biddy Mason" were higher than on the first segment of "Where the Ashes Are," [t (14) = 6.23, p < .001, and 2.75, p < .02], for comprehension without and with look-backs, respectively. On social studies, comprehension was higher on "Lewis and Clark" and "Ferdinand Magellan" than on the first segment of "World War I" [t = 5.17, 4.01, p < .01]. On science, comprehension without look-backs was higher on "Fireworks" and "Life Cycles of Stars" than on the first section of "Characteristics of Viruses" [t = 8.67 and 4.29, p < .001]. However, with look-backs, only comprehension of "Fireworks" was higher than that of the first section of "Viruses." Apparently, access to the text of "Life Cycles of Stars" and "Viruses" allowed students to recall what they had understood, but not remembered, when reading these selections.

As a result of the above comparisons, there are sufficient data indicating that the passages are of increasing difficulty. In all passage comparisons, the comprehension of the lower passage was one to two questions higher than that of the higher passage. In addition, on passages through third grade, children read with greater accuracy on the passages of lower readability. On expository passage comparisons of levels 3–4 and 4–5, students read with greater accuracy and greater acceptable accuracy on the lower passage. Comparing performance on the upper middle school and high school texts illustrates the difficulty that eighth graders had in comprehending the high school texts after a single reading and without access to the text. Allowing them to look back improved comprehension significantly, though even then, the greater difficulty of the high school texts were evident.

2. Are there comprehension differences on different text types? One of the theoretical foundations of the *QRI* was that it should find comprehension differences between narrative and expository passages. We conducted multivariate analyses of variance comparing conceptual-knowledge scores, retelling, and comprehension for children who read at least one narrative and one expository text at a readability level. Because each student read both a narrative and an expository text, passage type was a within-subjects factor.

Results of these analyses differed according to the readability of the passages. Table 16.4 presents the means and standard deviations of proportion-correct scores on conceptual knowledge, retelling, and comprehension as a function of readability and text type. Significant effects of passage type were found at all levels except primer, fifth, and sixth. At the pre-primer level, students retold, F (1, 14) = 17.10, p < .001, and comprehended, F (1, 14) = 5.78, p < .05, more on narrative texts, despite having higher knowledge scores on the expository text, F (1, 14) = 8.96, p < .01. At the primer level, no significant differences were found, and as Table 16.4 illustrates, all means were very close. At first grade level, students had more conceptual knowledge, retold more, and comprehended more on narrative text than on expository, F (1, 31) = 16.56, 24.16, and 22.07, p < .001. A multivariate analysis of covariance that removed the variance due to conceptual knowledge (*Beta* = .32), still found higher retelling and comprehension on narrative text, F (1, 30) = 9.23 and 9.50, p < .01. At second grade level, students retold and comprehended more of the narrative text, F (1, 18) = 45.60 and 11.53, p < .001 and .01, respectively, than of the expository text, despite almost identical conceptual-knowledge scores. At third grade level, students retold and

TABLE 16.4

Means and Standard Deviation of Proportion Correct Score on Conceptual Knowledge, Retelling, and Comprehension on Narrative and Expository Text as a Function of Readability Level

Readability Level	Conceptual Knowledge	Retelling	Comprehension
Pre-primer ($n = 15$)			
Narrative	.54**	.35*	.57**
	(.14)	(.16)	(.33)
Expository	.74	.15	.31
	(.23)	(.13)	(.18)
Primer ($n = 13$)			
Narrative	.58	.29	.72
	(.19)	(.16)	(.23)
Expository	.62	.33	.68
	(.11)	(.17)	(.16)
First ($n = 32$)			
Narrative	.67**	.26**	.76**
	(.14)	(.13)	(.12)
Expository	.54	.15	.50
	(.19)	(.13)	(.26)
Second ($n = 19$)			
Narrative	.69	.43**	.82**
	(.15)	(.18)	(.17)
Expository	.68	.22	.61
	(.19)	(.13)	(.19)
Third ($n = 26$)			
Narrative	.69	.34**	.77**
	(.16)	(.18)	(.16)
Expository	.66	.19	.58
	(.13)	(.11)	(.22)
Fourth ($n = 17$)			
Narrative	.46	.34*	.65
	(.29)	(.15)	(.20)
Expository	.47	.27	.71
	(.21)	(.13)	(.18)
Fifth ($n = 12$)			
Narrative	.52	.27	.74
	(.31)	(.13)	(.19)
Expository	.57	.24	.62
	(.20)	(.18)	(.21)
Sixth ($n = 13$)			
Narrative	.47	.28	.73
	(.21)	(.15)	(.15)
Expository	.40	.27	.62
	(.18)	(.13)	(.22)
Upper Middle School ($n = 15$)			
Literature	.60	.28	.67
	(.19)	(.15)	(.23)
Social Studies	.59	.23	.52
	(.22)	(.12)	(.25)
Science	.69	.17	.48
	(.24)	(.11)	(.16)
High School ($n = 12$)			
Literature	.42	.16	.49
	(.25)	(.12)	(.21)
Social Studies	.47	.09	.43
	(.17)	(.11)	(.25)
Science	.41	.11	.28*
	(.21)	(.11)	(.11)

*$p < .05$ **$p < .01$

comprehended more of the narrative than of the expository texts, $F (1, 25) =$ 21.31 and 12.32, $p < .001$, and .01, respectively, despite similar conceptual-knowledge scores. At the fourth grade level, students retold more of the narrative text, $F (1, 16) = 5.29, p < .05$, but differences between comprehension and conceptual-knowledge scores were not statistically significant. At fifth and sixth grade levels, there were no statistically significant differences on any measure. However, it should be noted that the number of students in these analyses was small (12). Leslie and Cooper (1993) found that average sixth grade readers retold more of the narrative text, $F (1, 53) = 12.85, p < .001$, than expository text, despite showing more prior knowledge of the expository text, $F (1, 53) = 68.13, p < .001$. No differences in comprehension were found. These findings corroborate those obtained with sixth grade level readers on the original *QRI*.

At the upper middle school and high school texts, comprehension differences across content remained. Although there were no differences in conceptual knowledge across content areas on the sections of the high school texts, some differences in comprehension were found. First, as indicated earlier, the proportion of propositions recalled was very low. In the face of the longer texts, students resorted to a gist retelling. When Parts 1 of "Where the Ashes Are," "World War I," and "Characteristics of Viruses" were compared, there were no significant differences in retelling. However, on Part 2, retelling was significantly higher on "Ashes" and "World War I" than on "Viruses," $p < .05$. On Part 3, recall of the "World War I" text decreased markedly and was significantly lower than that of the "Viruses" or "Ashes" text. The unfamiliar detailed account of the reorganization of countries after World War I resulted in low recall.

The differences in comprehension without access to text were significant across some content areas. Comprehension of Part 1 of "Where the Ashes Are" and "World War I" was greater than comprehension of the science text, "Viruses." Comprehension of Part 2 was highest on "Where the Ashes Are" [mean = 58], followed by "World War I" [mean = 47], followed by "Viruses" [mean = 22]. When students were allowed to look back in the text, total comprehension was not different among the content areas on Parts 1 and 2. However, on Part 3 the highest scores were found on "World War I" [mean = 95], followed by "Where the Ashes Are" [mean = 82], followed by "Viruses" [mean = 76]. These differences probably occurred because although students couldn't remember the organization of countries after World War I, they could easily find the answers to these questions when allowed access to the text. Users of these texts should realize that the content of the text dictates the type of questions asked, which affects the measures of comprehension.

In summary, an examination of the above findings, in addition to those on the original *QRI*, suggests that students *recall* more from narrative than from expository text through high school. Comprehension differences appear through third grade reading level at least. It should be noted that these differences are probably subject to instructional modification. That is, in schools where more emphasis is placed on reading expository material, the differences should be less pronounced, or ameliorated. Such may be the case in our current fourth level readers compared to the fourth level readers in our original sample.

3. **Is comprehension affected by interest in the topic?** We piloted an interest measure to assess the effect of interest on retelling or comprehension. Prior to reading, the student was asked, "If the title of the passage is '____,' how interested are you to read about '____'?" A four-point Likert scale was used: "very interested," "a little interested," "not very interested," and "not at all interested." Again, after students finished reading the selection, and before retelling, we asked them to rate, on the same scale, how interesting

the passage had been to them. Results indicated that the two interest measures were highly correlated with each other at all levels, thus establishing the reliability of the measure. Interest predicted retelling or comprehension on three out of four passages at the first and second reading level. It correlated with retelling or comprehension only once at the fourth level and twice at the sixth level. Because of the inconsistency of these results, we chose not to include the interest measure. It should be noted that interest was more likely to correlate with retelling than comprehension; thus it may be a measure of motivation to retell. Further research should be done to investigate this possibility.

4. Is comprehension affected by gender of character or gender of reader? The narratives above third grade level are biographies. The name of the person was the title of the passage and one of the concepts assessed in the prior-knowledge measure. Some of the biographies were about males, others about females. There was concern that students' interest in the characters might affect their comprehension and that the interest might be gender-related. We conducted a multivariate analysis of variance on the fifth grade data because there were two biographies of males and two of females. The reader's gender was the between-subjects factor, and the character's gender was the within-subject factor. The dependent measures were comprehension as measured by questions and total retelling. There were no significant effects of either of these factors, or of their interaction, on comprehension.

5. Are there differences in instructional levels obtained in familiar and unfamiliar text? We have used the same criteria for determining instructional level in familiar vs. unfamiliar material. To ascertain whether students' instructional level in familiar material was different from their instructional level in unfamiliar material, we performed analyses of variance with instructional level in familiar and unfamiliar material as the within-subject variable at all grades above third. We did not use the lower levels because many of these children did not have an instructional level in unfamiliar material (all the material was relatively familiar to them). We found significant differences between the levels for the children at all grade levels between fourth and junior high. At all readability levels, the mean instructional level in familiar material was one-half year higher than in unfamiliar material.

An examination of the percentage of students whose familiar instructional level was either the same or one or more levels higher than their instructional level in unfamiliar material showed differences depending on readability level. At the third grade and junior high levels, most students had instructional levels that were equal in familiar and unfamiliar material. In contrast, at all other levels, 67% showed an instructional level in familiar material one or more levels higher than in unfamiliar material.

This finding supports the use of materials of varying familiarity on the QRI–3. Because students will vary in their familiarity with material, a teacher or assessment specialist needs to be aware that students' instructional level may vary as a function of the familiarity of the material.

Rationale for Scoring Oral Reading Miscues

We recommend that examiners score miscues in two ways: (1) to find the total number of miscues and convert it to oral reading accuracy in percentage; (2) to determine the percentage of uncorrected miscues that change the authors' meanings. Studies by Leslie (1980), Leslie and Osol (1978), and Bristow and Leslie (1988) indicate that changes in miscue quality occur as the total number of miscues increases. Specifically, as the total number of miscues increases, the number of miscues that change the authors' meaning and are not corrected also increases. Research indicates that these changes may occur as the child reads with less than 95% accuracy (supporting the traditional criteria for instructional level), but these changes certainly occur if the student reads with less than 90% accuracy. The one exception to this finding occurs for children at the pre-primer instructional level. Data describing this exception are presented below.

1. What is the relationship between oral reading accuracy and retelling and comprehension? The correlation between oral reading accuracy and retelling and comprehension was examined at each readability level. At the pre-primer level, there were significant correlations between oral reading accuracy and both retelling and comprehension (r values ranged from .38 to .83). At the primer level, significant correlations were found on only one passage, "A Trip." At the first grade level, significant correlations were found on three out of the four passages (r values ranged from .36 to .66). There were no statistically significant correlations at the second grade level. Above second grade level, fewer subjects read orally, so the number of students on which the correlations are based is small, contributing to the lack of statistically significant correlations at those levels.

2. How accurate does oral reading need to be for instructional-level comprehension? The traditional oral reading accuracy scores used to determine instructional level have been between 90% and 95%. We analyzed our pilot data to determine the level of accuracy related to instructional-level comprehension (70%). In other words, how accurately does one need to read in order to comprehend, or how much meaning construction needs to occur for accurate oral reading?

Discriminant function analyses were conducted on pre-primer, primer, and first grade level passages and showed significant correlations between either total accuracy or acceptable accuracy and either retelling or comprehension. From the classification function coefficients, we determined the accuracy level that best predicted instructional-level comprehension (80% at pre-primer level, 67% at primer and first grade levels). At pre-primer level, a total accuracy score of 85% best predicted instructional-level comprehension on "Just Like Mom," whereas a total accuracy score of 80% best predicted instructional-level comprehension on "Lost and Found." This difference in accuracy level was expected from the mean accuracy differences between the two stories. Why was 80% comprehension associated with 85% accuracy on one story but with only 80% accuracy on the other? There are two obvious differences between the stories: picture vs. no pictures, and predictability of text. "Just Like Mom" had pictures, and "Lost and Found" didn't. One would expect that if pictures supported comprehension, the accuracy percent associated with instructional-level comprehension would be lower on the pictured than on the non-pictured passages. Given that the opposite was found, the "picture–no pictures" difference does not seem a likely explanation. Alternatively, the questions on "Just Like Mom" appear to be more open-ended, and thus, children with less accurate reading may have given answers from their knowledge base because they weren't able to construct enough meaning from the text or the picture. One author (LL), who gathered 90% of the pre-primer data, observed such responses. In contrast, on "Lost and Found," the questions did not elicit responses from prior knowledge but rather tapped key words that the children appeared likely to recognize in the predictable text (e.g., cat, dog, bed, table). Thus, if the children read these words correctly, they could comprehend at instructional level, even though they could not read other words in the story correctly.

An analysis of the accuracy score related to retelling of at least 20% indicated that on both pre-primer narratives, 88% acceptable accuracy was related to a retelling of at least 20% of the text. At the primer level, 87% total accuracy was related to a retelling of at least 20%. At first grade level, the accuracy percentage increased: 93% total accuracy was related to instructional-level comprehension, and 96% acceptable accuracy was related to a retelling of at least 20%.

In conclusion, **at the pre-primer and primer levels, children may read with less than 90% accuracy and still achieve instructional-level comprehension**. Whether it would be instructionally beneficial for children to spend a lot of time reading such challenging material is an empirical question. It would probably depend on teacher support, picture support, interest, and other factors. At the first grade level, however, the traditional criteria of at least 90% total accuracy and 95% acceptable accuracy were supported.

Reliability and Validity

An informal reading inventory should meet the requirements presented in the *Standards for Educational and Psychological Testing* (1985) written by the American Educational Research Association, American Psychological Association, and National Council on Measurement in Education. According to the *Standards*, a test is an instrument that evaluates some ability, and an inventory obtains data upon which no evaluation is made (such as a personality inventory). Thus informal reading inventories are tests, not inventories. We acknowledge this, but we call our instrument an inventory because it is structurally similar to other IRIs, however misnamed historically. No matter what you call this instrument, there are basic standards of any instrument that must be met. Following is a discussion of reliability and validity issues as they pertain to the uses of our instrument.

Issues of Reliability of an Informal Reading Inventory

Cross and Paris (1987) present an analysis of the relationship between test purposes and the statistical evidence necessary to document the reliability and validity of the test. Perhaps the most important contribution of this work is the illustration that evidence important to one kind of test may be irrelevant or detrimental to another type of test. The purpose of the instrument should guide the author and user to determine the relevant reliability and validity data for the instrument's purposes.

Because we designed the *QRI–3* for mastery (that is, determination of an instructional level) and diagnostic purposes, the essential test properties, according to Cross and Paris, are consistency, construct representation, and penetration. Consistency is a reliability property of a test that refers to the replicability of scores for a single individual. A score is consistent if, in the absence of growth or learning, an individual repeatedly obtains the same score. The *QRI–3* measures consistency of scores in three ways: interscorer reliability, internal consistency reliability, and alternate-form reliability. Construct representation and penetration are validity properties and are discussed in the validity section.

Interjudge Reliability (Consistency) of Scoring.
Aside from the purposes for which an instrument is used, one must have evidence that the test is scored consistently across examiners. Whenever there is a judgment, lack of consistency can develop. In our analysis of scoring reliability of the *QRI*, we

examined the reliability of judges' scores on total percentage of miscues, percent of meaning-change miscues, prior-knowledge concept score, total explicit comprehension score and total implicit comprehension score, and the propositional analysis of recall. All examiners had the same scoring manual to judge these scores. However, our expert scorers ($n = 3$) were reading teachers or specialists who had a master's degree. Thus our reliability estimates compare persons without extensive training by the test developers to those with training by the test developers. It should be noted that the experts did not receive their master's degrees from the program of either test author, but one test author trained the experts in the scoring of the QRI–II. We did not have two judges listen to the tapes of the children's oral reading unless the examiner was an undergraduate student. Thus we assumed that the transcription of the total number of miscues was correct. Hood (1975–1976) reports the reliability of two judges recording total miscues from tape to be .98+.

Estimates of the inter-scorer reliability of the new conceptual-knowledge questions found agreement on 299 of the 304 concepts sampled, for a 98% agreement. Scorers used the scoring instructions and examples found in Section 8. Estimates of inter-scorer reliability of total miscues, acceptable miscues, and explicit and implicit comprehension were assessed by examining data from 122 readings. These data were gathered across all readability levels and both types of text. Of the 122 readings, 49 were conducted orally. Thus the estimate of reliability for total miscues and acceptable miscues is based on 49 observations. The estimates of inter-scorer reliability were found using Cronbach's alpha (Cronbach, 1951). Alpha reliability estimates were .99 for total miscues, .99 for meaning-change miscues, .98 for explicit comprehension, and .98 for implicit comprehension. These reliability estimates indicated a high degree of consistency between scorers. Thus an examiner should be able to score the QRI–3 reliably without extensive training.

We used a sample of 393 passages to estimate the reliability of scoring the list of propositions for each passage. Again, all levels and types of text were represented. The alpha estimate of inter-judge reliability was .94. This indicates that the proposition data from which we built our passage maps were scored reliably.

Internal Consistency Reliability. This form of reliability examines how reliable the score is as an estimate of the true score. For example, when we measure total comprehension, how reliable is the score as an estimate of the student's true comprehension score?

The standard error of measurement of the total comprehension score was estimated through an analysis of variance with items (1–5; 1–6; 1–8; 1–10) as the within-subject factor and subjects as the between-subjects factor. Crocker and Algina (1986) recommended the use of the standard error of measurement rather than a correlational estimate of reliability for criterion-referenced tests where there is reduced variability in subject's performance. Remember that a correlation is based, in part, on variability. In our case, we did not give harder passages to students who scored as frustrated on easier material, and so we reduced variability. Thus a traditional correlational measure of reliability would not accurately reflect the reliability of the scores. Similarly, because the alpha coefficient is based on variability, it is subject to the same restrictions. Crocker and Algina (1986, p. 196) illustrate that the standard error of a criterion-referenced test can be very low (such as .001), indicating a highly reliable score, yet the reliability, expressed as a generalizability coefficient, could be very low (.00). This happens when there is no variability in the data. Because we have restricted variability, we chose to use the standard error of measurement. The formula for determining the standard error of measurement from analysis of variance data is

$$\text{Standard error of measurement} = \sqrt{\dfrac{\dfrac{\text{MS}_i - \text{MS}_r}{n_p} + \text{MS}_r}{n_i}}$$

where MS_i = mean square for items
MS_r = mean square residual
n_i = number of items
n_p = number of persons

According to Crocker and Algina (1986, p. 196), the standard error must be between .00 and $.25/(n_i - 1)$; the lower, the better. This maximum value is obtained by considering the maximum variance possible with a set of items. For example, if all examinees get half the items correct and the other half incorrect, we have the maximum item variance, which works out mathematically to be $.25/n_i - 1$. There were five comprehension questions on the pre-primer passages. For the primer and first grade passages, there were six comprehension questions; for second to sixth grade passages, there were eight; and for upper middle school and high school passages, there were ten. As the formula above illustrates, the more items, the more reliable the test will be, because you are dividing by n_i. Also, the more items, the less the SEM will affect instructional-level decisions.

Table 16.5 presents the mean, standard deviation, and standard error of measurement (SEM) of the proportion-correct total comprehension score for all passages. Consider the highest SEM for an eight-item test, .18 for "Wool: From Sheep to You" and "Sequoyah." A student with a score of 75% has a true score between 57% and 93%, 68% of the time. Because of the relatively large SEMs on any single passage, we recommend that an examiner give passages of the same type (such as narrative or expository) with which the student is familiar when attempting to estimate true score. When the examiner uses two passages, the percent correct is determined from sixteen items. The standard error is based on sixteen items and is reduced substantially. When we pooled data from children who read "The Trip to the Zoo" and "A Special Birthday for Rosa," the SEM for sixteen items was .10. Thus a child with a total score of 75% has a true score that lies between 65% and 85%, 68% of the time; this is a much more reliable estimate of true score than their separate SEMs of .15 and .14 based on eight items.

For similar reasons, we cannot recommend that users interpret scores for explicit and implicit comprehension on a single passage. First, these subtests do not contain enough items to be reliable indicators of the children's true scores in these areas if only one passage is used. Even when the examiner uses two passages, and the total number of explicit items from both passages is compared to the total number of implicit items from both passages, large differences are needed for reliable diagnostic conclusions. When we pooled explicit items from "The Trip to the Zoo" and "A Special Birthday for Rosa," we obtained a SEM of .13; the standard error for implicit items was .15. The standard error of the *difference* between these two is .20. (The formula is SEMdiff = the square root of the sum of the two squared SEMs.)

Thus, only if a student received scores of 75% to 100% correct on explicit questions and 0% to 25% correct on implicit questions can we be 95% sure that these scores do not overlap. If a student consistently receives scores that differ by as much as 50%, then conclusions that a student is better in answering one type of question than the other are reliable.

If the major purpose is to determine an instructional level, then it is important to have consistency in that level. Thus the reliability issue becomes, "If I find an instructional level of fifth grade on this test, would I find an instructional level of fifth grade if I gave the test tomorrow or next week?" This type of reliability is called *test–retest reliability*. The interest is in the consistency of test results over time or conditions. As many test developers have learned, there is a problem in giving exactly the same test over two time periods in order to assess test–retest reliability, because the student may learn something in the first administration that raises his or her score on the second administration.

An alternative method of estimating level reliability is to examine performance on two passages similar in design; this method is called *alternate-form reliability* (Crocker & Algina, 1986). In the *QRI–3*, this means that we would examine performance on two similar passage types (such as narratives or familiar expository). If performance on these indicates the same instructional level, we have evidence for alternate-form reliability.

In order to obtain the best estimate of alternate-form reliability of level, we examined the reliability of the total comprehension score to estimate instructional level across passages of the same type. The procedure used to estimate alternate-form reliability of criterion-referenced tests was Livingston's (1972) K^2. This index reflects the magnitude of the discrepancy of misclassification in judging the reliability of the decision. In our case, the question is "How close are the two comprehension scores to the cutoff of 70% for instructional level?" The formula for K^2 may be found in Crocker and Algina (1986, p. 203).

The reliabilities of our instructional-level decisions based on comprehension scores were all above .80; 75% were greater than or equal to .90. In addition, we examined whether the same instructional level would be indicated on the basis of the comprehension scores on each passage. Across the readability levels, 71% to 84% of the time the same instructional level would be found on both passages (specifically, at the primer level, 71%; first, 86%; second, 78%; third, 80%; fourth, 80%; fifth, 75%; sixth, 77%; and upper middle school, 81% of the time).

TABLE 16.5

Standard Error of Measurement (Proportion Correct) for Total Comprehension Scores for Passages

Passage Level and Name	Mean	S.D.	*n*	SEM
Pre-primer				
"Just Like Mom"	.65	.25	48	.22
"Who Do I See?"	.86	.36	36	.15
"Lost and Found"	.72	.29	25	.19
"Spring and Fall"	.62	.50	20	.19
"People at Work"	.30	.20	28	.20
Primer				
"A Trip"	.81	.21	12	.15
"Fox and Mouse"	.63	.33	21	.21
"The Pig Who Learned to Read"	.67	.23	19	.18
"Who Lives Near Lakes?"	.67	.19	12	.19
"Living and Not Living"*	.58	.17	25	.21
First Grade				
"The Bear and the Rabbit"	.72	.20	33	.18
"Marva Finds a Friend"	.70	.43	35	.17
"Mouse in a House"	.66	.19	14	.20
"Air"	.55	.27	18	.19
"What You Eat"	.40	.25	15	.19

TABLE 16.5 *(Continued)*

Passage Level and Name	Mean	S.D.	*n*	SEM
Second Grade				
"What Can I Get for My Toy? "	.82	.15	19	.13
"Father's New Game"	.73	.26	18	.14
"The Lucky Cricket"	.63	.45	15	.16
"Whales and Fish"	.68	.18	17	.17
"Seasons"	.50	.22	13	.17
Third Grade				
"The Trip to the Zoo"	.76	.18	22	.15
"A Special Birthday for Rosa"	.64	.48	12	.16
"The Friend"	.71	.19	20	.16
"Cats: Lions and Tigers in Your House"	.69	.21	20	.16
"Where Do People Live?"	.47	.30	11	.15
"Wool: From Sheep to You"	.45	.19	12	.18
Fourth Grade				
"Johnny Appleseed"	.81	.22	9	.13
"Amelia Earhart"	.67	.15	11	.17
"Sequoyah"	.53	.17	9	.18
"The Busy Beaver"	.71	.13	9	.17
"The City of Cahokia"	.74	.25	10	.15
"Saudi Arabia"	.75	.16	10	.15
Fifth Grade*				
"Martin Luther King, Jr."	.65	.21	32	.17
"Christopher Columbus"	.63	.24	31	.16
"Margaret Mead"	.66	.18	23	.16
"Getting Rid of Trash"	.59	.21	38	.17
"The Octopus"	.66	.19	32	.16
"Laser Light"	.54	.20	36	.17
Sixth Grade				
"Pele"	.71	.17	57	.16
"Abraham Lincoln"	.75	.17	16	.16
"Andrew Carnegie"	.47	.20	57	.17
"Computers"	.70	.15	57	.16
"Predicting Earthquakes"	.61	.22	20	.16
"Ultrasound"	.58	.24	19	.16
Upper Middle School				
Literature:				
"Biddy Mason"	.65	.23	18	.14
"Malcolm X"	.69	.24	18	.14
Social Studies:				
"Lewis and Clark"	.54	.16	13	.16
"Ferdinand Magellan"	.57	.30	13	.13
Science:				
"Fireworks"	.61	.30	12	.14
"Life Cycles of Stars"	.28	.20	12	.13
High School				
Literature:				
"Where the Ashes Are"—Part 1	.43	.21	20	.15
"Where the Ashes Are"—Part 2	.47	.22	19	.15
"Where the Ashes Are"—Part 3	.61	.19	16	.15
Social Studies:				
"World War I"—Part 1	.35	.24	22	.14
"World War I"—Part 2	.39	.26	17	.14
"World War I"—Part 3	.44	.24	17	.14
Science:				
"Characteristics of Viruses"—Part 1	.20	.15	25	.12
"Characteristics of Viruses"—Part 2	.37	.20	20	.15
"Characteristics of Viruses"—Part 3	.20	.18	20	.12

*Based on original piloting of the *QRI*.

Reliability (Consistency) of Diagnostic Profiles. The pertinent reliability data are somewhat different if the purpose for giving the test is diagnostic. In this case, the examiner seeks consistency in conclusions regarding the child's strengths and weaknesses in reading. For example, if the child's major reading problems appear to be in decoding words, support for that conclusion should come from several sections of the test. One should expect that the child will score low on word lists at or below grade level and have low oral reading accuracy scores on passages at or below grade placement. Thus consistency should exist between total accuracy in oral reading on a passage and performance on the word list at the comparable level of readability. This same child should comprehend material generally well if he or she is within instructional range on oral reading accuracy, or if material is read to him or her.

In another case, a child might have consistently high scores on oral reading accuracy but might have difficulty comprehending material at his or her grade level. Or perhaps a child will comprehend narrative material for which s/he has prior knowledge but will have difficulty with expository material.

Two judges examined test results from 108 children to assess the reliability of diagnostic judgments. The child's grade level, percentage accuracy on word lists, percentage oral reading accuracy on all passages read orally, and comprehension on all passages were available. In addition, the level and types of passages (such as narrative) were given. The two judges independently classified the student's abilities according to word recognition and comprehension. A sample judgment would be, "word recognition—excellent; has trouble comprehending in all types of material." Or, "word recognition problems at grade level, comprehension good when word recognition is within instructional range." Or, "word recognition good, comprehension okay in narrative material, but problems in expository material beginning at fourth grade level." The judges agreed on the diagnostic category for the student's abilities 87% of the time. An examination of misclassifications showed that in most cases, lack of agreement came in instances where the pattern of strengths and weaknesses was not clear. In other cases, one judge had a more stringent criteria than the other for word-identification difficulties.

Sensitivity to Change. Sensitivity to change refers to the responsiveness of a test to change or difference on the underlying construct being measured. We have conducted research on two aspects of the *QRI* that should be sensitive to change.

Regner (1992) used the *QRI* to compared progress made by two groups of children who were experiencing reading difficulties. One group has been identified as learning disabled, and the other group, though not significantly different in reading, as measured by the *QRI* and the *Woodcock Reading Mastery Test-Revised* (Woodcock, 1987), or in intelligence, had not been so identified. Regner (1992) followed the children for four months, examining their reading instruction. Pre-test and post-test performance in reading as measured by the above instruments showed significant gains for both groups but no difference between the groups. Thus the *QRI* was capable of measuring change in word recognition and comprehension over a four-month period. It should be noted that change was assessed by weighting the word-recognition and comprehension scores. For example, the total score on a word list was multiplied by its level (primer = .5, first = 1, etc.) and added to a word-recognition accuracy score in context weighted in the same manner. Comprehension was weighted by multiplying the percentage correct by the readability of the passage. The passage chosen for this procedure was the highest-level narrative passage at the student's instructional level. This weighting made the measurements more precise, and sensitive to change, than simply an instructional level.

The same weighting system was used in a study of the effectiveness of an early literacy intervention program for inner-city at-risk children (Leslie & Allen, 1999). The *QRI* was used to assess students three times per year, in early September before intervention, in December to determine whether they could graduate from the program, and in May to assess final progress. Longitudinal studies of these children have also used the *QRI* and compared it to the Wisconsin Third Grade Reading Test (WTGRT). The *QRI* has been found to be a sensitive measure of growth in instructional level, and weighted scores allowed Leslie and Allen (1999) to identify factors that contributed to students' growth during and after the intervention. Furthermore, performance on the *QRI* is highly correlated with performance on the WTGRT.

A three-year longitudinal study (McCarthy, 1999) of a first grade intervention found that children in the intervention group who began significantly below their classmates at the beginning of first grade were not significantly different from them in oral reading accuracy or comprehension on the *QRI-II* given in April of second grade. Rate differences continued into fourth grade.

Glass (1989) examined whether students' comprehension of two first- and second-level passages would be increased if they participated in a personal, analog discussion related to themes in the story. For example, on "Bear and Rabbit," the researcher engaged students in a discussion of why people are afraid of real bears, why animals would like to have friends, and why people become friends. These concepts are related to the theme of the passage and directly related to the most difficult comprehension question, "Why did the bear and the rabbit become friends?" Two groups of second grade students participated: sixteen average and sixteen below-average readers, reading the second- and first-level passages, respectively. Students' prior knowledge of concepts was assessed on two passages, and the analog discussion was held on one passage and not on the other. Whether the discussion was held on the first or second story was counterbalanced across students. Results showed significant improvement in comprehension when students participated in the analog discussion on a story (effect sizes were greater than 1 for students at each readability level). These results suggest that instruction directed toward the conceptual knowledge judged as important to comprehending stories can enhance comprehension on the lower-level *QRI–II* passages.

These findings suggest that the passages on the *QRI–II* are sensitive to immediate change (Glass, 1989) and long-term (3–7 months) instructional interventions (Leslie & Allen, 1999; Regner, 1992). Thus researchers may use the *QRI* as outcome measures of instructional research.

Issues of Validity of an Informal Reading Inventory

Content Validity. Content validity is the degree to which the sample of items, tasks, or questions on a test are representative of some domain of content (*Standard for Educational and Psychological Testing,* 1985, p. 10). This type of validity is usually judged by experts in the content field. In our case, the research literature described in Section 2 served as the basis for test development. Thus, to review our conclusions, we sought to represent the domain of reading more systematically than other IRIs. We chose narrative and expository material to represent the reading abilities from pre-primer through high school. We included passages with pictures at the pre-primer through second grade levels to represent more fully the type of materials children encounter in school and out. On the *QRI-3,* two pre-primer passages were written with rhyming text to examine children's ability to use a known rhyming word to decode a less familiar rhyming word. Passages were varied in their familiarity. In addition to presenting children with a variety of materials, we chose to measure their reading abilities in ways that reflect research findings and classroom practice.

Research suggests the powerful effects of prior knowledge, so we included a measure of prior knowledge. Oral reading research suggests that in addition to finding total miscues, examiners should attend to the proportion of uncorrected miscues that change the meaning of the passage; thus we scored oral reading accuracy in these two ways. Because of findings that comprehension may be measured by examining whether children can make inferences, remember information stated directly in text, and retain information in memory, we chose to include three ways of measuring comprehension: answers to implicit questions, answers to explicit questions, and retelling (including inferences). On the word lists we included words that can be decoded using the rules of English and those that must be memorized because their spelling is irregular. We measured children's rate of word recognition, in addition to their accuracy.

Whether we have succeeded in our attempts to present the domain of reading depends, in part, on one's view of the importance of the factors listed above. In addition, examinations of the pilot data provided us evidence of the construct representation and penetration we have achieved. Validity data for each part of the *QRI–3* are presented in the previous parts of this section called "Development of the . . . " (e.g., Word-Identification Tests). In addition, we have presented evidence of overall test validity below.

Criterion-Related Validity. Criterion-related validity demonstrates that test scores are related to one or more outcome criteria (*Standards for Educational and Psychological Tests*, 1985, p. 11). There are two types of criterion-related validity: *predictive* (where the test is used to predict future criterion behavior) and *concurrent* (where the test results are compared to a current criterion). According to the *Standards* (1985), "concurrent evidence is usually preferable for achievement tests, tests used for certification, diagnostic clinical tests or for tests used as measures of a specified construct" (p. 11). Thus concurrent validity is needed for the *QRI–3*.

We examined the correlation (within a grade) between the instructional level in familiar material obtained from the *QRI–II* and the student's NCE for Total Reading on either the California Achievement Test or the Iowa Test of Basic Skills. We conducted an analysis whenever we obtained data on at least twelve children at a grade level. Table 16.6 presents the correlations between instructional level in familiar material as a measure of standardized reading comprehension.

At all grade levels where we had sufficient data, there were significant correlations between a student's instructional level in familiar material and NCE. Results from the original *QRI* reached the same conclusions at grades 3, 5, 6, 7 and high school. Taken together, the results indicate that the instructional levels obtained on the *QRI–II* and *–3* and comprehension scores from standardized reading achievement tests are measuring some common factors and support the validity of the instructional levels obtained on the *QRI–II* and *–3*.

Regner (1992) found that weighted word-recognition scores from the *QRI* correlated .90 with a combined Word-Identification and Word-Attack scale score from the *Woodcock Reading Mastery Test-Revised* (WRMT-R, 1987). Similarly, weighted *QRI* comprehension scores (% correct on the highest instructional level in narrative text × the readability level of the passage) correlated .75 ($p < .01$) with Passage Comprehension from the WRMT-R (1987). Thus, when *QRI* scores are weighted to reflect the difficulty of the words or passages, they correlate quite highly with results from the WRMT-R (1987).

Construct Validity. Evidence of construct validity focuses on the test scores as a measure of the psychological characteristics, or construct, of interest. The

TABLE 16.6

Correlations Between Instructional Level in Familiar Material and Standardized Tests of Reading Achievement as a Function of Grade

Grade	Correlation	n
1	.86**	41
2	.65**	32
3	.48*	18
3	.61**	21
4	.66**	31
8	.52*	19

Note: Data from grades 1, 2, and 4 are correlated with the NCE for Total Reading on either the CAT or the ITBS. The third grade samples are correlated with Wisconsin Third Grade Reading Test. Although similar in content each year, the tests are different each year. The third grade samples above comprise different children. The eighth grade data are correlated with the Wisconsin Student Assessment System–Reading sub-scale. *p < .05; **p < .01.

conceptual framework specifies the meaning of the construct, distinguishes it from other constructs, and indicates how measures of the construct should relate to other variables (*Standards for Educational and Psychological Testing,* 1985, p. 10). At the most general level, the *QRI–3* measures word-recognition ability and comprehension. Depending on the stage of reading development, we should find different patterns of intercorrelations. Among beginning readers, we should find greater interrelatedness among word identification on word lists, oral reading accuracy in context, and reading rate than among those factors and comprehension. On the other hand, after students have achieved some degree of automaticity of word recognition, we expect correlations between our prior-knowledge measures and retelling and comprehension.

1. Correlations among factors on the QRI–3. We found support for the interrelatedness and uniqueness of several factors on the *QRI.* The intercorrelations among word identification on the word lists, total oral reading accuracy in context, acceptable accuracy in context, and rate of reading were consistently highly correlated, particularly among beginning readers (those with instructional levels at or below second grade). Word identification was also significantly correlated with retelling or comprehension through first grade level. Thus there is evidence for a word-identification factor in early reading.

The other construct in evidence was illustrated by the intercorrelations among conceptual-knowledge scores and prediction, with retelling and comprehension. Evidence for the role of prior knowledge in predicting retelling or comprehension began at first grade level (in expository text) and held through high school. At some levels, conceptual-knowledge scores correlated most highly with retelling or comprehension; at other levels (e.g., third grade), prediction was most highly correlated. Certainly we have evidence that the *QRI–3* measures at least two constructs that theorists have posited to be central to the reading process: word recognition and comprehension (Gough & Tunmer, 1986).

2. Are there diagnostic categories of reading (dis)abilities? To determine whether different factors predict comprehension of beginning readers compared to comprehension of more advanced readers, or that of students with good vs. poor word-identification scores, we divided our sample into three groups, organized by their instructional levels in familiar text. Group 1 comprised children with pre-primer, primer, or first grade instructional level. Group 2 included children with second or third grade instructional level, and Group 3 included students with fourth, fifth, or sixth grade instructional level. Next, within each group, children were further divided into two groups based on their word-identification score on the word list at their instructional level. Note that word-list scores are not used to judge instructional level. Those with scores on the word list at their instructional level of under 70% correct were called *poor word identifiers*, and those identifying 70% of more of the words correctly were called *good word identifiers*.

At each instructional-level grouping, stepwise regression analyses were conducted with acceptable miscues, rate, prior conceptual knowledge, and text type (whether the text read was narrative or expository) as the predictor variables and with total comprehension (on questions) as the dependent variable. We conducted the same analyses without acceptable miscues on the silent reading data. The summary below describes the variables that entered the regression equation and the amount of variance accounted for by the entering variables.

For children with pre-primer, primer, and first grade instructional levels and poor word-identification skills, nothing predicted comprehension (the number of students with such low word-identification scores yet with instructional levels within this range was only 13). For children who were within these same instructional levels and who had good word-identification skills, acceptable miscues accounted for 16% of the variance in oral comprehension ($n = 83$), and text type explained an additional 7% of the comprehension variance. For students with second and third grade instructional levels and poor word-identification skills, nothing predicted oral or silent reading comprehension, but again, few subjects fit this category ($n = 17$). For students at the same instructional levels with good word-identification skills, text type accounted for 26% and 16% of the variance in oral and silent comprehension, respectively. For students with fourth, fifth, and sixth grade instructional levels, prior knowledge accounted for 34% and 23%, respectively, of the oral and silent reading comprehension of good word identifiers. Again, small samples of students at these instructional levels with poor word-identification skills on the word list at their instructional level precluded accounting for variance in their comprehension scores.

In summary, at beginning reading levels, students' comprehension is best predicted by the percentage of miscues that retain meaning and by whether they are reading narrative or expository text. At the upper levels, comprehension is best predicted by conceptual knowledge that the reader possessed before reading the text.

Using the QRI–3 to Guide Instruction

In addition to the type of construct validity presented above, Cross and Paris (1987) describe how a diagnostic test must represent specific constructs to be of use to teachers. Construct representation assessed how well a construct is contained in the items. Construct representation is often uncertain because one test score is the result of many cognitive processes. Often achievement test scores have not been able to provide educators with direction for instruction. This inability is related to the fact that construct representation does not usually occur in a one-to-one relationship between a score on a test and a single cognitive process responsible for the performance on that item (Cross & Paris, 1987).

We have attempted to offer construct representation by providing the examiner with a set of passages that vary according to type of text and familiarity to the reader. In this way an examiner can determine why a child might comprehend one type of material well, but not another. In addition, we have assessed comprehension in several ways: retelling, answers to questions with the text absent, and answers to the questions with the text present.

Thus an examiner can separate what a student remembers from a text from what the student comprehends with access to the text. Furthermore, on the word lists, we have represented the construct of word identification by measuring the student's rate of identification and by including words that vary in decodability.

Data Supporting the Use of QRI Results to Guide Instruction

Leslie and Allen (1999) reported a study of the effects of an early intervention project that used the *QRI* to assess the children's reading abilities and to group them for instruction. Their evidence suggests that different instructional procedures were correlated with growth for children who entered the project at different instructional reading levels. For readers with less than a first grade reading ability, the number of rimes taught was the best predictor of growth, but for children reading at or above first grade, the amount of story grammar instruction best predicted their growth. These data suggest that reading acquisition is a developmental process that is sensitive to different instructional methods. The students' abilities can be assessed by the *QRI*, and relevant instructional decisions can be made.

A small instructional study was also conducted in 1991 to assess whether we have been successful at providing information that will help guide instruction at the upper elementary level. Sixth graders from a single classroom were given the *QRI*. Although all students were taught, only the data from students reading at a sixth grade instructional level in narrative text ($n = 16$) were used in the analyses. The mean pre-test scores showed that students retold more information from narrative than from expository text, $F (1, 15) = 15.71, p < .001$, although there were no differences in comprehension, $F < 1$, and the prior-conceptual-knowledge scores were higher for *expository* text, $F (1, 15) = 14.64$, $p < .01$. The teacher then taught four text structures to the students: cause–effect, problem–solution, sequence, and compare–contrast. The instruction in text structure occurred over one month and was integrated within a unit on Greek and Roman governments, which was particularly useful in teaching the compare–contrast structure. The instruction was composed of direct instruction on text structures, modeling how to determine structures in text, guided practice in finding structures in text, independent assessment of knowledge gained, and an application project. Post-testing with the *QRI* was conducted two months after the formal instruction had ended. Students read new (not used at pre-test) sixth grade narrative and expository texts. We also asked students to identify text structures of the expository texts. Although there were no differences between pre-test and post-test in students' abilities to identify different text structures, increases in their ability to recall expository texts were found, $F (1, 15) = 12.79, p < .01$. Mean retelling scores on expository text increased from .20 at pre-test to .30 at post-test, which made it non-significantly different from the retelling of narrative text (mean = .33). We cannot conclude that the instruction on text structures resulted in the improvement in retelling ability. Rather, the effect could have been a more general one. It may have been that the greater emphasis on constructing meaning in expository text was the decisive factor. The students certainly liked the unit, as we learned when one teacher came and asked what we were doing in social studies. Students had reported to her an excitement about the subject that she had not seen before. Although our results were less than conclusive, others have found that instruction in text structures can improve students' recall and comprehension of expository text (Armbruster, Anderson & Ostertag, 1987; Richgels, McGee, Lomax & Sheard, 1987).

References

Aaron, P. G. (1997). The demise of the discrepancy formula. *Review of Educational Research, 67*, 461–502.

Afflerbach, P. and Johnston, P. (1984). Research methodology on the use of verbal reports in reading. *Journal of Reading Behavior, XVI*, 307–322.

Allen, L. (1998). An integrated strategies approach: Making word identification instruction work for beginning readers. *The Reading Teacher, 52*, 254–268.

Alvermann, D. E., Smith, L. C., and Readance, J. E. (1985). Prior knowledge activation and the comprehension of compatible and incompatible text. *Reading Research Quarterly, 20*, 420–436.

Anderson, R. C., Reynolds, R. E., Schallert, D. L., and Goetz, E.T. (1977). Frameworks for comprehending discourse. *American Educational Research Journal, 14*, 367–382.

Armbruster, B. B., Anderson, T. H., and Ostertag, J. (1987). Does text structure/summarization instruction facilitate learning from expository text? *Reading Research Quarterly, 22*, 331–346.

August, D. L., Flavell, J. H., and Clift, R. (1984). Comparisons of comprehension monitoring of skilled and less-skilled readers. *Reading Research Quarterly, 20*, 39–53.

Baker, L. and Brown, A. L. (1984). Metacognitive skills and reading. In P .D. Pearson, M. Kamil, R. Barr, and P. Mosenthal (eds.), *Handbook of reading research* (vol. I, pp. 353–394). White Plains, NY: Longman.

Becoming a nation of readers: The Report of the Commission on Reading. (1985). Washington, DC: The National Institute of Education.

Bereiter, C. and Bird, M. (1985). Use of thinking aloud in identification and teaching of reading comprehension strategies. *Cognition and Instruction, 2*, 131–156.

Berkowitz, S. and Taylor, B. M. (1981). The effects of text type and familiarity on the nature of information recalled by readers. In M. Kamil (ed.), *Directions in reading: Research and instruction* (pp. 157–161). Washington, DC: National Reading Conference.

Betts, F. (1946). *Foundations of reading instruction.* New York: American Book.

Blanchard, J. S., Borthwick, P., and Hall, A. (1983). Determining instructional reading level: Standardized multiple choice versus IRI improved recall questions. *Journal of Reading, 26*, 684–689.

Bradley, L. and Bryant, P. (1985). *Rhyme and reason in reading and spelling.* Ann Arbor, MI: University of Michigan Press.

Brennan, A. D., Bridge, C., and Winograd, P. (1986). The effects of structural variation on children's recall of basal reader stories. *Reading Research Quarterly, 21*, 91–104.

Brewer, W. F. (1980). Literary theory, rhetoric and stylistics: Implications for psychology. In R. Spiro, B. C. Bruce, and W. F. Brewer (eds.). *Theoretical issues in reading comprehension: Perspectives from cognitive psychology, linguistics, artificial intelligence, and education* (pp. 221–244). Hillsdale, NJ: Erlbaum.

Bristow, P. S. (1985). Are poor readers passive readers? Some evidence, possible explanations, and potential solutions. *The Reading Teacher, 39*, 318–325.

Bristow, P. and Leslie, L. (1988). Indicators of reading difficulty: Discrimination between instructional and frustration range performance of functionally illiterate adults. *Reading Research Quarterly, 23*, 200–218.

Brown, C. S. and Lytle, S. L. (1988). Merging assessment and instruction: Protocols in the classroom. In S. M. Glazer, L. W. Searfoss, and L. M. Gentile (eds.), *Reexamining reading diagnoses: New trends and practices.* Newark, DE: International Reading Association.

Burge, P. D. (1983). Comprehension and rate: Oral vs. silent reading for low achievers. *Reading Horizons, 23*, 201–206.

Caldwell, J. (1985). A new look at the old informal reading inventory. *The Reading Teacher, 39*, 168–173.

Caldwell, J., Fromm, M., and O'Connor, V. (1997–1998). Designing an intervention for poor readers: Incorporating the best of all worlds. *Wisconsin State Reading Association Journal, 41*, 7–14.

Carroll, J. B., Davies, P., and Richman, B. (1971). *The word frequency book.* New York: American Heritage Publishing.

Carver, R.P. (1990). *Reading rate: A review of research and theory.* San Diego: Academic.

Chall, J. S. (1983). *Stages of reading development.* New York: McGraw-Hill.

Chou-Hare, V. and Smith, D. C. (1982). Reading to remember: Studies of metacognitive reading skills in elementary school-aged children. *Journal of Educational Research, 75*, 157–164.

Chrystal, C. (1991). Assessing prior knowledge across cultures. Unpublished doctoral dissertation, Marquette University.

Clark, H. H. and Clark. E. V. (1977). *Psychology and language.* New York: Harcourt.

Clay, M. M. (1985). The early detection of reading difficulties, 3rd ed. Portsmouth, NH: Heinemann.

Coté, N. and Goldman, S. R. (1998). Profiles in reading: Using verbal protocols to examine students' construction of discourse representations. Paper presented at the American Educational Research Association Conference, San Diego.

Coté, N., Goldman, S. R., and Saul, E. U. (1998). Students making sense of informational text: Relations between processing and representation. *Discourse Processes, 25,* 1–53.

Crain-Thoreson, C., Lippman, M. Z., and McClendon-Magnuson, D. (1997). Windows of comprehension: Reading comprehension processes as revealed by two think-aloud procedures. *Journal of Educational Psychology, 89,* 579–591.

Crocker, L. and Algina, J. (1986). *Introduction to classical and modern test theory.* New York: Holt, Rinehart and Winston.

Cronbach, L. J. (1951). Coefficient alpha and the internal structure of tests. *Psychometrika, 16,* 297–334.

Cross, D. and Paris, S. (1987). Assessment of reading comprehension: Matching test purposes and test properties. *Educational Psychologist, 22,* 313–332.

Dale, E. and Chall, J. S. (1948). Formula for predicting readability. *Educational Research Bulletin, 27,* 11–20.

Davison, A. and Kantor, R. N. (1982). On the failure of readability formulas to define readable texts: A case study from adaptations. *Reading Research Quarterly, 27,* 187–209.

Durkin, D. (1978–1979). What classroom observations reveal about reading comprehension instruction. *Reading Research Quarterly, 14,* 481–533.

Durkin, D. (1981). Reading comprehension instruction in five basal reader series. *Reading Research Quarterly, 16,* 515–544.

Ehri, L. C. and Wilce, L. S. (1979). Does word training increase or decrease interference in a stroop task? *Journal of Experimental Child Psychology, 27,* 352–364.

Ehri, L. C. (1991). Development of the ability to read words. In R. Barr, M. L. Kamil, P. Mosenthal, and P. D. Pearson (eds.), *Handbook of reading research* (vol. II, pp. 383–417). White Plains, NY: Longman.

Ehri, L. C. (1992). Reconceptualizing the development of sight word reading and its relationship to recoding. In P. B. Gough, L. C. Ehri, and R. Treiman (eds.), *Reading acquisition,* (pp. 107–143). Hillsdale, NJ: Erlbaum.

Englert, C. S. and Hiebert, E. H. (1984). Children's developing awareness of text structures in expository material. *Journal of Educational Psychology, 76,* 65–74.

Fry, E. (1977). Fry's readability graph: Clarifications, validity and extension to level 17. *Journal of Reading, 21,* 242–252.

Garner, R. (1982). Verbal-report data on reading strategies. *Journal of Reading Behavior, XIV,* 159–167.

Garner, R. and Reis, R. (1981). Monitoring and resolving comprehension obstacles: An investigation of spontaneous text lookbacks among upper grade good and poor readers. *Reading Research Quarterly, 16,* 569–582.

Garner, R., Hare, V. C., Alexander, P., Haynes, J., and Winograd, P. (1984). Inducing use of a text lookback strategy among unsuccessful readers. *American Educational Research Journal, 21,* 789–798.

Gaskins, I., Downer, M., Anderson, R., Cunningham, P., Gaskins, R., and Schommer, M. (1988). A metacognitive approach to phonics: Using what you know to decode what you don't know. *Remedial and Special Education, 27,* 36–41.

Gaskins, R., Gaskins, I., Anderson, R., and Schommer, M. (1995). The reciprocal relationship between research and development: An example involving a decoding strand for poor readers. *Journal of Reading Behavior, 27,* 337–377.

Glass, S. (1989). The effect of prior knowledge on reading miscues and comprehension of narrative text. Unpublished master's thesis, Marquette University.

Goldman, S. R. (1997). Learning from text: Reflections on the past and suggestions for the future. *Discourse Processes, 23,* 357–398.

Goodman, K. S. (1969). Analysis of reading miscues: Applied psycholinguistics. *Reading Research Quarterly, 5,* 9–30.

Gough, P. B. and Juel, C. (1991). The first stages of word recognition. In L. Rieben and C.A. Perfetti (eds.), *Learning to read: Basic research and its implications* (pp. 47–56). Hillsdale, NJ: Erlbaum.

Gough, P. B. and Tunmer, W. E. (1986). Decoding, reading and reading disability. *Remedial and Special Education, 7,* 6–10.

Graesser, A. C. and Goodman, S. M. (1985). Implicit knowledge, question answering and the representation of expository text. In B. K. Britton and J. B. Black (eds.), *Understanding expository text* (pp. 109–171). Hillsdale, NJ: Erlbaum.

Graesser, A., Golding, J. M., and Long, D. L. (1991). Narrative representation and comprehension. In R. Barr, M. L. Kamil, P. Mosenthal, and P. D. Pearson (eds.), *Handbook of reading research* (vol. II, pp. 171–205). White Plains, NY: Longman.

Hardy, N. D. and Jerman, M. E. (1985). *Readability estimator.* Seattle, WA: Berta Max, Inc.

Hare, V. C. (1982). Preassessment of topical knowledge: A validation and extension. *Journal of Reading Behavior, 15,* 77–86.

Harris, A. J. and Sipay, E. (1985). *How to increase reading ability: A guide to developmental and remedial methods,* 8th ed. New York: Longman.

Holmes, B. C. and Roser, N. L. (1987). Five ways to assess readers' prior knowledge. *The Reading Teacher, 40,* 646–649.

Hood, J. (1975–1976). Qualitative analysis of oral reading errors: The inter-judge reliability of scores. *Reading Research Quarterly, 11,* 577–598.

Hood, J. (1984). Stages of reading. In E. Forell (ed.), *Manual for student teachers: Children's Reading Clinic* (pp. 14–23). Iowa City: University of Iowa.

Huey, E. B. (1968). *The psychology and pedagogy of reading.* Boston, MA: M.I.T. Press (originally published by Macmillan in 1908).

Jett-Simpson, M. and Leslie, L. (1997). *Authentic literacy assessment: An ecological approach.* NY: Longman.

Johnson, N. S. and Mandler, J. M. (1980). A tale of two structures: Underlying and surface forms in stories. *Poetics, 9,* 51–86.

Johnston, P. H. (1984). Prior knowledge and reading comprehension test bias. *Reading Research Quarterly, 19,* 219–239.

Kavale, K. and Schreiner, R. (1979). The reading process of above average and average readers: A comparison of the use of reasoning strategies in responding to standardized comprehension measures. *Reading Research Quarterly, XV*, 102–128.

Kintsch, E. (1990). Macroprocesses and microprocesses in the development of summarization skills. *Cognition and Instruction, 7*, 161–195.

Klare, G. R. (1974–75). Assessing readability. *Reading Research Quarterly, 10*, 62–102.

Kletzien, S. B. (1991). Strategy used by good and poor comprehenders reading expository text of differing levels. *Reading Research Quarterly, 26*, 67–86.

LaBerge, D. and Samuels, S. J. (1985). Toward a theory of automatic information processing. In H. Singer and R. Ruddell (eds.). *Theoretical models and processes of reading*, 3rd ed. (pp. 689–718).

Langer, J. (1984). Examining background knowledge and text comprehension. *Reading Research Quarterly, 14*, 468–481.

Leslie, L. (1980). The use of graphic and contextual information by average and below average readers. *Journal of Reading Behavior, 12*, 139–149.

Leslie, L. (1993). A developmental-interactive approach to reading assessment. *Reading and Writing Quarterly, 9*, 5–30.

Leslie, L. Recall and comprehension of narrative vs. expository text. Unpublished manuscript, Marquette University.

Leslie, L. and Allen, L. (1999). Factors that predict success in an early intervention project. *Reading Research Quarterly, 34*, 404–424.

Leslie, L. and Caldwell, J. (1995). *Qualitative Reading Inventory-II*. NY: HarperCollins.

Leslie, L. and Caldwell, J. (1989). The Qualitive Reading Inventory: Issues in the development of a diagnostic reading test. In S. McCormick and J. Zutell (eds.), *Cognitive and social perspectives for literacy: Research and instruction* (pp. 413–419). Chicago, IL: National Reading Conference.

Leslie, L. and Calhoon, J. (1995). Factors affecting children's reading of rimes: Reading ability, word frequency, and rime-neighborhood size. *Journal of Educational Psychology, 87*, 576–586.

Leslie, L. and Cooper, J. (1993). Assessing the predictive validity of prior-knowledge assessment. In D. J. Leu, and C. K. Kinzer (eds.), *Examining central issues in literacy research, theory and practice* (pp. 93–100). Chicago, IL: National Reading Conference.

Leslie, L. and Osol, P. (1978). Changes in oral reading strategies as a function of quantities of miscues. *Journal of Reading Behavior, 10*, 442–445.

Lipson, M. Y. (1983). The influence of religious affiliation on children's memory for test information. *Reading Research Quarterly, 18*, 448–457.

Livingston, S. A. (1972). Criterion-referenced applications of classical test theory. *Journal of Educational Measurement, 9*, 13–26.

Mandler, J. M. and DeForest, M. (1979). Is there more than one way to recall a story? *Child Development, 50*, 886–889.

Mandler, J. M. (1984). *Stories, scripts and scenes: Aspects of schema theory*. Hillsdale, NJ: Erlbaum.

Markman, E. M. (1977). Realizing that you don't understand: A preliminary investigation. *Child Development, 48*, 986–992.

Markman, E. M. (1979). Realizing you don't understand: Elementary school children's awareness of inconsistencies. *Child Development, 50*, 643–655.

McCarthy, P. (1999). The effects of balanced literacy instructional training: A longitudinal study of reading performance in the primary grades. Unpublished doctoral dissertation, Marquette University.

McClean, M., Bryant, P., and Bradely, L. (1987). Rhymes, nursery rhymes, and reading in early childhood. *Merrill-Palmer Quarterly, 33*, 255–281.

McCracken, R. (1966). *Standard Reading Inventory*. Klamath, OR: Klamath Printing

Meyer, B. J. F. and Rice, G. E. (1984). The structure of text. In P .D. Pearson, R. Barr, M .L. Kamil, and P. Mosenthal (eds.), *Handbook of reading research* (vol. I, pp. 319–352). White Plains, NY: Longman.

Meyers, M. and Paris, S. G. (1978). Children's metacognitive knowledge about reading. *Journal of Educational Psychology, 70*, 680–690.

Myers, J. (1988). Diagnosis diagnosed: Twenty years after. *Professional School Psychology, 3*, 123–134.

Myers, J. and Lytle, S. (1986). Assessment of the learning process. *Exceptional Children, 53*, 138–144.

Myers, L., Lytle, S., Palladino, D., Devenpeck, G., and Green, M. (1990). Think-aloud protocol analysis: An investigation of reading comprehension strategies in fourth and fifth grade students. *Journal of Psychoeducational Assessment, 8*, 112–127.

Mulcahy, P. I. and Samuels, S. J. (1987). Problem solving schemata for text types: A comparison of narrative and expository text structures. *Reading Psychology, 8*, 247–256.

Nelson, K. E. (1986). *Event knowledge: Structure and function in development*. Hillsdale, NJ: Erlbaum.

Nicholson, T., Lillas, C., and Rozoskama, M. A. (1988). Have we been misled by miscues? *The Reading Teacher, 42*, 6–10.

Nist, S. L. and Kirby, K. (1986). Teaching comprehension and study strategies through modeling and thinking aloud. *Reading research and instruction, 25*, 254–264.

Olshavsky, J. E. (1976–1977). Reading as problem solving: An investigation of strategies. *Reading Research Quarterly, 4*, 654–675.

Olson, G. M., Duffy, S. A., and Mack, R. L. (1984). Thinking out-loud as a method for studying real-time comprehension processes. In D. Kieras and M. Just (eds.), *New methods in the study of immediate processes in comprehension* (pp. 253–286). Hillsdale, NJ: Erlbaum.

Paris, S. G., Wasik, B. A., and Turner, J. C. (1991). The development of strategic readers. In R. Barr, M. L. Kamil, P. Mosenthal, and P. D. Pearson (eds.), *Handbook of reading research* (vol. II, pp. 609–640). White Plains, NY: Longman.

Pearson, P. D., Hansen, J., and Gordon, C. (1979). The effect of background knowledge on young children's comprehension of explicit and implicit information, *Journal of Reading Behavior, 11*, 201–209.

Pearson, P. D. and Johnson, D. D. (1978). *Teaching reading comprehension*. New York: Holt, Rinehart and Winston.

Perfetti, C. A. (1985). *Reading ability*. New York: Oxford University Press.

Perfetti, C. A. (1991). Representations and awareness of the acquisition of reading competence. In L. Rieben and C. A. Perfetti (eds.), *Learning to Read: Basic Research and its Implications* (pp. 33–44). Hillsdale, NJ: Erlbaum.

Perfetti, C. A. (1988). Verbal efficiency in reading ability. In M. Daneman, G. E. MacKinnon, and T. G. Waller (eds.), *Reading research: Advances in theory and practice* (vol. 6, 109–143). New York: Academic.

Pinter, R. (1913). Oral and silent reading of fourth grade pupils. *Journal of Educational Psychology, 4,* 330–337.

Pinter, R. and Gilliland, A. R. (1916). Oral and silent reading. *Journal of Educational Psychology, 7,* 201–212.

Pressley, M. and Afflerbach, P. (1995). *Verbal protocols in reading: The nature of constructively responsive reading.* Hillsdale, NJ: Erlbaum.

Raphael, T. (1986). Teaching question–answer relationships, revisited. *The Reading Teacher, 39,* 516–522.

Recht, D. (1986). The effect of prior knowledge on the spatial performance, verbal short-term memory and verbal long-term memory of good and poor readers. Unpublished doctoral dissertation, Marquette University.

Recht, D. R. and Leslie, L. (1988). The effects of prior knowledge on good and poor readers' memory for text. *Journal of Educational Psychology, 80,* 16–20.

Regner, M. (1992). Predicting growth in reading in regular and special education. Unpublished doctoral dissertation, Marquette University.

Richgels, D. J., McGee, L. M., Lomax, R. G., and Sheard, C. (1987). Awareness of four text structures: Effects on recall of expository text. *Reading Research Quarterly, 22,* 177–196.

Rogers, T. (1991). Students as literary critics: The interpretive experiences, beliefs, and processes of ninth grade students. *Journal of Reading Behavior, 23,* 391–423.

Rowell, E. H. (1976). Do elementary students read better orally or silently? *The Reading Teacher, 29,* 367–370.

Rumelhart, D. (1977). Toward an interactive model of reading. In S. Dornic (ed.), *Attention and performance* (vol. VI, pp. 573–603). Hillsdale, N.J.: Erlbaum.

Schmidt, M. B. (1990). A questionnaire to measure children's awareness of strategic reading processes. *The Reading Teacher, 43,* 454–461.

Smith, W. E. and Beck, M. B. (1980). Determining instructional reading level with 1978 Metropolitan Achievement Test. *The Reading Teacher, 34,* 313–319.

Spache, G. D. (1974). *Good reading for poor readers,* rev. 9th ed. Champaign, IL: Garrard Publishing.

Spache, G. D. (1981). *Diagnosing and correcting reading disabilities.* Boston: Allyn and Bacon.

Standards for education and psychological testing. (1985). Washington, DC: American Psychological Association.

Stanovich, K. E. (1980). Toward an interactive compensatory model of individual differences in the development of reading fluency. *Reading Research Quarterly, 16,* 32–71.

Stanovich, K. E. (1991). Discrepancy definitions of reading disability: Has intelligence led us astray? *Reading Research Quarterly, 26,* 7–29.

Stanovich, K. E., Cunningham, A. E., and West, R. F. (1981). A longitudinal study of the development of automatic recognition skills in first graders. *Journal of Reading Behavior, 13,* 57–73.

Stein, N. L. (1979). How children understand stories: A developmental analysis. In L. Katz (ed.), *Current topics in early childhood education* (vol. 2, pp. 261–290) Norwood, NJ: Ablex.

Stein, N. L. and Glenn, C. (1979). An analysis of story comprehension in elementary school children. In R. O. Freedle (ed.), *Advances in discourse processes* (vol. 2): *New directions in discourse processes* (pp. 53–120). Norwood, NJ: Ablex.

Stevens, K. C. (1980). The effect of background knowledge on the reading comprehension of ninth graders. *Journal of Reading Behavior, 12,* 151–154.

Sulzby, E. and Teale, W. (1991). Emergent literacy. In R. Barr, M. L. Kamil, P. Mosenthal, and P. D. Pearson (eds.), *Handbook of Reading Research* (vol. II, pp. 727–758). White Plains, NY: Longman.

Swalm, J. E. (1972). A comparison of oral reading, silent reading, and listening comprehension. *Education, 92,* 111–115.

Taft, M. L. and Leslie, L. (1985). The effects of prior knowledge and oral reading accuracy on miscues and comprehension. *Journal of Reading Behavior, 17,* 163–179.

Taylor, B. M. (1979). Good and poor readers' recall of familiar and unfamiliar text. *Journal of Reading Behavior, 11,* 375–380.

Taylor, B. M. (1982). Text structure and children's comprehension and memory for expository material. *Journal of Educational Psychology, 74,* 323–340.

Thorndike, R. L. and Hagen, E. (1977). *Measurement and evaluation in psychology and education.* New York: Wiley.

Valencia, S. W. and Stallman, A. C. (1989). Multiple measures of prior knowledge: Comparative predictive validity. In S. McCormick and J. Zutell (eds.), *Cognitive and social perspectives for literacy: Research and instruction* (pp. 427–436). Chicago, IL: National Reading Conference.

Valencia, S. W., Stallman, A. C., Commeyras, M., Pearson, P. D., and Hartman, D. K. (1991). Four measures of topical knowledge: A study of construct validity. *Reading Research Quarterly, 26,* 204–233.

Vosniadou, S., Pearson, P. D., and Rogers, T. (1988). What causes children's failures to detect inconsistencies in text? Representation versus comparison difficulties. *Journal of Educational Psychology, 80,* 27–39.

Wade, S. E. (1990). Using think-alouds to assess comprehension. *The Reading Teacher, 43,* 442–451.

Weaver, C. A. and Kintsch, W. (1991). Expository test. In R. Barr, M. L. Kamil, P. Mosenthal, and P. D. Pearson (eds.), *Handbook of reading research* (vol. II, pp. 230–245). White Plains, NY: Longman.

Wheeler, L. R. and Smith, E. H. (1954). A practical readability formula for the classroom teacher in the elementary grades. *Elementary English, 31,* 397–399.

Wisconsin Department of Public Instruction (1986). *A guide to curriculum planning in reading.* Madison, WI.

Woodcock, R. W. (1987). *Woodcock Reading Mastery Test-Revised,* Circle Pines, MN: American Guidance Service.

Zabrucky, K. and Ratner, H. H. (1992). Effects of passage type on comprehension monitoring and recall in good and poor readers. *Journal of Reading Behavior, 24,* 373–391.

Zwaan, R. A. and Brown, C. M. (1996). The influence of language proficiency and comprehension skill on situation-model construction. *Discourse Processes, 21,* 289–327.

Index

Numerals in italics indicate test passages of the titles cited.

VIDEOTAPES ARE AVAILABLE
TO ACCOMPANY *QRI-3*

The Instructional Media Center at Marquette University is producing a 60-minute VHS color videotape. The tape demonstrates the use of *QRI–3* with three students: two primary grade children of different reading abilities and an eighth grade student to demonstrate the use of look-back and think-aloud procedures.

ESTIMATED DATE: October 1, 2000

Cost: $60.00 per tape

I wish to order:

_____ **videotapes @ $60.00 each** $ _____ **Total**

+ _____ **5.6% Sales tax**
(WI residents only)

$ _____ **TOTAL ENCLOSED**

NOTE: A check or money order payable to Marquette University must accompany your order. If a purchase order is attached, a $10 shipping and handling fee will be added to the total billed.

Name _____

School _____

Address _____

City _____ **State** _____ **Zip Code** _____

MAIL ORDER FORM TO
Lauren Leslie, Ph. D.
School of Education
Marquette University
P. O. Box 1881
Milwaukee, WI 53201-1881
ATTN: Video order
FAX: Forward purchase order number
to Coreen Bukowski at 414-288-3945.

For further information, call Coreen Bukowski 414-288-7235.